JUAN PERÓ.

JUAN PERÓN

The Life of the People's Colonel

Jill Hedges

I.B. TAURIS
LONDON · NEW YORK · OXFORD · NEW DELHI · SYDNEY

I.B. TAURIS
Bloomsbury Publishing Plc
50 Bedford Square, London, WC1B 3DP, UK
1385 Broadway, New York, NY 10018, USA
29 Earlsfort Terrace, Dublin 2, Ireland

BLOOMSBURY, I.B. TAURIS and the I.B. Tauris logo are
trademarks of Bloomsbury Publishing Plc

First published in Great Britain 2021

Cover design by Alice Marwick
Cover image: President of Argentina, Juan Domingo Perón,
1950. (© Universal History Archive/Getty Images)

A catalogue record for this book is available from the British Library.

A catalog record for this book is available from the Library of Congress.

ISBN: HB: 978-0-7556-0271-1
       PB: 978-0-7556-0272-8
       ePDF: 978-0-7556-0269-8
       eBook: 978-0-7556-0268-1

Typeset by Integra Software Services Pvt. Ltd.
Printed and bound in Great Britain

To find out more about our authors and books visit www.bloomsbury.com
and sign up for our newsletters.

For Andrés, with love

CONTENTS

ILLUSTRATIONS

PREFACE

Although outside Argentina Juan Domingo Perón has been overshadowed by his second wife, Eva (Evita), he himself was a remarkable and durable political figure whose influence persists over forty-five years after his death. It is impossible to understand Argentina without understanding Perón (and vice versa).

Within Argentina Perón continues to be the subject of exaggerated and diametrically opposed views – a dictator, a great leader, the hero of the working classes, a weak and spineless man dependent on his stronger-willed wife, a Latin American visionary, a traitorous bastard. Depending on the point of view expressed, he was responsible for dragging Argentina into a modern, socially just twentieth-century society or, conversely, wrecking a prosperous nation and fomenting class war and unreasonable aspirations among his client base. Needless to say, all these portrayals have some truth and much fiction, largely created by pro- and anti-Peronist propagandists whose versions appear mutually exclusive but in fact often represent different views of the same reality. This book proposes to present a more balanced and less extremist view of Juan Perón, a more interesting and subtle figure than the 'fake news' approach to him would suggest.

Although her early death at only thirty-three arguably gave Evita even greater cachet than her husband – who was forced to face old age, his many errors and the gulf between legend and reality as an eighty-year-old president – Perón remains a key figure in Argentine politics, still occupying so much of the political spectrum as to constrain the development of viable alternatives. With his diffuse ideology, he was able to attract and justify support from the left and right, and debates persist as to whether Peronism should be defined as left- or right-wing populism. Also unlike Eva, who was as sincere as she could be misguided, Perón was an altogether more cerebral, calculating and distant figure behind his genial exterior, whose convictions could be open to question. (As he himself was wont to say, 'I'm not Peronist. The boys are the Peronists.') Nevertheless, he was sincere in his desire to develop a 'new Argentina' characterized by 'social justice, economic independence and political sovereignty', and enjoyed many successes, despite the fact that Peronism became dependent on an entrenched patron-client structure, thus limiting the real gains of working-class independence. As David Michaelis would say of Franklin Roosevelt, 'it might be a shallow kind of caring, but within certain inauthentic men there was a base of genuine caring'.[1]

Perón remains a political icon whose legacy is still contested today, despite the 'negatives' associated with his extreme personalism. A more contemporary parallel could be found in the late Venezuelan president Hugo Chávez, a 'populist' figure marked by both self-interest and a sincere desire to improve the lot of his people, albeit on his own terms. While also tempted by the lack of institutional channels to improvise solutions bypassing institutions, his failure to create sustainable institutions and his creation of a system heavily dependent on his own personality cult have generated longer-term difficulties not dissimilar to those already experienced in Argentina. Moreover, the problems inherent in personalism were compounded by Perón's proclivity for surrounding himself with mediocre figures and gradually abandoning most of his more intelligent and competent colleagues; whether this represented an unassailable belief in his own intelligence or insecurity about the intelligence of others, it would produce unsatisfactory and sometimes tragic results. (It also ran counter to an opinion expressed early in his nascent political career, to the effect that 'to govern it is not necessary to be very intelligent, just intelligent enough to take suitable advice'.[2])

With renewed interest in the ill-defined and variegated phenomenon of 'populism', in both Latin America and elsewhere, in the wake of more recent political events, it is perhaps a convenient time to look more analytically at a figure who has often been seen as the personification of populism (accurately or not). Moreover, Perón's thinking has returned to the international stage, at least indirectly, in some attitudes voiced by Pope Francis, an Argentine once linked to one Peronist movement and who, like his whole generation, has been influenced by Perón throughout his career.

ABBREVIATIONS

AC	*Acción Católica* (Catholic Action)
ALN	*Alianza Libertadora Nacionalista* (National Liberating Alliance)
CGE	*Confederación General Económico* (General Economic Confederation)
CGT	*Confederación General del Trabajo* (General Confederation of Labour)
DNT	*Departamento Nacional del Trabajo* (National Labour Department)
ERP	*Ejército Revolucionario del Pueblo* (Revolutionary People's Army)
FAP	*Fuerzas Armadas Peronistas* (Peronist Armed Forces)
FAR	*Fuerzas Armadas Revolucionarias* (Revolutionary Armed Forces)
FORJA	*Fuerza de Orientación Radical de la Joven Argentina* (Radical Orientation Force of Young Argentina)
FRECILINA	*Frente Cívico de Liberación National* (Civic Front for National Liberation)
FREJULI	*Frente Justicialista de Liberación* (Justicialist Liberation Front)
GOU	*Grupo de Oficiales Unidos* (United Officers' Group)
JOC	*Juventud Obrera Católica* (Young Catholic Workers)
JP	*Juventud Peronista* (Peronist Youth)
PAN	*Partido Autonomista Nacional* (National Autonomist Party)
PJ	*Partido Justicialista* (Justicialist Party)
PPF	*Partido Peronista Femenino* (Women's Peronist Party)
UCR	*Unión Cívica Radical* (Radical Civic Union)
UCRI	*Unión Cívica Radical Intransigente* (Intransigent Radical Civic Union)
UCRP	*Unión Cívica Radical del Pueblo* (People's Radical Civic Union)
UES	*Unión de Estudiantes Secundarios* (Secondary Students Union)
UIA	*Unión Industrial Argentina* (Argentine Industrial Union)

Introduction

BACK TO THE FUTURE

Si ayer fue la Resistencia, hoy Montoneros y FAR,
Y mañana todo el pueblo en la guerra popular.
Con el fusil en la mano y Evita en el corazón
Montoneros Patria o Muerte son Soldados de Perón

If yesterday was the resistance, today Montoneros and FAR
And tomorrow everyone in the people's war.
With a rifle in our hand and Evita in our heart
Montoneros, Fatherland or Death! are the soldiers of Perón
Los muchachos peronistas (The Peronist March, Montonero version)

20 June is Argentina's Flag Day, but in 1973 the date represented a far more significant occasion: the return of Juan Domingo Perón, nearly eighteen years after a military coup sent him into exile. The subsequent years had been marked by coups and counter-coups, economic crises interspersed with periods of prosperity, the proscription of the majoritarian Peronist party, political polarization and, increasingly, left- and right-wing violence both targeted and indiscriminate. Perón himself, a polarizing figure during his first two presidencies and during his long exile, was now seen increasingly as a potential peacemaker, someone who could unite the warring factions and bring about reconciliation in the crisis-weary country. One of Argentina's most popular-ever political figures during his heyday, he arguably now enjoyed more consensus and embodied more hopes than ever before.

Although hopes had already been raised by recent political developments – the departure of the 1966–1973 military government and the election of Perón's proxy, Héctor Cámpora, to the presidency – some of them had already been dashed. Cámpora's inauguration on 25 May had failed to halt political violence, and indeed Perón's own evident disdain for his placeholder president only underscored Cámpora's weakness. With no solution in sight, consensus was mounting that the eighty-year-old former president was the only potential saviour on the horizon.

As such, Perón's arrival at Ezeiza International Airport on a charter flight from Madrid was a historic occasion, and one of celebration. For Perón himself, that return was the vindication he had long sought, while for his supporters it represented the culmination of eighteen years of often violent and often brutally repressed struggle. It also represented for many the first face-to-face encounter, not only with a mythic leader, but with an ageing man in ill health, rather than the popular but distant hero idealized by supporters thousands of miles away from his Madrid residence.

Even for a public life characterized by mass events, Ezeiza was to stand out: the largest mass mobilization in Argentine history. A huge platform had been mounted on an overpass near the airport, dominated by huge portraits of Perón and his second and third wives, Eva Duarte (known as Evita) and María Estela Martínez (known as Isabelita). A public holiday was declared and free transport laid on, in the best Peronist tradition. However, planning and security at the event were in the hands of the Peronist right, as were the lion's share of weapons.

As Joseph Page astutely observed, 'the dark shadow of violence, a constant factor in the development of Argentine history, followed Perón at a discreet distance' throughout his career.[1] This was not entirely coincidence, nor a circumstance in which Perón himself was innocent; throughout his career he had been prone at times to promise or encourage violence (almost invariably when he believed he could control it) before prudently retreating from it. In particular during his exile, Perón had frequently encouraged both the leftist and rightist factions of his movement to resort to violence as a means to an end. At Ezeiza, however, violence abandoned its discretion and took centre stage.

The detonator of what became known as the Ezeiza massacre is not entirely clear. Early skirmishes between leftist and rightist groups produced at least one death, but violence around the platform quickly mounted; the press and the orchestra hired to play fled among pitched battles and mounting gunfire, while the master of ceremonies, the singer and director Leonardo Favio, bravely tried to calm the situation and unarmed, unprotected participants panicked and began to stampede in an attempt to escape. A famous photo of the scene shows members of the far right on the platform waving guns, and a member of the left being dragged up by his hair. Without any confirmed reports, the number of deaths ran anywhere from 25 to over 100, with at least 400 injured. Moreover, security services continued to hunt down leftist activists, many of whom were taken to the airport hotel and tortured.

Amid the carnage on the ground, Cámpora's vice-president, Vicente Solano Lima, ordered that Perón's plane be diverted to the military base at Morón, depriving both Perón and his supporters of their great moment. The former president made a brief radio address thanking those that had attempted to welcome him, and his triumphal return ended in frustration and violence.

It is tempting to see Ezeiza as a metaphor for much of went before and after – notably, the illusion that Perón could unite and pacify the country, and that his return would mark a shift to a more optimistic future. (This in itself was not unique in Argentine history, marked by a predilection for individual saviours, from the Liberator General José de San Martín onward.) While it crystallized for many (including Perón) the conviction that Cámpora would be unable to halt the slide into chaos and that only Perón's return to the presidency could offer a hope of salvation, it should also have raised a warning flag over the folly of charging an ailing elderly man with sole responsibility for saving a drowning nation.

* * * * * *

A youngish, handsome and dashing colonel at the time of the June 1943 *coup d'état* he helped to engineer, Perón would rapidly become the somewhat improbable hero and protector of the working classes, using his support within the military to pursue pro-labour policies even as he used his rising clout with the trade unions to counterbalance potential competitors within the military. By 1945, when doubts were mounting among his colleagues in the armed forces, Perón had become synonymous with the protection of workers' rights. An army revolt that led to his arrest and removal from office prompted massive spontaneous popular demonstrations that culminated in the famous events of 17 October 1945. The protests on that date forced the armed forces to capitulate and ensured that Perón would remain in power for a decade, and at the centre of Argentine public life for far longer.

The unfavourable Anglo-Saxon view of Perón owes much to the hostility of contemporary US diplomats and journalists who in the immediate post-war period were more than willing to see him as a local variant of the recently defeated European fascism. This version owes much in particular to Spruille Braden, the US ambassador to Argentina during Perón's rise to power and subsequently Assistant Secretary of State for Western Hemisphere Affairs – and Perón's personal nemesis. Braden, who would accuse Perón alternately of fascism and communism, 'came to Buenos Aires with the fixed idea that he had been elected by Providence to overthrow the Farrell-Perón regime',[2] according to British Ambassador Sir David Kelly, and his unremitting enmity would provide Perón with dividends at home even as it cemented a negative view of him in the United States. British diplomats and journalists were less negative, sharing the Argentine perception of Braden as a cowboy; Kelly himself accurately described Perón as 'a brilliant improviser, with a strong political sense and much personal charm, but not in the least interested in Nazi or other ideology'.[3] Subsequent UK embassy officials would also take a more tolerant view of Perón (as did many later US diplomats), but the initial State Department assessment has tended to colour later views of Perón and Peronism in partial and negative ways. So, too, did his emphasis on state intervention in the economy, anathema to admirers of US-style free-market capitalism.

One defining characteristic of Perón and his career illustrated by Ezeiza, apart from the not-always-discreet attendance of violence, was his solitariness. In June 1973 he was perceived as the sole person possibly capable of governing Argentina, just as he had earlier been the single man of destiny shaping the nation: 'the great Argentina San Martín dreamed of is the reality we owe to Perón', in the words of the Peronist March. This carried over into his private life. A lonely boy raised by distant parents in the remote and inhospitable south before being sent off to school in Buenos Aires, throughout his life Perón lived among crowds, but essentially alone. Popular with the men under his command during his military career, and with his supporters and collaborators during his political career, Perón 'loved his dogs and was loved by a great part of his country'[4] but was close to almost no one. One impression that stands out from a close look at his life is that of loneliness. In part his insecurities, which led him to prefer relationships with inferiors, were to blame, but it is hard not to conclude that the premature deaths of both his first and second wives must have hardened that shell and cemented his natural distrustfulness. To paraphrase Perón himself, 'in times of misfortune, he tend[ed] towards introversion as he tend[ed] towards extraversion in times of dominance'.[5]

In fact, with the exceptions of his first two wives, Aurelia Tizón and Eva Duarte, and his early collaborator Colonel Domingo Mercante, it is difficult to discern close and affectionate relationships in Perón's life. Although rarely alone, much of his life after Eva's death in particular appears to have been spent in the company of hangers-on, acolytes, opportunists and admirers, some of them sincere but few of them intimate.

That solitary nature may also have been key to Perón's chameleonic qualities that allowed him to appear to be all things to all people – and to a tendency to fantasize, both to impress others and, most likely, to colour in a life that, while remarkably full, was sometimes difficult to live, especially in childhood and old age.

Hints to that intrinsic nature can also be found in the books Perón professed to keep by his bedside, gifted to him by a father with whom he had almost no apparent relationship. He would later claim that Plutarch's *Lives*, the Argentine gaucho epic *Martín Fierro* and *Lord Chesterfield's Letters to His Son* were his constant bedside companions. The relevance of Plutarch's history of singular, disciplined, extraordinary lives to Perón's image as the man of destiny is obvious. However, arguably the latter contains the most interesting insights into Perón's character; his father inscribed the book to him 'so that you will learn to move among people'. Chesterfield's 'pious mission was not to raise the level of the multitude, but to lift a single individual upon a pedestal so high that his lowly origin should not betray itself'.[6] His advice to his son (illegitimate, like Perón), to 'remember to have that constant attention about you which flatters every man's little vanity' and 'that attention and civility please all those to whom they are paid; and that you will please others in proportion as you are attentive and civil to them', effectively defines much of Perón's public persona.[7] Equally, it is also likely that in Chesterfield 'he found norms of urbanity that he wanted to apply in his undisciplined Argentina'.[8]

Similarly, although the point of referencing *Martín Fierro* as part of Perón's '*criollo*' appeal is evident, it is not hard to see the relevance of the gaucho's famous warning – 'the brothers must be united … because if they fight amongst themselves they will be devoured by those from outside' – to Perón's discourse on nationalism and the importance of unity (albeit around his own figure). Perón was in fact almost obsessive about unity, despite the fact that he often deliberately fostered disunity for his own ends. Admittedly, disunity is not difficult to foster in Argentina, a country long characterized by polarization: a series of conflicts between Unitarians and Federalists, civilization and barbarism, personalist and anti-personalist Radicals, of which Peronism and anti-Peronism were only one manifestation, albeit an extremely durable one. While Perón played on that polarization when it suited him, it is hard to avoid the conclusion that he also found it deeply frustrating, resisting as it did his proposals of a military-style unity in favour of the common good.

Apart from these possible insights into his thinking, Perón's frequent references to his preferred reading matter are also in line with his lifelong vocation as a teacher and as a would-be intellectual. An intelligent man, Perón was not an especially original thinker but was adept at adapting the thoughts of others and applying them to best use (the author has described him elsewhere as an 'ideological string-saver'[9]). Indeed, notable intellectuals are rarely successful politicians, and the quality of the true intellectual would have added little to Perón's quite remarkable political talents. He was also a prolific writer, who left behind him a large body of works expressing what he thought and represented at any given time – or at least what he believed it expedient to think or represent, which is not necessarily the same thing. He wrote as a professor of military history at the Superior War Academy, and would subsequently produce many books either on his political 'theory' or of an autobiographical and self-justifying nature, the latter revealing little of the human being behind the public face except perhaps, on occasions, his unquiet state of mind. His thoughts and representations would evolve considerably, if not consistently, over time, shifting from a more traditional military mentality earlier on to a worldview more in keeping with the Non-Aligned Movement and the Third World in the 1960s, although with a continuing if inconsistent thread of anti-imperialism.

This skill in *aggiornamiento* that allowed Perón to appear forward-thinking as an elderly man was with him throughout his life, but his sometimes visionary ideas alternated with frankly old-fashioned and shopworn concepts and a closed mindset that appeared sometimes to have remained trapped in his glory days of the 1940s. In part this reflects his environment. Born in the late nineteenth century in a largely rural country, his early education was in a backward-looking military nostalgic for the Prussian modes of the Bismarck era. Yet Argentina modernized rapidly in the twentieth century, from 1914 in particular, and Perón was not isolated from the political, social and economic trends of his day. He understood instinctively how to apply them to advantage, both his own and that of others (which he sometimes confused). Absent from Argentina between 1955 and 1973, he doubtless erred in many of his perceptions of its realities, but his years in Europe gave him a perception of international trends that perhaps eluded many who spent those years in Argentina.

The combination of military and academic experience was crucial to Perón's character and style. The British Embassy would note in 1973 that 'it is worth remembering that he is by training a soldier, accustomed to analyse problems in the manner of a military appreciation'.[10] Yet he was also convinced of the need to educate and to persuade in order to bring people with him. The combination of problem-solving (which he sometimes sought to reduce to an unrealistically simple level) and persuasion was key to his style.

At the same time, his teaching experience and pedagogical bent doubtless contributed to Perón's great skill as a communicator, whether one-on-one or to a mass audience. A sober, disciplined man of regular habits, he came alive before a crowd, demonstrating his improvisational gifts, as well as the ability to sense and interpret what the crowd wanted to hear. If this were not enough, as already noted, he communicated his message through books, pamphlets and newspaper articles, and was also the first Argentine president to make constant and effective use of mass media – print, radio and newsreel. While the Peronist machine's creeping dominance over the media highlighted an increasingly authoritarian bent, the use of media for political propaganda purposes would soon become widespread globally, and the effective use of media a key political asset.

Clearly one of the most frequent charges levelled against Perón has been that of being a 'populist', an amorphous term applied to figures as diverse as Huey Long, Hugo Chavez, Viktor Orban and Donald Trump. While recognizing some points in common among all these figures – an ability to channel popular frustrations and anger, an ability to shape media narratives and political 'realities' to fit their agendas, skill in recognizing genuine social demands and an authoritarian bent – in practice any term applicable to all can only be of limited use as a definition. Perón clearly embodied elements of 'populism' – demagogic outbursts, mass mobilization, authoritarian elements, lack of ideological structure, a tendency to be all things to many people and a focus on grievances as a uniting force – but he also represented a pragmatic recognition of the need to expand the concept of 'society' to the large segments previously marginalized. Those segments played a useful role both as producers and consumers, and as political supporters, but also as elements of Perón's 'organized community' designed to function for the benefit of the whole. Although this can be interpreted at least in part as an authoritarian concept, it also contained a large degree of idealism, something that characterized Perón and his followers, offset his cynical side, and most likely contributed greatly to his frustration and bitterness over its failure.

Moreover, much of the so-called ideology surrounding Peronism was deliberately vague; as Perón was fond of saying, 'If I define, I exclude'. Yet Peronism was never able to be all-inclusive, not only due to innate Argentine factionalism and bitter opposition in some sectors, but above all because it was defined essentially as an opposition posture itself, pushing back against enemies such as the 'oligarchy', 'obscure forces' and the lackeys of imperialism. If these had supposedly been banished with Perón's election, the threat of their return was both useful and realistic, as was demonstrated following his overthrow by the self-styled 'Liberating Revolution', which did its utmost to expunge Perón from Argentine history and succeeded primarily in cementing his legacy and the belief that his government had represented a golden age.

That legacy (which needless to say owes much to many actors other than Perón himself) is mixed, but its achievements cannot be disregarded. How many of them would have come to pass without Perón is unknowable, but the failure of the labour movement to produce its own leaders created a vacuum into which he stepped with enormous success. However, this created its own problems: Perón depended on military support, but also increasingly on the trade unions he was seen to represent. Straddling those two worlds was possible only thanks to his ability to reflect what his audience wanted to believe. However, this also limited his ability to shape any serious and concrete ideology had he wanted to. Perón and Peronism increasingly became what others wanted or believed them to be, rather than what they were. This is also a challenge for any would-be biographer.

With his successes and failures, his virtues and defects, Perón was a fascinating individual and one who left a lasting impression on a highly individualistic society. An opportunist, ambitious and unscrupulous at times, Perón also perceived the need for social justice in an unequal society where it was sadly lacking, and took serious steps to redress that inequality, marking 'the first time any Argentine government has seriously interested itself in the conditions of the working classes at all'.[11] He had the ability to make people who had largely been forgotten feel cared for; 'many men and women in Argentina felt that their lives were richer and fuller when they had him at their side'.[12]

One of Perón's favourite aphorisms was 'the only truth is reality'. However, 'reality' lies in the eye of the beholder to at least some degree. For the worker who saw his real wages and purchasing power increase, who was able to take his family on holiday, buy a radio or take out a mortgage credit for the first time, the 'reality' was that the Peronist government brought great gains and a new sense of dignity. ('I became Peronist because I no longer needed an umbrella to go to the toilet.'[13]) For the person unable to find work because they did not have a party card, or the opposition legislator dinned into silence or pushed into exile, or the bus driver punched because he would not shout 'Viva Perón', the 'reality' was that the government was corrupt, repressive and destructive. All of those realities contain truth. The difficulty is finding the balance between diametrically opposed and arguably equally valid realities.

Chapter 1

A BRIEF CHILDHOOD

Dónde estará mi arrabal? Quién se robó mi niñez?
Where has my old neighbourhood gone? Who stole my childhood?
Tinta roja (tango), Cátulo Castillo and Sebastián Piana[1]

Founded in 1802 in the environs of a fort constructed in 1779, the town of Lobos, Buenos Aires province, lies around 100 kilometres southwest of the city of Buenos Aires (and around 65 kilometres from Ezeiza airport). The fort, constructed at a time when settled ranching was beginning to supplant wild cattle hunts in the Pampas area, was one of a series of similar installations designed to keep hostile Indians at bay and was staffed by cavalry militias known as *blandengues*, later incorporated into the army post-independence. It was built close to the *Laguna de Lobos*, a large lagoon given its name by a Jesuit mission that visited a few years earlier, apparently owing to its large population of otters (known as water wolves, or *lobos de agua*). By 1871 the railway line had reached Lobos, by then a centre of well-established cattle ranching. Three years later, Lobos came to prominence following the killing there of Juan Moreira, a famous gaucho-turned-outlaw, who is buried in the cemetery there and who would come to play a further supporting role in the early years of Juan Domingo Perón.

With a modern population of around 31,000, the town of Lobos is a popular weekend destination for fishing, as well as its aerodrome, rural activities, camping facilities and restaurants. Its other key tourist attractions include a natural history museum and a second museum, located at 482 President Perón Street and billed as the birthplace of Juan Domingo Perón, on 8 October 1895. The house contains a fairly modest collection of Perón's belongings, most of them from his adulthood, including some furniture donated by his widow, as well as the skull of Juan Moreira. However, like the so-called birthplace of Eva Perón in Los Toldos, around 180 kilometres to the west, this is a misnomer. As Perón would later say, the house was that 'of my early years, where I crawled, where I started to take my first steps, but certainly did not see my birth, because that happened in Roque Pérez, Saladillo district.[2] (Unhelpfully, if typically, at other times Perón would just as vigorously assert that 'I was born in Lobos, when my brother Mario was already four years old' – i.e. in 1895.[3])

Located some 30 kilometres south of Lobos, Roque Pérez, currently a town of around 11,000 inhabitants, was and is a backwater, although the area was important enough to the agricultural export sector for the railway to arrive in 1884. The town also boasts another 'birthplace of Juan Domingo Perón', this one with a greater claim to have seen his birth, though on 7 October 1893. It is a modest adobe house with a corrugated tin roof and stone floors, not dissimilar to Evita's childhood home in Los Toldos, and also sparsely stocked for a museum. (The Roque Pérez house, which at the time of Perón's birth was registered in his mother's name, was declared of historical interest as his birthplace in 1996.) The key question is perhaps why the confusion over Perón's date and place of birth has persisted, although it is not out of keeping with the facts of the rest of his life, which are often strangely elusive.

Perón was the second son of Mario Tomás Perón and Juana Sosa Toledo; Mario Avelino had been born in 1891 in Lobos at his mother's home there and was recorded in the civil registry of Lobos as the 'natural' son of Juana Sosa, aged seventeen and single. In effect, Mario and Juana were not married and would not marry until 1901, when their sons were already eight and ten; Juan Domingo was baptized in Lobos as Juan Domingo Sosa, the natural son of Juana Sosa, although he received his father's legal recognition and surname on his parents' marriage. Perón would later claim that his baptism certificate correctly stated his date of birth as 7 October 1893 but had 'accidentally' been damaged and rendered illegible. (It is not entirely clear who purportedly caused the 'accident', but it is notable that documents relating to key life events of both Perón and Evita proved remarkably accident-prone over the years.) While uncertain, it is possible that the document may have been rendered illegible in order to facilitate Perón's entry into the military academy, where proof of his illegitimacy would likely have disqualified him.[4]

For whatever reason, his father did not go to the registry office in Lobos to record his birth for two years; certainly it was not to conceal Juan Domingo's illegitimate status given that his parents did not marry for a further six years. In light of Mario's somewhat lackadaisical attitudes in many areas of his life, it may not have seemed important, or he may have begrudged the little money the trip would cost. Perón may have been correct in later years when he said that it was not seen as urgent given his robust state of health; Mario Avelino's more precarious health had made it expedient to register his birth in case it soon became necessary to register his death. In any case, when asked by the registrar when his son had been born Mario apparently said 'yesterday', prompting the birth record giving a date of 8 October 1895.

The reason for having registered Juan Domingo in Lobos may have been quite straightforward: at the time Roque Pérez had no registry office, and births should have been registered in the district seat of Saladillo, substantially further away than Lobos. Moreover, Mario had work in Lobos and visited it fairly regularly, with registered domiciles in both Roque Pérez and Lobos, while Juana's family continued to live there. Although the reasons for the two-year delay are less certain, Mario may also have had a logical reason for claiming that his son had been born the day before: having delayed the birth registration far beyond the legal deadline of three days, he could have been subject to a stiff fine.

Mario and Juana came from substantially different ends of the social spectrum, in a country that lacked an aristocracy but already maintained considerable class snobbishness over who came from the *criollo* oligarchy, the merchant middle classes, the immigrant communities (themselves divided among the northern European, often British, immigrants who worked with the railways or utilities and the southern European, darker-skinned migrant labourers) or descended from indigenous groups. Although the oligarchy might look down on the expanding and politically ever-more-demanding middle classes, Argentina already had a reputation as a country where people could work hard for a better life and see their sons exceed them in social standing and prosperity ('my son the doctor' was a popular phrase, especially among immigrants).

In this respect, Perón's grandfather Tomás Liberato was a success story, even if his grandson may have exaggerated his achievements as he exaggerated his own. Born in 1839 to an Italian father and a British mother, Tomás Liberato Perón Hughes studied medicine and gained a respectable standing in Buenos Aires society as a doctor and chemistry teacher. He married an Uruguayan widow of French Basque descent, Dominga Dutey (or Duteil), who already had two daughters, Vicenta and Baldomera Martirena; Tomás and Dominga would have three sons, Mario, Tomás and Alberto. Perón would later claim that his grandfather had fought in the key battle of Pavón in 1861, which saw the reincorporation of the secessionist Buenos Aires into the new Argentine Republic under President Bartolomé Mitre, leader of the victorious side. He would also say that his grandfather served as a senator, an envoy in France and president of the National Health Department. Certainly he served as a provincial legislator in Buenos Aires province and owned a property in Ramos Mejía, an area home to many of the well-to-do, notably those of British descent, and now part of Greater Buenos Aires.

Tomás Liberato's upward trajectory was not copied by his eldest son, Mario, who made a vague attempt at studying medicine before going to Lobos to work as overseer at the La Porteña ranch, owned by a colleague of his father, Dr Eulogio del Mármol. Mario also officiated as justice of the peace in Lobos and in Roque Pérez, where he met the adolescent servant Juana Sosa. (Del Mármol, for whatever reason, was in possession of the skull of Juan Moreira and gave it to the Perón family, where it would become a somewhat macabre plaything for Juan Domingo during his childhood.)

Unlike Mario, whose inherited respectable standing gave him his employment as overseer and justice of the peace, Juana was of full or part indigenous ancestry on both sides; her father may have come from the northern Santiago del Estero province, while her mother's family, the Toledos, were established in the Lobos area and were reportedly of Tehuelche origin. (During the nineteenth century, most notably following the so-called Conquest of the Desert in Patagonia in the late 1870s, many indigenous people from the south were transported to Buenos Aires province, including Lobos and Los Toldos.) Photos of her both as a young woman and in old age show an attractive woman of warmth and apparently strong character. After Mario Avelino was born, Juana and Mario set up home together in Roque Pérez, where she gave birth to Juan Domingo, although Mario was footloose and often away from home, frequently staying in his mother's home in Buenos Aires. (His father, Tomás Liberato, had died of tuberculosis in 1889, apparently contracted from a patient.) Some time later they seemingly spent some time in Lobos, where Mario continued his functions as justice of the peace, and it is possible that they lived for a time in the house later identified as Perón's birthplace (despite the fact that the house was not constructed until 1894, the year after his real birth date, and was owned and occupied uninterruptedly by the Moore family from 1894 until it was expropriated in 1953 due to its 'historical significance' and turned into a museum and library). While the circumstances are unclear, it has been suggested that Juana and her younger son may have stayed in the house while she acted as wet nurse to Moore's wife, who was Del Mármol's daughter. Thus, Perón's later claim that he had 'taken his first steps there' and the reason why the house might have been chosen as his 'birthplace' years later, to maintain the secrecy surrounding his illegitimacy and ethnic origins.[5]

There seems to have been no contemporary doubt as to the children's illegitimacy; Juan Domingo was known locally as Juancito Sosa and the neighbours called him Sosita. However, with relatively few people of exceptional social status in Roque Pérez (indeed, Mario would have been one of the more respected as a justice of the peace), there seems to have been little prejudice against the children for their 'natural' status or mixed ethnicity.

Although during most of his public life Perón would make little reference to his mother or her ethnicity, later in life he would speak of her in suspiciously glowing terms (given what is known about their relationship) and also her indigenous origins, noting that his background was the archetype of the 'overused phrase "melting pot" .... My family did not escape the norm. The Old World's ancestral culture mixes with local passions.'[6] The convenience of tying his origins in so neatly with those of the country as a whole is clear and self-serving, as is his observation that his government had passed a law giving 'natural' children the same rights as legitimate ones. Nevertheless, his defence late in life of women discriminated against 'when in reality their only sin was the courage to be single mothers' while 'the father was exonerated of all guilt and the son found the doors to his future closed', if perhaps containing a note of self-pity, was lucid and ahead of its time.[7] Perón would also note that he was aware of 'the existence of a cultural clash within [his] own family, a fact that could probably be extended to Argentine society as a whole'.[8]

Curiously, conflicting versions of Juana Sosa's origins appear to be equally designed to highlight Perón's 'Argentineness'. While Hipólito Barreiro would insist that Juana was full-blooded Tehuelche, Ignacio Martín Cloppet would claim that she had Spanish ancestry that could be traced back to the Conquest. Given how few Argentines are of purely indigenous ancestry, the suggestion that Juana had both indigenous and Spanish origins is highly likely. Yet both versions seek to underscore Perón's claim to being an authentic Argentine *caudillo*; Barreiro celebrates the fact that he did not take after his father's fair-skinned and 'foreign' family, while Cloppet (who also treats Mario somewhat offhandedly) attempts to highlight Perón's ancestral links to the 'Cross and the Sword' of the Conquest – the Catholic and Hispanic heritage that tied him to a nation with pretentions, at least in some quarters, to inherit the mantle of Catholic, Hispanic leadership in Latin America.[9]

In 1901 Juana formally ceased to be a single mother, apparently at the behest of Mario's mother Dominga, who had learned that her son had a concubine and two small children. Mario and Juana married at a registry office in Buenos Aires on 25 September of that year, and Mario gave legal recognition to his sons. However, this did little to strengthen the family bond. Mario continued to travel and Juana continued to work outside the home, leaving her children in Lobos to the care of relatives. Juana in particular was charged with looking after the family's sheep, due to Mario's still delicate health and frequent absences, and was known as a hard worker and a fearless horsewoman.

The situation would only worsen after Mario, who according to his son felt that Lobos was becoming too urban for his liking, decided to move the family to the distant southern Patagonia region where he proposed to take up management of a remote sheep ranch. While the trek was in preparation, Juan Domingo and Mario Avelino would be left in Buenos Aires in their grandmother's house, where seemingly their father's errant ways, their illegitimate birth and the origins of their mother made them the subject of some scorn and isolation. Buenos Aires itself, already a modern city of some 660,000 with a thriving port, railways, museums, theatres, railways, trams, gas and electricity, shops, factories and a sharp divide between the elites and poor workers crowded into tenement housing, must have been intimidating for two small boys from a rural village, in particular when they were not especially well regarded even in the family home. By his own later accounts, Juan Domingo greatly missed his life of liberty in Roque Pérez, spent on horseback and in the company of the rural workers, notably his friend Don Sixto Magallares ('el Chino'), who taught him to ride.

A year later, Juana and Mario returned for their sons and the family began the lengthy voyage to Patagonia. Arriving in Puerto Camarones, some 1,600 kilometres from Buenos Aires, in what was then the territory of Chubut, the family moved to the La Maciega ranch where Mario was to act as overseer. However, the property was sold a short time later and in 1902 Mario would take his family 1,000 kilometres further south, to the Chank-Aike sheep ranch in the territory of Santa Cruz. The area is still only sparsely populated today; at the turn of the last century, with minimal communications and a bitterly harsh climate, it must have seemed the end of the earth.

Although Perón would later tell the writer Tomás Eloy Martínez that his father had installed all the creature comforts at Chank-Aike, a former inhabitant of the area told that author that the Perón family lived in a corrugated metal house with wooden panels within, in a climate where temperatures below −20 were normal in winter.[10] Perón would also idealize his time there as a childhood of great liberty, in which he and his brother rode horses, hunted with dogs and went out to work with the labourers, most of them Chileans, some of whom would also be charged with acting as his early tutors and would teach him that 'it is better to learn good things than to learn a lot'.[11] He would later describe them, and the workers they had known in Lobos and at La Maciega, as 'magnificent people' and 'like family', 'in their infinite humility there was a greatness that I had difficulty finding later in more evolved people'.[12] To this he would attribute his early efforts to improve the lot of rural workers when he came to power some forty years later. For the child, the workers, horses and dogs were his earliest friends and teachers; he would retain a lifelong love of dogs and a respect for their intelligence and loyalty that he rarely displayed in the case of human beings. (Despite his praise for the sheepdogs and greyhounds of his youth, in later life his great predilection was for poodles, of which he always had several – a somewhat counterintuitive choice for the leader of such a *machista* society and a person so proud of his manly fortitude.) His mother would also ride out with them all day to hunt guanacos, a physically and mentally dauntless figure. One of the few women in that frontier area, she ran both the home and many of the ranch's activities, did all the cooking for the workers, hunted, and acted as nurse and as midwife on occasion.

Perón would also note, perhaps not entirely accurately, the influence his father had on his early life and thinking, describing him as severe and austere but also humane and decent towards his workers and the indigenous inhabitants of the area who had survived the Conquest of the Desert and the banishment of many family groups to other parts of the country. (The so-called Conquest of the Desert, led by General and later President Julio Roca, in 1879, had largely decimated the indigenous and Chilean migrant population in Patagonia, opening up some 8 million hectares of land that, as had happened earlier in the Pampas region, were largely distributed among a small group of landholders numbering around 400. Most of the remaining Indians were either limited to special reservations or handed over into servitude.) In his renewed capacity as justice of the peace, Mario would seek to give them some protection, saying to his son 'now we call the Indians thieves and forget that we are the ones who stole everything from them'. If Perón is to be believed, his father was given to musings on the evils of landowning oligarchs that deprived both the indigenous and immigrants of access to land, 'the origin of these people's poverty. Today's poor are treated like strangers in the land that belonged to their ancestors.'[13] Whether or not accurate, the discourse that Perón would employ (and put into practice, with tangible results) had its origins in these early experiences.

Despite Perón's late portraits of his mother and father as, respectively, his closest friend and confidant, and an austere, disciplined and authoritative paternal figure, the hardy Juana seems to have been far more energetic and decisive than her wayward and sometimes sickly husband. (If anything, it appears more likely that the highly disciplined Perón learned more from his father's seeming lack of self-discipline than from his supposedly positive example.) A former neighbour who played with Perón as a child would later say 'Don Mario liked his sons to be very *macho*. But him, who knows. Around here they said his wife paid no attention to him.' The same person would report that, on arriving at the house early with Juan Domingo one day in 1911, when he was at home during the school holidays after becoming an army cadet, they found Juana in bed with one of the workers. Thereafter, Juan Domingo would return to Buenos Aires immediately and had little to do with his mother for the remainder of her long life.[14]

After three years of endurance at Chank-Aike, Mario moved the family back to the area of Punto Camarones, to an isolated ranch called El Porvenir, although the family's accommodation was reportedly even more primitive than at Chank-Aike, a small adobe hut. The difficulties of finding viable lands for ranching in Patagonia were complicated by both the climate and, as noted above, the fact that much of the region was in the hands of a few large landholders. (The settlers of the Welsh colony who arrived in Chubut in the 1860s experienced a similar problem, discovering that they had been sold lands that were arid and barren, treeless and without water supplies, although the gradual introduction of irrigation and water management techniques would eventually produce a successful arable and pastoral agricultural economy – something that Mario and most other settlers failed to achieve.)

Mario again found a post as justice of the peace in Punto Camarones, occasionally travelling to the town and leaving his family at the remote ranch with sheep, dogs and pumas for company. However, this phase of Juan Domingo's life would be relatively short. With no schools in the area and their parents seemingly enduring a difficult marital relationship, Juan Domingo and Mario Avelino were sent to school in Buenos Aires, to the unwelcoming household of grandmother Dominga Dutey. They were deposited there by their parents, who soon returned to Chubut, in a home that also housed a school run by Dominga's daughter Vicenta, located at San Martín 458 in central Buenos Aires.

Mario Avelino and Juan Domingo would begin their formal schooling in Vicenta Martirena's establishment, along with other children also housed there. They included their cousins, the children of Mario's deceased brother Tomás – Julio and María Amelia – as well as two boarders, girls named Gabriela and Rosalía. The cousins were all around the same age and would play together; María Amelia years later recalled that 'Mario Avelino was serious and quiet. Juan Domingo, however, was chatty, everyone's friend, naughty, very entertaining',[15] perhaps in a bid for greater acceptance. However, relations with Julio were patchy, apparently because he seemed to look down on his cousins from the south with their irregular background. Juan Domingo could be aggressive, once pushing his brother down and breaking his tooth, and enjoying frightening his cousins with Moreira's skull. After an early childhood in the inhospitable Patagonian desert, with its privations but also its great freedom and physical activity, a Buenos Aires household run by a schoolteacher and a middle-class grandmother might have been less physically uncomfortable but must have been in many respects stifling and disconcerting for small boys used to a more elemental existence.

Not long after the brothers started primary school – their first experience of formal schooling despite being eleven and thirteen at this time – Mario Avelino, who disliked the city and did not take to study, became ill with pleurisy and returned to Chubut permanently, where his parents finally settled on a ranch some 180 kilometres south of Punto Camarones named La Porteña after Del Mármol's Lobos property. This left Juan Domingo alone and uncertain at an early age. By his own admission he was only a middling student; although he received warm comments from his teacher during his first year, his reports would decline thereafter. In part it would appear that he felt disparaged both at home and at school due to his mixed parentage, rustic rural upbringing and his father's unimpressive career. (He would later express the belief that another cousin, Mecha, rejected him as a potential suitor because he belonged to a 'somewhat murky branch of the family'.[16]) Moreover, he was older than most of his fellow students, which contributed to his isolation; one would years later describe him as 'dominating and bossy'.[17] However, it may also have contributed to other characteristics of his adult life and career, notably his attitudes of being both a bully and a protector. As the oldest male in his grandmother's household after his brother departed, he would early on come to play the role of 'man of the house', for example, leading his grandmother and the household to attend the wake of former President Bartolomé Mitre in 1906.

Although it is unclear that he had a greater than average religious fervour, Juan Domingo would also serve as an altar boy during his school days. Under the 1884 Lay Education Law, which guaranteed free and obligatory primary schooling, religious education was not allowed during the regular school day but priests would give classes in Catholic doctrine in the afternoons; this too was arguably an environment in which Juan Domingo could feel more 'included' and perhaps more 'Argentine'. Catholicism was identified with nationality (as opposed to the waves of immigrants of Protestant or Jewish origin or non-religious beliefs such as anarchism) and, like the military, a means of forging an Argentine identity among the children of immigrants. As the grandson of immigrants on his father's side and the son of an at-least part-indigenous mother, such a distinction was important for a youth who found it difficult to fit into the Buenos Aires society into which he had been thrown.

Indeed, it was following the secularizing legislation of the 1880s (which also included civil marriage and the removal of birth, marriage and death records from church to civil authorities) that efforts to identify the Catholic Church and the army as the nation's foundational institutions began to increase. The relatively limited strength of the Catholic Church doubtless contributed to the perception of liberalizing legislation in the 1880s as anticlerical, and of the Church itself as under attack. The reaction thus sought to link Argentine national identity with Catholicism rather than foreign settlers and their foreign beliefs. This would, in the early twentieth century, increasingly coalesce with a certain cult of nationalism surrounding the army, and its identification also with nation rather than immigrant.

On entering secondary school, Juan Domingo's situation would begin to change. On the one hand, he appeared to have developed an increasing taste for discipline and concentration that would keep him out of trouble with teachers. On the other hand, secondary school opened up the possibility of participating in sports, which throughout his life he enjoyed and excelled at, and in which he was likely favoured by being older and taller than most of his schoolmates. He began to take part in rowing and football (the latter never one of his favourite sports, either as a player or as a spectator), bringing him some renown and at least an appearance of belonging; later he would take up fencing, boxing, gymnastics and skiing with considerable success. However, in later years he would insist that he had attended the elite international boarding school in Olivos, on the river to the north of the capital, rather than the Cangallo Polytechnic School in the centre of Buenos Aires which his cousins and friends would insist was his real alma mater – yet another example of his sometimes mystifying need to be cavalier with the truth, perhaps based primarily on the desire to keep the truth about his 'murkier' origins undiscovered. (The street then named Cangallo, where he actually attended school, is now called Juan D. Perón.)

As Juan Domingo came near the end of his secondary school he began to consider studying medicine, following in his grandfather's footsteps, and he studied anatomy with that in mind. However, the family's finances could not fund a lengthy university degree and he was forced to reconsider his career options. (He would nevertheless maintain a lifelong interest in medicine and fancied himself something of an expert, offering free medical advice that was probably worth what it cost.) As he would later note, a number of his companions had enrolled in the military academy (*Colegio Militar*), and the young Perón, attracted by the discipline and elegant uniform, decided to accompany them. A career as an army officer also provided a social step up for the children of immigrants and the less materially blessed. 'We definitely did not belong to the social class that was common in the *Colegio Militar*. I was a strange animal and was lucky enough to continue to be one.'[18]

Here, too, however, he would face obstacles: officers were required to be born into 'constituted families'; that is, they were required to be the legitimate offspring of legally married parents, and, as in the case of medicine, his mother's ethnicity would also have raised a serious obstacle. His grandmother would eventually obtain a false birth certificate dated 8 October 1895 which inaccurately documented his parents' legal wedlock; she would also have to obtain a study grant given the family's inability to finance his tuition. Perón's entry into a military career would thus give him greater social status than he had previously enjoyed, but at the cost of his humiliation at knowing that his secret might disqualify him if the untruth were uncovered. In later years he would arguably become less troubled by convenient untruths, but the entry into the *Colegio Militar* would mark yet another crucial phase in the construction of Juan Domingo Perón. It would also mark the end of an odd and truncated childhood and of any residual tie to his family.

> I said farewell to the last shreds of the tie that bound me to my family. My grandmother Dominga ... went with me on the first day and with a kiss left her grandson, proud to think that he would be educated for the fatherland, in an environment that otherwise would have been adverse and hostile to us because it was inaccessible.[19]

Already at this early age, Perón could be said to have experienced many situations that were common to many Argentines, and some that were emblematic. Even for urban Argentines, both the Pampas and Patagonia are seen as iconic regions, romantic, untamed and characterized by the honest and dignified qualities of the 'gaucho' as embodied by Martín Fierro. Perón's earliest experiences were among those rural icons (people who might be scorned in reality by urban dwellers

Figure 1 Perón (left) with his brother and mother, around 1899 (Archivo Gráfico de la Nación, Wikimedia Commons)

but idealized as an image) and among those broad, flat and sparsely populated horizons; he was familiar from birth with people and places seen as central to Argentine national identity. He had an understanding of their people (both as their pupil and, to a degree, as their social superior, 'the boss's son') and of the hardships of their lives, as well as the disparagement and marginalization they felt when they came to the city – eventually in large numbers – to give up those rural freedoms and hardships for the more oppressive urban hardships of the factory and the tenement. These early experiences would be crucial to his later career and his apparently instinctive understanding of the people who would form his key support base.

Perón would later reflect on the effects of his early life and how his isolation and autonomy had generated maturity and independence, at least on some levels. 'At the age of ten I did not think like a child but almost like a man.' 'This early maturity would be a refuge for many of my companions and a hiding place for my weaknesses. They thought they saw society reflected in me, and in reality it was only a mask that hid a profound need for affection, arising from the early separation from my parents' home.'[20]

Chapter 2

THE ARMY

Y nuestros granaderos, aliados de la gloria,
inscriben en la historia su página mejor.
Cabral, soldado heroico, cubriéndose de gloria,
cual precio a la victoria, su vida rinde, haciéndose inmortal.
Y allí salvó su arrojo, la libertad naciente
de medio continente.
¡Honor, honor al gran Cabral!

Our grenadiers, glory's allies, write history's finest page.
Cabral, heroic soldier, covering himself in glory
Gives his life as the price of victory, becoming immortal.
And his daring saved the nascent liberty of half a continent.
Honour, honour to the great Cabral!
Marcha de San Lorenzo, military march (Cayetano Alberto Silva and Carlos
   Javier Benielli)

Juan Domingo Perón entered the *Colegio Militar* on 1 March 1911 at the age of
seventeen (officially fifteen), beginning his incorporation into an institution that
would become a source of the stability, security and camaraderie lacking in his
early life. This did not make it a welcoming institution: the academy was still
characterized by brutal hazing and 'baptism' of new cadets by the second- and
third-year students, designed in theory to build fortitude and obedience. The
new boys saw their new uniforms stolen and replaced by old, worn-out clothes,
and they were beaten and forced to 'run the gauntlet' as they were kicked and
battered by older cadets; one fellow student would later recall Perón, naked and
on his hands and knees, being 'ridden' around the patio by an older boy across
frozen paving stones. Perón himself would later recall that the older cadets were
'allowed to torture the new arrivals physically and psychologically, as a catharsis
and as compensation for what they had suffered in previous years', and that the
psychological damage this left implied that 'it was better that that person did not
wield much power, because the consequences are incalculable for those who have
no choice but to tolerate them'.[1] Typically, Perón would later give himself great
credit for having halted these practices, claiming to have headed a delegation of

cadets to argue against them before the head of the academy, who accepted their arguments and banned such behaviour.

Although Perón was later scathing about the abuse, rigidity and the quality of teaching at the *Colegio Militar*, he would recall the importance of the organization and friendship he found there, saying that the only people outside his family with whom he was on familiar terms were his fellow cadets, in particular those who like himself lacked illustrious families and had to make common cause. (Despite his claim to have forged lifelong friendships there, however, his fellow students were largely absent from his later life and career.) His early years in Patagonia had made him resilient enough to cope with physical hardships and cold winters, and his sporting prowess became an asset at the academy and throughout his military career. By the time of his second year, he was no longer among the new cadets on the receiving end of punishments and bullying, and could even begin to indulge his preference for endearing himself to subordinates by offering discipline, advice and protection rather than insults and beatings. Also in the second year, cadets were required to choose the branch of the army they would enter; like others of more modest socio-economic origins, Perón chose the infantry rather than the more elite cavalry, despite his early experience with and fondness for horses.

Perón's time at the *Colegio Militar* coincided with significant changes both within the army and society. By 1911 French military instructors had been replaced by those taught in the German model, while Germany was also the source of arms purchases, notions of discipline and use of more martial images such as a new uniform and the goose step.

Politically, although the landed elite maintained its social and economic dominance, shifts were underway that had begun to undermine the old order. Notably, huge waves of immigration from the 1880s in particular had begun to change both the social structure and the demands of an expanding middle class. Although most immigrants came from Spain and Italy, substantial numbers also came from Eastern Europe (many of them Jewish refugees), the Middle East and the British Isles, the latter often employed by the railways or British-owned utilities, or seeking lands on which to farm.

For the more successful families, who entered the middle classes as merchants, small business owners or nascent professionals as the sons of immigrants gained access to higher education ('my son the doctor'), political and economic participation became matters of importance. In 1889 the *Unión Cívica* was founded by a range of disparate interests including members of the expanding urban middle classes; an attempted 'revolution' the following year was easily put down by the government but made it clear that new political interests would demand a greater say and greater opportunities in future. Further activism led by the *Unión Cívica Radical* (UCR), founded by political leaders including Leandro Alem and his nephew, Hipólito Yrigoyen, would increasingly undermine the position of an elitist government. The so-called Sáenz Peña Law providing for universal male suffrage for citizens over eighteen was adopted in 1912. Although the new law still left women and the foreign-born disenfranchised, it marked a significant shift in the political landscape. Indeed, in the first votes held after its adoption, in Santa Fe and the city of Buenos Aires, the UCR won and the Socialists ran second.

Perón graduated fortieth in his class of 110 cadets at the end of 1913, after participating in military exercises commanded by Colonel Agustín P. Justo and designed to test the mettle and endurance of the now rigidly disciplined students. A 20-kilometre march under the summer sun of Entre Ríos province, while carrying heavy packs, left a number of the cadets, including Perón, collapsed and requiring assistance (although he would subsequently claim to have completed the march and even helped carry the pack of another exhausted cadet). Like the rest of his class, on graduation he was given the rank of sub-lieutenant and ordered to his first posting, with the Twelfth Infantry Regiment based in Paraná, Entre Ríos. This became the next stage of his life and chosen career, one to which he seemed increasingly suited and dedicated, with ten NCOs and eighty soldiers under his command.

So well did the routine of military life suit him in fact that Perón was seldom to be seen enjoying social activities in Paraná with his comrades, who were seen as good marriage material by the daughters of provincial society. While others enjoyed their free time at weekends in the city, Perón spent most of his days off in barracks, in line with the solitary streak that characterized so much of his life. However, his early career did not seem to promise great things; although he was rated 'very good' for physical fitness, he was less well regarded by his superiors in other respects and was punished for infractions on various occasions. His physical fitness and passion for sports nonetheless stood him in good stead; he took up boxing with some notable success. He also wrote and organized plays in which the men under his command took part, and enjoyed, as usual, a good relationship with his subordinates if not always with his superiors.

As Perón himself would later note, this experience served as much as a political apprenticeship as a military one. His time in Paraná brought him face to face with the social deprivation affecting much of the country; 'in a country with 50 million cows, 30 percent of conscripts were rejected for service because of physical weakness, and those who did join were semi-naked, coming from the deepest poverty'. 'At that time I began to see patriotism not as love of our ancestors' land, … but of our Argentine brothers, who deserve most and need most.'[2] His recognition of the miserable state of many compatriots would stay with him in later life, and indeed would be expanded by his many protracted assignments in Argentina's poorest provinces (referred to in Buenos Aires as 'the interior'). Those experiences led him to perceive what he described as 'on the one hand, the indiscriminate and corrupt management of public assets; on the other, the social injustice and abominable distribution of wealth that produced pockets of poverty wherever you looked'.[3] At the same time, he would note that these years led him to understand that his calling in the military was as a 'conductor', that is, a leadership, intellectual and didactic role, rather than as a 'troupier', a soldier or troop commander spending his life in barracks. This, again, was in line with his intellectual pretensions, capacity for study, solitary nature and preference for relationships of a teacher-to-pupil nature.

Perón was promoted to lieutenant two years later, when his regiment was also transferred to Santa Fe. Here his military career began to flourish further. On the one hand, he became personal assistant to the head of the regiment, Lieutenant

Colonel Ernesto Mastropietro, who encouraged his social life by inviting him to gatherings attended by local families. On the other hand, he found himself under the orders of Captain Bartolomé Descalzo, who for many years would become a mentor, friend and protector, as well as a significant personal influence. Descalzo 'knew how to form the souls of the young officers .... A large part of what I have been able to do in my life should be credited to the account of that captain.'[4]

During Perón's service in Santa Fe, in 1916, the first presidential elections were held under the new Sáenz Peña law, in which Perón voted for the eventual winner, UCR candidate Hipólito Yrigoyen. (Given his already apparent tendency to inflate or distort the truth about himself, his family and his exploits, one of his comrades in arms reportedly said that 'he is such a liar ... that we'll never know who he voted for',[5] possibly suspecting that Perón would have wanted to be seen to be on the winning side.)

Yrigoyen's victory was a watershed. The first genuinely popularly elected president, members of the public unhitched the horses from his carriage at his inauguration and pulled the carriage themselves. It also marked the end of the stranglehold on political power held until then by the conservative elites united in the *Partido Autonomista Nacional* (PAN), although the PAN retained control of Congress and a number of provincial governorships. This partial separation of economic and political power would see the elites increasingly intransigent in maintaining their hold on economic power in order to subvert political power. This they did through their control over business and the newspapers – and eventually, from 1930, through the armed forces. At the same time, the popular euphoria surrounding Yrigoyen's election prompted expectations of political and economic policy changes that were not met in practice. Yrigoyen lacked both the economic control and the focus on working-class interests that might have led to more popular policies, concentrating instead on his middle-class constituency whose interests lay more in access to higher education and public-sector jobs. The frustrated expectations would prompt a sharp rise in social tensions and labour activism under Yrigoyen which would be met by rising repression by the police and the army.

As so often, Perón's own experience of that repression is somewhat uncertain, although there is no question that he saw it at first hand. In January 1919 the country was shaken by the events of the 'Tragic Week', in which police repression of a metal workers' strike led to violent clashes and a week-long general strike in Buenos Aires punctuated by fighting between workers and upper-class, anti-Semitic youths calling themselves the *Liga Patriótica* (Patriotic League). The final death toll of the Tragic Week was in the region of some 700; despite its more popular colouring, the Yrigoyen government did nothing to support the workers and indeed ordered the armed forces to restore order. Perón himself was assigned to the Esteban de Luca arsenal in Buenos Aires to provide weapons to the security forces, although it can reasonably be assumed that he was also called onto the streets. He would later cite the experience of conflict between an 'owners' economy' and a 'workers' economy' as an object lesson in the need for a 'national economy' coordinated by the state that could mediate between mutually dependent but sometimes mutually exclusive interests. He would attribute the events to 'a sick society, where abundance and marginality co-existed brazenly', but also to the machinations of 'pseudo labour organisations … mixing demands for rights with foreign ideological positions', in other words, something that his later trade union policy would seek to eliminate.[6] However, he would also say that 'they said [the strikers] were communists, pro-Russians; I am inclined to think they were just poor Argentines scourged by physiological and social misery'.[7]

On various occasions Perón would claim to have learned of the events of the Tragic Week only from newspapers and telegrams owing to his presence at another labour conflict, this one relating to the British-owned La Forestal, which operated in both Villa Guillermina, Santa Fe province, and in Tartagal, in the northern province of Salta. La Forestal processed quebracho wood to produce tannin for leather tanning, and its forestry operations in both Santa Fe and Salta were plagued by often violent labour disputes over several years during this period. (Given the time frame, there is no reason why Perón could not have participated in both the Tragic Week and La Forestal.) Worker grievances related to the dangerousness of the work, low wages, poor accommodation and the fact that they were paid in coupons that could be used only in the company store. The company's response to labour strife on various occasions was to close down the company stores, leaving them without any supplies, and to call in the army to repress violent protest.

Yet again, it is not entirely clear whether Perón was involved in Tartagal, in Villa Guillermina or both; he himself spoke of the latter but not the former. When interviewed many years later, former employees of La Forestal could not agree; some said that he had been in Tartagal but not Villa Guillermina, others reported having spoken to him in Villa Guillermina and others had not seen him but said that years afterward, when he became president, others would remark that he had been there. It is perhaps unsurprising that decades later people would have unclear recollections of someone who at the time was an unknown junior officer, or that after he became president some might have believed or wished to believe that they had met him in his younger days. (According to one witness, 'I was a young girl and don't remember very well, but everyone said that a lieutenant had come who was in favour of the workers and years later they all remembered that it was him.'[8])

However, although as usual Perón's own account of his role is perhaps more heroic than that of other witnesses, all statements largely coincide in crediting him with a positive approach that helped to alleviate tensions. In command of a patrol sent into the estate to deal with armed strikers, he ordered his men not to draw their weapons, engaged with the strikers, discussed their grievances and then sought to mediate with the managers to ensure that at least some demands were met. He would be praised for his calm and bravery in speaking with the strikers and intervening in various fraught situations to calm nerves; he later attributed his approach and his grasp of dealing with individuals to the example and his knowledge of Plutarch. (He would later claim to have ordered the frightened storekeeper to open the company store against his employers' instructions and even to have forged a fine relationship with the owners, to the point of being invited to stay in their home, although he preferred to stay in the humble accommodations of one of the workers.) Perón would later say that La Forestal subsequently failed to honour the accords he had brokered, leading to renewed conflicts and, although 'we understood each other on the basis of dialogue, others came [after] who did not do things that way and let the weapons of the fatherland do the talking'.[9] However, it further convinced him of the need for mediation between the demands of capital and labour, and increased his experience of the deprivation rampant in many parts of the country; Salta in particular, where the agricultural economy was virtually feudal, would become a detonator for later events in Perón's career.

At the same time, Perón would later recognize the effect on the army of being used for internal security, as a sort of para-police force deployed to defend the interests of the oligarchs rather than to defend the country from external threats. This approach ran counter to his perception (and that of earlier military leaders) of using the army to create a national identity and 'Argentinize' both the children of immigrants and the poor of the interior who had been excluded, rather than to use it to repress them in favour of elite and often foreign interests. In addition to its purported role in defending the population, the army was also an institution that provided a degree of social mobility for some of those individuals, including Perón himself, and its use as a weapon to shore up elite interests no longer able to manipulate election outcomes so easily would become an increasing bone of contention for Perón and others, after the 1930 coup d'état in particular.

After a brief period back in Santa Fe under his friend Descalzo's command, in 1920 Perón was promoted to first lieutenant and assigned to the Sergeant Cabral non-commissioned officers (NCOs) school at Campo de Mayo in Buenos Aires. This represented an important career step for the young officer, allowing him to become increasingly involved in teaching, as well as putting him in greater contact with soldiers and candidates for promotion to NCO. One of his first functions was to participate in a trip to the deeply impoverished northern province of Santiago del Estero to interview potential candidates, many of whom suffered from poor physical and intellectual development and to whom he would dedicate extra didactic efforts such as teaching them about hygiene and table manners or lending them money to allow them to go out when on weekend leave. He also made systematic efforts to ensure that they would use those skills and leave time to seek out 'more refined' social settings to improve themselves. Another of his key functions at the school was to expand its sports and physical education programme. He started basketball and athletics teams and himself became deeply involved in gymnastics and fencing, winning a number of military and other competitions in the latter sport and establishing a gymnastics team that won a city competition.

All of these activities were beneficial to the men under his tutelage, and to Perón as well, increasing his prestige, his self-confidence (if only with inferiors) and his teaching and persuasive skills. His prowess did not go unnoticed among his superiors, with one report noting that 'he lives his profession intensely and is always willing to do more. Excellent instructor and very good troop commander'.[10] This didactic turn in his career also allowed him to indulge his interest in reading, his passion for history (especially military history) and his intellectual pretensions, encouraging him to begin publishing some writings of his own. The academy

Figure 2 Perón (right) as the army's fencing champion (AFP via Getty Images)

would initially publish his translation of a German manual of physical fitness exercises (illustrated by himself), as well as a few chapters of the academy's manual for aspiring NCOs, touching on issues such as correct hygiene, and an article on the 1810–1814 military campaigns in Upper Peru. For the rest of his life Perón would be a prolific, if not always profound, author, and would maintain a passion for setting out and explaining his philosophies and concepts to his military audience and political followers alike.

As if his military activities were not sufficient to keep him occupied, during these years Perón also founded a sports club for underprivileged children in the Flores neighbourhood, where he had moved to a house on Lobos Street, near the corner of San Pedrito, and near the home of some of his mother's relatives; a few years later his parents would also move to the house when his father became too ill to remain in Chubut. The eponymous Juan Domingo Perón football club also included boxing among its activities, with the recently promoted Captain Perón supplying the necessary kit and also organizing social activities for the children. It is hard not to view the football club initiative as an outgrowth of his interest in sports and leadership, his concern over the physical condition he saw in many poor youths across the country and, perhaps, a reflection of his solitariness and truncated childhood.

His fine record as an instructor at the NCOs' academy, capacity for hard work and his already significant written output would stand Perón in good stead; in 1926 he was promoted to the *Escuela Superior de Guerra* (Superior War School) for the advanced training of promising officers in line for promotion. Perón would join the *Escuela* as both a pupil and an instructor, teaching intensive courses and also travelling around the country for reconnaissance and training purposes. In this more exalted post he would also continue to study and to publish, demonstrating a particular predilection for the works of Napoleon, Von der Goeltz and in particular Count Alfred von Schlieffen, whose strategy was based on the element of surprise and the use of an unexpected move to defeat one enemy in order to be able to concentrate on another. Schlieffen's strategies would be visible in Perón's later political manoeuvres and his influence on Perón's writings would also be considerable; Perón followed Schlieffen in writing on the history of the Russo-Japanese War, and his sceptics would later note that his work would gradually evolve from frequently quoting Schlieffen to simply setting out his ideas without attribution, suggesting that Perón was in fact their original author.

Perón's career progress and rising prestige within the army also allowed him during this period to permit himself more social activity and enjoyment, frequently going to cabarets and other entertainments with a group of friends who became known as 'the four P's' (Perón, Pedernera, Pelufo and Pirovano). However, it was his superior officer and friend Bartolomé Descalzo (also a teacher at the *Escuela*) who pointed out to him an obstacle in the way of further advancement: the assumption that officers should have a respectable family life involving a suitable wife. Apart from having shown romantic interest in his cousin Mecha, who apparently rejected him due to his 'murky' connections,

Perón has thus far shown little zeal for marriage, devoting himself to his career to the extent that he often spent weekends in barracks rather than joining comrades at social events where local young ladies were looking for likely candidates among the young officers. Like others, he is generally assumed to have paid prostitutes or, in his more prosperous latter days at the *Escuela*, cabaret girls and dancers also available for hire, yet whether due to feelings of inferiority, his habit of solitude or his immersion in a military career, he had seemingly given little thought to the next step in the conventional trajectory of a respectable and ambitious man.

By his own later admission, Perón not only listened to Descalzo's advice but asked him to help find a suitable candidate, believing that Descalzo's opinion on the matter would be correct and adequate to the task at hand. Descalzo did indeed agree to do so, and within a short time invited Perón to a social event at which he introduced him to the suitable, pre-approved candidate.

Aurelia Tizón, known in the family since childhood as Potota (a childish mispronunciation of 'precious'), was born on 18 March 1908, making her some fourteen years Perón's junior. A former convent school pupil, at the time of their meeting she was working as a teacher at the República de Honduras state school in the Palermo neighbourhood. Quietly attractive and shy, Potota had studied piano and classical guitar, painted, spoke some English and French, and could be considered an entirely admirable wife for a rising military officer. (Although Perón would later claim she had been a concert guitarist, she seems to have devoted herself to music and painting more as private passions suitable to a respectable young woman, rather than as a public performer, although during their marriage she would have some private music and art students, including her husband.) Moreover, her father owned a photography studio in Palermo, was well connected in the UCR and was seen as a fine example of middle-class propriety and distinction. For the time, neither Potota's youth nor the age gap with Perón was a matter for concern or comment; girls customarily had a 'coming out' party at fifteen, when they were considered to be of marriageable age, and the fact that a husband was older was considered appropriate given his ability to guide and educate a less-experienced spouse.

Yet again, the exact circumstances of their first meeting are somewhat uncertain. According to some versions, Descalzo and his wife held a small social gathering at their home or at the barracks in Palermo and invited both Perón and Potota; in other versions, Descalzo and his wife invited the two to accompany them to see Rudolph Valentino in *The Son of the Sheikh*. Perón would later claim to have met her first when riding in Palermo Park, coming across her as she sat sketching for her drawing class. He would claim to have introduced himself, telling her that 'you have dazzled me, first with your beauty and then with your drawing', noting that he could 'discern in her face a great internal strength, as well as an excellent predisposition for the arts'.[11] Whatever the precise circumstances of that first encounter, it is clear that Aurelia would have been scrutinized and approved by Descalzo or other senior officers, as was usual for the possible wife of a promising young officer. For her part, Aurelia was apparently smitten with the

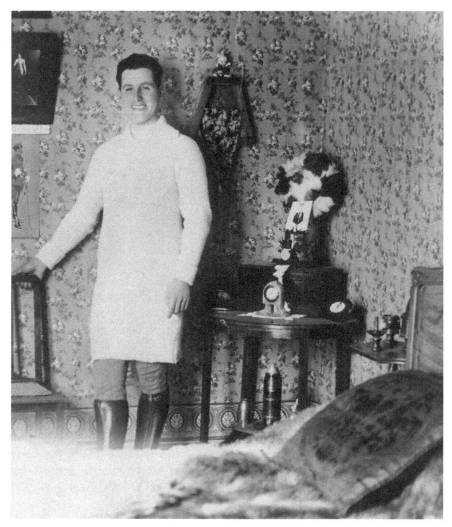

Figure 3 Perón as a young man (Bettmann/Contributor)

handsome young officer; one of her sisters would recall years later that after their first meeting, Potota had been trembling when she came home. 'We asked if she felt ill and she said she was fine. Very emotional, she had a fever that night, she was sick with love.'[12]

Following their initial meeting, Potota and Perón quickly became officially a couple, and Perón would call for her every Saturday afternoon to 'walk out' before coming back to chat with her father. He rapidly became a fixture in the Tizón family home in Belgrano, where he easily ingratiated himself with her parents and two sisters. His tendency towards verbosity was complemented by her timidity, and her sister would much later comment that Potota 'had great tact, … and was already prepared to be the wife of a man so studious and full of ideals as he'.[13] If it was not a deeply passionate relationship, Potota would seem to have fallen in love with the attractive and courtly captain, while Perón was delighted to find himself loved and respected by a cultured young woman and her family. In April 1928 Perón and Aurelia's Radical father Cipriano Tizón could share their enthusiasm at the re-election of Radical leader Hipólito Yrigoyen to the presidency, and also a more personal event, when Perón formally asked Cipriano for Potota's hand in marriage and their engagement was confirmed. The stage appeared to be set for a new and successful phase in Perón's life and career.

Chapter 3

POTOTA AND POLITICS

Alta en el cielo un águila guerrera, audaz se eleva en vuelo triunfal,
azul un ala del color del cielo, azul un ala del color del mar.
Es la bandera de la patria mía del sol nacida que me ha dado Dios.

High in the sky, a warlike eagle audaciously rises in triumphant flight,
One wing the blue of the sky, one wing the blue of the sea.
It is the flag of my fatherland, born of the sun, that God has given me.
Aurora (Hymn to the Flag), Héctor Panizza and Luigi Illica

Perón and Aurelia planned to wed in October 1928, but their plans were delayed by the arrival of his parents from Chubut, owing to his father's deteriorating health. Mario and Juana arrived in Buenos Aires in mid-1928 as Mario was by now too ill to remain in the harsh southern climate, and moved into Perón's Flores house. Mario Avelino stayed behind to take over the running of the ranch in Sierra Cuadrada, where he and his family would remain. Now wheelchair-bound, Mario died on 10 November, just before his sixty-fourth birthday. The wedding was pushed back to 5 January 1929; even then it was a subdued affair, with the religious ceremony held at Aurelia's parents' home, in keeping with the fact that the family was still in mourning. Aurelia's father Cipriano and Juana acted as best man and matron of honour. There was no reception, and the couple went immediately on their honeymoon. Juana would remain in Buenos Aires for some time, before returning finally to Chubut in early 1930, where a few years later she would marry the much-younger Marcelino Canosa, the ranch hand with whom Perón had purportedly caught her in bed. Unsurprisingly, he reacted to events with displeasure, and his relationship with Juana returned to being distant and sporadic. After her departure, Perón opted to move with Aurelia to a flat in the Palermo district, located at Santa Fe 3641.

Coinciding with his marriage, Perón graduated from the *Escuela Superior de Guerra* and received a posting as assistant to Colonel Francisco Fasola Castaño, a member of the army high command, marking a new advance in his career. However, the new position must have come as a mixed blessing for Potota. Having already been deprived of a wedding celebration, Potota now found herself alone much of the time, with a husband who would later have been characterized as a workaholic. Seemingly she had already foreseen this situation, telling her sister before her wedding that she feared being left alone: 'his head is somewhere else. He is a military officer and can only think about his career.'[1] This would prove to be a constant. Although all sources indicate that Perón and Potota were a devoted couple, and that he was an affectionate and attentive husband (when time permitted), his dedication to his career would imply that his wife spent much time alone while he worked, whether in the War Ministry or at home, or undertook missions in remote parts of the country – one of which, in 1931, lasted three months and took him to the Bolivian border. Both her sister and Perón's cousin's wife (a neighbour in Flores who became close to the couple) would remark that Potota became a virtual hermit, unwilling to go out in case her husband came home and found her gone, yet at a loose end in an empty flat. While she did not seemingly suspect him of being unfaithful, his work proved a more demanding competitor for his time and attention than another woman.

Of course, long days with an absent husband were considered normal for military wives, and indeed for the wives of many working men, given the assumption that married women would stay at home if their husbands were able to provide (although Potota briefly continued to teach in the early days of their marriage). However, it was also assumed that those days would be occupied by children, an assumption that Potota must have shared. Yet she became increasingly frustrated and downhearted as the months came and went and there was no sign of a pregnancy. (Her state of mind cannot have been helped by her beloved mother, who frequently asked her 'when? when?' – doubtless with good intentions but underscoring the fact that the question had no answer.) According to her sister María, after more than a year of waiting in vain, during Perón's long stay in northern Argentina in mid-1931 Potota would face the humiliating experience of consulting a doctor, whose examinations revealed no reason to suppose that could not conceive. It was suggested that, this being the case, she should urge her husband to be examined, but she refused to do so to spare him any humiliation.

The question of Perón's inability to have children has remained a vexed and durable one over many decades. Statements by Potota's sister to the author Tomás Eloy Martínez make it clear that she at least believed Perón was sterile.[2] The fact that, over the course of three marriages with women of childbearing age and relationships with other young women, none of them was ever demonstrated to have become pregnant (despite unproven claims that both his second and third wives might have suffered early miscarriages) suggests that this is likely. In fact, some sources point to a specific event as the possible cause: a 1913 gymnastics competition at the *Colegio Militar* in which he suffered an accident during an exercise and landed heavily on the parallel bars, causing injuries to his groin area that doctors warned might affect his fertility. This issue would be hotly debated in a society in which the condition could be seen as a slur on his masculinity, and indeed Perón himself appeared keen to believe that he might have fathered children, later claiming that he might have had a child with an Italian woman with whom he had a brief relationship during his European stay in the late 1930s. Hipólito Barreiro would also dispute the claim, saying that on a visit to Roque

Pérez in 1938 Perón had told a young boy that he had a four-year-old daughter whose mother did not allow him to claim her.[3]

The most persistent claim to Perón's putative fatherhood came to public attention after his death, in the form of Martha Holgado, a lady who insisted vociferously and persistently that she was his illegitimate daughter. (She also insisted, even more dubiously, that they maintained a relationship for many years after he himself explained her paternity to her, and that she had been present at various well-photographed historical events, despite the fact that she seems to have been invisible.) It has been claimed that Perón had an affair with Martha's mother, María Cecilia Demarchi, whom he met at the home of the Peróns' friends Isidro and Luisa Martini. Born in Italy, Cecilia was attractive and well-off, and at the time separated from her husband, Eugenio Holgado. (Divorce was not legal in Argentina until 1986, apart from a brief period during Perón's second term; as such, remaining in an unhappy marriage and separation were the only options available during the 1930s, with the latter implying scandal and social disapproval. Even for an independently well-to-do woman, maintaining the façade of respectable marriage was often the lesser evil.)

According to some versions, the affair risked a scandal that could have ended Perón's military career and damaged that of Martini, and thus the relationship ended when Perón undertook another border exploration mission, this time in the southern territory of Neuquén. Cecilia thereafter returned to her husband, who recognized Martha as his own child when she was born in July 1934. This could well have been the source of Perón's purported claim in 1938 that he had a four-year-old daughter whom he was not permitted to recognize (although according to Holgado he refused to recognize her to avoid damaging his career). This would also presuppose that he had at some point been unfaithful to his wife, despite the fact that he was not much prone to philandering. However, whether or not he had a relationship with Cecilia Demarchi and whether or not she told him her daughter was his, there is no certain way he could have known this in the pre-paternity-testing era, although his desire for it to be true might have made him believe it. In 2003 three DNA tests were carried out, one of which was inconclusive and two of which determined that Martha Holgado was not Perón's daughter – and, indeed, that there was a 99.98 per cent certainty that she was the full-blooded sister of Eugenio Holgado, the other child of Eugenio Holgado and Cecilia Demarchi, whose paternity had never been attributed to Perón.[4]

Given the contemporary state of medical knowledge, it is perfectly plausible that in the 1930s no doctor could have been certain of the fertility of either Perón or Potota, nor of how to address fertility problems that might in later decades have had medical solutions, and that Potota's doctor might have erred in telling her that she had no impediment to conceiving. Either way, Perón left no demonstrable descendants and in all probability had none. This is a likelier theory than assuming that none of his three young wives was capable of having children, despite claims by some historians that Eva had gynaecological problems from early in her life that would have prevented her becoming pregnant – claims that contradict other statements that she suffered a miscarriage early in her relationship with Perón.

Whatever the truth, it can have mattered relatively little to Potota, for whom the reality remained that her marriage was doomed to be childless, leaving her alone much of the time and seemingly suffering from anxiety and depression that made her reluctant to leave the house even when her husband was away. For her, too, the question of having children was an important one, both given the societal value placed on motherhood (and the commensurate disparagement of its lack) and her own personal desires. Coming from a large family and with a background in teaching, it is likely that Potota had seen motherhood as a key ambition in her life; although far less accustomed to family life, Perón too was known to like children and was both fond and somewhat envious of his brother's numerous offspring. In addition to the implicit slur on his virility, their lack must have seemed inexplicable and sad, although his more unconventional upbringing perhaps meant that his expectations of marriage were vaguer or more limited than his wife's. That childless marriage was also another factor that separated him from most of his colleagues and isolated him from 'normal society'. However, with his career in the ascendant and his professional activities often occupying him well into the night, Perón most likely felt the lack less keenly than his wife, for whom children were expected to be the most important part of life, and of marriage.

Early married life thus jogged along in the regular and predictable routine that Perón tended to favour, with much of the young couple's social life revolving around his military colleagues and their spouses, such as Martini, Descalzo and Fasola Castaño, Perón's immediate superior and a convinced proponent of fascism as a system appropriate to an orderly polity. With Potota increasingly reluctant to venture out in case her husband (to whom she habitually referred, both personally and to third parties, as 'Perón') were to return and find her gone, her contacts with her own sisters and Benita Escudero de Toledo, the wife of Perón's cousin in Flores, would become more infrequent. Perón's military and intellectual career were on an upward trajectory with his duties at the high command and his teaching of military history at the *Escuela Superior de Guerra*, which also allowed him to indulge his enthusiasm for writing and publishing articles and books for the illumination of his pupils and colleagues. He himself would note that his 'permanent vocation for study' placed him in 'the double role of teacher-student', a role that would later develop in his political style of absorbing ideas and feelings from his interlocutors and reflecting them back.[5]

It was during this period, when his studies into theories of war and leadership and his experience as a teacher were beginning to form his views of 'the leader' (or *caudillo*), that Perón also became caught up in politics for the first time. Although Perón, his in-laws and millions of others had celebrated Yrigoyen's return to the presidency in 1928, popular expectations were rapidly dashed and by 1930 the political climate was at boiling point. Yrigoyen, known as *el peludo* (armadillo), had always been a somewhat secretive and unreadable figure, given to gnomic utterances and contact with a reduced circle of advisers, but by this time he was also elderly, widely believed to be suffering from dementia and perceived as completely out of touch with the times. Those times had also become increasingly adverse. Whereas Argentina (or at least some sectors) had enjoyed a period of economic and cultural bonanza in the 1920s, and the initial phase of Yrigoyen's second term remained favourable to his middle-class support base, the 1929 Wall Street crash had a disastrous impact on export prices and demand, as well as capital inflows. After one of Yrigoyen's rivals within the UCR, Mendoza Governor Carlos Washington Lencinas, was murdered by an Yrigoyen supporter in November of that year, political uncertainties mounted yet further; shortly thereafter an individual attacked Yrigoyen outside his home with seemingly murderous intentions and was killed by his guards. Thereafter Yrigoyen became even more secluded from public view, isolated and seldom venturing out except under guard. Although Yrigoyen received 840,000 votes in the 1928 elections, in the 1930 mid-terms his party's vote fell to only around 600,000, and the now opposition-dominated Congress blocked whatever limited initiatives the government sought to take.

Already by 1929 rumours of an impending coup were flying, propelled both by the conservative elites who had lost the elections at Yrigoyen's hands and by mounting hardship as companies dismissed workers and the government was unable to pay the salaries of the bloated public sector that formed Yrigoyen's key support base. Efforts to curb public spending only worsened the recession, as unemployment and poverty rose and the government could do little to ease the crisis. The Depression had made clear how fragile Argentina's economic success really was, depending primarily on external circumstances it was unable to influence. Moreover, with dictatorships established in Spain and Italy – countries with strong societal and cultural ties to Argentina – there were precedents for replacing a floundering civilian government without waiting for elections. The army was also increasingly opposed to Yrigoyen on the grounds that he had politicized military promotions to favour partisanship over performance, and that he had more than once called out the army to undertake repressive measures such as the Tragic Week or the intervention of provinces led by opponents (such as the case of Mendoza under Lencinas), as well as inciting military rebellions when he was still in opposition prior to 1916. Arguably the key factor delaying a coup was the splits within the armed forces as to who should lead it and what form it should take.

Perón would later find himself in something of a quandary when speaking of his role in Yrigoyen's overthrow, admitting to regret at having played a part in the fracturing of the democratic order (once he too had become the victim of a coup) but seemingly trying to strike a balance between minimizing his responsibility and playing up his role in order, as ever, to make it seem more significant than it was. In practice, as a captain with no troop command, his involvement appears to have been somewhat marginal, and also undermined by his attempt to avoid committing to any side that might lose. But the experience was his first in the field of political plotting, one for which he would develop both a taste and great talent.

In June 1930 Perón was invited by a colleague to a political meeting to be addressed by General José Félix Uriburu, a German-trained and Germanophile officer widely referred to as 'Von Pepe', who led one of the two factions forming parallel coup plans. Uriburu, who was admired by Perón's friend and mentor Bartolomé Descalzo (although Descalzo was far more sceptical of many of his co-conspirators and refused to back the movement), proposed a break with civilian politics and the imposition of a military government that would modify the 1912 Sáenz Peña law providing for universal male suffrage, which had undermined 'the natural hierarchies', in order to avoid the kind of popular experiment represented by Yrigoyen and characterized by nepotism and pork-barrel politics. Uriburu proposed to exclude civilian participation from the coup (avoiding the civil-military alliances that arise when civilian politicians 'knock on the doors of the barracks', in the popular phrase), and to bide his time until he could count on the support of 80 per cent of the active officer corps. Clearly authoritarian in his concepts, Uriburu nevertheless impressed Perón and other officers as being well-intentioned and concerned with the national good rather than personal benefit.

Uriburu's main competitor in the coup stakes was General Agustín P. Justo, who had served in the 1922–1928 Radical government of President Marcelo T. de Alvear and who proposed to maintain the participation of civilians and political parties in an electoral process once Yrigoyen was removed. Seen as overly liberal and too interested in personal ambitions by Uriburu's followers, Justo was nevertheless a more attractive figure for the political class, for obvious reasons, and for military officers who either did not want the armed forces to be diverted into politics or who wished to have wide popular support for any post-Yrigoyen regime rather than a military-imposed and controlled dictatorship.

Within days of that first meeting Perón had been incorporated into a 'revolutionary command' and tasked with setting out tactical objectives for the anti-Yrigoyen movement. Disconcerted by proposals to kidnap the president from his home, Perón would also rapidly become concerned over the disorganization of the movement and Descalzo's advice to avoid involvement in an operation that he believed would fail. Those concerns were cemented when he was told to report to a colonel supposedly involved in the plot to receive orders and discovered that the colonel denied any knowledge of or participation in a coup plan.

As Perón's doubts over Uriburu's success mounted, he became increasingly attracted to Justo's faction, in which Descalzo was also involved. Descalzo indicated that a plan to merge the two factions was in train, and indeed Uriburu accepted Justo's insistence that a military government would only remain in place long enough to organize new elections, apparently in order to ensure wider backing for the coup. Perón finally joined Justo's faction on 4 September, claiming to have informed Uriburu's men with implausible bravado that he was dissatisfied with their leadership and could 'not accept that we are playthings of their ineptitude and lack of conscience'.[6] On 6 September the coup was launched, with the support of the *Colegio Militar*. Yrigoyen was taken into custody and eventually confined on Martín García island, while citizens threw flowers at the troops in the streets and set fire to Yrigoyen's belongings. Captain Perón's own participation was very much in a secondary role (or less), printing copies of the military proclamation, urging uncommitted troops to remain in barracks, marching on the *Casa Rosada* (the 'Pink House' or government house) with a troop of grenadiers, posting guards at the entrances to the *Casa Rosada* and subsequently participating in patrols during the night. Later that night, despite his sudden change of sides, he was informed that he had been named private secretary to the new war minister, Francisco Medina. Uriburu was proclaimed provisional president and declared martial law until June 1931.

Perón would later note that the coup had come close to failing, and that only the extent of popular support had saved it – a lesson about the need for both civilian and military backing that he would digest and remember years later. He would say that 'amid their last death rattles, the liberals had not just tried to save the last traces of a past that could not return. The attempt to create a bourgeois democratic republican model with strong oligarchic overtones in our country would soon be destroyed by an unstoppable popular force.'[7] He would claim that the so-called revolution had 'no support, … foundation or content. Uriburu was a conservative and carried out the coup exclusively against Yrigoyen. We young officers had a deeper vision: we rebelled against a situation before which Yrigoyen had been impotent.'[8] Of his own role, he remarked that 'I was destiny's plaything, like everyone. But some let themselves be swept along by destiny and by others. I let myself be swept along by destiny and by myself.'[9]

Indeed, many of the measures taken by Uriburu's 'oligarchic nationalist' government and its successors during what would become known as the 'Infamous Decade' were laying the groundwork for Perón's own rise in the following decade. Uriburu himself would survive in the presidency only until November 1931, when conservatives managed to impose elections that brought his rival Justo to power at the head of an alliance known as the *Concordancia*, including the conservative oligarchy, anti-Yrigoyen Radicals and the other main congressional parties, the Independent Socialists and the National Democratic Party, which would become synonymous with corruption and electoral fraud.

Perón himself was thriving, and would describe the period 1930–1935 as 'the most fertile of my intellectual and teaching life', with his promotion to professor of military history.[10] However, it was not without its setbacks: shortly after the coup he was replaced as private secretary to the war minister as Uriburu purged his government of Justo's supporters. (Also at the end of 1930, his grandmother Dominga Dutey died.) Between March and June 1931, he was sent as part of an extended mission to the northern provinces, while Descalzo was also dispatched to a posting in Formosa. Perón's mission involved international border demarcation and reconnaissance, on the one hand, and intervention in another case of social upheaval in Chaco, involving reported sexual abuse of indigenous women and the murder of the accused rapists. He would eventually return from the far north ill and suffering from pleurisy, at least allowing Potota to enjoy his company and to look after his health for a period of several weeks, but the rigours of the mission led him to conclude that it also constituted punishment by Uriburu for his change of loyalty in the days before the coup. Uriburu's departure from office would provide a welcome relief for Perón, who was promoted to major on 31 December.

Although Perón thrived, the same could not be said for much of society, affected by the Depression, instability and a corrupt and fraudulent government. Justo and the *Concordancia* brought with them the return to power of the traditional landed elites, thanks to electoral fraud and the proscription of the UCR. The popular expectations surrounding the coup were rapidly dashed, to such a degree that when Yrigoyen died in 1933 his funeral produced the largest popular demonstrations seen until that time. Falling commodity prices, a weak exchange rate and declining agricultural production and exports prompted the government in 1933 to negotiate the Roca-Runciman treaty with Great Britain, in essence obliging Argentina to remain an exporter of raw materials while importing finished products. This prompted both a negative impact on nascent domestic industries and a backlash against the creation of a virtual neo-colonial state, although currency controls and declining exports would soon give an unexpected boost to import-substitution industries. At the end of 1933 the government would unveil an economic restructuring plan that included a programme of public works and production welcomed by the *Unión Industrial Argentina* (Argentine Industrial Union, UIA). Necessity would thus come to the aid of small-scale industrial development, not least because it was largely labour-intensive and thus both alleviated unemployment and required limited investment in machinery. (Large-scale industrial investments during the period were largely made by US and British companies in areas such as meatpacking, which also fed into the nationalist narrative that began to take hold.)

The economic shifts of the 1930s would also prompt shifts in political thinking, at least on the margins. One of the most important intellectual and political trends in the nationalist and 'revisionist' vein was embodied by the *Fuerza de Orientación Radical de la Joven Argentina* (Radical Orientation Force of Young Argentina, FORJA), a group of leftist Radicals whose calls for popular sovereignty, economic emancipation and social justice would become Peronist slogans in the 1940s and whose historical revisionism would vindicate figures such as Juan Manuel de Rosas, the nineteenth-century 'restorer of the laws' who had hitherto been defined by liberal elites as a dictator rather than a nationalist hero. Rosas, a large landowner with a strong gaucho following, had been governor of Buenos Aires intermittently between 1829 and 1852 and he and his powerful and politically active wife Doña Encarnación would later be seen as the 'bloody precedent' for Perón and Evita, in the words of US journalist Fleur Cowles. He also made use of his ties with both the Catholic Church and the army to maintain control over a lawless society, and was regarded by the Enlightenment-influenced intelligentsia of his time as the embodiment of 'barbarism' as opposed to the civilization implied by European influence. The revisionist version of him as a strong nationalist leader would offer another example to whom Perón could look in his definition of an Argentine identity and tradition.

In addition to political tendencies such as the FORJA, another institution seeking to reinterpret Argentine culture and its own role was the Catholic Church, which had welcomed the 1930 coup against a supposedly anti-clerical and overly secular government. The decade also marked the Church's first tentative efforts to influence the working classes, based on papal encyclicals such as *Rerum Novarum*, although these were restricted to a handful of priests and one or two bishops and had, for the time being, only limited success. However, the curtailment of political activism in the 1930s saw a rise in middle-class Catholic activism, driven by a religious intelligentsia including Monsignor Gustavo Franceschi, director of the influential journal *Criterio*. They saw Catholicism as immutable and central to national life and identity; Franceschi in particular considered that liberalism and democracy were impracticable in the Argentine context. Catholic integralism in Argentina was informed by events in Italy and Spain during the period, following the 1929 concordat between Mussolini and the Vatican that made Catholicism the state religion in Italy and made religious education compulsory. The 1929 Lateran Treaty recognized the Holy See and an independent state with the Pope as its sovereign head, and Pope Pius XI regarded Mussolini as 'a man free of the prejudices of the "Liberal" school'.[11]

In Spain, tensions between the Church and the Republican government were marked by strongly anticlerical legislation and the burning of churches, while during the Civil War some 7,000 members of the clergy, including thirteen bishops, were killed. By contrast, General Francisco Franco's government would be officially Catholic, and the Spanish episcopate endorsed his nationalist position in a 1937 Pastoral letter. In Argentina Catholic nationalist thought viewed the Spanish Civil War as an example to Latin America generally, representing 'the alternative between the high religious and cultural values of the West and Marxist barbarity'.[12]

At the institutional level the Argentine Church created two lay bodies to expand its influence, the *Acción Católica* (Catholic Action, AC) in 1931 and the *Juventud Obrera Católica* (Young Catholic Workers, JOC) in 1933. The latter, the Church's only official attempt to address the rapid expansion of the urban working class and to expand its role within organized labour, had limited political weight, but would become the only official Catholic body that initially gave its unequivocal support to Perón after 1943. AC, a middle-class lay organization initially intended only to propagate religion, began to move into the political vacuum of the 1930s.

AC's organizational activities were at least partly responsible for the holding of the International Eucharistic Congress in Buenos Aires in 1934, welcomed by the Justo government as a means of legitimating its political position. The Vatican's representative, Cardinal Pacelli (later Pope Pius XII), was greeted by hundreds of thousands of flag-waving Argentines; as Noreen Stack noted, the flags 'were moved by hands that voted'.[13] This was a consideration that, eventually, would not be lost on Perón.

The governments that followed the 1930 coup were not particularly favourable towards industry or towards working-class aspirations or organization (a base never courted by the traditional oligarchy – a key reason why after 1912 it was unable to win elections except via fraud and military intervention). However, by the mid-1930s economic trends were beginning to favour both, as the worst effects of the Depression began to ease. The continuing slump in the industrialized West reduced the availability of manufactured imports, prompting an increase in import-substitution industrialization and thus also expanded factory employment. This process would continue and expand following the outbreak of the Second World War. Unusually, it also brought a coincidence between the interests of the landed oligarchy and nascent small industries, which facilitated a gradual shift to government policies more favourable to industry. By contrast, the UCR, still considered the majority party and largely urban in its base, remained anti-industrial, somewhat paradoxically in favour of an agricultural economy that would finance the public and service sector employments common among its members.

At the same time, bad harvests in 1937 and 1938, combined with low international prices, hit the value of exports and prompted the imposition of import permits, favouring domestic production as the only alternative.[14] Moreover, the resulting slowdown required some stimulus for industry as a means of resolving rising unemployment and goods shortages. By 1940, the so-called Pinedo Plan attempted to balance both agricultural and industrial interests: on the one hand it provided for the state to purchase agricultural produce unable to be sold abroad, while on the other hand it sought to stimulate both construction and manufacturing, arguing that, at least temporarily, 'the country must have recourse to its industry to substitute as far as possible what cannot be imported or paid for and avoid the grave problem of unemployment'.[15]

Simultaneously with these trends, the flood of European immigrants slowed to a trickle during the 1930s, affecting the supply of urban labour. This coincided with the difficulties faced by rural economies within Argentina, which prompted significant migration from the countryside to urban factories. Despite the rising need for industrial workers, however, wages would stagnate over the period and unions gained little bargaining strength, with strikes producing little in terms of improvements in wages and conditions.

According to some theories at least, falling immigration and greater migration from the provinces would see the working classes become more homogeneous and less partial to imported doctrines such as anarchism that had traditionally characterized foreign-born labour activists. The traditional argument sustained that the 'older' workers from Europe or established in Buenos Aires had a class identification that made them less susceptible to a supposedly 'populist' or 'totalitarian' appeal such as that which would be ascribed to Perón. By contrast, the 'new' workers from the interior were taken to represent an 'available mass' for such a movement and to be pre-disposed to follow a *caudillo*, in particular given the theory that the migration to the city had destroyed or damaged their traditional social structures, leaving them vulnerable to the blandishments of populism. In practice, most of the native Argentine workers who came to Buenos Aires during the Depression had first migrated to provincial cities and factories and were already more homogeneous and disciplined than sometimes argued, although their identification was more likely to be based on shared experiences such as poverty, rather than class consciousness or ideology.[16]

Although Argentina's first trade unions dated back to the mid-nineteenth century, the employers' organization, the UIA, refused to recognize collective bargaining or the right to organize, and the surplus of labour contributed to weakening unions' bargaining position and thus their ability to attract members. Indeed, the limited appeal of 'foreign' ideologies such as anarchism or communism may have had less to do with the nature of the domestic labouring class than with the fact that trade unions had made few gains and thus held limited appeal. By the end of the 1930s only around one-third of industrial workers and 10 per cent of white-collar workers were unionized. These figures highlight the weakness of the union movement, but also indicated that the industrial working classes would inevitably become a political actor once they found an effective leader.

These trends in Argentine society and politics must have affected Perón, although he did not yet affect them from his professorial position at the *Escuela Superior de Guerra*. Nor did his publications, which included various articles and the books *The Eastern Front in the World War in 1914, Notes on Military History* and *The Russo-Japanese War*, all published between 1932 and 1934, and the book *Patagonian Place Names of Araucanian Origin*, published in 1936 after several lengthy stays in Patagonia that again took him away from Potota. These did, however, add to his prestige within the military and also form much of his military and political thinking – not least *Notes on Military History*, which focused on Colman von der Goltz's theory of 'The Nation in Arms' and contributed to Perón's views on social organization and mobilization, not only in the sphere of national defence but also that of politics (arguably, the continuation of war by other means).

Perón's work on Patagonia led him to deliver a lecture in 1935 warning of the risks attached to the lack of attention paid to the south, in a context of purported expansionist tendencies on the part of Chile; he would later claim that his harsh diagnosis was not well received by the high-level military and government figures to whom the lecture was addressed. Soon thereafter, however, in early 1936, he was named military attaché to the Argentine embassy in Santiago, a feather in his professional cap and a delicate assignment given bilateral disputes over the Beagle Channel and suspicions of Chilean intentions in Patagonia. The assignment was also doubtless a source of happiness and relief for Potota, who would accompany her husband to Santiago where he might be expected to be less peripatetic. It was a difficult time in her life, with the death of her mother, to whom she was extremely attached; that too implied that she had all the more need to have her husband at home, away from political intrigue in Buenos Aires and itinerant assignments to faraway points of Argentina.

The two of them set off for Chile by road, in a 1935 Ford acquired for the journey, one which marked the start of their longest period together. During the long trip across the Andes, through Mendoza province and the Uspallata pass, Perón would teach Potota to shoot, apparently at her request, and she took to carrying a .22 calibre pistol in her handbag. They arrived in Santiago in March 1936 and settled easily into life there, moving to the comfortable neighbourhood of Providencia and forming an equally comfortable social and professional life with the embassy staff and others. Perón would quickly form a good relationship with the ambassador, Federico Quintana, whose daughter María Teresa many years later recalled that 'Perón was very likeable and won the affection of my father, with whom he got together at least twice a week at the ambassador's residence. He was very amusing and had very refined manners. Of all the embassy staff I think he was the one closest to my family'.[17] His position allowed Perón to join the exclusive Ñuñoa social club, where he and Potota would go frequently for receptions and sporting activities – a far more active social life than they had enjoyed in Buenos Aires, with Perón working and Potota lingering alone in the flat. They also travelled frequently to other parts of Chile, with Potota able to accompany her husband now that he was not undertaking more physically challenging missions to remote areas. Both of them seemed to enjoy the lifestyle, with Potota pleased to play the role of the wife of a military officer and diplomat – a role for which her education, artistic interests and personality made her ideal – and Perón predictably enjoying both the camaraderie and the admiration and respect. For perhaps the first time in their married life, they were able to share considerable 'quality time' and both seemed very content with this arrangement. Potota's family also visited them for a long stay, providing the excuse for a tour of southern Chile. Even so, they were relatively austere and did not have domestic help, with Potota doing the cooking and cleaning and Perón sometimes helping out.

Perón's good manners and good humour made him equally popular with the Chileans in his circle (not always favourably impressed by Argentines), possibly making the Chilean sojourn the first time he had found himself so easily popular and sought after. To his Chilean friends at the Ñuñoa club and elsewhere he became known as 'Che Panimávida', the latter a brand of mineral water to which he was extremely partial, from a spa and hot springs in the Maule region not far from Santiago. (The very Argentine expression 'che', used frequently for emphasis or as an interjection along the lines of 'hey', has often caused the nickname 'Che' to be bestowed on Argentines living abroad, the most obvious example of course being Ernesto 'Che' Guevara.) Having such a good-natured sobriquet was probably also a first for someone whose life had been characterized by an air of solitude and 'outsider' – although he would have many other nicknames thereafter, not all of them affectionate, Che Panimávida would seem to have been his first as an adult, since he had been known in his family as 'Pocho' as a child.

During his stay in Santiago Perón also continued his climb up the ranks, being promoted to lieutenant colonel at the end of 1936, for which occasion the ambassador hosted a dinner in his honour. (One of the less gratifying moments of the year, however, was the news that his mother had married her younger labourer Marcelino Canosa, hardly the kind of family news he wished to share with his friends and colleagues.) While such promotion was relatively routine for officers who stayed out of trouble, the distance from Buenos Aires may have proved a blessing in that respect: Perón's friend Bartolomé Descalzo was arrested after calling on President Justo to take more decided action against communism, and Fasola Castaño was also at odds with the president, prompting disciplinary action.

However, Perón's role in Chile was predictably not purely social or diplomatic; with security ties between the two countries traditionally strained, part of his role as military (and now aeronautical) attaché was to prepare confidential reports on Chilean military developments, some of which information could only be obtained through clandestine channels. The fact that the role contained more than an element of spying was surely known to both governments (and the Chilean military attaché in Buenos Aires doubtless undertook similar activities). However, this aspect of Perón's stay would provoke a scandal and longer-term damage. Perón was assiduous in intelligence gathering, forming a network of informants and even supposedly paying a maid at his own embassy to hand over documents found in wastebaskets. In 1937, he entered into an agreement with a former Chilean officer to purchase documents and maps outlining a purported military move against Argentina. He cleared the move with the high command in Buenos Aires, which forwarded the funds to complete the transaction. However, Perón's assignment in Chile was drawing to a close, and the deal was to be finalized by his successor as military attaché, Major Eduardo Lonardi.

Lonardi and his wife Mercedes Villada Achával arrived in Santiago in April 1937 and were met at the station by Perón and Potota, with whom they would enjoy a three-month crossover. Perón and Potota moved to an address closer to the Lonardis and the four of them spent considerable time together for personal as well as professional reasons. Mercedes (known as Mecha) would later say that Potota was 'a very agreeable woman, and with her partner formed an exemplary marriage. We were with them from morning to night.'[18] Potota would warn her new friend about Chilean women, whom she felt were audacious and 'dangerously effusive' with men, and once commented to her how handsome both their husbands were, presumably making them potential prey for the effusive Chileans.

According to Mecha later, the deal entered into by Perón to acquire documents from a Chilean informant was a trap created by a Chilean military interested in provoking a border incident with Argentina and thus gaining congressional support for an increased defence budget. It is entirely likely that Perón suspected this and thus decided to leave the operation in the hands of his successor. In any case he told Lonardi to carry out the deal at a flat near the Plaza de Armas where they were both living, hand over the money and photograph the documents. Shortly after their departure, as Lonardi photographed the documents as instructed, Chilean security forces arrived and detained the participants, prompting a diplomatic incident that saw Lonardi declared persona non grata and expelled from Chile, forcing him to return to Buenos Aires in disgrace. In an attempt to safeguard his career, Mecha enlisted the aid of Ambassador Quintana, who refused to intervene and suggested that she had 'imagined' the raid. Fearing that her husband could be court martialled, Mecha went to the Peróns' flat in Buenos Aires to ask Perón to accept responsibility. She was dumbfounded when he told her that Lonardi was at fault, having been told explicitly by Perón not to photograph the documents while at the flat, and that she and her husband had both misunderstood his instructions. Although Perón would later declare to the military authorities that the events were unfortunate but not derived from any 'lack of discretion or prudence on my successor's part', and Lonardi was spared punishment, the events would bring a dramatic end to their friendship and would come to the fore again in 1955, when Lonardi would lead the coup that ended Perón's presidency.[19]

Even before their return to Buenos Aires, Potota had begun to have recurring episodes of pain and illness that worsened with time; she suffered haemorrhaging that led her to visit Buenos Aires for medical consultations several times before their final return, but received no clear diagnosis. In Santiago, according to Mecha, Perón 'took her to see all the Chilean doctors. He was a good husband.'[20] She spent some time in a clinic near Santiago before their return, which provided an opportunity for rest but did little else except cause her distress at being separated from her husband. After they returned to Buenos Aires her health improved for a time, although she was ordered to rest, and Perón was able to begin a new posting, teaching classes on 'combined operations' at the Naval Academy.

Despite the brief improvement, Potota's health again deteriorated, and she was eventually diagnosed with uterine cancer. Perón, unusually, began to neglect his work and was upbraided for 'mediocre' preparation of his lectures. After one of his lectures the Academy's director, Captain Eduardo Vernengo Lima, stood up and pointed out a number of serious historical errors in Perón's presentation (most likely not for the first or last time, although he would seldom be called out for those errors). An emergency operation at the Marini clinic in Buenos Aires was unsuccessful, and Potota remained in hospital with Perón at her side, despite her protestations that she wanted to spend her last days at home. Two months later, on 10 September 1938, she died aged only thirty. Hours before her death, she would beg Perón to marry her sister María after she was gone, a promise he made despite having no real intention of doing so. ('What could I do', he would say later, 'she was dying'.[21]) It is not clear whether María had other expectations of the promise, although after Perón married Eva Duarte in 1945 she had Potota's remains removed from the Perón family crypt in Chacarita cemetery.

Not the most overtly emotional of men, even in a society in which masculine emotion was expected to be controlled, Perón was deeply grieved by Potota's death, calling it 'the only misfortune you gave me in ten years'.[22] If not apparently deeply passionate, their relationship was affectionate and stable, unlike most of the years he had lived before, and the marriage gave him the companionship and secure framework that allowed him to pursue his career, even if sometimes at the expense of Potota's loneliness. The fact that his much younger wife should be taken from him at only thirty must have been difficult to comprehend, leaving him more solitary and directionless than ever before. It was at around this time that he made the visit to Roque Pérez and Lobos, perhaps looking for his roots and memories of childhood, during which Hipólito Barreiro suggested he had chatted with a local boy and told him both that he had been born in Roque Pérez and that he had a daughter. Subsequently he was invited by his superior, Colonel Juan Carlos Sanguinetti, to take part in a long road trip through Patagonia, which allowed him to revisit other childhood settings and to make a favourable impression on his superior officer.

Despite these episodes, Potota's death left a vacuum in Perón's life that he was unsure how to fill. However, shortly the fact that he was at a loose end and available for new assignments would let him fill it in unexpected ways, and ones that would begin to influence the reshaping of his life and career, and of Argentina's modern history.

Chapter 4

TURNING POINT?

*Que el mundo fue y será una porquería, ya lo sé, en el quinientos seis y en el dos
  mil, también.*
*Que siempre ha habido chorros, maquiavelos y estafaòs, contentos y amargaòs,
  valores y dublés.*
*Pero que el siglo veinte es un despliegue de maldá insolente, ya no hay quien lo
  niegue …*

I know the world was and always will be trash, in 1506 and in 2000 as well.

That there have always been thieves, Machiavellis and dupes,
The happy and the bitter, true and false.

But the 20th century is an exhibition of insolent wickedness, no one could deny it ….
Cambalache (tango), Enrique Santos Discépolo[1]

In April 1939 Perón would depart for his first visit to Europe, on a mission whose characteristics again depend on the source consulted. Perón had evidently requested a mission overseas in a desire for a change of scene and new responsibilities following Potota's death, and he was sent to Italy to train with Alpine troops and study military strategies. Perón himself would inevitably offer a more self-aggrandizing version of the mission, saying that the war minister, General Carlos Márquez, had summoned him and told him that the armed forces needed more information about the coming war and the international politics that surrounded it. He ordered Perón to go and study the political situation, purportedly saying that 'I think you are the right man to send me the information I need. Choose where you want to go.'[2] Proud of his Italian heritage and proficiency in the language (which he claimed to speak as well as he spoke Spanish), Perón opted for Italy, also noting the historic changes occurring there and the formation of what he described as an attempt at national socialism (by which he meant an autochthonous form of socialism as opposed to international Marxism, not Nazism). He would also later observe that his own movement, focused on social issues, had been influenced both by the Russian Revolution and by Mussolini's 'national socialist' experiment, while adapting both to a domestic context. He may perhaps also have had other hopes for his voyage; on saying their farewells his friend Fasola Castaño's wife, Nancy, suggested that he might well find great success and perhaps a new love among the Italian women (although he purportedly feared might it hinder his military career if he were to marry a foreign bride).[3]

Perón sailed on an Italian ship, the *Conte Grande*, and arrived in Genoa three weeks later, then travelling to Merano, near the Austrian border, where he was to be stationed as an observer of the Alpine troops of the Second Tridentine Division. He was shortly joined by a second Argentine officer, Captain Augusto Maidana, with whom he would form a friendship and share travels and social gatherings. A fine athlete, Perón adapted easily to the Alpine exercises and became a proficient skier, as well as ingratiating himself with his Italian colleagues. Nevertheless, whatever his later desire to hint at a more important mission, it is difficult to imagine that a remote Alpine ski force was at the centre of the feverish military and political events of the day, or that Perón could have been expected to gather important intelligence or observe the political situation at close quarters in that location. Indeed, given his very minimal political experience until this time, beyond his not wholly successful sojourn in Chile, it is hardly clear that he would have been the obvious person for such a job, particularly given that he did not speak English, French or German. His posting to Italy appears far more likely to have been part of the experience offered to army officers with good career prospects, with his knowledge of Italian a helpful assist in forming contacts there. Perón would be assigned to various Alpine regiments over the next year, and seemingly did well at all of them. The military attaché, Virginio Zucal, would report to Buenos Aires that opinion among the Italian officers with whom he served was that Perón was 'an outstanding leader, both militarily and intellectually', while on his departure from Merano his commanding officer there described him as 'a brilliant officer', among other flattering words concerning his manners, education and love for Italy.[4]

Perón apparently visited Germany at some point during his time in Europe, where his impression of the Nazi regime was that of 'an enormous machine which functioned with marvellous perfection'.[5] He would also claim later to have visited Germany extensively and to have made a number of visits to Soviet territory in the company of German troops, although the date he would sometimes later give for these visits – early 1938 – is inaccurate and the claims are not wholly plausible. (There is of course no absolute evidence that he did not visit at some later date, either, but given Perón's frequent infidelity to the truth his memories of long-ago events are best approached with tongs and a healthy dose of scepticism.) He even claimed on occasion to have entered Paris with German troops in June 1940, despite the fact that he is known to have been in Rome at the time. He may also have visited other parts of Eastern Europe and even France, although again there is no official record to demonstrate this.

At least as implausible was Perón's much later claim that he had met Mussolini, either on a visit to Rome or in Milan (in one version, the meeting took place on the very day Italy entered the war). He had already become deeply impressed by Mussolini's emphasis on 'fatherland', an 'organized community' and a 'third position' between capitalism and communism, ideas that would become central to Peronist doctrine a few years later. He would also claim to have studied political economy while in Italy, perhaps suggesting that his military duties were not overly burdensome. Although it is most likely that Perón saw Mussolini addressing the crowds in Rome while visiting the city, the notion that the Italian leader offered an interview to a mid-ranking Argentine officer on the day Italy declared war on France appears exceedingly fanciful even among the half-truths and outright inaccuracies that often characterized Perón's later memories; under the circumstances *Il Duce* might be expected to have had more pressing things on his mind. Indeed, his friend Maidana would tell the writer Tomás Eloy Martínez years later that, while they had hoped to meet Mussolini, this had proved impossible and they had to content themselves with a brief courtesy meeting with his son-in-law and foreign minister, Count Ciano. Maidana would also dismiss Perón's claims to have visited the front, saying that he had spent his time after leaving the Alpine troops at the embassy in Rome, although he backed Perón's later claims to have expressed criticism of Italian military strategies to Italian officers, saying that they had had considerable respect for Perón's views in that area.[6]

According to Perón, Mussolini himself explained to him that he had begun life as a Marxist, and also told him in some detail of the usefulness of propaganda and the ubiquity of a leader's image in cementing popular support for that leader. Mussolini's socialist beginnings are hardly unknown and Perón would scarcely have needed *Il Duce* himself to reveal this information to him. Nor indeed, being observant and intelligent, would he have required Mussolini to offer him helpful tips on propaganda to recognize the effectiveness of having public spaces festooned with posters depicting a charismatic leader striking heroic attitudes. (The aesthetic of later Peronist propaganda, with brawny workmen, smiling children and teeming factories would indeed be similar to both fascist and Soviet political art.) Despite the extreme unlikelihood of this meeting having taken place, Perón was clearly deeply impressed by *Il Duce's* charisma, apparent effectiveness as a leader and social and political successes, describing him as looking like 'a demigod out of Roman mythology'.[7]

A less welcome incident also occurred during his time in Italy, when he was informed by the military attaché that he would be required to serve five days' arrest owing to an incident that occurred shortly after he returned from Chile, when Perón had been temporarily assigned to lecture at the Naval Academy during Aurelia's final illness. Another officer had accused him of plagiarism due to the inclusion of another text without attribution in a publication written by and published under the name of Perón and a second officer. On this occasion Perón claimed innocence on the grounds that he was himself the author of the publication cited and therefore did not believe the inclusion represented plagiarism, but he was still obliged to accept the brief loss of liberty, although he escaped the threat of a court martial. Whatever the facts of the plagiarism case, Perón's tendency to adopt, rehash and repeat the writings or theories of others, as in the case of Von der Goltz and the nation in arms, would recur throughout his life. This would be evident not only in his writings, but also in his formulation of 'Peronist doctrine', which indeed included many nods to Mussolini and to Marx, but also to the Papal encyclicals and the post-war Labour government in Britain.

Perón's favourable impression of Italy and Germany and his frequent recycling of some of Mussolini's phrases and writings (not to mention the aesthetic of mass demonstrations and heroic images) would cause his critics, both contemporary and subsequent, to accuse him of being a fascist, although in practice it would be more realistic to say that he was a pragmatist who used what he deemed useful and overlooked that which was not useful or downright inconvenient. Perón was hardly the only outside observer impressed by the political and economic turnaround in both countries in the pre-war period, when many of the darker elements of European fascism had yet to become as clear; given how widely the Holocaust was overlooked until well into the 1940s, Perón was hardly alone in his ignorance. While Germany was a far more alien culture to him, and his lack of the language would have limited his perceptions somewhat, like other Argentine officers Perón had been trained by German military instructors who had imparted an admiration for German (not Nazi) militarism and his own preference for military philosophers such as Von der Goltz also predisposed him to look admiringly on German methods. (Many years later, he would remark to his physician that he was an 'admirer of Prussian rationalism'.[8]) Moreover, as will be discussed in later chapters, Perón in power actively courted Argentina's large Jewish community, and the ethnic and religious persecution elements of Nazism were entirely absent from Peronist doctrine, which in fact had a more idealistic view of including all Argentines within an overarching national identity (albeit, of course, a Peronist identity).

Italy, by contrast, was a far more familiar context – not just to Perón but to many Argentines – and in that respect perhaps even more impressive. Some 30 per cent of Argentines, including Perón, were of Italian descent; the country had received hundreds of thousands of Italian immigrants between the 1880s and 1920s in particular, and the vast majority had come escaping severe poverty at home, not motivated by a desire for adventure. Thus, for Argentines accustomed to thinking of Italy as a poor and underdeveloped country (despite its status as a cultural icon), the Italy of the 1930s appeared a remarkable feat of organization and development. Even Italian military 'success' in Ethiopia, not visible at close range, may have seemed impressive for Argentine officers whose own experience of actual warfare was non-existent. Although it had begun to recover from the Depression, Argentina in the late 1930s was a flailing economy governed by a corrupt, inept and fraudulently elected elite whose claims to be 'democratic' did no credit to the concept of democracy. (The Anglo-Saxon democracies of the United States and Great Britain were in general considered less relevant, given the prevailing Argentine attitude of the 1930s in favour of the Hispanic, Catholic tradition.)

In contrast, an Italian government that had not only made the trains run on time but had seen the country begin to prosper and advance economically could easily be construed as being more beneficial to its people than a farcical democracy open to derision. The wreckage of war and the evils of genocide were not yet so visible during Perón's grand tour of Europe, and it is not difficult to understand that he was impressed by German and Italian achievements on the surface. However, despite sharing with Mussolini his charisma as an orator and verticalist ideas of organizing the state, Perón did not share his aggressive public image nor cultivate the cult of masculinity that surrounded *Il Duce*; there was none of the jutting chin, stern poses or exaggerated virility that characterized Mussolini's public persona.

Despite adopting at times an aggressive tone, Perón's public image in general was far more genial and approachable, while advances for women in society under his government were real.

It was also during his Italian stay that Perón met a woman, as Nancy de Fasola Castaño had predicted. Perón met Giuliana dei Fiori during his visit to Rome in July 1939, when both of them coincided at the Argentine embassy. Giuliana lived and worked nearby, and had a friend who worked at the Argentine embassy whom she had gone to meet when she encountered Perón. Little is known about Giuliana, except that she had been born in the north of Italy; the few photos extant show a healthy looking and attractive young woman. She and Perón would maintain a sentimental relationship throughout the remainder of 1939 and 1940, during the last six months of which time Perón was attached to the embassy. In late November 1940 Perón and the rest of the Argentine officers in Europe were ordered back to Buenos Aires on account of the war. At the beginning of December she accompanied him as far as Barcelona by car; they spent some days in Barcelona and Zaragoza before saying their final farewells. The relationship would leave its mark on Perón for many years, perhaps primarily because he claimed to be convinced that Giuliana had been pregnant and that he had a child somewhere in Europe. It is less clear why he did not ask her to return with him, apart from the suggestion noted above that he believed that a foreign wife would undermine his career. In any case, after their farewells at the end of 1940 nothing further is known of Giuliana or any supposed offspring. As late as 1970 Perón charged his friend Jorge Antonio with trying to find her (them) in Italy, but despite persistent and extensive efforts Antonio was unable to find any trace of Giuliana in either Spain or Italy. Given the time elapsed, the destruction left by the war and the fact that no one even knew whether she had returned to Italy, and if so where, his failure was hardly surprising. However, Perón evidently felt the lack of children keenly enough to cling to some hope of having fathered a child either with Giuliana or with Cecilia in Buenos Aires several years earlier, despite all the apparent evidence against this. Like his stories of interviewing Mussolini, this seems to reflect Perón's wish for what might have been rather than what actually took place.

Unlike Italy and Germany, the Spain that Perón saw at the end of 1940 showed clearly the effects of its civil war and the vengeance inflicted by the Franco government. Here, far from showing any enthusiasm for the Spanish brand of fascism, Perón was lastingly appalled by the devastation and often spoke of his aversion to such destruction – one of the motives to which he attributed his refusal to fight against the 1955 coup that would depose him. He would often say thereafter that his conscience was clear because he had refused to allow thousands to go out and die for such a cause.

After a relatively brief period in Spain, Perón and the other Argentine officers sailed on a Portuguese vessel, the *Serpa Pinto*, from Lisbon to Rio de Janeiro, reaching Buenos Aires at the end of 1940 after nearly two years away. His time there would be brief; on 8 January 1941 he was sent to Mendoza province as an instructor for mountain troops, and shortly thereafter promoted to colonel and named head of the Mendoza Mountain Instruction Centre.

The posting was a logical follow-up to his time with the Alpine brigades, and allowed him to indulge his taste for both skiing and teaching (as well as suggesting that his time in Italy had indeed been designed to strengthen his skills in mountain operations rather than for intelligence-gathering or other more important political functions, on which he would scarcely have had time to report before departing for the Andes). Perón himself would later claim that he had returned from Europe eager to share what he had learned with his comrades and to warn that 'what had happened in Europe would happen ten or fifteen years later in Argentina' if the social situation were not addressed, and that he gave a series of closed lectures on his experiences. These, he said, led the 'caveman sector' of the military to think he was 'some kind of nihilist, a socialist with a bomb in each hand', prompting his rapid transfer to Mendoza.[9] Whether or not this is entirely accurate, the reaction to some of his political proposals a short time later would be along similar lines.

In Mendoza, as usual, he would become known for his obsessive work ethic, in his office every morning by 6.30, as well as his athletic pursuits, which in addition to skiing again included fencing and riding (although boxing appears to have become a thing of the past). Perhaps predictably, the rather tranquil posting left considerable time for such an industrious and ambitious man to reflect on matters beyond his military duties. He himself would say that 'the provincial life in Mendoza gave me time to reflect on historical themes, but more specifically on history as a discipline imbued with life force, nothing like the history they sold to us'. In large part this meant the role of the military in Argentine history, which had been minimized to a degree by the political elite but would later be somewhat exaggerated by military devotees of historical revisionism. However, later on, as his time in Mendoza drew to a close, he would note that it was the end of 'a phase of my life in which peace, calm, days without real worries would be definitively replaced by something that all men crave, secretly or openly: power'.[10]

Perón rented a house in the city centre, where he appears to have felt much at home in the mountainous region and arid climate. The city of Mendoza, near the Chilean border and in some ways more similar to Chile than to the rest of Argentina, was a modern and prosperous one, much of it rebuilt after an 1861 earthquake. The agricultural economy, focused to a large degree on vineyards and olives, was also modern, having benefited from the creation of a water department to administer the scarce resource in 1885 and from the arrival of many foreign technicians who designed advanced irrigation systems. More than many of Argentina's remoter provinces, Mendoza was also heavily influenced by immigrants from Spain and Italy in particular; for many years a provincial agent in Buenos Aires was paid one peso for every immigrant who opted to go to Mendoza, and nearly 100,000 arrived between 1880 and 1914. It was also Argentina's first oil-producing province, albeit on a small scale. Thus, the province had a thriving middle-class and a settled population of largely Mediterranean origin.

Mendoza was also something of an outlier among the Argentine provinces with respect to its politics (as was neighbouring San Juan, where women's suffrage was introduced for provincial elections in 1927). Between 1916 and 1930 provincial politics were dominated by the Lencinas family under Governor José Néstor

Lencinas and his sons. A Radical who was elected the same year that Hipólito Yrigoyen first won the presidency, Lencinas would split from Yrigoyen and Mendoza would suffer several federal interventions removing its elected officials from office. As noted earlier, Lencinas' son Carlos Washington, who was elected to but blocked from entering the national Senate twice and who succeeded his father to the governorship in 1928, was assassinated in 1929, allegedly on the orders of Yrigoyen, which contributed to the president's overthrow in the 1930 coup. *Lencinismo* was widely defined as populist, as Peronism would be in later years, but the Lencinas government adopted significant social legislation during its truncated administration, including regulations on minimum wages, working hours and pensions that would not be translated to the national level until Perón came to power two decades later. Whether or not Perón was influenced by this, he could scarcely have been unaware of *Lencinismo* during his time in Mendoza and indeed claimed to have socialized with members of the Lencinas family.

In Mendoza, again, Perón would prove a social success, having gained considerable confidence since his early days in the *Colegio Militar*. A handsome, well-travelled worldly widower in his forties with a flourishing career, personal charm and elegant manners, he was predictably in demand within provincial society, notably among the available women and daughters of marriageable age. Yet the relationship he formed there was not with one of Mendoza's eligible ladies, but rather with a young woman called María Cecilia Yurbel, the daughter of a carpenter. They met at the inauguration of the local branch of the National San Martín Institute, where Perón was invited to give a history lecture and to become a founding member. Born in February 1924, María Cecilia was seventeen when they met, an aspiring actress who was already part of the resident theatre company at the local university and who appears to have considered that the relationship would eventually allow her to move to Buenos Aires to pursue her career. Perón would refer to her by the nickname 'Piraña', supposedly due to her voracious appetite.

Despite the thirty-year age gap and the fact that some later claimed that Piraña had been handed over to Perón by her family as a servant or for other less above-board services, in point of fact she would seem to have been a rather resolute young lady who fell in love with Perón and also saw him as a useful career prospect. However, the fact that he would later tend to introduce her as his daughter or his niece during their time in Buenos Aires suggests that he was aware that the age difference, and the fact that they were living together without benefit of marriage, would have raised eyebrows and perhaps done little for his career – although a more surreptitious relationship that did not involve cohabitation would have done him no harm and perhaps even raised his stock among some comrades in arms. (The fact that cohabitation was frowned upon but infidelity in a married man was largely considered acceptable and perhaps even positive points to a dubious sense of morality and double standards common in society more widely beyond the armed forces.) As in the case of Giuliana, there are only a few known photos of María Cecilia, showing a petite, attractive but seemingly unremarkable young woman. However, the relationship was reasonably stable and lasted until 1944; Perón did take Piraña back to Buenos Aires with him on his return in March

1942, where they lived in a flat at the corner of Coronel Diáz and Arenales in the Palermo neighbourhood and she made sporadic efforts to pursue her acting career, with little success.

During this period, Perón was again joined by his friend Maidana, who like him was transferred to the mountain instruction centre following his time in the Alps. But he also formed two other relationships in this time that would prove more durable and more important to his career than that with Piraña: those with General Edelmiro Farrell and, later, Lieutenant Colonel Domingo Mercante.

Farrell, born in 1887 to a family of Irish origin, was at the time director of the training centre for mountain troops in Mendoza, and like Perón had been attached to an Alpine regiment in Italy during the 1920s. Not known for his addiction to hard work, which seemingly interfered with his preferred pursuits such as socializing, drinking, playing the guitar and womanizing (although he was married for sixty-six years to Conrada Victoria Torni and had three children), Farrell was pleased to have a subordinate like Perón who was so willing to take up much of the slack. Although he was also generally thought to have less than an incisive intellect, Farrell was a genuinely warm and sociable man who developed a considerable affection for the genial Perón and was largely happy to be led by his more highly developed astuteness. Farrell was not a significant influence in Perón's life, but his pliability and higher rank would make him a key instrument in Perón's rise to power from 1943.

At the end of 1941 Farrell was transferred to command the inspectorate of mountain troops in Buenos Aires, and shortly thereafter he arranged Perón's (and Maidana's) transfer, in March 1942. A few days later, Domingo Mercante was also transferred to the inspectorate at Farrell's request. They had become acquainted some time earlier when Mercante was based at Covunco Centro, in the then territory of Neuquén, in early 1941 (apparently in 'punishment' for a falling out with a superior officer). Covunco Centro also fell within the inspectorate of mountain troops, and Mercante had served as Farrell's aide during an inspection tour there in 1941. In an apparent goodwill gesture, Farrell brought Mercante back to Buenos Aires, ending his virtual banishment in Covunco Centro and the separation it implied from his wife and children.

Although they had met before when Perón had taught at the NCOs' school, this was the first time he and Mercante got to know each other well. They rapidly came to respect each other's intelligence, capacity for hard work and complementary qualities; Mercante was arguably more rigorous and had advanced further in forming his political beliefs, but Perón was more charismatic and had greater leadership qualities. Both men also shared a penchant for Plutarch and experience of the rigours of life in Patagonia, and as in the case of Mendoza their workload appears to have left them with time on their hands for other matters (perhaps unsurprisingly, given that the inspectorate of mountain troops in Buenos Aires was located hundreds of miles from anything that could be described as a mountain). Mercante would become a close collaborator, an ideological influence, governor of Buenos Aires province and, at least until 1949, Perón's virtual second-in-command and anticipated successor, referred to by Evita as 'the heart of Perón'.

Domingo Alfredo Mercante was born in Buenos Aires in 1898, to parents who were both the children of Italian immigrants and were dedicated to hard work and personal advancement. His father, José Domingo, began working in the British-owned railways as a young man, first cleaning locomotives, then as a stoker and finally as an engineer. While José Domingo worked his way up in the Ferrocarril Oeste railway, his wife Flora devoted herself to saving money and investing it, and by 1901 they owned various rental properties. Flora's grandson, Mercante's son Domingo (known as Tito), would later recall that they had been scrupulous about not becoming slum landlords, renting out decent accommodation at fair prices to decent families who paid for them.[11]

Although his younger brother followed their father into the railways, Domingo Mercante was attracted to the army – as was his mother, who saw it as a good road to professional advancement and a step up to the middle classes. He graduated from the *Colegio Militar* in 1919 as a sub-lieutenant in the artillery. He rapidly became one of the favourite pupils of the academy's director, Colonel Agustín P. Justo, whose competing bid to lead the 1930 coup would attract Perón away from General José Uriburu's cabal and prompt a glitch in his career. Justo's enthusiasm for civil engineering would encourage Mercante's own, and during his first posting in Córdoba he also completed a degree in engineering at the university there – suggesting that he shared with Perón a considerable capacity for hard work and application. Also during that posting he would marry the 20-year-old daughter of Italian immigrants, Elena Caporale.

Yet despite pursuing a military career and enjoying a prosperous youth, Mercante remained linked to the problems of working-class life in Argentina. Mercante's father was a member of the engineers' union, the socialist-led *La Fraternidad*, while his brother Alberto joined the other railway workers' union, the *Unión Ferroviaria*. Those contacts with trade unions and their concerns would become invaluable in the early 1940s, at a time when Perón and Mercante were seeking to reach out to unions deeply suspicious of military men.

In practice, Perón had been absent from Buenos Aires for some years by the time he returned in early 1942, virtually since his posting to Chile six years earlier. (The months between his return from Chile and his voyage to Italy had been largely occupied by Aurelia's final illness and death.) Although Mendoza was a comparatively more tranquil city, somewhat isolated from the political currents affecting Buenos Aires, the capital was more than ever seething amid the effects of the 'Infamous Decade' (by this time twelve years old), a new downturn in the late 1930s and concerns over the effect the Second World War would have – not least given its impact on Argentina's main export market, Great Britain, and the possibilities for trans-Atlantic shipping.

In 1938 President Justo had been succeeded by another fraudulently elected candidate of the *Concordancia*, Roberto Ortiz, a former member of the UCR who had been public works minister in the government of 'anti-personalist' Radical President Marcelo T. de Alvear (1922–1928) and treasury minister under Justo. Somewhat to the surprise of his cohorts, Ortiz never denied charges of irregularities in the elections, but took advantage of his office to attempt a democratic shift and to clean up politics. However, Ortiz was severely ill from diabetes and nearly blind, and became increasingly forced to delegate to his vice-president, Ramón Castillo, who in effect assumed presidential powers in 1940. Ortiz would finally resign in 1942, shortly before his death, amid increasing military disquiet not only about his debility, but also his pro-Allied leanings and accusations that he had restructured the army, purging nationalist elements and promoting 'liberal' currents linked to the Radicals. There were already deep splits in the military between those favouring the Allies, the Axis, or neutrality (which meant that the latter largely prevailed as a policy default), and those pressures had prevented Ortiz from declaring war on the Axis. Castillo, a conservative oligarch from the northwestern province of Catamarca, at least initially appeared more pliant to the demands of both the military and the conservative elites who could no longer win clean elections but who continued to hold economic sway.

Another concern for both the military and the elites by this time was the fear of working-class activism and, in particular, the threat of some kind of communist or other violent revolution (precisely the sort of consequences Perón had warned of on his return from Europe). Inequality had been rising in the first decades of the twentieth century, and, despite some economic recovery from the mid-1930s following the 1929 crash, GDP per capita continued to fall throughout the decade. The wage-rent ratio in the 1930s was below 60 per cent of the level in 1911, pointing to the fact that living costs continued to mount far more rapidly than wages.[12] Moreover, despite the recovery in GDP, income concentration increased, with the top 1 per cent accounting for 25.9 per cent of income in 1943 – up by 50 per cent in the decade.[13]

By 1940 there were some 350 trade unions active, with a membership of around 473,000, although this accounted for a small percentage of industrial workers. Most union members were concentrated in relatively skilled heavy industries, primarily around the cities of Buenos Aires and Rosario, and most unions remained dominated by leftist leaders. The umbrella *Confederación General del Trabajo* (General Confederation of Labour, CGT) had a number of communists among its leadership, and unions became increasingly militant as the ranks of industrial workers expanded and labour shortages boosted wages and expectations. In 1942, there were 113 strikes, only 45 of which resulted in pay increases, and the CGT had split into two factions: the CGT-1, led by José Domenech, the socialist leader of the *Unión Ferroviaria*, and the CGT-2, dominated by socialists and communists and led by the municipal workers' leader Francisco Pérez Leirós. Arguably the main reason the unions had failed to become more effective, despite their numbers, was the fact that they had yet to identify a leader who could unite them and push them in a more coherent and successful direction.

By 1942 there were some 7 million industrial workers, out of a total population of around 27 million, highlighting the reason that the large number of strikes prompted disquiet in the ruling sectors. However, one of the reasons for the sharp rise in industry was the new increase in import substitution prompted by the Second World War. This process gained greater impetus with the war, which stemmed the flow of manufactures from Britain in particular, now converted to wartime production rather than the manufacture of refrigerators. While deplored by many of the landed elites who regarded Argentina as an exporter of foodstuffs and an importer of finished products, many in the military took a different view, seeing the key to national development as lying in a broader process of industrialization. Coupled with their often more pro-German views than the British-aligned elites, this would increasingly put the more modern and modernizing sectors of the armed forces on a collision course with the *Concordancia* governments that had become increasingly focused on maintaining political power and policy-making in the hands of the traditional oligarchy – anathema to many younger officers who saw modernization and industrialization as the only course to make Argentina a major power.

Indeed, the moment was ripe for such a modernizing movement. Some industries had begun to flourish and some manufactures were even being exported: by 1943 around 20 per cent of exports were industrial or semi-industrial goods, and industry had for the first time exceeded livestock and agriculture as a percentage of GDP. The war had raised questions over the sustainability of exports and the export model; despite a sharp rise in foreign sales there were fears that they would again collapse post-war, as had been the case after 1918.

In these respects, despite the revolutionary fears of many within the military, many officers found common ground with the industrial working classes, who were still marginalized from political power and from any attempt at a construct of 'national identity', exposed to the vagaries of global economic developments against which they had no defence and to the perceptions of self-interest of the elite. Added to this, the rising number of strikes prompted concerns within the military as to the efficacy of that elite's handling of the potentially explosive social system.

To make matters worse, within the military tensions mounted further following Pearl Harbor, with Washington increasing pressure on Buenos Aires to abandon its policy of neutrality and declare war on the Axis (pressure instrumentalized in part by US military sales to Argentina's regional competitor, Brazil, which had joined the Allies). In practice US pressure ran counter to British interests, favoured by Argentine neutrality that reduced the risk to its shipments of meat and wheat to Britain. However, following the US entry into the war Washington would become increasingly concerned about the potential risks attached to neutrality among its hemispheric neighbours; although both Argentina and Chile remained neutral, Argentina was known to allow espionage and other activities by Axis agents, and its military's close links with Italian and German traditions made it all the more suspect. While some officers favoured declaring war on the Axis – not least as a means to facilitate arms purchases from the United States – US pressures tended to have a counterproductive effect that if anything undermined their position vis-à-vis those who favoured neutrality or even an actively pro-Axis posture.

As the 1943 elections loomed, these issues were compounded by the deaths of Ortiz and of the *Concordancia's* two likeliest presidential candidates, Justo and Alvear. The absence of a weightier candidate led Castillo to light on another presidential hopeful, Salta Senator and landowner Robustiano Patrón Costas.

Patrón Costas would prove entirely unacceptable across much of the military, both because of his pro-Allied position and because of his record as a virtually feudal figure, the owner of vast sugar plantations where conditions were reminiscent of those encountered by Perón at La Forestal years earlier. For such a figure to win the presidency, widespread fraud would again be necessary, and the social reaction unpredictable.

By this time, a number of mid-ranking officers were already forming a secret organization to attempt to influence events, although as yet it had no high-ranking officer in place to lead any bid for a key role. This time, the ambition would go beyond a coup against a government perceived as corrupt or incompetent: it would involve a lengthier and deeper role for the military, not only in government, but in an attempt to create an overarching national identity. This would reflect not the landed elite view imposed for decades, but an identity in which the armed forces, the Catholic Church and, increasingly, labour would be seen as united as the pillars of the Argentine nation. Although the plotters did not realize this at the time, that attempt at national identity would become identified with Peronism.

Given his experience, work ethic, writing skills and penchant for politics, Perón would soon be in contact with the initial group, eventually with remarkable results. With the political and social climate increasingly effervescent, and some military and labour concerns beginning to coincide, events would take a surprising turn: both labour and the military would find the leader that had been lacking, and it would prove to be the same person.

Chapter 5

IN THE ASCENDANT

Si habrá crisis, bronca y hambre,
que el que compra diez de fiambre hoy se morfa hasta el piolín ....

Al mundo le falta un tornillo ...
Que venga un mecánico, pa' ver si lo puede arreglar!

There's so much crisis, anger and hunger,
That anyone who buys a bit of salami even eats the string ....
The world has a screw loose ...
Call a mechanic to see if he can fix it!
Al mundo le falta un tornillo (tango), Enrique Cadícamo and José María Aguilar[1]

On 4 June 1943 a military coup ended Castillo's presidency, the protracted Infamous Decade and any plan to engineer the fraudulent election of Robustiano Patrón Costas to succeed Castillo. Grandiloquently referred to thereafter as the 'Revolution of 4 June', the coup differed from the overthrow of Hipólito Yrigoyen nearly thirteen years earlier in that it was a purely military affair, without the participation of civilian interest groups 'knocking on the doors of the barracks'. Indeed, this is hardly surprising, given the expanding political vacuum and widespread contempt for traditional political groupings that had deepened following thirteen years of fraudulent elections and disarray within the parties. This reduced popular resistance to a military coup, as well as the need to incorporate discredited political figures as a sort of democratic 'fig leaf'. It also chimed with the fact that at least some of the powers behind this coup wanted a lasting change in the political landscape, rather than a restoration of one or another political faction.

Popular reaction (or lack thereof) was also coloured by the fact that Patrón Costas was widely seen as a corrupt businessman as well as one who exploited his workers. Those who visited Salta or worked there were often shocked by the 'sub-human' living conditions of his workers, miserable wages and lack of health care or rest entitlement, and the fact that, as in the case of La Forestal, they were paid in vouchers that they were required to spend in the (overpriced) company store. Moreover, there were widespread rumours that he stood to be relieved of substantial debts on his election, which hardened much military and popular opinion against him, even above and beyond his reputation as an exploitative and virtually feudal overlord, the antithesis of what many officers hoped would become the face of modern Argentine industry.

However, while these characteristics doomed Patrón Costas's presidential aspirations, at least in part, they lent themselves nicely to the narrative that Perón would later construct (both rhetorically and practically) of the need to defend the workers from exploitation. Perón would later describe Patrón Costas's Tabacal sugar complex as a '"true fiefdom", with its own currency and police', and Patrón Costas as 'a man of the pro-English northern oligarchy [who] belonged to a dying political class, disposed to reorganise itself in order not to die'.[2] For his part, Patrón Costas would later be claimed to have said: 'what I will never forgive Perón is that during his government and also afterward, the *negrito* who came to fight for his wages dared to look us in the eye. He didn't ask anymore; he argued!'[3] In social and political terms he would become the perfect nemesis and foil for Perón. Those views, as ascribed to Patrón Costas, would be shared by factory owners as well, less perturbed by the financial cost of the benefits gained by their workers than by their empowerment.

Nor were the alleged conditions at Patrón Costas's installations by any means unique, as the La Forestal case also indicated. A report prepared by the National Labour Department in 1938, on conditions in northern Argentina, noted that 'the children who do not perish in their first months begin to develop in deficient conditions …. When they reach school age, malnourished, … they are already weak. Rural schools teach concepts that are later of no use to them, when they have to leave school early, without having completed their physical development.'[4] That report was presented to Socialist leader Alfredo Palacios, who made it public but lacked the political support to act on its findings. Those findings might have seemed remote to the comfortably off in Buenos Aires, but not to other expanding urban sectors – the workers who had come from impoverished rural areas and provincial cities during the Depression to look for work in Buenos Aires. Many were now living in similarly parlous conditions in crowded and over-priced tenements and working in dangerous and unhealthy conditions in factories and slaughterhouses where they lacked guarantees, health care, paid holidays or the possibility of unemployment benefit. Those urban working classes lacked, as yet, effective union backing or political weight – the political elites and fraudulent elections of the *Concordancia* not requiring mass support – but their increasing size would imply that it was only a question of time before they became an attractive political constituency. By 1943 the industrial working classes had reached substantial numbers, and most were now native-born Argentines and thus eligible to vote, if they had had someone appealing to vote for.

While the coup leaders sought to avoid being co-opted by the interests of 'corrupt' political parties, Castillo's overthrow was not without its shambolic aspects. Although it has variously been attributed to the military's desire to prevent the rise of Patrón Costas or to its aim of thwarting any declaration of war on the Axis, in practice it involved a number of different groups and interests which were in some cases in conflict and in others simply ignorant of the existence of other plotters. (Patrón Costas himself was variously believed to be a pro-Nazi who employed German managers on his plantations, or pro-Allied as an industrialist who needed access to machinery imports.) At the same time, despite the political vacuum and mounting rumours, the coup came out of the blue for most observers; the British Embassy sent a telegram on 4 June itself describing rumours of a coup to prevent Patrón Costas' candidacy, and the following day noted that 'this sensational development has taken us completely by surprise'.[5]

Although not the only party to the coup, unquestionably one of the most significant was a shadowy group of mid-ranking officers that, while then largely unknown, would become known as the GOU. Even its title had some air of mystery; debates persist over whether the initials stood for *Grupo de Oficiales Unidos* (United Officers Group), *Gobierno! Orden! Unidad!* (Government! Order! Unity!) or *Grupo Obra de Unificación* (Group for the Task of Unification). Equally unclear was its political orientation, which was believed by some to be pro-Nazi and others to be primarily informed by nationalism or that strand of 'cross and sword' Catholic nationalism that had gained steam during the 1930s. In practice the GOU seems to have been somewhat heterogeneous in its views, 'a mix of ideas extracted from geopolitical theories, professional admiration for the German military, and nationalism with industrialising tendencies'.[6] What is unquestionable is that its early members included Perón and Mercante.

Mercante may in fact have been Perón's first recruit to the GOU when both were working with Farrell in the long-distance inspection of mountain troops in Buenos Aires. Mercante would often find Perón drafting documents late at night in the office, and in their talks would become increasingly persuaded by Perón's arguments that economic exploitation and working-class ignorance might pave the way to communist revolution; Mercante himself already shared Perón's views on the need for economic and social justice, and indeed had probably influenced them. Although Perón initially rejected Mercante's assistance with his late-night dactylography, he eventually shared with him the documents he was drafting, which Mercante viewed as 'a call for revolution' with which he was in agreement and 'ready to act to change the situation'. Mercante would subsequently say, 'I concurred with the principles of the movement and agreed to join the group. Perón's emphasis on social justice, which, in his opinion, had to be established in the country, coincided completely with my own convictions'.[7]

Although Perón would later claim to have pronounced that 'I am the GOU',[8] it is not at all clear that this is the case. However, after joining he would rapidly become seen as a first among equals and the likely author of many of its documents. For Perón, 'the GOU was necessary so that the revolution did not lose its way, like the revolution of 6 September [1930]'.[9] His increasingly close ties to Mercante and the energy displayed by both would also solidify that influence; as Perón would later say, 'the reason why we imposed our authority ... was very simple: all of them were "one" while we were "two" – Mercante and me'.[10]

An early report on the GOU's activities prior to 4 June, prepared by Lieutenant Colonel Juan Carlos Montes, noted the group's concerns relating to Argentina's internal and international difficulties, owing in part to its neutrality in the Second World War as well as to the corrupt political class. The GOU appears to have begun in earnest only in February 1943, following the announcement of Patrón Costas's candidacy. Montes reports February discussions with Perón, Mercante and other 'comrades of recognized patriotism' with a view to 'immediately initiating the task of bringing together and unifying the ranks of the army, so that we could all work together tirelessly, without distinction between different political ideas or sympathies for the various belligerent parties to the war, for a common ideal, the welfare of the fatherland and its greatness'.[11] A second meeting in February ended with the GOU having twelve members, each of whom was charged with recruiting a further four, who would each recruit a further four, etc., each from a lower rank.

The GOU's earliest foundational document, dating from February or March 1943, shows signs of having been written by Perón, not least in the penchant for classical references. The document highlights the perceived risk that Argentina could be pushed towards war by US pressures, at a time of internal weakness and division. It also notes the fear that elections could favour the current dominant forces, producing either continuity in the policy of neutrality or a shift that could force Argentina into the war – or alternatively, the victory of a 'popular front' that could bring about communist revolution. The GOU's primordial mission is to 'save the army' by 'neutralizing' discordant elements and to this end one of its goals is to ensure that the War Ministry is in the hands of 'one of ours'. This mission of 'saving' the army is by definition seen as a means of saving the country; the GOU's members 'have no personal ambitions: their only ambition is the welfare of the army and the fatherland'. This requires in turn (perhaps somewhat ironically) that politicization of the army be avoided at all costs but that its members understand politics. 'This would have avoided communism in Russia and the Spanish Civil War. In both, … officers often repeated "I don't get mixed up in politics" and, consciously or unconsciously, closed their eyes to the red menace that would devour them.'[12]

One of the more often-highlighted points of this document is the fact that all members of the GOU had signed resignation letters, which were held by Perón – an obvious form of leverage to be used as necessary. One of the less widely noted points is that it includes the phrase 'for a military man there should be nothing better than another military man' – a phrase which a few years later would become 'for a Peronist there should be nothing better than another Peronist'.[13]

Bearing in mind that a group of junior officers would be unable to lead any action 'when the time comes', this document recognizes the need for a senior officer; if the army chiefs failed to take up the role, 'we will designate him ourselves'. In practice this is what happened; although the first general they approached to take over the de facto presidency, Martín Gras, declined on the grounds of ill health, the GOU lighted upon three generals who could be parachuted into a leadership role: Arturo Rawson, Pedro Ramírez and Perón's friend Edelmiro Farrell. Rawson, commander of cavalry at the key Campo de Mayo garrison near Buenos Aires, was the first to be chosen; on 4 June he led a column of 10,000 troops to the Casa Rosada, proclaimed himself president and dissolved Congress and the Supreme Court. (Perón, characteristically, was not very visible until the success of the coup was clear; Mercante, by contrast, was charged with preventing loyal troops from entering the city and among other things did so by ordering the stationmaster at Once station, at gunpoint, to stop a troop train from arriving from Mercedes.)

However, Rawson immediately fell foul of the GOU, which discovered him to be closely linked to the conservative elites whose removal from power had been a key goal (his predilection for alcohol was also said to be a factor). His suggestion of several conservative politicians to join his cabinet clashed with the GOU's 'new broom' approach to politics. Moreover, he was believed by some to have Allied sympathies, and by others to be an Axis sympathizer who also suggested pro-German names for his cabinet – although, adding to the confusion, his first speech as president sounded a more militant Catholic note in opposition to lay education. (Rumours that the 'entirely Argentine and completely non-political' Rawson was preparing a decree to sever ties with the Axis may have hastened his departure.[14]) If he believed himself to be in command, he was in for a rude awakening; only two days after assuming the presidency Rawson was forced to resign by the GOU and replaced by Pedro Ramírez, an uncharismatic figure known as 'Palito' (little stick). Somewhat embarrassingly, this manoeuvre required the GOU to remove references to its loyalty to Rawson from its written records; instead, it promised allegiance to Ramírez and 'to collaborate strongly in maintaining the army in the hands of his minister of war, General D. Edelmiro J. Farrell'.[15] Later in the year Perón's friend and supporter Farrell would also be named vice-president.

Ramírez was recognized by both the United States and UK within the week, despite the State Department view that the new government was composed of 'fence-sitting non-entities' unwilling to cede to US pressure to abandon Argentina's neutrality.[16] For his part, British Ambassador Sir David Kelly presented an amusing but less than flattering portrait of Ramírez, saying that 'it is clear that he began to intrigue against his chief [Rawson] almost immediately' and that he 'is not a strong man, and he has a record of unreliability which some might call treachery'. As if that were not enough, Kelly remarked that Ramírez is 'an insignificant looking little man; and he drinks more alcohol than is good for him'.[17] Clearly the 'revolution' could not be left solely in the hands of so unprepossessing a figure.

Shortly after Farrell's appointment as war minister, a brief and largely overlooked communique announced that Colonel Juan Domingo Perón had been named as head of the war minister's secretariat. (Mercante was also seconded to the Ministry.) Perón at this time remained largely unknown, but by the end of 1943 this would by no means be the case. (One of the first public mentions of his name came in early June, in which 'a general officer' told British Embassy sources that the coup had been Rawson's idea but that Farrell and Perón had been involved.[18]) In terms of his military constituency, Perón already had considerable support among the junior officers, both due to his cordial relations with former students and subordinates and to the perception that he had greater experience of the world than many of his contemporaries. He would build on this support as Farrell's secretary (and later successor), by supporting improved pay and promotion prospects for officers, military industrialization measures and the creation of an air force, all policies that interested and favoured the army. However, his increasing profile was not universally welcomed; suspicions also increased that he was motivated by personal ambitions (explicitly rejected by the GOU) rather than the institution or the nation as a whole. Those suspicions and the distaste they prompted would continue to expand in tandem with Perón's power.

At the same time, Perón's interests had already extended well beyond the welfare of the army. According to Mercante years later, at a May 1943 meeting of the GOU 'Perón spoke at length and in general there was agreement with his words. But at a given moment his tongue ran away with him and he said "we are going to make a revolution". Most of the comrades were surprised and I realised that Perón had been too hasty.'[19] While at least some of this concern reflected fears that a communist revolution could become inevitable, and that the social situation was thus also a security situation, his perception was that the government must take a hand in resolving gross inequalities and social demands. '[T]he great landowners enrich themselves at the cost of the peasant's sweat …. The cities and countryside are filled with lamentations that no one hears; the producer strangled by the monopolist, the worker exploited by the boss and the consumer literally robbed by the tradesman.' The proposed solution was, however, a controversial one (and one that would be central to Perón's first government – 'the removal of political, social and economic intermediaries. For that the government must become the regulator of wealth, director of politics and social harmoniser. This implies the disappearance of the professional politician, the elimination of the monopolist and the removal of the social agitator.'[20]

With Perón not as yet the well-known and divisive figure he would become, popular reaction to the coup and subsequent internal adjustments largely fluctuated between ennui and scepticism. However, one of the coup's strongest supporters was the Catholic Church, or at least strands of Catholic nationalist opinion. Bishop Gustavo Franceschi, the director of *Criterio*, welcomed the 'revolution' as 'a purifying wind through the social environment', saying that 'the providence of God wanted our armed institutions to come forward in time and save us'.[21] This in part reflected the Church's long-standing resentment of what it saw as decades of 'anti-clerical' legislation, such as the enshrining of civil marriage and lay education, as well as, internationally, its relations with Mussolini's Italy and Franco's Spain.

It is not clear to what extent Perón and his GOU colleagues were deeply influenced by Catholic thinking, although some of the GOU's documents specifically rejected freemasonry and quasi-masonic entities such as the Rotary Club (as well as secret societies more generally – ironically given the GOU's own provenance). Catholic influence appears evident in a number of GOU documents, in particular in relation to statements attacking the masonry and Jewish business groups. However, the absence of similar sentiments in Perón's later discourse suggests that Perón saw Catholic thinkers as useful rather than as sources of ideology.

It is likely to have been around this time that Perón first came in contact with a priest who would become a long-time ally and (according to his own statements) a major intellectual influence, the Jesuit Hernán Benítez. Benítez, who would become Eva Perón's confessor, would claim to have helped to shape Perón's social policies and highlight their debt to Papal Encylicals such as *Rerum Novarum* and *Quadragesimo Anno*, which focused on the conditions of workers and the role of workers' organizations in the social and economic order. Again, these contributions appear to represent grist to Perón's intellectual and ideological mill, as he sought content for a 'revolution' that would become increasingly associated with him, rather than any profound feeling for Catholic dogma. Perón himself would say later that the majority of Argentines were Catholics, 'but this does not mean that Argentine Catholics' faith reflects primitive fanaticism. We believe intelligently, we are more doctrinaire than practising.'[22]

Another element that showed some enthusiasm for the new de facto government was the dissident Radicals of the FORJA, as mentioned in the previous chapter. Historical revisionists, the FORJA's intellectuals rejected liberalism as a discredited and foreign-inspired ideology and considered that its mirror image – a nationalist, Hispanic, Catholic tradition – was thus to be adopted and celebrated in its place. Perón would hold discussions with some of the FORJA's leaders, including Arturo Jauretche and Raúl Scalabrini Ortiz (despite the GOU's aversion to talking to politicians), who would add some further intellectual ballast to the projects he was beginning to mull. In particular, the FORJA's slogan of popular sovereignty, economic emancipation and social justice would be adopted by Perón and Peronism.

Amid the crossed international pressures with regard to Argentina's position on the Second World War, labour unrest was also stirring in the wake of the 4 June revolution, with little faith on the part of trade unionists that the military government would do anything to benefit the workers. As noted above, however, Perón and Mercante had already begun to think in terms of new approaches to labour – an area in which Mercante's family background and union ties would prove invaluable. This was in line with Perón's belief in the need for both social justice and a greater and more interventionist state role in the economy: 'intelligent state intervention in labour relations, to achieve the collaboration of all those who contribute with their muscle, their intelligence or their capital to the economic life of the nation ….'[23] This in turn owed some intellectual debt to Perón's experience of Mussolini's Italy, although it also reflected his belief that the economic dislocation prompted by first the Depression and subsequently the Second World War had made such intervention and collaboration increasingly urgent.

At the same time, it was in line with a nationalist view in the military that the government should boost domestic heavy industry. It did so relatively successfully, as well as favouring smaller businesses by increasing access to credit that had previously been concentrated among the landowning classes and large businesses, notably through the creation of the Industrial Credit Bank. Above and beyond the fevered activity of Perón (and Mercante) over the next two years, the government would come to issue a total of 20,000 decrees, many of them focusing on attempts at modernization and diversification of an economy originally constructed on the unsustainable basis of exporting agricultural goods and importing manufactures. While this process was already under way from the 1930s, the de facto government sought to give it impetus, reducing the obstacles it had hitherto faced from the elite interests behind the 'Infamous Decade's' governments – notably from a landed oligarchy seeking to maintain its traditional power as its share of the national economy declined.

Perón had already encouraged Mercante to begin making contact with unions from their early days in the War Ministry, no easy task given the military government's initial repressive measures against communist and socialist leaders and memories of the military's role in repression during the Tragic Week in 1919. The situation deteriorated in August 1943 after the government promulgated the Law of Professional Associations which severely curbed unions' political activity, and intervened in the two railway unions with which Mercante had ties, the *Unión Ferroviaria* and *La Fraternidad.*

Also in August, in his capacity as secretary to the war minister, Perón was required to intervene in a strike by the meatpackers' union for which the union's leader, communist José Peter, had been imprisoned. Perón and Mercante took a different tack, negotiating with the union rather than repressing the strike, and reaching agreement on a five-cent-per-hour pay rise and the liberation of Peter. The success of this intervention not only bolstered Perón's position, but increased his perception of the trade union movement as a potential power base that could complement (and counterbalance) the military. Both had the capacity to act as organized forces, and both were important to a vision of Argentina as a modern industrial nation organized on corporatist lines.

Not long thereafter, in October 1943 Perón successfully sought the post of director of the National Labour Department (DNT), a hitherto largely dormant office focusing primarily on collecting labour data. Perón's appointment implied the sidelining of another colonel, Carlos Gianni, who had taken up the post only three months earlier, and who had also begun the work that would be continued by Perón: building up relations with trade unions and the profile of the DNT itself. The fact that Perón retained his post at the War Ministry raised some suspicions as to the suddenly visible rise of the ambitious colonel, with the apparent backing of the CGT, although it was generally assumed that the DNT was a somewhat uninteresting 'toy' of which he would soon tire. At the same time, those who suspected Perón's ambitions (including President Ramírez) took some comfort from the thought that the DNT was a dead end in the corridors of the Interior Ministry and that it would take Perón far from the centre of power and the public eye.

Nothing could have proved further from the truth. The sleepy DNT would rapidly become a hive of activity, and would bring Perón to the attention of a far wider audience. Within days of his appointment, the British Embassy would report on the event in the context of strikes that had closed the Swift and Armour meatpacking plants, noting its suspicions that Perón and his clique were using the strike for their own ends and the fact that his plans already included a 'unified syndical movement'. Only a few weeks later, on 6 November, Ambassador Sir David Kelly sent a telegram to London referring to Perón as 'reputedly the strong man of the new government' and saying that he had begun contacting known Radical politicians, 'aiming at an election leading to his own election as President'.[24] In a subsequent report on Argentine personalities in 1943, Kelly would describe

Perón as 'intelligent, capable and energetic, he is good-looking and has a sense of humour', and as 'a likely future President'.[25]

Perón quickly found capable and active assistants for his plans, both within the DNT and outside it. He brought Mercante with him from the War Ministry, who brought his own cousin, Hugo Mercante, and his young secretary and mistress, Isabel Ernst. Isabel, the attractive blonde daughter of German immigrants who had once been a nursery teacher, would rapidly take responsibility for union relations, meeting union delegations and preparing reports on their goals as a reference for Perón. Perón was also able to engineer the appointment of Mercante as the new government intervener in the two railway unions, much to the satisfaction of their leadership – notably Luis Monzalvo, a leader of the *Union Ferroviario* and one of Perón's first union backers (although he noted Perón's 'ability to leave his listeners satisfied without promising them anything'[26]).

Another aide who joined the DNT at around the same time as Perón was Blanca Luz Brum, an Uruguayan poet and journalist who had recently moved to Argentina after spending a number of years in leftist circles in Peru, Mexico and Chile. Blanca Luz had been one of the founders of the Peruvian magazine *Guerrilla*, together with Socialist Party leader José Carlos Mariátegui, in 1926, and had subsequently joined the Communist Party in Mexico while married to communist artist David Alfaro Siqueiros. In 1943 she took up residence in Argentina and became part of the propaganda team at the DNT, where she would write some of Perón's speeches and influence his labour policies, contributing to suspicions within the government that he might have communist sympathies.

Within the DNT Perón found José Figuerola, a Spanish-born lawyer and technocrat with a deep knowledge of the labour legislation that had earlier been drafted and shelved, or adopted and forgotten. Figuerola, one of the founders of the Spanish Ministry of Labour in 1920, had been chief of statistics at the DNT for over a decade and had developed wide expertise in labour law and Argentine labour issues in particular that had thus far awakened no interest in putting his ideas into practice. In Perón he found just the person to do so.

Within a few weeks of Perón's arrival, the DNT was promoted to the Secretariat of Labour and Social Welfare, making Perón a member of the cabinet for the first time. His public debut in this role came with a radio speech on 2 December, in which he ably set out his political stall as the arbiter of unity among the state, employers and workers, key to the resolution of Argentina's social and economic ills. The Secretariat, it was made clear, would henceforth be responsible for employer-labour relations; it would, he claimed, be even-handed in that role, although initially 'historical injustices would have to be remedied by giving greater benefits to workers than to employers. Far from being accepted by employers as a necessary evil to ensure social peace and avoid revolution, this preference to the unions would earn Perón widespread and intransigent resistance from employers and their organizations.

However, Perón's success with the unions would be far greater, as the Secretariat took an increasingly active role in enforcing and expanding labour legislation (much of it proposed or even passed by the Socialist Party in the early part of the century but rarely implemented). The Secretariat established labour courts, paid holidays and sick leave and minimum wages, and arbitrated in labour disputes (almost invariably to the benefit of labour rather than management); arguably its most important step was the creation of a pensions system for workers. Over the next two years it would set up oversight of child labour and training and even extend those labour rights to the 'feudal' rural workers whose plight had been symbolized by Patrón Costas. Moreover, it would encourage unionization, in sharp contrast to past government practice which had been repressive rather than permissive. Organization, in both non-unionized sectors and areas in which union leadership had been disputed or under communist control, would soar, due to the government's blessing and to the fact that union membership now brought tangible benefits as the government sought to swing the pendulum to labour's side to redress long-standing inequalities. The number of trade unions would more than double between 1941 and 1945, from 356 to 969, although membership would rise much more slowly in this period, from 441,412 to 528,523 (of whom by far the largest number was in the food-processing industries). It would not be until after Perón assumed office that membership would seriously take off, reaching 1.5 million in 1947 and 3 million by 1951. That the largesse with which the Secretariat met union demands – often granting more than was asked – was far greater towards unions led by Peronist sympathizers than to opponents would eventually become a matter of concern, as would the gradual suppression of opposition-dominated unions. But in the early months of the de facto government and Perón's stewardship of the Secretariat, these issues were marginal compared to the new benefits the working classes were beginning to enjoy.

Those benefits remained, in 1943, largely confined to the urban working classes, notably those in labour-intensive and mechanised sectors; despite the expansion of industry and the rise in employment in the early years of the 1940s, such benefits had been slow to be felt. An April 1943 report from the DNT had noted that 'in general, the situation of the Argentine worker has deteriorated, despite the rise in industry. In spite of remarkable profits, the majority of the population is forced to reduce their standard of living.'[27] Benefits would now begin to be felt, and from 1944 they would be extended. Unions working in foreign-owned industries were also attracted to the new secretary of labour, whose nationalist rhetoric struck a chord. The success of Perón's blandishments and support for generous settlements in avoiding strikes were undeniable, although his dealings with labour contained a fair element of 'divide and conquer', which often involved changes of union leadership to new figures considered loyal to Perón and who could thus bring benefits to their members. This was relatively straightforward given the factionalism and often violent conflict to which the struggling union movement was prone. As noted earlier, the CGT, which accounted for around two-thirds of organized labour at the time, had split into two factions in 1943 – with CGT-1 aiming to form a Labour Party potentially useful to Perón, and CGT-2, dominated by communists and socialists. CGT-2 was finally suspended by the Secretariat and most of its members joined its Perón-allied competitor. (In 1945, Decree Law 23.852 would allow only one union in any sector to have legal recognition, ensuring that those with Peronist leadership would get the nod.) Although Domenech, a socialist, would have a somewhat cooler relationship with Perón than leaders such as Cipriano Reyes and Luis Monzalvo, he would remain at the CGT for some time to come and would in fact be the first to say that 'the colonel is the First Worker of the Republic'.[28]

Despite some doubts over these – as yet – minor issues, with Mercante's help and boosted by his own efforts, Perón would fairly rapidly win over sceptical union leaders (in part due to his support for replacing communist or socialist leaders with others who had long been seeking to challenge them). Cipriano Reyes, the combative meatpackers' leader who was a rival of José Peter and who was encouraged by Perón to set up a competing union, would come to say that 'at first, Perón didn't appear to be an authentic revolutionary, but his intelligent sensitivity stood out .... [H]e had the innate qualities of a leader (*caudillo*) and ... the vital charisma to stand out among his peers.'[29]

Reyes himself, a key figure in the origins and cementing of Peronism, was a complex man whose background and beliefs made him a quintessential figure of the autochthonous type of trade unionism mooted if not originated by Perón. Born on 7 August 1906 (the day of San Cayetano, the patron saint of labour), Reyes as a small child worked in his father's circus. At the age of twelve he was apprenticed in a glass factory in Buenos Aires, where he was taken under the wing of a Catalan anarchist and labour organizer who early on began to take him to labour meetings. He experienced the events of the 'Tragic Week' at first hand and later described the ferocity of the 'cossacks' brought from the northern provinces of Corrientes and Chaco to repress protesting workers, as well as the *Liga Patriótica* that attacked workers and union offices, and the sight of the dead and wounded in the street. Subsequently he worked in a meatpacking plant in Zárate before spending a few years 'globetrotting' as he put it, travelling around the country and working in a variety of jobs that included agricultural labour, a bakery, as well as journalism, poetry and the establishment of cultural societies for workers.

Reyes' respect for the working poor in both the countryside and factories was deep and based on personal experience (if grandiloquently expressed in his writings), and he understood the rural poverty and hopelessness that drove people to look for factory work and possibly a better life in the cities. Although he honoured the struggle of workers' activists of whatever ideological persuasion, he was also strongly anti-communist and decried the Russian Revolution as 'the blackest and bloodiest tyranny under the regime of state capitalism, now converted into a new imperialist colonialism'.[30] Working both in the ports of Necochea and again in meatpacking plants in Berisso, he was frequently imprisoned for his organizing activities. He became an opponent of José Peter, refusing to accept the settlement that allowed for Peter's release from prison without the guarantee of better pay and conditions, and establishing the competing Autonomous Syndicate of Meat Industry Workers. Tough-minded, nationalist and anti-communist, he was, at least initially, the perfect foundation of the nascent Peronist movement.

Only six months after the 4 June coup and only two months after taking over the DNT, Perón ended 1943 as the most prominent face of the new government and its most popular figure, among the working classes if not the elites. This meteoric rise gained him the notice of a foreign ambassador as a potential presidential candidate and of military and union leaders as a force for change. 'This all came about when Perón opened the doors of the Secretariat of Labour to the labour movement, respecting and promoting union freedoms, proclaiming a programme of social justice, not just as a political statement, but with real deeds.'[31] In his first two months at the DNT (and later Secretariat), Perón had established the bases for what would become a remarkable shift in social and economic policy that would change some aspects of Argentine society forever. There would be much more to come.

Inevitably, the suspicions surrounding Perón were growing in a number of quarters along with his reputation. Some saw in his affection for corporatism and Mussolini's successes the threat of Nazi influence, while others (despite the frequent references in GOU documents to the need to avert a communist threat) believed him to be a communist agent. This was one of the suspicions harboured by President Ramírez, who distrusted both Perón's politics and his ambitions, although the president also found himself easily persuaded by his talented subordinate; whenever he decided to remove him, he would find that Perón would talk him out of the idea. (This pattern became so established that Ramírez's wife supposedly suspected that Perón was drugging her husband's coffee when they met.) More generally, fellow officers were becoming deeply concerned by his apparent personal ambitions as well as by his overtures to some representatives of the political class who had been specifically sidelined by the 4 June coup.

In practice, it could be argued that Perón's shifts represented an evolution rather than a pre-planned strategy to gain power. While the grab bag of ideological influences he chose from included a range of seemingly mutually exclusive positions, all of them provided him with ideas that shaped an eventual project as well as the intellectual heft to justify that project. This was nothing more nor less than an attempt to establish a vision of an inclusive Argentine national identity, something previously lacking. Concepts of national identity had traditionally focused on the idea of a prosperous agro-export model, one which excluded the vast majority of the population; the number of immigrants who had come to Argentina also made it difficult to find an identity to which all could sign up. Arguably the most systematic effort to create such an identity into which the children of immigrants could be incorporated was the system of conscription.

Perón's evolving notion of Argentine national identity that would eventually include all of its parts would be highly controversial, not least given the fact that it would increasingly become a Peronist identity (which itself would require identification of an oligarchic enemy that would thus by definition be excluded). However, there was no other serious alternative on offer, for a country lacking a clear self-image. And Perón's vision had its attractions, positing a harmonious, prosperous, modern and industrializing nation in which both workers and employers would benefit. At the same time, that vision was formed not only by the range of intellectual and political influences, but by his own early life and experiences – which, unlike political leaders of the past, were experiences shared with a wide range of Argentines, for whom they had resonance. Thus, Perón's notion of national identity was one that actually had appeal and relevance for many of his compatriots; his political thinking was influenced by, and influenced, the lives they had lived. Was this vision a convenient servant to his desire for power, or was his increasing ambition for power a recognition of the fact that political power was indispensable to implement a major economic and political project? It seems likely that the two priorities merged in his mind; his interest in power and his desire to implement a great national project went hand in hand, even as his belief that he was the person to implement that project (and to know what project would most benefit Argentina) became more expansive and more questionable.

The remarkable level of activity sustained by Perón leading up to and after 4 June can have left little time for a social or personal life as opposed to the political. Unlike Mercante, who despite his own workaholic tendencies had a wife and son, a mistress and a number of social activities as well as poker games with fellow officers, Perón's habits seemingly returned to the nocturnal writing and studying that had characterized his early years at the *Escuela Superior de Guerra*. He continued to attend boxing matches, a sport that still fascinated him, sometimes with María Cecilia. There are few references during this period to the kind of outings to cabarets and restaurants he had once enjoyed with colleagues, and it can only be assumed that María Cecilia spent a great deal of time at home alone or contemplating how to advance her acting career. Although 'Piraña' was reputed to have character, their relationship appears to have been largely domestic and perhaps somewhat superficial; like Aurelia before her, Perón's work took precedence and María Cecilia took a back seat and a marginal role. (Unlike Aurelia, her youth and the fact that they were living together unmarried also made it advisable for Perón to keep her out of the public eye or to pass her off as a young relation.) In this respect, Perón had begun 1943 as an unknown and ended it as a rising political star, but his personal life had not kept pace and could be said to have stagnated. That would soon change: the start of 1944 would see changes in Perón's political and personal life that would arguably represent the high water mark in both spheres, and would leave their long-term impact on Argentina.

Chapter 6

SAN JUAN

Que tendrás en tu mirar,
Que cuando a mí tus ojos levantas
Siento arder en mi interior una voraz llama de amor?

What is in your look, that when you lift your eyes to me
I feel a devouring fire of love burning inside?
Pasional (tango), Mario Soto and Jorge Caldara[1]

The start of 1944 would be a crucial moment in Perón's personal life and political career, and thus for Argentine political history.

On 26 January Argentina was finally pressured into breaking relations with Germany and Japan, prompting a political crisis that forced President Pedro Ramírez to resign a few weeks later, on 24 February. In his (unpublished) resignation speech, Ramírez denied that US pressure had prompted the rupture, but claimed instead that it was due to German and Japanese espionage activities in the country. He would claim that he was unable to convince the army (presumably the GOU) of this, as 'intrigue was more powerful than reason'.[2]

Ramírez was replaced by General Edelmiro Farrell, who in turn was replaced as minister of war (and in July, as vice-president) by his friend Colonel Juan D. Perón, already secretary of labour. Two days after Ramírez's departure, the British Embassy noted prophetically that 'Colonel Perón, the right-hand man of the Vice-President, will greatly gain in power by President Ramírez's withdrawal'.[3] A telegram from the British Embassy in Chile also noted that in Santiago 'Minister of War says that GOU colonels are a bunch of Nazis but army opinion seems to be that Perón will eventually be president and it is better not to quarrel with his faction'.[4]

The ouster of Ramírez was indeed engineered by the GOU, which curiously enough dissolved itself at the same time, leaving its members 'free of the oaths and commitments they had undertaken' in line with earlier documents produced by the group, which committed them to 'follow General Pedro P. Ramírez, support and protect his work until its objectives were fully realised'.[5] Months earlier, these events had been foreshadowed in earlier GOU documents, which outlined a possible coup against Ramírez in September 1943 should he abandon Argentina's neutrality and included a draft decree naming Perón as vice-president and war minister. Plans were shelved at the time, when after a tense meeting with members of the GOU Ramírez agreed to maintain neutrality and make changes to his cabinet, but the drafts of his resignation and of Farrell and Perón's promotions remained on file and at hand.[6]

Even before Perón's sudden political promotion, however, more fundamental events were already underway. On the evening of 15 January 1944, an earthquake of some 7.4 on the Richter Scale virtually destroyed the western city of San Juan, 875 kilometres from Buenos Aires. Some 10,000 were killed and a third of the provincial population left homeless, making it Argentina's worst national disaster until that time and prompting a national wave of sympathy.

Perón's Secretariat of Labour and Welfare was charged with overseeing relief efforts, and Perón personally took charge of operations, further raising his public profile. Speaking on the radio, he called for a public meeting of various important sectors for 17 January to coordinate fundraising efforts. Among those who took part were a delegation of actors including a young radio actress called Eva Duarte, who crossed Perón's path for the first time. According to his much later memories, she strongly rejected suggestions of a benefit concert, saying 'this is no time to organise a show, or a tea or a bridge party. Old outdated things that do nothing but justify hypocrisy.' 'I looked at her and felt that her words conquered me, I was almost subjugated by the warmth of her voice and her look.' 'When I met Evita, I was not attracted by the beautiful woman, but by the good woman. Of course, she had both extremes: beauty and goodness. .... From the first I realised that I had before me an extraordinary being.'[7]

Although Eva's suggestion of a street collection went ahead successfully, a benefit event a concert was also hastily organized for 22 January, at the Luna Park stadium in Buenos Aires, in which many of the most famous performers of the day took part. Despite her rejection of the idea of a benefit, Eva Duarte also attended, albeit not as one of the famous performers. High-ranking members of the military government, from Ramírez down, were also present, while less important members of the entertainment world were largely on the sidelines. Accounts differ as to how Perón and Eva ended up sitting together at Luna Park, given that she was not in theory destined for the VIP section. Various versions suggest that she abandoned her escort and brazenly approached Perón or usurped the seat next to his; others say Mercante, who had met her in her role as a founder of the Argentine Radio Union, introduced them, possibly having noted Perón's interest following their brief exchange at the 17 January meeting. (Mercante's role was ostensibly one of the reasons the two enjoyed a warm relationship for some years.) However their meeting came to pass, the Luna Park event would become Eva's 'marvellous day'; she and Perón left together and would from that day become a couple. Whether in fact she said to him 'thank you for existing', as has been claimed, the two were immediately smitten.

*****

Much has been written about Eva Duarte, later Eva Perón or simply Evita (including by this author) and much more probably deserves to be written. While this is not the place to rehash it, Eva's arrival in the life of Perón would mark the key moment in both their lives and in the ideation and myth of Peronism. Eva would define Peronism's lasting image and enduring popularity to an even greater extent than Perón himself, becoming both an icon and a lightning rod for much of the opprobrium that would otherwise have focused more strongly on its eponymous founder. Perhaps her most outstanding quality was that her life history was common and widely shared – what set her apart was an uncommon energy and determination to rise above it and to take others with her.

Eva's early history was not unlike Perón's in some respects, both of them beginning as illegitimate children in small towns surrounded by the vast Pampas (and both of them influenced by a strong mother and a more irresponsible father). Eva was born Eva María Ibarguren on 7 May 1919 near the village of Los Toldos, the fifth and last child of a prosperous rancher, Juan Duarte, and his cook and long-standing mistress Juana Ibarguren. Although Duarte recognized their first four children – Blanca, Elisa, Juan and Erminda – for whatever reason he did not recognize Eva. When she was still a toddler he returned to his legitimate family of eight children in the town of Chivilcoy, some 150 kilometres away, possibly as the result of his wife's death. Duarte himself died a few years later, in 1926, and Juana's determination to attend the funeral with her children led to a humiliating snub. Following his return to Chivilcoy, Doña Juana, as Eva's mother was known, had to return to Los Toldos with five children, no support and an immoral reputation. However, she was resourceful and determined, and took a course in sewing that allowed her to maintain her five children in a two-room brick house, largely thanks to a contract with the local school to supply the smocks worn by all schoolchildren.

Although they were housed, clean and fed, the Duarte/Ibarguren children were looked down on and isolated due to their irregular parentage and the fact that their mother was widely believed to have various 'protectors' who helped her, in part by getting her the sewing work and eventually getting Elisa a job at the post office. Following the 1928 elections, however, her conservative protectors had lost office to new Radical incumbents who were not similarly helpful. In early 1930 Doña Juana managed to get Elisa transferred to Junín, a larger city some 50 kilometres away, where she rented a bigger house and began to cook for the unmarried men working in local government or the army base there. Recasting herself as a respectable widow, she succeeded in marrying off her older daughters to middle-class professional men, a significant achievement in a class-conscious semi-rural society.

However, in Eva, Doña Juana encountered an indomitable spirit more like her own. After finishing primary school, Eva, a pretty but shy young teenager, was bent on going to Buenos Aires to find work as an actress; in early 1935, shortly before her sixteenth birthday, she did so. Although she had no special thespian talent (a characteristic she shared with most of the young actors in Buenos Aires at the time), she succeeded relatively quickly in finding occasional bit parts on the stage, although she suffered difficult periods of unemployment and deep poverty. It was later generally assumed that she won her acting roles based on sexual availability rather than talent – something that was often the case, not only for Eva but for other young women working in the theatre, in factories or as domestic servants.

In some cases, it would appear that her relationships with older benefactors involved (at least on her side) a genuine romantic attachment, possibly the result of an absent father and a desire to find a real protector. Many testimonies suggest that she had an affectionate, vulnerable and generous side to her nature that made her real friends and found people genuinely willing to help her, even though her talents were never likely to bring her great success. According to others, her life history of poverty, rejection and marginalization had – understandably – also made her deeply resentful.

In part thanks to her brother Juan, who was working as a salesman for a large soap company, Eva began to get radio work in the dramatic serials that became known as 'soap operas' due to their sponsors. She also won a few small film roles and some modelling work, but radio would become her metier; even before meeting Perón she earned a comfortable living at Radio Belgrano and had leading roles in several series, although her listeners were more likely to be the maids doing the housework than the more cultured middle and upper classes. Already in September 1943 she was announced as the star of a new series of radio dramas portraying the lives of famous women in history that began broadcasting the following month, a step up often attributed to her relationship with either the owner of the sponsor, Radical Soap, or Colonel Aníbal Imbert, the head of the Office of Posts and Telecommunications. A later British Embassy report would claim that she was unsuccessful 'despite her many friendships with directors, impresarios and actors' although she obtained work and 'was able to hold her position as the result of the favours she bestowed on successive directors'. The unflattering note would also call her 'common, almost completely illiterate but physically attractive. She was also extremely foul-mouthed.'[8]

When Eva met Perón she was nearly twenty-five, a young woman of limited education, a famously vulgar vocabulary and a reputation for ambition and the willingness to use sexual favours to further it. (Her detractors saw nothing amiss in regarding an unemployed young woman as a sexual predator, while regarding the men who exploited her as respectable and correct – after all, they did not bring her home to meet their wives nor contemplate marrying her.) Many, such as the writer Jorge Luis Borges, would insist that she had been a 'common prostitute' and that her mother had run a brothel in Junín, although most saw her as a regular occupant of the casting couch rather than what would now be called a sex worker; even that was bad enough in a conservative society. Her admirers would later turn this image on its head, seeking to portray her as a virginal and saintly Madonna figure, an equally implausible image.

Although insecure and somewhat fragile in health, Eva was determined, impetuous and possessive, unlike the cautious Perón. Uncultured and largely uneducated (albeit, with her primary school education, no more so than many women of her time), she was also intelligent and intuitive. Shortly after their meeting, she arrived at Perón's flat with her belongings, only to find María Cecilia still installed there. After her initial surprise, she would later tell a friend that 'since he [said he] liked decisive women – I hadn't forgotten that – I packed her things in a suitcase and sent her back to her province without any further formalities.'[9]

However, rather than remaining in the Arenales Street flat, Eva found a flat for Perón adjoining her own, in Posadas Street in Recoleta, to which he moved with alacrity. They would use one flat for political meetings (which Eva rapidly began to attend, to the consternation of Perón's colleagues) and one as their residence, making it abundantly clear that they were living together.

While Perón's cohabitation with Piraña was not regarded favourably, the relationship had been a much more discreet one in which she rarely appeared in public and played no apparent role in his military and political career. Eva had no intention of being unobtrusive and Perón seemingly did not trouble to make her so, openly presenting her to his comrades in arms (and, at times, sneaking her into his rooms at Campo de Mayo in the boot of his car) and allowing her to participate actively in political discussions. She rapidly became bold about expressing her views, to the dismay of those present. This would have been acceptable even from an army wife, who would have been expected to retire decorously while the men made decisions; for an actress of doubtful reputation, it was entirely scandalous and seriously damaged Perón's own reputation within the forces.

In some respects, the romance had points in common with the past relationships of both: Perón was drawn to young women towards whom he often displayed his pedagogical bent, while Eva's more serious relationships had been with older, influential men. However, while Perón bent the rules when he brought Piraña back from Mendoza, he had never before had a relationship deemed so entirely unacceptable and damaging; this was a man who had rejected thoughts of marrying a foreign wife, however respectable, on the grounds that it could damage his career. Aurelia had been the model wife for an army officer and Piraña's discretion made her a reasonably acceptable mistress, even as a live-in companion. Eva was neither, and indeed she was despised not only for her background but because she was believed both to be taking advantage of Perón and of dominating him – a humiliating image for the man widely regarded as the most powerful in the government.

What is perhaps most striking is that Perón did not seem to care. Did he now believe himself to be so powerful as to be untouchable? It is possible, but it seems that the strongest reason was simply that he was in love with Eva. Hitherto a wary man who tended to avoid deep commitment, at the age of fifty he was confronted by a beautiful young woman who adored him and was willing to take great risks to get him. She deeply admired him and entered enthusiastically into one of the roles in which he liked to cast his romantic partners: that of pupil to his teacher. Their contrasting personalities would work well together at both the personal and political level, balancing impulsiveness and calculation, passion and reason. Given that Perón was prudent and astute enough to realize that such an unsuitable relationship could undermine his position, possibly fatally, it is implausible that he entered into it so openly without being in love.

Inevitably, there has been much speculation over the sexual relationship between the two, most of it disparaging, and veering wildly from rumours that Eva had conquered Perón with the sexual wiles learned as a prostitute, to claims that neither had any interest in sex at all, but only power. There is perhaps an undercurrent to these assumptions that considers that Perón could not have sincerely 'loved' so unworthy a woman and that therefore the enduring link could only be explained by her sexual prowess – and indeed, a suggestion that Eva did not love anyone but saw him coldly as the best meal ticket she would find. Possibly more convincingly, Eva's confessor Hernán Benítez would later observe that their love grew out of 'the encounter of two people profoundly wounded in their sex. Joined together by sad, puritan childhoods .... I think love had surprised both of them: Perón because he thought it was a subject over and done with, and Eva because she had never known it before.'[10] In practice, Eva's later claims that 'we loved each other because we wanted the same thing' would seem to be the most accurate, despite the fact that they might not have known it at the time.[11]

Not a sympathetic writer, José Ignacio García Hamilton would suggest that 'while he hid the humiliations and pain of his infancy with a style of permanent seduction, she fascinated him with her shifts between belligerence towards the world and a certain delicacy towards the few she loved'. Moreover, he noted persuasively that 'Perón saw that the girl's eloquent combativeness expressed and completed a volcanic part of his own personality that he had always tried to dissimulate'.[12] The dress designer Paco Jamandreu, who would begin to dress Eva during this phase of her career, would describe it differently, saying that 'I felt there were two Eva Peróns: the sweet, kind girl I designed clothes for ... and joked with; and another, totally different. I have always thought that that second Eva Perón was inhabited by another spirit.' He explained in this way – some kind of possession – the fact that she could transform into a completely unexpected and dominating personality, something that for Perón also must at times have appeared inexplicable and unexpected. 'Evidently she had a dual personality. In the dressing room, chatting with her friends, she was incredibly fragile and feminine. In the Plaza de Mayo that fragility became an irresistible force .... I have never been able to believe that both Evas were the same person.'[13]

Equally, Eva could fairly be said to have acted decisively to avoid losing a far 'better catch' than she could ever have hoped for. But her fascination with him was real and her love and gratitude genuine – he was arguably the first man who had ever valued her and thought her worth spending time and conversation on. She would prove a model pupil and sounding-board (one who in some ways would outshine her teacher); her intelligence and experience in public exposure would allow her to assume a role that Perón probably did not originally intend, but which he enabled her to develop to an unexpected degree. Even educated and middle-class women found it difficult to enter the public sphere successfully (Argentina's earliest female doctors had been forbidden to practise their profession due to their gender), and for Eva to conquer the public sphere so fully, with Perón's blessing, was unprecedented. Moreover, this was one of Perón's few relationships in which his partner's energy and workaholic tendencies equalled or even surpassed his own.

Following a meeting with Eva in 1948, the wife of the then British Ambassador would say somewhat disparagingly that 'had she allowed herself to be guided in the right way, her energies could have been used more constructively'.[14] Yet it is hard to imagine who else would have taken it upon himself to guide her; it is more likely that those remarkable energies would simply have been squandered.

In these early days the relationship was not widely known to the public (and indeed Eva was moderately well known but far from a household name), but it rapidly became known in circles that mattered. Only a few days after the Luna Park concert, on 26 January Perón and Mercante visited Eva at Radio Belgrano, eliciting some magazine coverage and prompting Radio Belgrano's owner, Jaime Yankelevich, to offer her a new contract for a record monthly salary of 35,000 pesos (then some 8,750 dollars). It is clear that at this stage Eva was still concentrating on her acting career as well as Perón, and was not above using the relationship to advance it; also in early 1944, it was announced that she would have a role in the film *La cabalgata del circo* (Circus Cavalcade), supporting the established stars Hugo del Carril and Libertad Lamarque. Her casting in a relatively important film owed much to the fact that raw celluloid, imported from the United States, was rationed, and the fact that Eva could obtain it through her relationship with Perón made her an interesting commodity. (In other respects, her contribution to the film is unremarkable, although during the course of filming she would for the first time dye her naturally dark hair to the pale blonde that would be her signature.) In parallel with the filming, she continued her series of famous women with portrayals of Queen Elizabeth I and Sarah Bernhardt. In fairness, she was not yet aware that a new career awaited her and was thus keen to achieve greater things in her existing one – and, indeed, she could not be certain at this stage that the relationship would last. Given the insecurity of her position as the mistress of a prominent man who could easily choose to end the affair if it damaged his own career prospects, she may have felt that her best course of action was to do everything possible to shore up her acting career in case she had to fall back on it later.

However, Eva's radio career would also take a more directly political turn, and one that supported the career of her partner. Beginning in June 1944, she would take the leading role in a propaganda series called *Hacia un futuro mejor* (Towards a Better Future) that exalted the achievements of the 4 June 'revolution' and of Perón himself. Eva played 'the woman', a woman of the working classes who called on Argentines to support the revolution; her speeches would be intercut with excerpts from Perón's own speeches. Her role would represent the beginning of her later identification as 'the woman of the people' and as her husband's chief propagandist, as well as another step in her political education; her message in *Hacia un futuro mejor* would essentially vary little when her artistic career was behind her and she became a political leader second only to Perón. 'I am a woman like you, mothers, wives, girlfriends or sisters …. The redeeming Revolution came for many … reasons, hunger, [...] the fatherland, forgotten and thirsty [...] and injustice and exploitation of the workers.'[15]

Another, not insignificant by-product of *Hacia un futuro mejor* was that it brought together the radio writers, including Francisco Muñoz Azpiri, who would subsequently become key influences in crafting the speeches of both Perón and Eva. Although Blanca Luz Brum had already begun writing speeches for Perón, the greater media savvy of Muñoz Aspiri (newly designated as director of propaganda in the Presidency's information office) and Perón's later media 'czar', Raúl Apold, would increase Perón's expertise in using radio as a tool of propaganda and mass communication.

Apold, a journalist, writer and aviation enthusiast who had also worked in the government of Yrigoyen and as a theatrical agent, had been born in Buenos Aires in 1898. He began working as a producer (and later director of press and publicity) at the studio Argentina Sono Film in the mid-1930s, where a very young Eva Duarte had a small role in the film *Segundos afuera* in 1937; Apold is said to have been a contact and possibly even her agent, and there are rumours that he may have facilitated her initial contacts with Perón. A deeply private man who went largely unnoticed during the peak of his career, as early as 1943 he had become instrumental in aiding Perón to make use of the media – all the more important given that the largest newspapers and periodicals of the time, notably the daily broadsheets *La Prensa* and *La Nación*, were opposed to the government and later to Perón in particular and did what they could to ignore or belittle their achievements. In October 1943 Perón was behind the creation of the government's first communications office, the Under-Secretariat of Information and Press, which was designed to 'centralise and coordinate official information and organise government propaganda'.[16] Subsequently, Perón would organize a press office at the Secretariat of Labour, run by a journalist from *La Razón*, Oscar Lomuto. While the move was subsequently attributed to Perón's ambition to present himself as a presidential candidate, it also reflected the rising political importance of mass media across the world. In any case, what it certainly did was ensure that Perón's undertakings on behalf of social justice and working-class betterment (not least in the wake of the San Juan earthquake) did not go unnoticed.

Although such mass communication for political purposes was unprecedented in Argentina at the time, and prompted comparisons with Nazi Germany, in fact the increasing presence of radio in households across the country made it an obvious and effective instrument for political communication, just as it made it an obvious and effective instrument to increase soap sales. Perón's (and later Eva's) natural charisma and dexterity in public speaking would make it a key tool throughout the Perón era, not least thanks to Eva's connections and experience in the medium. However unfavourably this was viewed by some sectors of opinion, radio would become an indispensable tool for a leader to communicate with his or her public in relatively direct and sometimes simplistic ways (such as, for example, Roosevelt's fireside chats), in the same way as effective use of television – and later of Twitter – would subsequently become a necessity and virtually an art.

Also at around this time, Eva began to take a relatively small but active role in the Secretariat of Labour and Welfare, becoming something of a fixture and, perhaps unsurprisingly, generating frictions with Blanca Luz Brum. By contrast, the relationship with Isabel Ernst was at least initially far more cordial; Isabel's political education had at the time advanced further than Eva's and Eva was still happy to learn from her example. In addition, Isabel was even younger than Eva and also occupied the position of mistress to a rising army officer, and as such they had more in common – and Isabel was less threatening – than the worldly, intellectual and glamorous Blanca.

Slightly later, in October 1944, Perón would create a women's division at the Secretariat, to be headed by Dr Lucila Gregorio de Lavié, a professional and feminist who suffered considerable criticism from others in her upper-class circle for collaborating with Perón and his proposals for 'suffrage by decree'. They argued that women who had fought for the vote for years should not accept it from a de facto government as a virtual gift; rightly or wrongly, it was precisely the women's suffrage movement that would be hostile to Perón's efforts to bring about votes for women. Gregorio de Lavié herself supported the notion of a decree, although these frictions meant that the women's division was less effective than it might have been, even in its key function of improving women's working conditions. Yet the early move towards women's suffrage both discounts efforts to portray the eventual law (in 1947) as largely an initiative of Eva's, and highlights the fact that even at this early stage Perón had a forward-thinking (if perhaps utilitarian) view of the potential role of women outside the home – not least, of course, as a potential voter base, something that in theory he did not require, as a member of a military government who disclaimed personal ambitions. (Perón would later attribute this at least in part to Eva's influence and the impact she had made on him, saying that 'I wondered whether it wasn't time for women to be involved in national matters, if only to show that they would not do any worse than we did.'[17])

Both her radio work and her insertion at the Secretariat would advance Eva's political education during these months, and Perón would further it even more with his own brand of personal tutoring. He would later describe her as promising 'raw material' whose formation went beyond the usual education: 'she had an artistic training that greatly developed her sensitivity, making her capable of applying it in real life. In other words, I received material already partly finished, with a sufficient intellectual level to "understand" as well as sufficient development to "proceed".'[18]

In spite of his preoccupation with Eva during 1944, Perón continued to maintain a remarkable level of activity in both the Secretariat and the War Ministry (to which the vice-presidency was added in July 1944). One of the Secretariat's most notable measures in this year was the adoption of the *Estatuto del Peón* (rural workers' statute, signed on Perón's 'official' birthday of 8 October), which extended the benefits already granted to industrial workers such as minimum wage and rest day rights, sick pay and pensions. The British Embassy would later note that this was the government's 'most revolutionary and controversial piece of labour legislation …. It must not be forgotten that this statute for the first time granted the rural workers legal conditions of work, housing, medical attention, wages, holidays and so forth.'[19] In the case of rural workers there were less unionization and less oversight, and those rights were thus less rigorously upheld, but the measure itself prompted outrage among the landowning classes (as suggested by the remarks attributed to Patrón Costas above). Traditionally it had been the case that rural workers were entirely dependent on landowners and there had been no attempt on the part of the state to meddle in those hierarchies. The suggestion that rural workers should have labour rights upheld by law was socially revolutionary even if the real effects did not match the psychological impact. The measure also strengthened support for Perón among rural working constituencies as well as urban unions; in particular, the sugar workers of Tucumán, who were encouraged to form the trade union FOTIA, would become key backers of Perón and the backbone of Peronism in the northern provinces.

At the same time, as the earlier Patrón Costas quote suggests, the differences in worker-employer relations under Perón at the Secretariat went beyond formal changes and the tangible benefits linked to pay, holiday and sick leave and pensions. Workers and their unions were now able to negotiate with employers on an equal basis, which implied gains in self-respect as well as pay, while Perón characterized their demands as 'social justice' and their just due, rather than gifts to be dispensed by employers (or the Secretariat itself) at their own whim. Perón himself would insist that the Secretariat 'is a body which should have close ties with both labour and employers' institutions, seeking in the best possible way the welfare of the working class and the tranquillity of the factories'.[20]

Another measure already mentioned, Decree Law 23.852 (signed in October 1945), could be argued to be substantially less beneficial to the trade unions – or at least to trade union independence. The Law of Professional Associations governed the formation of trade unions and accredited only one union as the sole authorized representative of workers in its sector. The law encouraged the establishment of rival unions in sectors where existing union leaders were not Perón enthusiasts and refused to be swayed by his blandishments and the tangible benefits accorded to pro-Perón unions; those rival unions would then be accredited and the original union would lose its legal standing and right to undertake collective bargaining. While an evident move to reduce trade union independence, it was less controversial at the time than might have been expected, given that most unions were making far greater gains than had ever been the case in the past. If those benefits implied that it was prudent to elect leaders of the correct persuasion, this was not a major consideration in many eyes.

A key event in this eventful year was the protracted strike by the meatpackers led by Cipriano Reyes in Berisso against Armour, which would also extend to Swift. The two companies, of British and US ownership, were of course heavily involved in supplying meat to the Allied forces, and strike action was denounced as an anti-Allied stance designed to damage the companies and halt deliveries of food to the anti-Axis troops at a crucial time of the war. In practice, the attitudes and labour practices of the meatpacking firms would also prompt elements of anti-Allied sentiment among workers that had less to do with ideological beliefs than the conviction that the US and British employers were exploiting their Argentine workers in order to maximize their gains in the opportune moment provided by the Second World War. Similar positions and crossed accusations had arisen during the First World War, and working and monopoly conditions in the meatpacking industry had been the subject of an investigation led by Progressive Democrat Senator Lisandro de la Torre in the 1930s that prompted an attempt on his life and the fatal shooting of his Senate colleague Enzo Bordabehere in the chamber in 1935.

Among the practices against which Reyes organized union resistance was the common one of taking on temporary personnel and then dismissing them the day before their ninety-trial period was up, at which time they would have to be made permanent; they might then be rehired for a new ninety-day period before again being dismissed. Although prohibited by law, such practices were common among large companies and the government had thus far proved powerless to stop them. On 1 June 1944, the Secretariat of Labour issued a decree signed by Farrell and Perón, noting that the companies' behaviour contributed to the perception that 'social demands cannot be attained except by imposition' and ordered a ten-cent-per-hour wage increase, the guarantee of at least sixty hours work per fortnight and payment of overtime for both permanent and temporary workers. Perón and Mercante would visit Berisso a few days later to be received by enthusiastic crowds, to whom Perón would claim that the government was seeking to 'free the country from the claws of the great foreign monopolies'.[21]

According to Reyes, despite the huge popular acclaim for Perón, the union leaders in Berisso made clear to him that 'we will be with the government if the government is with the workers, because we are convinced that the emancipation of the workers … is the task of the workers themselves'.[22] While this sounded a warning as to the limits of their loyalty to Perón, it was also a recognition that the government would only be able to achieve reforms if labour unions continued to strengthen their own position and demands – 'we were obliged to feel the military and national revolution to be ours, and to defend the government that represented it in order to defend ourselves'.[23] This would prove to be true, when the companies' failure to comply with the government's decree prompted new strikes, which the Secretariat initially supported and then declared illegal, seemingly under political pressure.

In part due to the meatpacking dispute (which both the US and British Embassies suspected Perón of using for his own ends), Perón's hope for close ties with both labour and employers would prove largely a chimera; despite his continuing efforts to convince them, most business sectors (with the exception of heavy industry, which benefited from the military government's efforts to expand the industrial base) were unconvinced and gave the labour secretary and his policies the cold shoulder. His attempts to convince them that violent class conflict could only be avoided if employers were willing to cede part of their lion's share of the cake largely fell on deaf ears, and the British and US Embassies were similarly unimpressed (though at least in part this reflects the socio-economic circles from which their contacts were largely drawn).

In a famous speech to the Stock Exchange on 25 August 1944, Perón set out a lengthy defence of his labour policies and explained some of their underlying motivations. The speech can be seen as cynical and self-serving – not least given the opening comment that 'my words, if not qualified by great knowledge, are qualified, on the other hand, by absolute sincerity and totally disinterested patriotism', which perhaps unintentionally invites the listener to infer the opposite. However, it can equally be seen as an intelligent, if somewhat ingenuous, attempt to set forth a rational argument of the benefits that could accrue across society as a whole if economic actors allowed themselves to be guided and instructed by the state.

Perón begins by recognizing the doubts attached to his person and his politics: 'on the one hand, they have said I am a Nazi, on the other they have claimed that I am communist; all of this makes me certain that I have found the perfect balance I am seeking in my work at the Secretariat of Labour and Welfare.' Then he comes rather quickly to the nub of his message for business: that social instability can only be resolved by 'consciously working to find perfect regulation between the working, middle and capitalist classes, securing a perfect harmonisation of forces …. Wealth without social stability can be powerful, but it will always be fragile.' He justifies the Secretariat's policy on the grounds that 'the inorganic mass is undoubtedly the most dangerous. Modern experience shows that the best organised working masses are without question those that can be directed and best led.'

Later in this speech Perón again refers both directly and indirectly to the fallout from the Spanish Civil War that he had seen there, as well as to Russia. '[T]he government's immediate objective must be to ensure the country's social tranquillity, avoiding at all costs a possible cataclysm of this nature, because if it happened, accumulated wealth, assets, lands and cattle would be worth nothing.' To this end, he proposes that business organizations, like trade unions, designate delegates to engage in tripartite work to ensure social justice, as well as undertaking their own 'social work'; 'they will thus be the ones who gain the affection, respect and consideration of their own workers.'

The main thrust of this lengthy speech is that only social justice, not repression, can avert crisis, and that the government's policies should therefore be welcomed by business. It contains a stark warning: 'it is necessary to know enough to give up 30 per cent in time to avoid losing everything afterward':

> It is in our hands to stop the situation before reaching that extreme, where all Argentines will have something to lose. The loss will be directly proportional to what each one has: he that has much will lose everything, and he who has nothing, will lose nothing. And given that those who have nothing are far more numerous than those who have much, at this moment the problem is at a crisis point so grave that few can imagine it.[24]

In spite of the dire warnings it contains, one of the more striking things about this speech is its inclusiveness; whereas later Perón would increasingly make use of division and cast opponents (including, often, business) as enemies, in this speech he is at pains to stress the need to work for the benefit of all. This does not include only the stated respect for business, but 'the need for unity among all Argentines, and when I say all Argentines, I mean all men who were born here or who are tied to this country with bonds of affection or citizenship'. The only 'enemy' defined as such here is communism, and even that is cast more as a symptom of social ills than as the disease. Despite some obvious defects in the concept and its execution, the stall Perón seeks to set out in this speech is indeed largely moderate and logical. It is a clear outline of the contemporary phase of what would later become Peronist doctrine: something which might more usefully be described as progressive populism than downright authoritarianism. Its key defect is the belief that deep-seated problems have simplistic solutions (and the inevitable disappointment when those solutions are at best short-term) and that they can be imposed from above rather than percolating from below, a system that works effectively in the military but not in a civil state.

The speech, which Perón believed to be reasonable and rational in the extreme, was received badly by those who felt they were being threatened with losing everything and being coerced into a pact with a military government whose policies they largely disliked. Rather than being taken as an invitation to collaborate for the wider benefit, it was seen as a threat to be pushed back against – albeit a threat limited by the fact that economic power was lined up largely on the side of the audience rather than the speaker. Yet if Perón was widely accused of a fascist bent by some sectors (notably in the United States), it should be noted that the greatest opposition he faced in Argentina came precisely from the right wing of both the military and the private sector. Indeed, some believed that he was actively compromising with the United States in a bid to reach the presidency and avoid being overthrown by officers on the far right,[25] and in his communications with US interlocutors he was usually at pains to draw parallels between his programme and President Roosevelt's New Deal rather than with Mussolini's fascist state. These parallels were not entirely unrealistic, and in fact Roosevelt had also come in for intense criticism that the New Deal was statist, interventionist and even downright communist. (Both Roosevelt and Mussolini, however, benefited from the fact that the First World War had already introduced the notion of a far greater state role in the direction of the economy, production and labour – something that did not apply in Argentina, which was not involved in the war.) Nonetheless, the perception abroad that Perón was a Nazi or fascist sympathizer was no small matter in 1944 and the early part of 1945, as he was increasingly recognized as the strongman of the de facto government and a possible president.

Relations between Argentina and the United States had seldom been cordial at the best of times, Buenos Aires having seen itself historically as Washington's competitor for regional leadership. The overt US interference in Argentina's foreign policy, which seemed (Ramírez's claims to the contrary) to have forced the breaking of relations with the Axis, had done nothing to ease those tensions, while Argentina's persistent refusal to declare war on the Axis stoked fires in Washington. US military assistance to Argentina's rival Brazil, which had declared war, was also a driver of anti-US feeling.

In the case of Perón himself, US suspicions were raised yet further by a lecture he delivered in June 1944 at the University of La Plata, where a new professorship of national defence was being inaugurated. The speech, on 'The Meaning of "National Defence" from a Military Viewpoint', expounded on a number of subjects dear to Perón's heart: Von der Goltz and the 'nation in arms or total war'; his experience in Europe at the start of the war; and the need 'to establish a perfect truce in all internal problems and struggles, whether political, economic, social or of any other type, to pursue only the objective that will save the fatherland: to win the war'. Perón's basic thesis is that 'war is an inevitable social phenomenon; so-called pacifist nations, such as ours, must prepare for war if they want peace; and that national defence of the fatherland is an integral problem which includes all activities, which cannot be improvised at the moment that war is knocking on the door.' Perón also reiterates that the Argentine economy has been almost exclusively dependent on primary agriculture, whereas heavy industry is required for economic development and wealth (in which context he notes with satisfaction the military government's creation of a direction of military industry, *Fabricaciones Militares*).

Much of this content might be seen as relatively uncontroversial, and indeed straying little from Perón's lectures during his years as a teacher. Yet Washington in particular fixated on sections of the lecture that could be construed as hostile, for example, the observation that

> the nations of the world can be divided into two categories: the satisfied and the unsatisfied. …. In the latter, they lack something to satisfy their needs: markets for their products, raw materials to process, … a political role to play …. If politics does not get them what they need or desire, they will not fear to go to war to attain it.[26]

The speech was taken as proof of Perón's hostility and dangerous intentions, and prompted the recall of the US ambassador to Washington for 'consultation'. (As Joseph Page noted, the reading in Washington did not even give Perón credit for his intelligence, with an Office of Strategic Studies report suggesting that he was too ignorant to have written it and that it must have been ghosted by someone more 'erudite' – apparently disregarding his long tenure as a professor of military history and the repetition of similar themes in much of his past work.[27]) Perón was probably in the right when he claimed to have been misinterpreted in Washington, but the dispute reflected long-standing suspicions and, not least, the distaste felt by Secretary of State Cordell Hull, who throughout his tenure was convinced that the GOU and the de facto government were pro-Nazi and that Argentina would soon be a safe haven for Nazi war criminals as well as for the undoubted espionage activities that had taken place largely uncontrolled throughout the war.

US-Argentine tensions and the ratcheting up of US pressure on Buenos Aires and on Perón in particular would continue through 1944 and increase in 1945. In some respects diplomatic pressure would achieve its ends – at the Chapultepec conference in February 1945, Argentina agreed to declare war on the Axis and suppress the activities of its agents within Argentina, in exchange for US support for Argentine entry into the soon-to-be-formed United Nations. (Argentina declared war on Germany and Japan on 27 March 1945, and the United States resumed normal diplomatic ties days later.) Yet more generally, and predictably, US pressures more often than not provoked the opposite result to that intended, and would allow Perón to bolster support in many quarters. The year 1945 would be yet another watershed for Perón and for Argentine politics, and it would be a US ambassador who would play the role of main antagonist and virtual opposition candidate as Perón's own presidential candidacy became more inevitable.

Perón's collection of political posts, high-profile and ceaseless trade union and other welfare activities, and his skilled use of mass media, had given him personal power and name recognition that buoyed some and appalled others. That in itself, together with rising rejection within the armed forces of his relationship with Eva and the apparent influence she and her family exercised, would be enough to crystallize opposition to Perón and his probable presidency in mid-1945. However, that opposition, whose factions had few points in common beyond their rejection of Perón, would make a number of unforced errors that, as in the case of US pressures, would backfire and cement precisely the power they feared.

Chapter 7

SAN PERÓN

Los muchachos peronistas, todos unidos triunfaremos
Y como siempre daremos un grito de corazón:
Viva Perón, Viva Perón!
Por ese gran argentino que se supo conquistar
A la gran masa del pueblo combatiendo al capital.
Perón, Perón, qué grande sos, mi general, cuánto valés!
Perón, Perón, gran conductor, sos el primer trabajador!

The Peronist boys, united we will triumph
And as always will give a cry from the heart: Viva Perón, Viva Perón!
For that great Argentine who conquered the masses by combating big capital.
Perón, Perón, how great you are, my general, how great your worth!
Perón, Perón, great leader, you are the first worker!
Los muchachos peronistas (Peronist march), attributed to Oscar Ivanissevich

By the start of 1945 Perón enjoyed a seemingly favourable position in both the political and personal spheres. In the political sphere, he had in his hands three key posts – secretary of labour, war minister and vice-president – and had for the time being seen off the most dangerous competitors for power. In particular, the strongly pro-Axis interior minister, General Luis Perlinger, appeared to have been defeated as a rival to Perón's power. Also a candidate for the vice-presidency in July 1944, Perlinger had lost to Perón by only six votes among the group of army officers who chose the candidate and had been replaced in the Interior Ministry by a Perón ally, Admiral Alberto Teisaire. This had staved off any real challenge to Perón, and indeed the threat of a far more authoritarian and pro-Nazi shift in the government, despite Washington's view that Perón represented that danger. For the time being Perón had no serious rival or coordinated opposition within the army, although during 1945 that would begin to change, in large part due to his blooming personal life and domestic arrangements.

From the time she and Perón had moved in together shortly after meeting, Eva Duarte had increasingly insinuated herself into all areas of his life. Despite their reputation for ambition and desire for fame, both Perón and Eva enjoyed the regularity of domestic life and fell rapidly into what in some respects could be described as a rather staid domesticity (were it not for the absence of a marriage licence). As during his life with Aurelia, Perón appeared to relish a stable family home and was not averse to helping with the cleaning and cooking, preparing salads or a steak. Eva, who had had little experience of a stable family life since leaving her mother's house in Junín, also enjoyed preparing basic meals, which they would often eat in bed on a tray if no one else was present. Eva would later say that most of the friends and political contacts who came to meetings at the flat would not stay to eat, and that they spent many of their evenings happily alone. She would also describe Perón as a romantic rather than as a leader, 'strong and tender at the same time. …. He made me feel like a different person. …. There is a flower on my pillow every morning. …. I don't know where he gets it or if he brings it when he comes home and I don't see it, but every morning I have a flower.' 'Just in love? … I'd give my life for him anytime.'[1]

If her acting career was nearing both its peak and its end, Eva's political education and controversial nature were expanding over the same period. As soon as they 'broke all conventions' by moving in together, she began to act as hostess to both his friends and political, military and union men who met in the flat. She recognized that they saw her as a 'fish out of water' and did not 'understand how a woman could be there, with Perón, learning'. Perhaps more uncomfortably for them, 'I look them straight in the eye, because afterward they go and I stay.'[2] Certainly they were not 'accustomed to the presence of a woman, not as a decoration, but as a participant in everything happening around her'.[3] Yet for many the disquiet went beyond any *machista* reaction, however much this was also part of the picture. Trade unionists, military men and political figures were startled that she would often express forceful political opinions, including about possible political and union appointees, frequently in very denigrating or vulgar terms. Although she would later become the idol of the trade union movement, at this early stage she lacked the contacts or the grasp of labour issues she would later display, and the tough men who had already begun to give their trust and affection to Isabel Ernst were unimpressed with Eva's high-handedness and her often shrill and trenchant views on their business.

Unlike the unions with which she would forge strong ties only a relatively short time later, Eva's relationship with the military would never improve, in part but by no means exclusively due to her inappropriateness and the brazenness of her cohabitation with a senior figure in the army and government. Her abrasiveness and lack of protocol also genuinely shocked officers used to correct behaviour and 'not accustomed to such things'. Worse, there was a widespread perception that her family were also becoming influential – primarily her brother Juan, always known as a dubious character, who was suspected of using his contacts for speculation and black market purposes. Here, too, there was a genuine perception within the army that the institution itself, as well as the government, was being affected by 'interference, first in [Perón's] life and then in the affairs of state that he managed, of the Duarte family, that family of obscure origins.'[4] Moreover, the relationship with Eva and her family represented a break in the discipline that had always characterized Perón which weakened and degraded him in the eyes of military colleagues who considered that leaders must be able to exercise personal discipline in order to have the right to impose it on others.

Both Perón and Eva may have begun to feel invulnerable, a pardonable error of hubris that would bring its own risks. (Alternatively, if Eva was dabbling in the black market, it may have reflected her underlying fears, given that, without the benefit of marriage and facing some uncertainty over the future of the military government and Perón himself, her good fortune and security might be only short-lived.) Not only had Perón seen off competition within the military and within the trade unions, but the opposition was divided and leaderless. Moreover, the UCR, which Perón and others wooed periodically in a bid to form an alliance for eventual elections, remained intransigent in its refusal to negotiate, clinging to its self-perception as the historical majority party and one unable to compromise on principle.

However, Radical intransigence also worked against Perón, who sought to gain some support from that quarter that could benefit him in pursuing electoral ambitions – not least given disaffection among junior officers in particular, in large part due to the 'Eva question', as well as the loss of support among 'nationalist' sectors following the break with the Axis. Perón would hold clandestine contacts with various Radical leaders over the middle of 1945, reportedly offering that, once elections were held, the party could choose candidates for all elected posts except the presidency, an offer that was rebuffed. Only a few Radicals would accept the offer of closer collaboration with the de facto government, including Hortensio Quijano and Juan Isaac Cooke, who would respectively become interior and foreign ministers later in 1945.

Nevertheless, in part due to the desire to sustain the improvement in relations with Washington, following a wave of detentions in April 1945 justified on the grounds of a supposed anti-government plot, on 23 April Perón took the apparently counterintuitive decision to issue a statement to the effect that 'he did not aspire to be a presidential candidate and disapproved of official backing for any candidate', and that 'I will energetically oppose any efforts to make me a candidate'.[5] This was the type of statement that generates more worries than it soothes – someone genuinely not planning a presidential bid would be unlikely to deny such a plan – although allies of Perón would tell both the US and British embassies that Perón had meant what he said and that his eventual candidacy was 'forced by the blindness of the Opposition'.[6] As such, it did little to ease his increasingly tense relations with sectors of the military or to reassure the broad but fractious civilian opposition. However, not unlike the way in which organized labour had latched onto Perón as a leader when it had failed to generate one of its own, the opposition would soon latch onto its own leader, from a most unlikely quarter. That leader would be the new US ambassador, who arrived in Buenos Aires following the measures taken by the Farrell-Perón government to patch up relations with Washington – Spruille Braden, who presented his credentials on 21 May 1945.

Perón and other allies would later observe that 'if Braden hadn't existed, we would have had to invent him',[7] and that is true to some degree. Yet before he became a foil who could be turned into an electoral weapon, Braden was a serious enemy and one who, barring some major miscalculations, might have welded the disparate opposition groups into a force capable of putting up a serious fight. Even as Perón had become a leader and conduit for a dispersed trade union movement, so Braden would become the leader of a diffuse and sometimes contradictory opposition – with the obvious drawback that casting a foreign diplomat in that role was a risky move, not least because he was clearly unable to be a candidate for national office in Argentina.

Spruille Braden, a robustly undiplomatic diplomat who in the eyes of some personified the 'ugly American' so unloved in Latin America, would later say that 'never have I expected to occupy the White House but I qualified for occupancy by being born in a log cabin,'[8] in Elkhorn, Montana in 1894. His father was a mining engineer who became one of the founders of the Braden Copper Company in Chile in 1904; although the family no longer had financial interests in the company, it was eventually nationalized in 1971 and became part of Chile's state copper company Codelco. Braden would spend much of his early life in Mexico and Chile and married a Chilean wife in 1915. In addition to Braden Copper, he was also an important shareholder in and later lobbyist for the notorious United Fruit Company, the 'octopus' that controlled much of the economy of Central America in the first half of the twentieth century, giving rise to the term 'banana republic'. Later in his career he would be involved in orchestrating the 1954 coup d'état against Guatemalan President Jacobo Arbenz, whose programmes were considered deleterious to the United Fruit Company's interests, and would have a notably warm relationship with Nicaraguan dictator Anastasio Somoza Debayle.

Prior to his arrival in Argentina, Braden had begun his diplomatic career as part of the US delegation at the inter-American conference in Montevideo in 1933, where he developed an intense dislike of 'Carlos Saavedra Lamas, the enormously egotistical Argentine foreign minister, [who] intended to stir up as much trouble as possible for the United States'.[9] (His long tenure in Chile and family ties there probably also predisposed him to a negative view of Argentines.) As a representative of Standard Oil he also intervened in the 1932–1935 Chaco War between Bolivia and Paraguay (in which Saavedra Lamas's mediation caused him to receive the Nobel Peace Prize, 'the source of a distasteful memory to me'[10]). In the late 1930s and early 1940s he served as ambassador in Colombia and Cuba. Corpulent, bull-necked and square of jaw, Braden was a fluent Spanish speaker and had no hesitation in speaking his mind in either English or Spanish. He would later recall with evident pride 'the editorials that called me "a bull in a china shop" in diplomatic affairs because I got tough with Perón, State Department appeasement of dictators having already become the official fashion'.[11] Clearly his mind was already made up about Perón and the government of which he was part, and to which Braden was accredited. Instead of acting as a foreign diplomatic representative to that government, his programme 'was to keep on attacking [it] by every means until they were pushed, stage by stage, into self-destruction'.[12]

Braden would note that 'the last commission signed by President Roosevelt was that naming me Ambassador to Argentina'.[13] Shortly after his arrival there, 'encouraged and flattered by the Opposition, especially the more wealthy "society" members, he launched out into a series of violent speeches against the regime'. Although British Ambassador Sir David Kelly would rightly believe that 'his campaign must eventually defeat its own object by rallying the forces of nationalism and anti-American feeling round Colonel Perón', for a time it appeared as though Braden might succeed in his campaign to turf him out of office.[14] In the longer term, Braden did indeed undermine what he set out to do and encouraged Perón to take a less conciliatory line towards business than he had done earlier in his tenure: 'he was willing for some time to reach compromise arrangements with the business community, but the hysterical hatred of the wealthy, and the ill-judged campaign of Ambassador Braden, so strengthened his hold on the masses that he was able to dispense with any other support'.[15] From an entirely opposite viewpoint, Cipriano Reyes would also note that Braden 'only managed to deepen the abyss that had opened between the workers and the country against the unscrupulous oligarchy that represented the great anti-national interests'.[16] This entrenched the mindset that was already undoing the traditional elites: 'the oligarchy did not have the intelligence to join this process, giving up some of its privileges in order to retain the most important'.[17]

Unsurprisingly, Perón and Braden would later recount entirely different versions of their few meetings. Braden would note that, having learned some friends were among around 1,000 political prisoners being held, when he arrived in Buenos Aires he made a point of asking loudly in front of the official welcoming committee as to why his friends were not there to greet him. On arriving at his hotel, he would be informed that one close friend he had named had already been released. 'Thus ended my first encounter with Perón', Braden observed, although Perón had not been part of the delegation. The following day, at a press conference Braden stressed the commitment to defending basic freedoms, which, he said, had resonance for Argentines who now felt that 'the United States was not, after all, indifferent to their plight'. Later that day, he met their 'oppressor' for the first time, at a reception at which he claimed Farrell told him many stories 'contrasting his alleged stupidity with Perón's intelligence, but more of them making fun of Evita's past in the oldest profession'.[18] While some of this conversation seems highly unlikely – Farrell was a friend and genuinely fond of Perón, and it seems doubtful that he would make such offensive comments about his girlfriend to a complete stranger, and the US ambassador at that – it reflects accurately Braden's attitude towards the Argentine government and Perón in particular.

During his subsequent conversation with Perón at the same reception, Braden would recall that Perón became insistent on the need for US military materiel and support for Argentine industrialization, to which Braden replied that Argentina must first comply with its obligations under the Chapultepec Agreement. The same topic would return in their second meeting a few weeks later, at which, according to Braden, Perón promised to turn over confiscated Nazi assets, as well as Nazi agents, to the United States and to have 1,203 political prisoners released. Perón, in turn, asked for Braden's intervention over 'lies' printed in the US press and was angry with his failure to act accordingly. On 29 June, a new meeting saw Perón accuse US journalists of involvement in plots to overthrow him and the government; after several disputes that Braden would characterize as childish arguments, he would claim that Perón in effect warned him that those US citizens involved could be subject to attack by 'fanatical' supporters outside his control. In Perón's own versions of these conversations, it was he who always came out on top, with Braden always vanquished and fuming. (Perón would claim that in early July Braden had promised that Washington would not stand in the way of a Perón presidency if he met Washington's commercial and espionage-related demands, to which he supposedly replied that in Argentina 'people who sell out the fatherland are called sons of bitches', to Braden's fury.)

Whatever the relative truth of these conflicting views, Sir David Kelly appears to have made a sober assessment of Braden's self-destructive approach in becoming the darling of anti-government elites and stirring nationalist and anti-Yankee sentiment. And indeed, it would appear that his frictions with Perón related not only to his higher calling to bring democracy to Argentina, but also to pressures on the government to take measures beneficial to US corporate interests with respect to domestic market access (not least for US airlines) and control over seized German and Japanese interests. However, his presence gave new impetus to opposition forces; in June 319 of the largest business and agricultural organizations took out full-page newspaper advertisements attacking the government's social policies – singling out the Secretariat of Labour for particular criticism – and calling for new elections. The Confederation of Rural Societies would also publish an advertisement warning that the *Estatuto del Peón* 'eliminates the landowner's hierarchy, leaving to the mercy of the workers or any professional agitator ... the tranquillity and the life of the families and honest men who work in the countryside'.[19] Such statements allowed Perón to accuse the organizations of seeking to reimpose the rule of the oligarchy and 'another Tragic Week', but they also strengthened the cohesion of the forces opposing the government.

The effect of these pressures and the US ambassador's campaign was such that at an armed forces dinner on 6 July (at which Perón also spoke briefly), Farrell announced that the government planned to call elections in the near future and would do everything possible to 'ensure completely free elections and that whoever occupies the presidency will be the one the people choose'.[20]

Days later, a newly reconstituted UCR would issue a document criticizing the de facto government for 'turning its back on the will of the people, in open violation of constitutional rights and guarantees', adding that the workers' gains over recent years did not require 'the continuation of governments or force nor the violence of social conflicts'.[21] A subsequent secret meeting of high-ranking officers, on 28 July, would issue a resolution that seemingly favoured a Perón presidential candidate, stating that

> faced with the refusal of the leaders of political parties to collaborate and respect the work of the Revolution, the government shall seek the means by which the will of the popular majority, which we believe favourable to the Revolution, can be expressed freely and democratically so that the President elected is the expression of that popular will.[22]

The other effect of opposition pressures, strengthened by the UCR's statements, was to convince union leaders, if they needed further convincing, that the departure of the government would see the end of its labour and other social reforms. A few days later, on 12 July workers demonstrated in front of the Secretariat of Labour carrying signs that read 'Perón for President' and chanting a slogan aimed directly at Braden's Nazi claims – *ni nazis ni facistas, peronistas*, or 'neither Nazis nor Fascists – Peronists', the first time the term 'Peronists' had been used. The union leaders who spoke expressed support for the government's policies without mentioning Perón by name, but the placards and chants made it clear who the participants supported. Once the leaders had departed, calls for Perón to appear were answered by the secretary himself, who made a speech extolling the achievements of the Secretariat, modestly if unconvincingly claiming that not even he himself was indispensable to the progress of social justice. Possibly even more disturbingly, a few days later a large group of several hundred 'spontaneously' assembled outside Perón and Eva's flat calling on him to stand for president.

A few days later, an accident at a Braden Copper Company mine involving hundreds of deaths allowed Perón's followers to mount a new assault on the ambassador, despite the fact that he was no longer involved with the company. Moreover, when Braden gave a lecture in Santa Fe in late July, he was met with thousands of leaflets lampooning him – although, more importantly to him, he was also met by 'the Mayor, the Governor, the president of the university and a number of leading citizens'. On his return to Buenos Aires he was met by 'some five thousand people', also of the great and the good, who shouted his name and, according to Braden, wished 'to demonstrate their repudiation of the vicious attacks on the United States and myself'.[23] What was clear already was that the presidential campaign was getting underway, with the US ambassador as leader of the opposition. This would not play out the way Braden, whose contacts were limited to business and social elites critical of the government, anticipated.

The entire month of August would be marked by opposition protests, above all by university students, and by rising tensions and occasional violence. No member of the government attended the Rural Society's annual agricultural show, one of the most important social and economic expositions of the year, at which the rich and powerful chanted anti-government slogans and a few cavalry soldiers who participated were roundly booed. For its part, with elections apparently on the horizon, the UCR issued a statement coyly accepting 'action in harmony with the democratic parties' but without 'in any way reducing its independence and autonomy' and, in somewhat contradictory terms, stressing that 'the Radical party is opposed to any kind of electoral alliances or pacts'.[24]

In September 1945, just as the political heat was rising yet further, Braden would leave the ambassadorship to become assistant secretary of state for Western Hemisphere affairs, implying his return to Washington if not the end of his vendetta against Perón. Before leaving, on 28 August he would give an electrifying speech to a gathering of the wealthy at 'a great banquet at the Plaza Hotel [where] several hundred guests stood on their chairs screaming applause and shouting "bravo" and "Viva Braden" for minutes on end'.[25] Braden's furious denunciation in that speech culminated with the promise that 'the voice of liberty has been raised in this country …. I shall hear it from Washington with the same clarity with which I have heard it here in Buenos Aires. My policy will not vary at all when I am in Washington, and if anything I will be able to accentuate it as I will have greater possibilities to do so.'[26] According to the anti-government newspaper *La Prensa*, which transcribed Braden's speech in full, some 800 people attended, with demand for access far outstripping supply.

Already prior to Braden's departure, as noted earlier, from July a disparate and cumbersome opposition alliance had begun taking shape with his encouragement, including conservatives, parts of the Radical party, communists, socialists and other entirely unsuitable bedfellows. By the time of Braden's departure that opposition was uniting around calls that the government be handed over to the Supreme Court, and on 19 September a mass demonstration, the March for Constitution and Liberty, was called to back up those demands. Gathering in front of Congress, the march passed Perón's office in the War Ministry and headed for Plaza Francia, in the heart of the elite Recoleta district, with placards and shouts of 'the military to barracks' and 'the government to the Court'. Estimates of participation varied wildly between 65,000 and half a million, but it was almost certainly one of the largest marches yet seen in Buenos Aires, despite a transport strike that aimed to thwart it. According to his own memoirs, Cipriano Reyes was prompted by the event to begin planning for a major pro-government demonstration as a show of counter-force, something that would be put into practice only a month later.

The March, unsurprisingly, was widely and glowingly reported in the opposition press, typically describing it as 'essentially an occasion of the people … a remarkable demonstration of spontaneous and concerted action by a people in the mass on a scale only possible under the uniting influence of some deep common experience or sentiment'.[27] The press also made much of the fact that, despite the generally orderly nature of the proceedings, 'such hostile cries as were uttered, were all directed against the person of the Vice President and Minister of War, Colonel Juan Domingo Perón'.[28] However, the Argentine press signally failed to note that 'the people' represented on the occasion were almost exclusively middle and upper class, and the public opinion they represented was one strand only, and in direct contradiction to another important (and overlooked) segment. Nevertheless, the March, and the opposition press reaction, would also strengthen the rising resistance to Perón among the officer corps, most of whom came from middle-class families and social circles and read newspapers such as *La Prensa*.

Perón's public reaction to the March was relatively controlled, calling on the workers to stay calm and avoid potential clashes, and to adhere to the Peronist slogan of 'from home to work and from work to home' in order to avoid the risk of violence with the anti-government forces. The possibility of a state of siege was considered and discounted, and the anti-government march was authorized. Yet the government was aware that behind the scenes a military conspiracy was forming behind the short-lived former de facto president Arturo Rawson to overthrow Farrell and Perón. That attempt, to be launched from Córdoba a few days later, was discovered and rapidly snuffed out without bloodshed, although it provided the excuse for a return to state of siege on 26 September.

Despite the number of arrests that followed the state of siege, opposition initiatives would begin to increase, with students occupying universities across the country in early October with the slogan '*alpargatas* [rope-soled canvas shoes used by the poor] no, books yes'. (An attempt by Perón to speak to the students in a radio broadcast to bring them on side would prove ill-considered and spectacularly unsuccessful.) Moreover, the Supreme Court, perhaps emboldened by the calls for it to assume government, began to issue rulings declaring measures by the Secretariat of Labour unconstitutional, among them the establishment of labour courts. Clashes between different factions would lead to the murder of one student in Buenos Aires and rising tensions that brought concerns within the officer corps to a greater pitch. However, unease over the rocky road to possible elections and the future of Perón might have remained under control had not a final outrage caused it to explode. That outrage came not in the form of concern over civilian opposition or rising repression, but in the form of an 'unacceptable' intervention by Eva Duarte into government affairs.

The actual touch paper that lit the remarkable events to come might seem of lesser importance. The post of director of the Department of Post and Telegraph was to be vacated by Colonel Aníbal Imbert, a former contact and supposed former lover of Eva Duarte's. Eva would propose that he be replaced by Oscar Nicolini, a friend (and also, supposedly, a possible former lover) of her mother's from Junín and the contact who had facilitated her own 'in' with Imbert when as a radio actress she had needed his approval for scripts to be broadcast. In point of fact, unlike many public sector appointments based purely on contacts rather than professional capacity, Nicolini was a career employee of the postal service and could be said to have had some qualifications for the post. However, this counted for nothing in military eyes, given both the fact that one of their comrades in arms had wanted the post and the fact that Perón's widely detested mistress had intervened in the process. Perón, who approved Nicolini's promotion, prudently had Interior Minister Hortensio Quijano sign the designation on 1 October, although this fig leaf scarcely represented deniability when he was confronted by his outraged fellow officers. Moreover, there were rumours that Nicolini had been involved in cases of corruption, along with Eva and her brother Juancito, who were said to be dealing illegally in petrol ration coupons.

The commander of the Campo de Mayo garrison, General Eduardo Avalos, a former member of the GOU and friend of Perón, would be charged with confronting Perón about Nicolini and the 'Evita situation' more generally. Avalos, initially a supporter of Perón's political activities, was by this time deeply suspicious both of Perón's labour activities and of Eva's influence; he was also increasingly seen as a possible political competitor. Following Nicolini's promotion, on 6 October Avalos confronted Perón in his office at the War Ministry and conveyed to him the ire the decision had aroused. Perón initially attempted to blame Quijano for the decision, but said it could not be reversed, prompting Avalos to demand that the president intervene. At Farrell's suggestion, Perón and Avalos again faced off at Perón's flat, where Eva's intervention to insist that Perón not back down only worsened the situation. The only conclusion reached was that Perón would receive a delegation from Campo de Mayo at his War Ministry office to hear their objections, after he refused to go to Campo de Mayo owing to fears for his safety. Despite his refusal to withdraw Nicolini's appointment, Perón was angry and distressed and spoke to Mercante of his possible departure from politics.

The meeting at the War Ministry took place on Monday 8 October, Perón's (official) fiftieth birthday. Perón received Avalos and his delegation in his office, where they found about forty of Perón's supporters already gathered. He again rejected any reversal of Nicolini's appointment and offered to resign from the army and government if a majority of those present so decided, proposing that if the vote went in his favour then Avalos should resign. Perón and Mercante departed his office to attend his birthday lunch and to allow discussion over his future; given his careful assembly of a substantial number of supporters, the vote, unsurprisingly, went in Perón's favour. However, Campo de Mayo was in no mood to accept the result, and Avalos was persuaded to step back from his promise to resign, although he himself managed to persuade the more irate younger officers not to march on the Casa Rosada to force Perón's removal. Avalos himself promised to confront Farrell to demand Perón's departure from government and the calling of elections, the conduct of which was to be guaranteed by the military.

Despite having gained the upper hand over Avalos, Perón in fact seemed uncertain as to how to proceed, unwilling to lose the support of any faction of the army which would be needed if he were to make a success of any future career. Moreover, Perón was characterized throughout his life by an innate caution (described by some as cowardice) and had little desire to be martyred in the cause of the revolution, suggesting to some collaborators that he would be willing, if Farrell requested it, to resign and return to private life. (Concerned over mounting tensions and the possible risk to his own security, on the 9th Perón suddenly cancelled a planned visit to the War Academy where, as it turned out, a number of armed officers were waiting to assassinate him.) He was encouraged in this by Eva, who at this stage was more concerned for their own safety than about the future of social policy, and who pleaded with him to go to Uruguay. However, he was equally unwilling to resort to violence being committed on his behalf, and rejected proposed plans to mobilize loyal troops against Campo de Mayo.

At a meeting with Farrell at Campo de Mayo on 9 October, Avalos made clear that Perón's departure was non-negotiable and rejected any suggestion that he should be allowed to take time to consider resigning. Faced with the implacable position of Avalos and other officers at Campo de Mayo, Farrell first offered his own resignation, which was rejected, before accepting the conditions imposed and offering Avalos the post of war minister following Perón's departure. A delegation sent by Farrell to the War Ministry, led by Perón's friend General Juan Pistarini, communicated the decision to him, and Perón sat down and wrote two notes, resigning his government posts and asking for his retirement from the army; he wrote them out himself, he said, so that it could be seen that that hand had not trembled. It seemed that his meteoric and apparently unstoppable career was suddenly over. Given that the crisis of recent days had not been reported to the public, the announcement that Perón had left the government was even more surprising, both for his supporters and detractors.

However, Perón had not entirely surrendered, and supporters such as Mercante and Reyes were even less inclined to do so. On the evening of 9 October Perón spoke with Farrell by telephone and asked to be allowed to give a farewell speech to his supporters at the Secretariat, to which Farrell readily agreed – including to allow the speech to be broadcast on the radio. Thanks to the organizational skills of Mercante, Reyes and telephone workers' leader Luis Gay in particular, the broadcasting equipment, a public address system and a crowd of thousands chanting Perón's name were in place by the time Perón arrived at the Secretariat to deliver his speech on the 10th, and a delegation of union leaders was on hand to meet the outgoing secretary.

Perón's supposed farewell speech was a fine example of his oratorical skill, enumerating the gains made by workers since he took over at the Secretariat only two years earlier and announcing that before departing he had signed a decree increasing both salaries and the minimum wage and providing for company profit-sharing with employees, which would be approved by the president. In less pragmatic and loftier terms, he went on to remind his listeners that they should continue to defend the Secretariat because the emancipation of the workers could only come from the workers themselves, and promised that 'our struggle may last one year or ten, but we will win in the end'. He said that he would now 'put himself at the service of the people and if necessary he would join a union and fight on with us wearing a worker's overall'. He ended by asking his supporters to disperse peacefully, but with the warning that 'if it becomes necessary to ask for war, I will ask for war'.[29] Despite the fact that his supporters heeded his request to disperse peacefully, there were clashes with members of the opposition now emboldened by Perón's apparent departure. However, to the observant, it would also become apparent that the workers were not the only sector whose support Perón still enjoyed; when he went to the Federal Police headquarters to bid farewell to the chief of police, an ally, police officers stood and shouted Viva Perón. That support would also become crucial in coming days.

Still concerned for his own safety amid numerous assassination rumours (which had only been fuelled by anger over his 'farewell speech'), Perón decided to leave Buenos Aires that night and to go with Eva to the country home of a supporter, Román Subiza, in San Nicolás. He left with Mercante a note to Avalos (now his replacement as war minister) confirming these plans and saying that he was taking a leave of absence. Late that night they departed along with Eva's brother Juancito and Rudi Freude, the son of a friend and Nazi agent, Ludwig Freude, but not before reassuring Mercante that the move represented a strategic feint rather than a final departure. In the end they did not go to San Nicolás but instead to Freude's retreat in the Tigre Delta, on Tres Bocas island. Rudi Freude and Juancito would return to Buenos Aires, leaving Juan and Eva alone to enjoy a peaceful setting for a brief respite. The house was well appointed, well stocked and attended by a German butler, Otto, who spoke no Spanish, thus guaranteeing their privacy and comfort.

For his part, Mercante, who had also been forced to resign from the Secretariat but still retained access, went into action, searching out trade union leaders throughout the Greater Buenos Aires area and exhorting them to attend a meeting at the Secretariat on Friday 12 October, a legal holiday. (Columbus Day, or *El Día de la Raza*, would play its own role in labour pressures for Perón's return; employers rejected demands for workers to be paid for the day as a legal holiday, telling them to 'go and ask Perón' for the lost day's wages.) Seconded by Isabel Ernst and his cousin Hugo, Mercante received some eighty trade unionists in the Secretariat on the morning of the 12th and urged them to call a general strike to ensure the return of Perón to office and the continuity of labour's gains over the previous two years. However, union leaders were dubious, hesitant to provoke clashes with the government before its labour policies became clear and unwilling to yoke themselves to the career of an officer whose star might have faded. The meeting was broken up by military and police officers who removed Mercante and other employees from the Secretariat, perhaps providing a hint that the new authorities would be less sympathetic to organized labour.

Simultaneously, a different event was taking place a short distance away, at the elegant Plaza San Martin, where a large group of well-heeled and irate demonstrators gathered outside the *Círculo Militar*, the officers' club, and began insulting, threatening and even attacking the officers present. Protesters reiterated demands that the government be turned over to the Supreme Court, something that even the most anti-Perón senior officers were unwilling to accept, believing it to be the duty and the honour of the military to oversee an electoral end to the de facto government. The elite crowd outside, who began to bring food and drink as well as ire to the scene, became increasingly strident as the afternoon wore on, and a group of aristocratic women went so far as to assault an army colonel. Efforts to placate the crowd were shouted down angrily, leading the officers inside to grow concerned over the treatment that might be meted out to them if the opposition were to come to power – a consideration that for many made Perón look more palatable than he had only hours before. Eventual police action to repress the crowd prompted a pitched battle that led to one death and a number of wounded on both sides, a further hint that no transition of power was likely to be amicable.

The respite enjoyed by Perón and Eva was very brief at best. Farrell ordered Perón's detention on the 12th, apparently in an attempt to safeguard him from an assassination attempt rather than to punish him. Mercante and the new chief of police – another Perón supporter, Colonel Aristóbulo Mittelbach – led a police delegation to Tres Bocas, where they found the couple walking along the shore with their arms around each other. Mittelbach informed Perón that he was to be detained, probably on Martín García island (where Yrigoyen had also been held following his ouster) and the group returned to the Posadas Street flat in sombre mood, with Eva sobbing on the back seat. Perón, Eva and Mercante were allowed to enter the flat without police guard, and Mercante rapidly reported to Perón on his own organizing efforts on his behalf, not least to discourage him from considering the possibility of fleeing to Uruguay, as Eva had urged.

Before long Major Héctor D'Andrea arrived to escort Perón to the gunboat *Independencia* which would take him to Martín García. As they were to depart, Eva stormed into the room and became hysterical when she learned that Perón was being detained. She was unceremoniously shut out of the lift and left weeping in the hallway, as Perón, D'Andrea and Mercante drove to the port. Mercante said his farewell as Perón boarded, urging him to keep up his courage, while Perón asked him to look after Eva. As Perón disappeared onto the gunboat, Mercante saw that the sailor standing guard was in tears; he would say later, 'I suddenly felt tremendously calm. I knew with absolute certainty that we were going to win the wager!'[30] However, Mercante's own activism would be temporarily halted a few hours later when, on the morning of 13 October, he was detained at the War Ministry and held in custody at Campo de Mayo for the next four days.

Now ensconced in Martín García, in the same chalet that had housed Yrigoyen, Perón would be seized by the urge to write, sitting down to produce both a self-justifying text to be published as a pamphlet, and a series of letters both personal and professional. Two of them were to Avalos and Farrell, asking to be informed of the charges against him and for his retirement from the army to be expedited. A third letter to Mercante, who years later handed it over to the historian Felix Luna to be published in its entirety, maintained the note of self-pity but was to a large degree a detailed recognition of Mercante's loyalty and utility. Complaining that he was unable to sleep due to the fact that his 'nerves have reached crisis after these two years of such intense sensations' and that his enemies had him incommunicado, Perón noted that 'however, I have what they do not: a loyal friend and a woman who loves me and whom I adore'. He asked Mercante to look after Eva 'because the poor thing's nerves are destroyed and I am worried about her health. When they give me my retirement I will get married and go to the devil.'[31]

Perón would also write two letters to Eva, one of which may or not have reached its addressee and has never been made public, and a second, given to Luna by an army officer who found it in a bedroom drawer at the presidential residence following Perón's 1955 overthrow, which has been widely published. It reiterates many of the same themes of his letter to Mercante, including his plan to retire from the army, marry Eva and 'go away somewhere to live in peace'. The tone of the letter is touching and deeply affectionate. 'Since I left you there with the greatest pain you can imagine I have not been able to calm my sad heart. Now I know how much I love you and that I cannot live without you.' 'Nothing must happen to you because then my life would be over.'[32] Although Perón may have believed that the letter would be intercepted and read by third parties, and therefore wished to give the impression that he was preparing to retire quietly, it appears primarily that his main concern had shifted now that his political future was at best uncertain. It seems that his primary focus was returning to Eva, and 'if my retirement comes through we'll get married the next day and if not I will arrange things some other way, but we will end this lack of protection that you face now'.[33] For someone who was always someone reticent in his emotions, it is a remarkably passionate letter; it is, for example, impossible to imagine Perón having written a similar one to Potota.

With the exception of the one letter to Eva that is lost, all of these letters were sent back to Buenos Aires with Perón's personal physician, Captain Miguel Angel Mazza, who was allowed to visit him on 14 October on Martín García despite his supposed incommunicado state. As noted above, doubts have been raised as to whether the letters were genuine expressions or designed by Perón to make it appear that he planned to give up politics and retire to Chubut. Certainly, he expected that Mazza would be searched and the letters read by more than their intended addressees. Nevertheless, at the very least they eventually reached their addressees' hands, and it appears likely that they expressed Perón's genuine (if at times somewhat incoherent) feelings. More than likely, as Joseph Page suggests, he was attempting to leave his options open, and he might have stuck to his offer to retire to Patagonia if it proved to be the best option available.

In addition to acting as courier, Mazza's visit served other practical purposes. For one, he brought Perón messages of support from some fellow officers, which suggested that an attempted return would enjoy some backing. For another, it provided a pretext to insist that Perón be moved back to Buenos Aires on the grounds that the damp climate in the Tigre Delta was damaging his health. On the afternoon of the 14th Mazza would visit Farrell, accompanied by an old X-ray of Perón's lungs, to claim that he must be moved on account of a health condition. Admiral Vernengo Lima was also present, and as both Perón's foe and putative jailer (given that he was in the hands of the navy at Martín García) he demanded that an independent medical commission confirm the diagnosis. Farrell, who was far more willing to see his friend returned home, agreed, and the commission was designated to visit Perón two days later, on Tuesday 16 October.

As Perón had feared, during these few days Eva was alone, at a loose end and under threat. She had been informed at Radio Belgrano that her services were no longer required, whether out of spite, a desire to remove a divisive figure or simply a desire to maintain good relations with the new authorities going forward. Many myths have since arisen as to her activities during these days and the extent to which they helped in the organization of the events of 17 October. She herself would later say in her autobiography, 'I launched myself into the street in search of the friends who could still do anything for him. ..... I honestly never felt so small, so insignificant, as in those eight memorable days. .... As I went from the proud and rich neighbourhoods to the poor and humble the doors began to open generously, with greater warmth.'[34] According to her and to other reports, she was recognized in a taxi on one occasion by a group of students who dragged her out and beat her; she would sometimes stay in friends' homes at night. However, despite later efforts to portray her as the heroine of the events of 17 October, in practice her role was limited by her lack of experience and contacts with labour organizations.

One of her few demonstrable contributions to events was her visit to Juan Atilio Bramuglia, a labour lawyer who had been designated as the de facto government's intervener in the province of Buenos Aires and who was one of Perón's most able and dedicated allies. Eva approached Bramuglia to ask him to present a writ of habeas corpus for Perón, which he refused on the grounds that she might seek to drag him off to exile and away from the political fray. Eva would never forgive

Bramuglia, with negative consequences later as her hostility truncated the career of one of Perón's most able cabinet ministers. Beyond this, though, she was largely condemned to watch and wait from the sidelines, uncertain of her own fate or that of her partner.

In denying later claims that Eva had been central to the 'rescue' of Perón and had collaborated actively with the unions, Reyes would subsequently go to the extreme of claiming he had never even met her at the time of 17 October and had no real dealings with her thereafter, although he was careful to applaud her 'immense work in favour of the humble and dispossessed' and to say in his usual exaggerated language that 'no one can imitate her, nor detract from her human values, nor obscure the greatness of her glory'.[35] Given that there is evidence that Reyes had attended meetings at the flat she shared with Perón, the statement that they had never even met is not credible and appears to be of a piece with Reyes's own later claim to have pulled off 17 October virtually single-handed. Nevertheless, the point that she was not, as she was later cast in Peronist myth, one of the authors of the event is valid; for someone of as activist a disposition as she, the inability to do more than sit and wait must have been galling. Indeed, this most momentous occasion would be one of the few in which neither Perón nor Eva would play a leading role. It would rarely happen again.

Meanwhile, the ruse of the X-ray, combined with Farrell's good will, would succeed in bringing Perón closer to the centre of the action; in the dawn hours of 17 October he was transferred to the military hospital in the Palermo district of Buenos Aires, where he was soon installed in the chaplain's rooms on the top floor, changed into his pyjamas and prepared to rest, receive visitors and await events. At the same time, over the night of the 16th the CGT had finally agreed to call a general strike for the 18th, although the strike call would carefully avoid reference to Perón's release, or even his name, instead demanding elections, maintenance of the labour rights granted over the previous two years, the lifting of the state of siege and for the government not to be handed over to the Supreme Court.

This reluctant eleventh-hour move by the CGT would be rapidly overtaken by events. Already on the night of the 16th a few thousand had attempted to walk to the centre of the capital from the industrial suburb of Avellaneda, although they were halted by the police and few got through. Meanwhile, in the northwestern province of Tucumán the sugar workers' union FOTIA declared an indefinite strike, while some strikes broke out in the industrial suburbs of La Plata and Córdoba. However, on the morning of the 17th events would pursue a course never before seen in Argentina and rarely elsewhere.

From early morning workers in Avellaneda began congregating with homemade banners; instead of entering the factories they continued walking towards the capital, gathering numbers as they went. On superior orders, the police raised the bridge over the nauseous Riachuelo, more an open sewer than a river, and the marchers then began to improvise rafts or even to wade across, until the bridge was mysteriously lowered. Similar marches were coming from other industrial suburbs in the southern areas of Greater Buenos Aires and by 10.00 am thousands had already reached the city centre. Further columns came from Berisso and

Ensenada, the focal points for the shipyards and meatpacking plants that were Reyes' stronghold. Similar marches were also taking place in other cities across the country, in Córdoba, Tucumán, Salta and Zárate, as apparently spontaneous as the throngs pouring into Buenos Aires. Some workers took over buses and trams and forced them to turn back into the city centre; the railway workers downed tools and joined the marchers. They began to congregate in the historic Plaza de Mayo, in front of the Casa Rosada. According to various trade unionists later, the processions and the meeting point were entirely spontaneous, with the army of Perón's supporters taking the decision to march on Buenos Aires despite the CGT's reluctant call for a general strike the following day. By noon there were some 15,000 in the Plaza de Mayo, and Buenos Aires had come to a halt, with many of its more well-heeled residents taking cover behind the shutters to watch the invasion. The police did little, if anything, to halt the marchers, often smiling and shouting Viva Perón themselves.

Apart from the genuinely awe-inspiring sight of thousands of self-led marchers, the 'Peronist hordes' or 'zoological deluge', as some detractors called them, represented something the *porteños* had never seen and never hoped to see: the appearance of the invisible classes from the slums and the impoverished interior. Even more strikingly, the marchers did not come bent on revenge, as many feared, 'there was no rancour in them, just the joy of becoming visible and demanding their leader'. They sang songs with invented lyrics such as 'Perón isn't a communist, Perón isn't a dictator. Perón is a son of the people and the people are with Perón.'[36] These invaders (who also included women and children) were not dressed like Buenos Aires office workers and their lack of jacket and tie was widely mocked – although in fact photos touchingly reveal that many had dressed in their best for their first visit to the city centre, and jackets were much in evidence although sometimes being carried rather than worn on the hot spring day. Most famously, some would take off their shoes after the long trek and soak their feet in the fountains in the Plaza de Mayo, which would become an iconic anti-Peronist meme for decades to come.

As people continued to arrive in the Plaza de Mayo, several hundred also found their way to the military hospital, where by now Perón had managed to speak to Eva by telephone and to talk with a number of visitors, including Mercante. Genuinely surprised by events, he was astute enough to delay any appearance, continuing to wait at the hospital while the crowds increased at the Casa Rosada, to the apparent amusement of President Farrell and the horror of Avalos – together with Vernengo Lima, one of only two cabinet ministers who had not resigned, and one who saw his apparent advantage of only a few days earlier disappearing rapidly. The crowds continued to swell, chanting slogans such as 'With Perón and Mercante Argentina will go forward' and 'Farrell, Perón, two hearts that beat as one'. And, increasingly, 'we want Perón'.

As the evening wore on and the crowds got ever larger, it became increasingly urgent to try to calm the anger that some clearly felt against those who had moved against Perón, notably Avalos. (Avalos himself, who had hoped to engineer an electoral solution to the morass, had to a large extent been undermined by the intransigence of the Radicals, notably Amadeo Sabbatini, whom he had tried to persuade to lead a presidential ticket.) Mercante was brought to the Casa Rosada and asked to placate the masses; in a clever bid to do precisely the opposite, Mercante stepped onto the balcony, took the microphone and began by saying 'General Avalos. ...' The name prompted an immediate and deafening chorus of boos and hissing and Mercante retreated inside with the air of a man defeated. Shortly thereafter, another figure appeared on the balcony, Eduardo Colom, editor of the only pro-Perón newspaper, *La Epoca*. Colom announced to a cheering crowd that Perón was well and would soon appear, hardly the message Avalos had wished to convey. Avalos would then make the pilgrimage to the military hospital, where after an interview with Perón he telephoned the Campo de Mayo barracks to inform them that Perón would speak from the balcony of the Casa Rosada later that night.

Perón continued to delay, in order to allow the crowd to reach a peak (which, although never definitively estimated, appears to have been somewhere between 200,000 and 500,000). He would occasionally ask those around him if it was really true that there were so many people. Finally, at around 21.30 he phoned Eva and then dressed, arriving at the presidential residence a short time later before travelling with Farrell to the Casa Rosada. At 23.10 he came out onto the balcony, to be greeted by the sight of hundreds of thousands of supporters, many of them holding flaming newspapers as torches, shouting his name. 'The people appeared to have gone mad: they shouted, they jumped, they wept and sang slogans with ever hoarser voices. There was the man they had risked everything for. Safe and sound. The victor. And they cheered their leader but also their own victory.'[37]

Farrell spoke first, promising elections and presenting Perón, the man 'who has won everyone's hearts'. Another deafening ovation followed. Taken by surprise but quick-thinking, Perón asked the crowds to sing the national anthem, giving him time to gather his thoughts. He returned inside and then stepped back onto the balcony, prompting yet another ovation with his first word: 'Workers!' Thereafter, Perón and the crowd engaged in an odd dialogue, with supporters demanding to know where he had been. Although there is no recording of this dialogue and reports of it vary, what remains is among the most effective and emotional speeches of his career, in which he announces his retirement from the army before reaching the rank of general, in order to remain Colonel Perón and to place himself 'at the full service of the authentic Argentine people .... to mix with the suffering and sweating masses that produce the labour and the greatness of the fatherland.' He speaks of 'the indestructible brotherhood between the people, the army and the police' and makes two rare references to his mother – one in which he wishes to embrace the crowds 'as I would my mother' and one in which he recognized that his followers had suffered his absence 'with the same pain and the same thoughts that my poor old lady must have had'.[38]

Following various minutes of dialogue interrupted by cheers and applause, Perón asked the people to disperse peacefully, remembering the presence of women and children, and to adhere to the general strike the following day. He asked them to remain for fifteen minutes more to allow him to look on the 'wonderful spectacle a while longer', and said that he would rest a few days in Chubut before returning to the struggle. Joyous and satisfied, the marchers began to chant 'Tomorrow is San Perón. Let the boss work!' before slowly beginning to disperse and to make their way back, exhausted, to their homes where a day of rest awaited them.

The emotive nature of 17 October is difficult to set out in words. It was a visceral and emotional response to the loss of a man who had come to embody the hopes of millions of Argentines and the gains in both material position and pride that he had helped to bring them. Its effect would be to cement a bond of love and loyalty between those people and their leader that would endure for years to come. Cipriano Reyes would describe it as 'the march of the relegated, the persecuted, those who carried and carry the weight of social injustice, a meek people full of faith that went in search of its hopes, aiming to find its destiny'.[39]

Yet while Reyes would rightly claim credit for much of the agitation that brought the marchers onto the streets, it was the spontaneous, word-of-mouth quality that was a key characteristic of 17 October. As Eva would later say, 'no one gave the call to come out. The people came out on their own.'[40] Her gratitude would also form an enduring bond between herself and the *descamisados* ('shirtless ones'), prompting the vortex of social action she would develop over coming years. The event would be a key moment in the virtual canonization of Perón and, eventually, Eva as the patron saints of the *descamisados*. At the same time, however, it was arguably the last improvised, spontaneous act of a movement and a leader hitherto characterized by spontaneity and an ability to improvise. Over time it would thereafter become increasingly orchestrated, inflexible and ultimately sclerotic, with sometimes grave consequences.

Although many did not realize it at the time, 17 October was a point of inflexion in Argentine history, in which the previously marginal working classes came into public view and political life for the first time, never to leave it. It would also mark a shift in the relative weights of Perón's power bases; trade unions would, at least for a time, outweigh the military in the balance of power. But perhaps most significantly, it was a show of love of a kind that few political leaders have seen. 'That October day, when he looked out on the Plaza de Mayo and received, in an unforgettable roar, the purest and most beautiful thing a man with a political vocation can aspire to: the love of his people.'[41]

Chapter 8

CANDIDATE

Fue mi sueño de purrete ser igual a un barrilete
Que, elevándose entre nubes, con un viento de esperanza sube y sube ....
Yo quise ser un barrilete buscando altura en mi ideal,
Tratando de explicarme que la vida es algo más que un simple plato de comida.

It was my childish dream to be like a kite
That, rising among the clouds, rises and rises with a wind of hope ....
I wanted to be a kite, seeking height in my ideals,
Telling myself that life is something more than just a plate of food.
Sueño de barrilete (tango), Eladia Blázquez[1]

Following the watershed events of 17 October, the *Review of the River Plate* would observe two days later that 'it thus becomes obvious that the country is in virtually the same position as it was a fortnight ago', a somewhat astonishing conclusion that highlighted the continuing blindness of significant sectors of Argentine society to what was happening around them. This would lead the opposition to commit errors that would cost them whatever chance they had of winning the looming presidential elections.

For the government itself, the turn of events was accepted with some apparent satisfaction by Farrell, and Perón's power within the government was quickly restored (with Mercante named secretary of labour). With a view to expediting an orderly transfer of power, the government brought forward the election date from 6 April to 24 February 1946, and the armed forces committed to ensuring that the process was free and fair. However, although the government continued to insist that it had no 'own' candidate and would only seek to ensure that the popular will was respected, Perón had an evident advantage, apart from throwing up a constitutional issue. Although the government was a de facto one, the constitution did not allow a second consecutive term for either the president or the vice-president and his candidacy was thus arguably illegal. This was certainly the interpretation of the opposition. However, instead of taking the constitutionally logical course of refusing to participate for that reason, they opted to establish an electoral coalition, in the mistaken belief that Perón was an unpopular figure and their candidate would easily prevail. By doing so, they would lose any moral high ground from which to argue that the process was unconstitutional.

On the surface at least, Perón also took the day's events in his stride, following up the 17th with a few days with Eva in San Nicolás and 'later at the *quinta* in San Vicente, which I had had for many years, to work on organising the campaign'.[2] The *quinta* (weekend home) at San Vicente would represent an important refuge for Perón and Eva over the next few years, where they would spend relaxing weekends away from the whirlwind of daily activities, riding or walking, talking and drinking *mate*, with Perón cooking steaks and Eva making salad and relaxing in Perón's pyjamas with her hair in braids. What is notable, apart from the peace and quiet they sporadically enjoyed, was the fact that Eva was already accompanying Perón not only in his private life, but also in the preparation of the next phase of his public life.

San Vicente would not be the only refuge, or the only priority: on 22 October Perón fulfilled his promise to marry Eva. The civil marriage was held at the Posadas Street flat (despite claims that they had married in Junín), with Mercante and Juancito Duarte as witnesses, although it was not without complications. Given that she would have to present a birth certificate showing that she was an illegitimate child with the surname Ibarguren, Eva went to some lengths to obtain a falsified birth certificate giving her name as María Eva Duarte and her date of birth as 7 May 1922 (a date after the death of Juán Duarte's legal wife which could in theory have allowed for him to have wed Doña Juana). There were practical as well as personal reasons at play; with Perón set to become Argentina's elected president, acknowledgement that his wife was an illegitimate child would have been deeply scandalous (albeit primarily for those who would not support him anyway). The marriage certificate also identified Perón's legal status as 'single' rather than 'widowed' for reasons that are less clear. A subsequent religious ceremony in La Plata was aborted on 29 November following reports of death threats, and only held on 10 December. It was presided over by Father Hernán Benítez, who had given last rites to Potota and would subsequently become Eva's confessor. Thereafter, the couple made a brief return to San Vicente for a short pre-campaign honeymoon marking one of their last quiet times alone, before moving temporarily into a house Eva had bought in Teodoro García Street in the Colegiales district.

Her illegitimate origins were not the only element of her past that Eva would try to bury. Considerable exertions were made to recover publicity photos from her acting career from Radio Belgrano and other sources, and director Mario Soffici would present her as a wedding gift with the final cut of her last film, *La Pródiga*, her only starring role, which would not be seen in public until some three decades after her death. (The film, in which she played a wealthy woman seeking to compensate for her misspent youth by becoming a benefactress to the poor, represented no loss to the cinema, but did represent an odd foreshadowing of what her career would become from here.) As Felix Luna would note, her marriage 'certified the death of the actress María Eva Duarte and the birth of a woman named Eva Perón'.[3] Her intense love for and gratitude to Perón – and, by extension, to the *descamisados* who had saved him on 17 October and returned him to her – would mark an intense and remarkable career ending with her death less than seven years later.

Figure 4 Perón and Evita's civil marriage ceremony, October 1945 (Wikimedia Commons)

(*Descamisados*, or 'shirtless ones', was a derogatory term used by the socialist newspaper *La Vanguardia* after the overheated 17 October marchers were seen to take off their jackets, and was taken up as a rallying cry by Perón, who would take off his jacket and roll up his sleeves during political speeches thereafter.)

With the elections approaching, the leadership of the UCR – still the unchallenged majority party in their own eyes – came under increasing pressure to form an electoral coalition with other opposition parties; with considerable reluctance, on 14 November the party's directorate voted in favour of joining the *Unión Democrática* (Democratic Union) with an uneasy range of other opposition groupings including the communists, socialists, Progressive Democrats and the old-guard conservatives first supplanted by the UCR in 1916. From the start the alliance suffered from many weaknesses that made it largely unviable, even above and beyond the obvious ideological incompatibility of its component parts.

One of those weaknesses, clearly, was its belief in its own invincibility, which was sufficient to overlook many errors in its strategy – including its single campaign slogan, 'For liberty, against Nazism'. As a slogan it represented a respectable viewpoint, but the fact that it implicitly branded the government (and Perón) as Nazis made any eventual accommodation impossible. That, and the inability to do anything but oppose even government measures that had benefited millions of workers whose interests in theory were of concern to the socialists and communists, became a trap from which those parties would arguably never extricate themselves.

One example of this difficulty was the December announcement that the government had issued a decree in line with Perón's promise, during his 'farewell' speech at the Secretariat in October, of profit-sharing for workers. The eventual Decree 33.302 in fact fell short of enshrining profit-sharing, but it contained a number of key elements, including the so-called '13th month' of annual wages (*aguinaldo*), across-the-board pay rises of between 5 and 25 per cent depending on income, and the imposition of paid holidays and sick leave and increased indemnity payments for dismissal or death. Predictably, it was widely resisted by employers and by the conservative press, but as such the *Unión Democrática* also felt obliged to denounce it – not as a questionable pre-election manoeuvre, which would have been reasonable, but as an unsustainable burden on employers. A lock-out by employers in January in rejection of the move failed to overturn the measure but in the eyes of many workers tied the *Unión Democrática* to intransigent capitalists impoverishing their workers.

Another critical defect was the fact that the alliance was valid for the presidential elections only; governors, members of Congress and other elected posts would be the subject of competition among those parties, making a broad legislative alliance impossible from the start. Moreover, the *Unión Democrática*'s presidential slate was composed of two Radicals, with no participation from the rest of the alliance. On 27 December, the slate was confirmed: José Tamborini and his running-mate, Enrique Mosca, were two old-school Radicals, eminently respected but seemingly relics from another era – not inappropriate, given the number of their supporters who wished to return to a pre-war past, but impractical for a country that had already moved beyond that time. Notably, they were ageing and dull, in contrast to Perón's charisma and infectious energy. In practice, however, many of these weaknesses appear largely irrelevant given that public opinion was so sharply divided that political platforms and propaganda would do little at this stage to shift voter loyalties.

Although the *Unión Democrática* lacked charismatic leadership and attractive platforms, it produced large amounts of election propaganda, not least through printing thousands of pamphlets containing dire warnings of the dictatorship to come and often scatological criticisms of Perón. These included amended poems and lyrics to famous tangos referring to Perón as a 'dog, criminal, and I know you are rotten like no one before' or 'the candidate of the riffraff' (or, in another case, of the 'residue of the latrines'), as well as somewhat dubious attempts to draw parallels between his career and that of Hitler. Again, in addition to being somewhat short on humour, these pamphlets were at least as insulting to Perón's supporters as to the man himself and did nothing to draw them towards the *Unión Democrática*; indeed, they only confirmed the perception that the elites were snobbish and anti-worker, and that they would do little to defend working-class interests.[4]

In early October 1945, shortly before the chain of events that would give the measure salience, Law 23.852 had given trade unions the right 'to participate from time to time in political activities where this has been resolved by a general assembly or a congress'.[5] This would pave the way to the foundation of the *Partido Laborista* (Labour Party) in late October, whose charter specified that it would be composed of trade unions and other labour organizations, political organizations and individual members and would focus its platform in precisely the areas of social policy that had characterized Perón's activities at the Secretariat of Labour. It represented elements of the CGT's political interests in particular, allowing it to act as a political party as well as a union movement. Given that Perón did not as yet have his own political party and elections were fast approaching, the creation of the *Partido Laborista* represented a realistic option, although not the only one. Perón continued to seek alliances with elements of the UCR linked to Quijano in particular, and was offered the candidacy of the *UCR-Junta Renovadora* as well as the *Partido Laborista*. This arrangement suited a leader who was seeking to broaden his base, in terms of both size and class composition, but required delicate compromises to keep both parties on side.

In January a *Partido Laborista* congress formally nominated Perón as its candidate for president, but the question of his running-mate was more vexed; the unions were reluctant to accept the imposition of Quijano as a means of keeping the Radical factions on side, and proposed the names of both Luis Gay and Cipriano Reyes before suggesting Mercante for vice-president. Although in some respects a logical choice, Mercante would have represented a second army officer on a supposedly civilian presidential ticket, and without party support to bring to the table. While his candidacy was rejected, the move served to unblock the nomination of Quijano, and also gave the unions a bargaining chip in the discussion over candidates for the governorship of Buenos Aires, for which Reyes proposed Mercante over Perón's preferred choice of the Radical Alejandro Leloir, who would have stood with Juan Atilio Bramuglia as his candidate for vice-governor. (According to some reports, Mercante's candidacy also had strong backing from Evita, due to both her warm affection for Mercante and her strong dislike of the more bourgeois Leloir and Bramuglia in particular.) The manoeuvre succeeded, but would keep alive frictions between the two civilian pillars of Perón's support.

The *Partido Laborista* would prove fundamental to Perón's eventual victory but would also carry the seeds of its own later demise, proving more independent than Perón would have liked. Indeed, one of the elements behind its creation was the idea of a potential alternative to Peronism, should that become necessary. Eventually, following the elections, both the *Partido Laborista* and the *Junta Renovadora* would be dissolved and combined as a newly named *Partido Unico de la Revolución* (Sole Party of the Revolution), which in its turn would shortly be renamed the *Partido Peronista* (Peronist Party) – the first political party to be named so baldly and clearly after its founder and leader, still very much alive and in power.

The presidential campaigns would get underway during the hottest period of the year in Argentina. Tamborini and Mosca would undertake their first tour in the so-called Victory Train which set forth from Buenos Aires on 21 January 1946, covering much of the north of the country. The tour consisted of a number of brief stops and briefer speeches by Tamborini, many of them marked by hostile shouts, stone-throwing and in some cases gunshots, while crowds of supporters were also attacked on various occasions; the Victory Train would return to Buenos Aires eight days later pocked with bullet holes and the impact of stones. These mishaps dented the rolling stock far more than the optimism of the *Unión Democrática*, convinced of victory.

Perón himself began his grand tour slightly earlier, departing Buenos Aires on 26 December for the stifling northwest (his train would be known as *La Descamisada*). Shortly thereafter Eva would travel to join him in Santiago del Estero for New Year's Eve. As with so many other aspects of their political partnership, this would represent a first, as no candidate's wife had ever accompanied him on a campaign tour before. Although not yet a political figure, she was known as a radio actress and their recent marriage added an element of romance to the proceedings; her presence was a positive. While she kept largely in the background, she was tireless in smiling and waving to crowds, whether at whistle stops or as the train chuntered through the baking hot northwest. She would even continue when Perón wearied and stopped for a nap (being replaced by a railway official who resembled him and who would keep up the smiling and waving while the train was in motion). The honeymoon was thus as unconventional as their early relationship and subsequent marriage would be, but if it was not intimate it allowed them to spend time together and for Eva to continue increasing her involvement in her husband's political project. That involvement in Perón's political and personal life was already closer and more intimate than anything Potota had managed in their ten years of marriage, much of it spent waiting for her husband to finish work. While the trip was in some ways reminiscent of the time Perón and Potota had spent together on their honeymoon and en route to Chile, it began to establish Eva as an integral part of Perón's career rather than an often-excluded spectator.

Unlike Tamborini, Perón (and his attractive new wife, in her background role) was received euphorically; despite the treatment meted out to Tamborini, Perón's speeches focused on the campaign's peaceful nature, calling for collaboration rather than conflict. Their train was also subjected to at least two serious attacks; dynamite was found on the line on one occasion, while on another six people were wounded when a crowd of supporters awaiting Perón's arrival was fired on.

Arguably the peak of the tour was a triumphal visit to Tucumán, the first province in which the general strike prior to 17 October was declared. Unlike most of the northwest, Tucumán had a solid industrial history arising from both the sugar mills and the railway workshops in Tafí Viejo, and the Peronist message arguably thus far had greater salience there than in the more traditional provinces. The (majority) opposition press, predictably, gave little attention to Perón's peregrinations; although in theory he enjoyed an advantage as the government's virtual candidate, in practice he received almost no publicity in the print media and he lacked the deep-pocketed supporters who financed the *Unión Democrática*'s propaganda, printing thousands of leaflets and posters. Nevertheless, their second and third campaign trips, one to the west by train and the other north to Rosario and the northeast by boat, were equally enthusiastically received.

Eva would also make a less successful attempt at campaigning for her new husband, giving a speech to a meeting of his (still disenfranchised) female supporters at a rally at Luna Park on 8 February. Eva appeared as a stand-in for her husband, who was ill, and was poorly received by his enthusiastic supporters, who shouted her down including with slogans that she doubtless did not find amusing, such as *sin corpiño y sin calzón, somos todas de Perón* ('without bra and without knickers, we all belong to Perón'). Some little time would yet pass before she would become a political leader in her own right, in particular of the Women's Peronist Party that she herself would organize.

It was during the presidential campaign that Perón, and Apold, would take steps to bring more newspapers into the candidate's orbit. Initially, only the trade union-funded paper *El Laborista* and Eduardo Colom's weekly *La Epoca* were supportive, but they lacked wide circulation. During the campaign *La Epoca* would receive a 'loan' that allowed it to expand into a daily, with a circulation of some 50,000. At the same time, the newly founded *Democracia*, which supported ideas linked to Perón such as agrarian reform, also received funding reserved for government publicity; the newspaper, which had a circulation of only around 10,000, was the only one to cover Perón's campaign in detail, including sending a journalist on his campaign tours. (Apparently on Apold's initiative, *Democracia* would eventually be sold to Eva Perón.) If the ethics of these manoeuvres were dubious, the coverage of the traditional press was equally so; both sides would engage in partisan reporting that encouraged flare-ups of violence.

Although Perón received no support from the larger newspapers, he did receive substantial boosts from two slightly unexpected quarters. One was the Catholic Church, which on 17 November issued a pastoral letter warning, as was traditional, that Catholic voters must not vote for parties that supported the separation of church and state or supported the legalization of divorce or lay education. This was certainly not designed to benefit Perón, who many members of the hierarchy viewed with suspicion (not least due to his lengthy pre-marital liaison with Eva); the pastoral letter echoed warnings issued on other occasions. However, it happened that parties associated with the *Unión Democrática* were also associated with the policies rejected by the hierarchy (the Radicals having long been seen by the Church as anti-clerical), giving Perón a new opportunity to emphasize his (questionable) religious fervour and the fact that the military government had adopted policies such as religious education that had appealed to the bishops. Moreover, some clergy working in poorer areas were already enthusiastic about the government's social policies and were happy to press home the contents of the pastoral letter more emphatically than would otherwise have been the case. The letter was timed nicely in advance of Perón's tour of the more traditional northwest, allowing for a number of well-judged visits to cathedrals.

The other source of support was even more surprising, and more unintended. From his more distant but lofty perch at the State Department, Spruille Braden remained in close touch with his friends in Buenos Aires, and as determined as ever to play his role in ending Perón's political career. Braden maintained contact with the same political and social sectors, who continued to misinform him as to Perón's real popularity, in the probably sincere belief that, because their social circles rejected him, rejection must be widespread and deeply felt. The US press also kept up negative coverage, taking its cue from the former ambassador and from the traditional opposition press such as *La Prensa*, whose reporting throughout the campaign had been biased in the extreme. (More than 90 per cent of the campaign coverage in *La Prensa* and *La Nación* was devoted to the *Unión Democrática*.) *The New York Times* and magazines such as *Life* covered Perón's campaign and personal life in inaccurate and insulting terms that a later generation would surely have termed 'fake news' and a smear campaign. The overriding impression among US readers was that Perón was a Nazi, a totalitarian, probably a degenerate and certain to lose a fair election. Nevertheless, whether to finish the job or simply to ensure that his support was not greater than anticipated, the State Department entered the campaign with an eleventh-hour flourish that, if it did not alter the eventual election result, gave Perón an unintended boost of a dramatic nature.

Days before the 24 February elections, on 11 February the State Department published the grandiloquently named 'Consultation among the American Republics with Respect to the Argentine Situation', a 131-page document purportedly transcribing discussions with other Latin American governments over the situation in Argentina. In point of fact, the document, which rapidly became known as the 'Blue Book', was revealed to the governments supposedly consulted only days before its release. The Blue Book held little novelty, basically reiterating long-standing claims of Nazi sympathies and the alleged involvement of the de facto government in the 1943 Bolivian coup. It was picked up enthusiastically by the opposition press in Argentina; *La Prensa* and *La Nación* published it in instalments in its entirety, to the approval of many of their readers – none of whom changed their voting intentions as a result, given that they were overwhelmingly behind the *Unión Democrática*, which enthusiastically supported the Blue Book and adopted it as their own.

To be fair, the Blue Book did not switch many votes to Perón either; positions were by and large so entrenched as to be immutable. Yet the blatant and heavy-handed US intervention went down poorly with many and may indeed have shifted some undecided votes away from the *Unión Democrática* which the Blue Book was so evidently intended to benefit; much of its text was virtually indistinguishable from their campaign materials. Moreover, Perón's reaction showed the quality of his political instincts at their most unerring. In a speech to a large crowd on the day the Blue Book was released and its contents were reaching Argentina through the wire services, Perón was measured, citing Roosevelt and his struggle for social justice and going on to outline the differences between the 'fictitious' democracy of his oligarchic opponents and the 'economic democracy' he represented, describing himself as a conservative rather than a demagogue. Building up steam, he claimed that the oligarchy did not want elections or democracy and then announced that 'Mr Spruille Braden is the inspiration for, creator, organizer and real leader of the *Unión Democrática*'. He then stated baldly that 'anyone casting their vote for the oligarchic-communist conspiracy is giving their vote to Mr Braden. The alternative in this transcendental hour is this: Braden or Perón!'[6] The slogan 'Braden or Perón' would appear in speeches, on walls and in the scant pro-Perón media in the final days of the campaign, in essence erasing Tamborini and his own virtues and defects from the race. (The Blue Book bolstered Perón's anti-imperialist credentials not only at home, but also in neighbouring countries; Chilean British Embassy contacts suggested that it would both help him win the election and make Chilean sentiment more pro-Perón.[7])

As if that were not enough, on 22 February Perón would publish a reply, to be known as the Blue and White Book (the colours of the Argentine flag), which denounced the Blue Book as 'nothing more than an electoral manoeuvre designed to save the Argentine oligarchy, threatened by the first free elections held in the Republic since 1928'. Responding to the accusations contained in the Blue Book, it dismantles much of the so-called evidence presented therein, and claims that 'the party created through Mr Braden's efforts … has produced a heterogeneous conglomerate in the service of the forces of privilege, which in our country are traditionally anti-democratic and which confront Colonel Perón just as before they combated President Yrigoyen'.[8]

Perón ended his campaign on 22 February with a sober warning that the opposition was mobilizing public transport and money to bribe voters and bring them to the polling stations, saying that his own party was poor and had only spiritual values, making it impossible for them to reply in kind. He urged his supporters to avoid attending any event that might prevent them from getting to the polls early on the 24th, called on them to avoid drink and disturbance and to make their way to polling stations over whatever obstacles were placed in their way. Despite his position as the de facto government's candidate Perón had taken up the position of an opposition leader, a discourse he had maintained since 1943 and would maintain for many years after, despite the fact that he had never been in the political opposition and, until 1955, his party, born in power, would not occupy that position. This was not entirely double-speak: with most economic power ranged against Perón and his supporters, they did embody the opposition to an old pattern of power, and indeed his power in office would never be as great as it sometimes appeared.

Following a campaign marked by underhanded methods, violence and polarizing propaganda on both sides, the 24 February elections were widely acknowledged to be the fairest and most transparent Argentina could remember.

The fact that they took place at all was considered a relief by some, amid rumours that the elections would be cancelled due to the certainty that Perón would lose. The acknowledgement on all sides that the elections were peaceful, free and fair underscored not only the fact that the elections were indeed clean, but also the fact that both Perón and the *Unión Democrática* were sure of victory. Thus, when the results, made public only on 8 April, showed that Perón had won by nearly 1.5 million votes to 1.2 million for Tamborini, the opposition could not cry fraud. The Electoral College convened on 6 May gave 298 votes to Perón and 66 to Tamborini. Moreover, the two parties supporting Perón received two-thirds of the seats in the Lower House, all but two Senate seats and every governorship except Corrientes province. For the first time since 1912, the Socialist Party had no seat in the Lower House and indeed the party would for many years suffer from having aligned with conservative anti-Peronist parties rather than working-class interests.

Despite his huge congressional majority, the composition of Perón's support base would give rise to difficulties early in his term. Given the limited participation of the *Junta Renovadora*, most of the newly elected legislators had little or no political experience, and gaining that experience would come at a cost, facilitating criticism and intransigence on the part of the opposition. Some of them were doubtless corrupt or opportunistic, as the opposition would claim, but many others had good intentions yet faced a steep learning curve; some had legal or other professional backgrounds but many were trade unionists or young men lacking in experience overall. Among the more unusual was Ricardo Guardo, who would become president of the Lower House. Guardo, a young dentist and university lecturer, was inexperienced but cultivated, and married to the daughter of a wealthy industrialist, Lilian Lagomarsino. The two would suffer ostracism and abuse for their Peronist views, anathema to most of their social circle. Lilian would also become a close friend and confidant of Eva after meeting her in the period between the elections and the inauguration. Invited to San Vicente one weekend, the Guardos were privy to Perón's pre-inauguration planning, as well as to Eva's already well-informed interest. According to Lilian later, 'I was impressed by her, by her beauty and her special manner. She talked politics all day, about this one and that one, this post and that post. She knew all about everything.'[9]

If the *Unión Democrática* failed to achieve its expected victory – owing to a remarkable degree of self-deception based on weighing the views of its own supporters and media backers as though they were universal – its component parts also failed to undergo any serious period of reflection and self-criticism. The reduced opposition in Congress would become intransigently hostile to the new government, doing what it could to block Perón at every turn rather than exercising a responsible opposition. In particular, those traditional opposition forces persistently failed to understand the extent to which dynamics had shifted; they refused to engage in any debate over what the future should look like, remaining obstinately stuck in the past. Clinging to the slogan 'for liberty, against Nazi-fascism', they did not enter into the discussion over how Argentina had changed and where it might go from there. As such, they left that debate on the future exclusively to Perón and his supporters, facilitating their argument that the opposition only wanted to overturn working-class gains and the promotion of social justice in favour of returning to an oligarchic past.

That backward-looking quality was not only unattractive to the working classes, but also to sectors of the middle classes and nascent industrialists who viewed the future as one of modernizing the economy. It was a clear dichotomy: Tamborini and the *Unión Democrática* represented the past, and Perón represented the hope of a modern future. The majority chose to vote for something new and optimistic, with an eye to the future and a more modern and socially just economy based on broader incorporation of the population as both consumers and producers and a redistribution of wealth. However, winning the vote and a hefty slice of popular support would prove easier than implementing that promise.

Figure 5 Evita, Perón and Domingo Mercante reading the election coverage in Evita's newspaper *Democracia*, 1946 (Archivo Histórico de la Provincia de Buenos Aires, Wikimedia Commons)

Chapter 9

EARLY DAYS

Se acerca la comparsa, ya vino el Carnaval …
Los negros van bailando, bailando sin cesar ….

The procession is coming, Carnival is here …
The poor are dancing, dancing ceaselessly ….
Carnavalera (milonga), Homero Manzi and Sebastián Piana[1]

In the intervening months between the elections and his 4 June inauguration, Perón would remain occupied in preparing the new government and a plan of action. (Shortly before taking office, he would also be retroactively promoted to general, apparently at his own request.) Part of that plan of action consisted of forming a cabinet able to respond to the demands of a 'new Argentina', no easy task given the lack of political experience of many of Perón's collaborators and the fact that Mercante, as governor-elect of Buenos Aires province, was out of the running.

Arguably the standout was Juan Atilio Bramuglia, who would become a distinguished foreign minister, overseeing both the resumption of diplomatic relations with the Soviet Union and improved ties with Washington, negotiating Argentina's entry into the newly formed United Nations and subsequently chairing the UN Security Council during the Berlin blockade. Bramuglia's substantial ability would, however, be offset by Evita's continuing hostility towards him, after he refused her request for a habeas corpus petition during Perón's October 1945 detention. She would continue to hinder and oppose him throughout his cabinet term, seeking to denigrate his achievements in reports to Perón and even airbrushing him out of photos published in the government press. (Mercante's son Tito would recall years later that, on returning from a visit to Madrid with a sealed envelope for Bramuglia entrusted to him by the Argentine ambassador, he would be summoned to the presidential residence direct from the airport and forced to hand the envelope over to Evita, who opened it and only allowed it to be delivered to the foreign minister after she had scrutinized its contents.[2]) In all likelihood, the fact that Bramuglia's international reputation was by and large far more positive than that of the first couple only served to cement that hostility.

While it is perhaps not surprising, given their backgrounds, that both Perón and Evita were distrustful and insistent on loyalty, this focus on loyalty to the detriment of competence would also lead to poor appointments, often of people whose key attributes were their personal fealty and inability to represent a challenge to their superiors. Moreover, while Evita was also known for fierce loyalty towards her friends, Perón was much less so. Eva would seek to ensure that Lower House president Ricardo Guardo did her bidding in trying to undermine Bramuglia by warning him that 'I'm the one who will always defend you. The general won't. I'm a friend to my friends and I will defend those who are loyal to me.'[3] (Eventually this category would no longer include Guardo; in 1947 she warned Perón that he was a 'traitor' and should be kept at a safe distance.) Among the less competent but nominally biddable cabinet choices was Labour Minister José María Freire, a former member of the glassworkers' union whose functions as minister would be largely taken over by Evita on an informal basis. (Bramuglia had wanted the Labour Ministry; his deployment to the Foreign Ministry instead may have represented a shrewd use of his considerable capabilities, but at least as likely it reflected Perón's wish to avoid having an independent labour minister who might outshine him.) At the same time, Evita's brother Juancito Duarte would be named the president's secretary; Juancito was known for neither his intelligence nor his probity, but he was loyal to his sister and could be trusted to keep her informed of what was happening around the president.

Arguably the most important appointment was Miguel Miranda, Perón's 'finance czar', a successful industrialist who Perón believed would be similarly adept at managing the national economy, although 33-year-old Ramón Cereijo was technically economy minister. Miranda had already been appointed president of the newly nationalized Central Bank by Farrell after the elections, and was also the director of the nascent Argentine Trade Promotion Institute (IAPI), which would be expanded under the Perón government. Subsequently Perón would designate him as head of the National Economic Council in 1947. His performance would prove patchy at best, due partly to his own limitations and partly to the difficulties in policy-making imposed by both internal pressures and opposition intransigence. The frequent arbitrariness of that policy-making would ultimately be a key source of criticism levelled at Miranda, as well as a source of some of the economic turbulence that followed.

Nineteen days before taking office, Perón attended Mercante's swearing-in ceremony in La Plata, accompanied by Evita. Mercante won the governorship of Buenos Aires province with some 20,000 more votes than Perón received there in the presidential contest. Despite the size of Mercante's victory, the provincial legislature was far more diverse than the national Congress, with the UCR having a narrow majority in both houses. This may in part have influenced Mercante's approach to the opposition, which would prove far more conciliatory than that of Perón, and also the opposition's view of the new governor. While the Radicals remained staunchly against the initiatives of the Peronist government, Mercante commanded far wider respect and proved more adept at coaxing some measure of agreement. At this stage Mercante was still 'the heart of Perón' and the favourite of Evita – who when starting off in her new role as first lady and social welfare representative would often begin her day by travelling to La Plata early in the morning to consult the governor on the work of the Secretariat of Labour. On 17 October 1946, the first 'Loyalty Day', Mercante would be awarded the first 'loyalty medal' created by Perón.

Nevertheless, Mercante's inauguration would point to tensions to come. Feeling increasingly marginalized within the incoming government structure and still convinced of his virtual sole authorship of the 17 October events, Cipriano Reyes would use the occasion to give a display of power aimed at reminding the president-elect of his own influence. Numerous supporters attended the inauguration and cheered loudly for Reyes, interrupting the proceedings and prompting Perón to refuse to speak. Though scarcely the fault of Mercante, the challenge would probably represent one step in the gradual distancing between the president and the governor. Reyes himself, elected to the Lower House, was offered the presidency of the chamber in a bid to 'kick him upstairs' into a ceremonial post, but Reyes rejected the offer and promptly called a new meatpackers' strike.

As noted earlier, these skirmishes were threatening to weaken the position of Perón's party base (and Perón himself) and on 23 May he announced the dissolution of all the parties in his coalition, the redundancy of their leaders and the creation of the Sole Party of the Revolution. This was largely accepted by some of the components but not by Reyes and his Labour Party, who fought back and would resign from the Peronist bloc in Congress in July; thereafter, it was announced that Perón had 'consented' to the new party being called the *Partido Peronista* (Peronist Party), a title which left no doubt as to the command structure. The party would make itself increasingly present across the country through local delegations called *unidades básicas*, offering community and advice services, training classes and hairdressing facilities, political participation and affiliation for new members. While representing a useful service in areas where the state had been largely absent, this also represented part of a process of conflating the state and the ruling party, as well as the use of party membership for more coercive purposes – the party card would become increasingly needful for those seeking public sector jobs or services, with non-affiliates coming under pressure even in professions such as medicine.

Similarly, telephone workers' leader Luis Gay, who was elected leader of the CGT over Perón's preferred candidate, would rapidly find himself at odds with the new president, also refusing to accept a 'promotion' to head the new state telephone company and thus remove him from the CGT leadership. In January 1947 he would be accused of treason after receiving a delegation from the American Federation of Labor (AFL) on a self-styled investigating mission and resigned shortly thereafter. The entirely subservient José Espejo would become leader of the CGT, bringing it increasingly within the orbit of the government and with a remit to defend the interests of that government over those of the unions (although, officially at least, these were one and the same).

Some of these measures could be justified on the grounds that Perón's coalition was indeed wide, disparate and in some cases intransigent, a 'bag of cats' that would engage in infighting as much as collaboration and would make it extremely difficult to govern. Once the elections were over it became clear that in some respects the coalition was little more coherent than the *Unión Democrática*, apart from enjoying a semblance of unity around a single leader, and the conflicting demands would complicate even further a situation in which the opposition was deeply and unbendingly hostile and in which Perón would be forced to govern at least in principle for the country as a whole and not for the constituent parts of his coalition alone. That this political inexperience and factionalism forced him to assert his authority early on is unsurprising. However, his penchant for non-entities and incompetents who offered no competition would represent an early warning sign of a future malaise, as well as undermining the efficacy of the government from the start.

Another early warning sign was the impeachment of three members of the Supreme Court by the new Congress at Perón's behest; they were somewhat absurdly charged with having illegally recognized the de facto governments of 1930 and 1943 (the latter having brought Perón to power) and then with having unlawfully impeded measures taken by the latter. Perón was far from the only leader to attempt to pack his Supreme Court with loyalists (Roosevelt was also accused of attempting this, albeit unsuccessfully), but the manoeuvre undermined any image of a government willing to negotiate with the opposition or to play by the rules.

One of Reyes' signal attempts at resistance was the organization of a 'parallel' demonstration commemorating the first anniversary of 17 October, held in front of Congress, at which he made a defiant speech noting that the original protests had been held in defence of workers' gains, not of any individual politician. However, he was outnumbered and outflanked by an 'official' commemoration in the Plaza de Mayo, convened by the government to mark what would become known as Loyalty Day. This would be a fixture every year for the next eight years and, while worker participation remained enthusiastic, it represented another symptom of the increasing institutionalization of a previously fluid and spontaneous movement – while the original 17 October protests were largely self-convened, hereafter they would respond to a rigid protocol and would represent an obligatory event for many participants. (Reyes, who would leave Congress after losing his seat in the 1947 elections, would subsequently be accused, on no apparent basis, of plotting to assassinate Perón and Evita and would spend seven years in prison, where he was badly tortured, until after Perón's overthrow in 1955.)

Similarly, the Peronist government would 'colonize' the 1 May International Labour Day commemorations, decreeing that it was no longer a day of protest but one of celebration now that the government in power represented the workers' demands, needs and aspirations. It also became an annual opportunity for Perón to ask the assembled workers, rhetorically, if they were satisfied with the government, implying a level of involvement more symbolic than real. May Day would be marked each year by the crowning of a 'Queen of Labour', drawn from among women factory, shop or farm workers (Evita having 'graciously' ruled herself out of a competition she would have unquestionably swept). The Queen of Labour concept was not without logic – it sought to promote the notion that working women could be as proud, beautiful and elegant as their wealthier sisters, and indeed to strengthen the narrative of Evita as the patron saint of labour – but it also reflected the increasingly top-down organization of popular events and plans. Logically, a government could no longer operate in the largely spontaneous and improvisational way of the earlier movement, but equally the increasing rigidity and ossification of the structure would eventually make it fragile and prone to breakage.

Perón was sworn in on 4 June amid widespread optimism and a positive economic outlook. On the previous night Evita had caused some scandal (and numerous jokes) by wearing an off-the-shoulder dress to an official dinner at which her bare shoulder was seated next to Cardinal Santiago Copello, but in general terms the pomp and ceremony passed off successfully despite her evident nerves. (She would insist that seating be on the basis of strict protocol, except that she asked to have Lilian Guardo seated on her right, possibly for reassurance but also to deprive Bramuglia of what should have been his place.) Perón made a conciliatory speech promising inclusion, social justice and equity and saying that 'all the passions of combat have left my will, my mind and my heart, and I ask of God only that he grant me the serenity that the work of government requires'.[4]

This does not appear to have been pure public relations. Perón, a genuine patriot, came to the presidency with good intentions. He believed himself to have been chosen by his compatriots to lead the country forward to a greater future, and believed that he had the ideas, means, method and opportunity to do so (though also an element of hubris that would prove destructive). He did not perhaps consider the obstacles he would face, which would defeat objectives that were far more difficult to achieve than he in his enthusiasm and inexperience believed. The levers of economic power remained largely in the hands of an oligarchy strongly opposed to the new government, the productive bottlenecks and pervasive corruption that complicated economic reform were still in place (and in some cases increased), and an over-simplistic approach and an inexperienced team were inadequate to tackle much of what Perón and his supporters hoped to achieve.

After being sworn in before Congress, Perón returned to the Casa Rosada to receive the presidential sash and staff of office and again came out onto the balcony to greet thousands of cheering torch-bearing supporters. He announced that, as on 17 October, the following day would be a holiday 'so that tonight the *descamisados* can celebrate properly'.[5] He and Eva then went to the presidential residence, the 247-room Unzué Palace, with the Guardos where they explored the vast array of bedrooms, Eva got into her pyjamas and Perón and Guardo slid down the bannisters. Here, too, was an example of the often appealing informality and spontaneity that had thus far been much evidence but that would tend to diminish with time. Perón would later note that they had lived quite happily in their house in Teodoro García after the elections and that 'from the first I felt myself anointed by the popular spirit and didn't want any special treatment for myself or my family'.[6] This too would change in at least some respects.

As president, Perón did not vary from his accustomed work ethic. Up at 5.00 am, he would do some exercises before leaving for his office, where he was at his desk by 6.20. This was a novelty. 'My predecessors arrived at 10 in the morning and they left at 12 with a sense of having fulfilled their duty.'[7] Perón, by contrast, would sign papers until 8.00 and then receive ministers or delegations before returning to the residence for lunch with Evita and a nap, followed by a return to his office by 4.00 pm and another few hours of work before attending official events or going home for a quiet evening. He would remain absolutely wedded to the need for a strict working timetable. Years later, in 1965, he would advise his third wife to work in the same way: 'for example, receive people in the morning and spend the afternoon in other activities or resting. One day per week should be totally free in order to recover energy. Scrupulously respecting the timetable set is fundamental.'[8]

Still austere in his habits, Perón's preference was for a simple dinner and an early night, possibly after watching a film with Eva (usually a Western if he had his choice). Similarly, he would continue to enjoy the weekends with Eva at the *quinta* in San Vicente, either alone or accompanied by the Guardos, the Mercantes, Father Hernán Benítez or other collaborators, and he continued to indulge his passion for sports, including fencing, riding and sports cars and motorcycles (the latter in particular giving him a popular and somewhat celebrity image). Perón and Eva would also continue to attend sporting events when time permitted, notably auto racing and boxing matches, and would maintain cordial relationships with some of the sporting stars of the day, such as racing driver Juan Manuel Fangio and the boxer José María 'El Mono' Gatica. (With a few exceptions, such as the singer, actor and director Hugo del Carril, they did not have similarly friendly relations with most of the artistic community, probably reflecting Evita's own difficult relationship with it.) They would also attend football matches from time to time, football being the national sport and a national passion at least on a par with Peronism, although Perón himself remained less enthusiastic about it than about fencing and boxing; never a team player himself, he was arguably more at home with sports focused on outstanding individual performance than on those requiring a well-oiled team of equals. At least initially he would adhere to the habits of a lifetime, which doubtless helped to maintain the energy required for an ambitious and wide-ranging plan of government.

Much of the broad outline of that government was contained in the First Five-Year Plan, prepared by Figuerola and launched on 21 October 1946. The Plan, which aimed to represent a blueprint for a state-led economy, set out a state role in a range of sectors including education, health and culture, as well as in directing production and investment. In fact, the Plan may not have appeared overly optimistic when it was presented. The economic outlook at the time was unusually rosy: Argentina had ended the Second World War as a creditor nation owing to the exports of foodstuffs to Great Britain in particular, and its foreign reserves were at a high of nearly 1.7 billion dollars. The situation encouraged optimism (and perhaps too little caution), suggesting that both the political and economic changes in train would combine to produce real structural change. The stated aim sounded positive: 'The economies of colonial countries have been characterised by being at the service of capital and we want the opposite: capital at the service of the economy.'[9] So did the explicit recognition that the government did not want to destroy the balance of the economy, which it recognized would set back social progress for many years. 'We must work, build and produce, because if we don't produce, build and work, the problem will not have the happy solution we all want.'[10]

At the same time, the Plan would offer at least a symbolic opportunity for popular participation, with Perón encouraging citizens to write in with suggestions. This they did in huge numbers, and a similar 'consultation' process would occur in the 1949 constitutional reform and the Second Five-Year Plan in 1951. The approach boosted the feeling of popular participation, although there is no evidence that the thousands of letters prompted any changes in the government's proposed policies.[11]

On 9 July 1947 Perón would declare Argentina's 'economic independence' in the historically significant city of Tucumán, where independence had been declared in 1814. This was based on increased industrialization and, in particular, the processing of agricultural products to increase their value-added. It also contemplated, in theory if not in great detail, the need to invest in training of technical personnel. 'Economic independence' also included the nationalization of the Central Bank, which it was argued had focused its services on the domestic and international banking sectors rather than on productive lending (obliging borrowers to have recourse to international banks), and had contributed to inflation by printing money against gold reserves blocked abroad. Its nationalization in theory allowed the government to control credit, just as nationalization of foreign-owned utilities purportedly returned those services to the local market and their profits to the state, helping to finance social justice policies such as pensions, housing and the state healthcare system – the latter seeking to ensure all necessary access to medical care by all who needed it. 'Public health should have no spending limits. The limit is the need to cure all the sick in the country' – a potentially very costly ambition.[12]

The highly ambitious Five-Year Plan aimed to keep a remarkable number of balls in the air, with only limited detail on the means required to finance its ambitious goals in the longer term, assuming that production did not increase in line with expectations. However, the Plan failed to take into consideration the extent to which Argentina remained heavily dependent on global markets that it could not significantly influence, and that the goal of making it an independent economic power would face serious headwinds. At the same time, the Plan focused primarily on industry, which was not yet a key driver of the economy, and disincentivized agricultural production by seeking to use the sector to subsidize economic development in other areas. The IAPI represented a state monopoly over purchases and exports of foodstuffs, which undermined farmers' incentives to boost output. While intended to guarantee prices to producers and to generate revenues that the state could use for redistributive purposes, in practice it saw investment and output fall precisely when domestic consumption was rising. Rising consumption and reduced supply would inevitably generate inflation once price controls had to be eased. More broadly, whatever the rhetoric in favour of heavy industry, industrial policy remained focused on import substitution. This generated jobs and satisfied consumers whose purchasing power had risen, but maintained dependence on imported machinery which skewed the trade balance. In practice, some of the IAPI's early operations were profitable in the early post-war years, and averted some of the boom-bust risk that characterized the period after the First World War. However, its functioning was inefficient and wasteful, and shifts in the export climate further reduced its usefulness.

Dependence on agricultural exports to sustain the trade balance, in light of the failure to broaden industrialization significantly, represented a risk due to both internal and external factors. As noted above, producers were discouraged from increasing output both by the obligation to sell to IAPI and by the lack of investment in the sector; they were also subject to the vagaries of climate, and droughts in the late 1940s would force some changes in the Five-Year Plan to bolster the farming sector.

Internationally, the agro-export model was premised on the assumption that the world – primarily Europe – would have little choice but to buy from Argentina. However, the introduction of the Marshall Plan largely put paid to Argentine exports to a Europe that lacked money to pay for them; much Marshall aid was earmarked for purchases of the same food exports from the United States. An attempt by Miranda to refuse to sell grain on international markets on anything but Argentina's own terms saw two grain harvests unsold, generating losses and lack of foreign exchange.

At the same time, the government would find that being a creditor to the British government after the war was at best a mixed blessing. As part of its plan to nationalize public services (many of them British-owned), the Perón government initially sought to pay for the acquisition of the British-owned railways using the debt accrued for wartime beef exports and then blocked in London. However, in August 1947 London ruled that the funds could not be converted or used for purchases outside Britain. These decisions were unforeseen and uncontrollable, but had a significant impact on economic plans.

Perhaps Perón's (and Miranda's) most serious error in economic planning was the belief that the United States and the Soviet Union were heading not for a Cold War but for a hot conflict that would produce the Third World War, and thus yet again a global conflict that would drive demand for Argentine agricultural exports. Moreover, they believed that a major devaluation was coming in both the United States and Europe that might make existing foreign currency reserves virtually worthless. The assumption that the time horizon for the onset of a conflict was short, and that spending could prove more astute than saving, encouraged incautious use of existing financial reserves; it also highlighted the risk involved in planning exclusively on the basis of events over which Argentina had no influence. (Perón, a historian by background, shared with many historians the mistaken belief that the future can be predicted by analysing the past; while history is certainly cyclical to a degree, it does not repeat itself so predictably, and assuming that it does is indeed a dangerous basis on which to form national policy.)

Above and beyond these difficulties, Perón's vision for economic independence and national sovereignty was certainly premised on a programme of nationalizations during the first part of his government – not least on the relatively solid grounds that public services had long been run for the benefit of foreign investors rather than for users. The programme arguably also benefited those foreign investors more than it did users; Perón was wont to 'flash the cash' and to pay more than the nationalized assets were sometimes worth. The United River Plate Telephone Company was acquired from ITT in September 1946 at a cost of 95 million dollars, while on 1 March 1948 Buenos Aires took over the British-owned railways at a cost of 150 million pounds, paid for by beef exports rather than through the debts now frozen in London. The railways required substantial investment in infrastructure and rolling stock to make them viable, but the takeover was cause for national celebration and allowed Perón to boast of having kept his promise to bring the railways into Argentine hands. Nationalizations were popular even where inefficient, given widespread distrust of foreign capital. This was highlighted in a speech by Interior Minister Angel Borlenghi in October 1948, in which he noted that 'we mortgaged everything that was ours. We handed over ... all the important public services. Then they took our meat ... these clients paid us 400 million pesos .... And for the labour of taking it away they charged us 600 million pesos.'[13] While the tone of this speech was obviously self-serving, it reflected much popular opinion, which considered that foreign capital had taken away resources and given little in return.

Arguably an even worse deal for the state was the nationalization of the bankrupt Dodero shipping lines, owned by Alberto Dodero, a friend of the Peróns and a frequent contributor of money and valuable gifts. The purchase by the government, justified on the grounds that the shipping company provided a public service, was costly and gave rise to sharp criticism of the likely corruption involved, although it allowed Perón to claim that the government had gained shipping capacity of 1.5 million tonnes and thus reduced its shipping costs. (Other rumours of corruption in the regime included reports that Miranda received a 6.5-million-dollar payment from British American Tobacco to allow cigarette prices to rise, and that War Minister General Humberto Sosa Molina had brought sixteen Cadillacs and thirty refrigerators from a mission to the United States without paying tax on them, with the cars sold through his brother, a Buenos Aires Cadillac dealer.[14])

As president, Perón maintained his charisma and his ability to impress and charm interlocutors. As his personal physician and sometime cabinet minister Jorge Taiana once observed, 'I have seen persons opposed to him who had to interview him for the first time, and a few minutes later they would come out transformed, as if they had been touched by true magic.'[15] Yet as president his face-to-face contacts with individuals and small groups, such as union delegations, were by definition limited by the range of other duties he had to perform. He remained an exceptional public speaker who captivated audiences at mass events, but opportunities for the personal touch had become fewer. Into this breach stepped Evita, at first tentatively and then with an energy and bravado that at least equalled Perón's own. As his wife and a 'woman of the people' she fulfilled the requirements to an outstanding degree, while ensuring that more independent figures would not overshadow the president.

Starting out with an office in her friend Nicolini's Post and Telegraph Department, Eva shortly thereafter moved into her husband's old office at the Labour Ministry. Initially she began visiting factories and receiving delegations, usually in the company of Isabel Ernst or Lilian Lagomarsino. Before very long Isabel Ernst would be distanced from the scene, either because Eva no longer required her tutelage and did not want a competitor, or because she became for

Figure 6 Perón riding his horse Mancha in 1946 (Photo by Mondadori via Getty Images).

a time closer to Mercante's wife, Elena Caporale, who as first lady of the province would soon take up many of the same social work activities that obsessed Evita.

With Perón now carrying much wider duties of government and no longer able to act so directly as 'the people's colonel', Evita would fill the vacuum and even expand beyond it, rapidly becoming 'the engine and the executor of Perón's project, the best student, the best disciple [...] She was born to be a leader.'[16] Her enthusiasm for the role, as a means of expressing her gratitude both to Perón and to the *descamisados* who rescued him on 17 October, was boundless and her energies prodigious: from an early phase she would begin attending to delegations and individuals at the ministry immediately after lunch, continuing until well into the night. Her social work would soon go far beyond the trade union movement, building up to the monumental undertaking that would become the Eva Perón Foundation.

Evita's 'mission' would be to carry out 'social justice' instead of charity (although the distinction was in practice sometimes difficult to discern), arguing that charity was designed to make the benefactor feel gratified and the recipient feel humiliated. Early on she was denied the role usually reserved for the First Lady, that of president of the venerable *Sociedad de Beneficencia* (Beneficent Society) established in the 1820s to take on much social action including a major role in education, health and charitable infrastructure. Appalled at the thought that a young woman of Eva's background should hold the position, the ladies of the *Sociedad* apparently told her she was too young (and did not accept graciously her suggestion that her mother might take the role in her place), ostensibly motivating her vengeful decision to have the *Sociedad* closed down and take over its role herself. In practice, the *Sociedad* was an outdated institution without the funds, infrastructure or expertise to manage the services under its orbit, most of which were now being taken on by the state – as would normally be expected in a modern country. However, whether because of the snub or because of her own experience of the humiliations of charity, Evita would take it upon herself to do things bigger and better than ever before. (Her Foundation would eventually also undertake functions of the state, such as construction of schools and hospitals, although these were then handed over to the state to manage.)

In mid-1947 Evita would undertake a 'Rainbow Tour' to Europe, initially at the invitation of Spanish dictator Francisco Franco. The *generalísimo*, in need of political and, in particular, economic assistance, initially invited Perón to visit Madrid, but given Spain's diplomatic isolation and continuing efforts to strike a balance between the international factions of the Cold War era, it was deemed preferable for him to decline. (Bramuglia in particular opposed the visit, and also opposed the decision to send Evita, which did little to improve their tense relationship.) Evita, on the other hand, could be invited on a more informal though still extravagant basis, and would characterize herself as a 'rainbow' between the two countries. There has been speculation (including rumours that she had suffered a miscarriage) that Perón was worried about her health and wanted her to undertake the trip as a distraction. However, more than a distraction, it would galvanize her into even greater ambitions for her social projects, making her more of a political partner but less of a wife and personal support.

On 6 June Evita departed for Madrid accompanied by Lilian Guardo, Juancito Duarte, her confessor Hernán Benítez, Alberto Dodero (who financed much of the trip) and a large contingent. Her reception in Madrid was magnificent, and she rose to the occasion magnificently, showing astonishing aplomb for someone so young and unaccustomed to pomp and ceremony. Franco would have to suffer the indignity of being upstaged and upbraided for his lack of a social welfare programme, but in return received a substantial donation of wheat for his isolated and impoverished country – which in turn gave the Perón government the chance to show solidarity with a suffering population, and Argentines the chance to feel proud of their role in the world.

Evita and company would continue on from Spain to visit Italy, France, Portugal and Switzerland (at least in part to make the visit look less like a mission to Falangist Spain). Although she would receive a less dramatic popular welcome elsewhere, she would be granted an audience with Pope Pius XII – apparently with the intention of bolstering the Vatican's efforts to secure a haven for 'displaced persons' in the post-war era, some of them former Nazis and war criminals. Although members of the Argentine opposition had been at pains to bring to the Vatican's attention her 'scandalous' past (including photos taken during her most impecunious days) and she did not receive either a papal decoration or a photograph with the pontiff, she 'was accorded the most elaborate Vatican reception extended to a visiting dignitary since the war', 'in view of Vatican interest in Argentine assistance as a supplier of relief to Europe and a receiver of displaced persons.'[17] In France she would meet President Vincent Auriol and the Papal Nuncio, Angelo Roncalli (later Pope John XXIII), and oversee the signing of an Argentine loan to finance French imports of Argentine foodstuffs. Notably, a mooted visit to Great Britain did not proceed, supposedly prompting Eva to adopt an increasingly anti-British viewpoint.

Eva would return to Argentina, via a stop in Rio de Janeiro to attend the Rio Conference and Foreign Ministers' meeting at which the Inter-American Mutual Assistance Treaty was agreed, more than two months after departing, on 22 August. The trip would mark the end of her friendship with the Guardos (and Ricardo Guardo's fall from grace and replacement as leader of the Lower House by Evita loyalist Héctor Cámpora), but also a change in her style and mission. Previously fond of a more cinematic style of glamour, she would now become the Evita most widely remembered, dressed in tailored suits and with her hair pulled back in a classic chignon. Although she would still continue to wear spectacular ball dresses on gala occasions, for her day-to-day wardrobe the look was increasingly pared down and classically elegant. It was nonetheless costly, with many of her clothes now ordered from Dior and other European fashion houses – sometimes with greater success than on other occasions. Paco Jamandreu once told Eva that an elaborate new green dress recently arrived from Paris made her look like an artichoke, prompting Perón to roar with laughter and say that he also thought there was 'something vegetable about it, but I was torn between artichoke and asparagus'; her fury failed to quell his amusement.[18]

Moreover, the trip crystallized her views on social justice, in which she saw Europe as sadly lacking and backward: 'I have seen the Old World and have contemplated its desolation, the difficulties and the impoverishment that Old Europe offers.'[19] For both Evita and for many Argentines, this was also a source of pride and encouragement: Europe, long seen by wealthy Argentines as a spiritual home and a beacon of civilization and advancement, was now seen to be behind Argentina in social and economic aspirations (something that would not have surprised many of the impoverished Europeans who had reached Argentina as immigrants).

The trip would also strengthen Evita's convictions about the role of women – which, while in no way feminist in modern terms, were in many ways deeply practical and empowering. In her first speech after Perón's election she had already stressed that 'it is necessary to establish equal rights, as women have already sought and … gained equal responsibilities …. [W]omen must vote […] The women's vote will be the weapon that will make our homes the supreme and inviolable surety of public conduct.'[20] While in practice she had had little role in the long-established women's suffrage movement even after Perón came to office, she would become increasingly seen as the author of the women's vote, which became law on 9 September, days after her return from Europe. The law was promulgated on 23 September and symbolically handed over to Evita at a public ceremony. If she was not a real factor in the passage of the law (which Perón had already favoured in 1943), she would become the key driver behind the organization of the *Partido Peronista Femenino* (Women's Peronist Party, PPF) and the first exercise of the women's vote in 1951. Thus, as early as 1947, at the age of only twenty-eight, Evita was already a key actor in both the women's movement and the organization of social justice. This activity would increasingly take her away from private life, curtailing the weekends at San Vicente and the shared quiet times with Perón. It would also eventually make her as important a figure as her husband, and one whose authority had begun to encroach on both politics and the social welfare activities hitherto seen largely as the preserve of the Catholic Church.

The relationship with the Vatican aside, during this period the quasi-religious element of Peronism would become increasingly enshrined, a development that prompted enthusiasm in some quarters and alarm in others. The Argentine hierarchy had welcomed many of the de facto government's measures and wittingly or not had at least in some way supported Perón through the Pastoral instructions not to vote for any candidate who favoured separation of Church and State, divorce or lay education, and to vote for 'those who, in good conscience, appear most able to procure the greatest good for religion and the fatherland.'[21] Nevertheless, he had also been rebuked by the magazine *Criterio* for referring to the '*descamisados* of God' in his campaign speeches; the magazine observed that 'there is a Christian *democracy*, but not a Christian *demagogy*. We can speak of Christ's *poor* …, but we cannot speak of Christ's *descamisados*, because the phrase has *class* and *party* connotations, and Christ does not belong to any party or class.'[22]

While the hierarchy took a reasonably positive stance towards Perón during this period, among the clergy, members of the right wing who had hoped that

Perón would represent an Argentine Franco, such as Gustavo Franceschi of *Criterio*, were openly hostile, with some regarding Perón as a nascent communist. Other members of the clergy supported Peronism, either for its social content or for its anti-communism. The most influential was arguably the Jesuit Hernán Benítez, who was also the spiritual adviser to the Eva Perón Foundation and rector of the University of Buenos Aires, and would take credit for much of Peronism's doctrinal content.

The legislation adopted by the Perón government in its early years continued to favour Church interests, although it also increased the Church's dependency on the state. In 1946 legislation was brought requiring the registration of non-Catholic religious institutions and placing them under the control of a newly created General Direction of Religion (although Catholic clergy were also required to register, they were to be controlled by their own superiors). In March 1947 religious education was made compulsory in primary and secondary schools, to bring about 'the spiritual restoration of the Argentine school'.[23] Two months later the Directorate of Religious Education was established, under the control of two priests, to oversee religious education, appoint teachers and approve religious texts, as well as the texts for 'moral instruction' given to non-Catholic children. The expansion of religious education created employment prospects for priests and lay Catholics; however, they were employed by, and ultimately responsible to, the state.

Following the 17 October 1948 celebrations, the British Embassy noted that 'apparently Perón is now occasionally referred to as "Saint Perón"; he must have lost what common sense he had, for this is bound, I would have thought, to affront all Christians …. This auto-beatification has caused some scandal in devout circles'. While the jocular reference to the post-17 October holiday as 'San Perón' dated back to 1945 and was not intended literally, as time went on concerns would indeed mount over the increasingly heavy-handed parallels between religion and party. Another Embassy note would report on a segment of a speech by Evita in Tucumán the following month, in which she remarked that 'I happened to overhear a conversation between two workers of Tucumán. One said to the other, "I love Perón more than God, because Perón gave me all and God gave me nothing!" The poor fellow was forgetting that it was God who sent us Perón.'[24]

There is no evidence to suggest that Perón believed these flights of fantasy or even originated them; much of the hagiography clearly came from supporters or members of his government seeking approval. (As early as 1946 the CGT had named Evita Argentina's First Samaritan, and not long thereafter its magazine would define her in terms likening her to the Virgin Mary – most likely calculated to please her, as well as to boost her image and importance, so closely linked to the CGT's own.) Indeed, the semi-divine characterization did not sit well with Perón's down-to-earth, practical and amiable image nor with his penchant for expressing himself in colloquial and approachable terms. Yet equally he did nothing to arrest them, and the pseudo-religious element would hold him up to ridicule and undermine the seriousness of what the government aimed to achieve.

Despite many difficulties and more than a few alarm bells, economic performance and popular enthusiasm were strong in the first few years of Perón's government.

Between 1946 and 1949 GDP expanded by nearly 30 per cent and salaried workers represented 55 per cent of the workforce, while their salaries rose by an average of around one-third during the period. The policy of encouraging light industry ensured that those better-off workers had goods to spend their money on (notably radios, which provided both light entertainment and political propaganda), and the availability of cinemas, sports and holiday complexes also expanded to take in social sectors previously excluded from such enjoyments. Moreover, Saturdays increasingly became a non-work day, while the plethora of national, religious and purely political holidays also ensured that people had time to enjoy themselves. Pro-government publications also expanded, focusing on news, sports, fashion and even advice on 'how to spend it' – what to buy, what to cook, what to wear.

Figure 7 Perón and Evita attend a gala at the Colón Opera House in 1949 (Photo by ullstein bild/ullstein bild via Getty Images).

Those publications saw particularly big sales whenever they featured photos of the president and his wife, especially following any full-dress gala affair.

On a more serious note, the government invested in public health and education, including in schools, hospitals and clinics, training for healthcare workers and tertiary education for skilled workers and the children of the working classes. In practice, many of the Perón government's policies were adapted from those of the post-war Labour government in Great Britain, also engaged in constructing a welfare state. If the government could be described as populist, it could be described as a sort of 'progressive populism', seen to be standing up for the interests of the nation and its citizens, defending economic independence and incorporating hitherto marginalized groups through greater distribution of wealth and the enshrining of greater social and economic rights.

It would not take very long before some of the flaws in the system became clearer. Indeed, already during these years the supposed economic boom was punctuated by strikes, while increased production failed to keep pace with increased consumption, prompting shortages and inflation which Perón and Evita's exhortations to 'produce, produce, produce' were insufficient to overcome in what was becoming an overly top-down economy too dominated by often inefficient state intervention. Nonetheless, in many respects it was a buoyant time, when much of the population had 'never had it so good'; it was the first time in Argentina's history that the fruits of bonanza were distributed so widely across the population. As Felix Luna put it, Argentina was a *fiesta*. The opposition might inveigh and protest, sometimes rightly and sometimes not, but for many it was a time of optimism and pride, and they were unlikely to carp too much at the less positive developments.

Chapter 10

IF I DEFINE, I EXCLUDE

Con los principios sociales que Perón ha establecido
El pueblo entero, está unido y grita de corazón: Viva Perón, Viva Perón!
Por ese gran argentino que trabaja sin cesar
Para que reine en el pueblo el amor y la igualdad.

With the social principles that Perón has established
The whole country is united and cries from the heart Viva Perón, Viva Perón!
For that great Argentine who works ceaselessly
To ensure that love and equality will reign among the people.
Los muchachos peronistas

By the latter half of the 1940s increasing efforts were being made to codify the content of the Peronist party, and indeed what would become Peronist doctrine. As noted, much of this revolved around an increasingly controversial identification with Catholicism. At the same time, however, Perón was often at pains to stress that neither Argentina nor Peronism suffered from prejudice: as early as December 1945 he had stressed that 'we have no racial prejudices. Decent men of goodwill will always be welcome in this generous and kind fatherland', while 'the movement welcomes all sincere and honourable men.' 'For us race is not a biological concept. For us it is purely spiritual. ... For us race constitutes our indefinable and unmistakeable personal stamp.'[1] 'How could it be acceptable, how could it be explainable, that anti-Semitism could exist in Argentina. In Argentina there should be only one kind of men: men who work for the national good, without distinctions. They are good Argentines, whatever their origin, their race or their religion.'[2]

Curiously, despite the mounting efforts to identify Peronism with an overarching national cultural and religious identity, in practice Perón was quite tolerant of diversity when it did not represent a threat, perhaps a function of his unconventional side. In particular, he and Evita took an interest in spiritism that would prompt anger in clerical circles. On a very personal level, it also included an apparently warm and respectful relationship with the fashion designer Paco Jamandreu, who designed much of Evita's wardrobe; a flamboyant and spectacularly 'out' gay man, Jamandreu retained fond memories of Perón's friendly attitude, at a time when few military men in particular would have treated him with anything other than horror, contempt and possibly violence.

However, some sectors of the Catholic nationalist strand were even more offended by his good relationship with the Jewish community and with the state of Israel, and by Perón's frequent stress on freedom and equality of religion. Argentina had (and still has) the largest Jewish community in Latin America and one of the largest in the world; both the Jewish and Arab communities in Argentina numbered around 400,000 people in the 1940s and represented important groups to be wooed. In 1946 much of the Arab community voted for Perón while evidence suggests that most Jewish votes went to the *Unión Democrática*, probably because many Jewish voters had links to the Radical, Communist or Socialist parties. Thereafter, however, Perón made substantial efforts to reach out to the Jewish community to bring it within the bounds of Peronism. This was a first for any Argentine political leader, and is in marked contrast to claims that Perón had Nazi sympathies.

Unquestionably the Perón government, like others elsewhere, received former Nazis after the war, not least in a bid to attract skilled scientists and technicians; Perón himself would describe this as 'good business', saying 'what costs us a plane ticket cost Germany millions of marks invested in training those scientists and technicians'.[3] Many also found their way to Argentina through the offices of the Vatican and, in some cases, through the willingness of some Argentine diplomats in Europe to sell them Argentine passports. Later investigations in the 1990s would identify 180 Nazis and collaborators who entered Argentina after the war, of whom around 50 were identified as war criminals, notably including Adolf Eichmann and Josef Mengele (with whom Perón had at least one conversation about his genetic experiments).[4] This represented indifference rather than Nazi ideology on Perón or the government's part, although Perón's later failure to condemn the Holocaust or to support the Nuremberg trials (which he saw as vengeance by the victors against a vanquished foe rather than justice) was far more reprehensible and in line with his blinkered approach to many unsavoury facts that might have got in the way of useful allies or narratives.

Nevertheless, Perón was at great pains to try to attract the Jewish community and the Argentine Israelite Organization (OIA) was a Peronist organization, albeit one that lacked the sympathy of large sectors of the Jewish community who were at best suspicious of becoming too closely identified with Peronism. Nevertheless, many Argentine Jews owned businesses or small industries – and, increasingly, held professional and public sector jobs, including in government-funded hospitals – and were attracted by Perón's economic policies, which favoured smaller businessmen over the traditional dominant industries.

Both Perón and Evita would make many speeches lauding the contribution of Argentine Jews and condemning anti-Semitism, which they argued with considerable truth was a characteristic of the traditional oligarchy more than of the working classes. Both also frequently expressed the view that, as a historically oppressed people, the Jewish community was uniquely well placed to understand the message of Peronism. Indeed, various of the trade union leaders who supported Perón were Jewish and the former socialist Borlenghi, who was not, had a Jewish wife and was also seen as a friend to the community. (In later years the anti-Peronists would claim that Borlenghi was Jewish and had provoked the conflict with the Catholic Church for that reason; they would also criticize what they regarded as excessive Jewish and masonic influence in the government.) In 1948 Evita would say 'in our country the only ones who have used class or religious separatism have been the dreadful oligarchy who governed for fifty years'.[5] Perón, who made many similar statements, would seek to bring minority ethnic groups as well as the working classes within the mainstream of a more equal and multicultural society – doubtless in part to boost his own support base, as well as to debilitate the traditionally dominant and deeply hostile social sectors – and had no tolerance for long-standing claims that Argentine Jews had divided loyalties or be might downright traitorous in their attitude towards Argentina as opposed to the State of Israel.

Evita's own position was said to have been influenced by her good relationship with Jaime Yankelevich, the owner of Radio Belgrano where she had spent much of her acting career. (Yankelevich, a pioneer of radio in Argentina, would also introduce television to the country in 1951; the first televised broadcast was of the Loyalty Day celebrations on 17 October of that year.) The Eva Perón Foundation would send donations of food, medicines, clothing and blankets to assist the Jewish immigrants arriving in Israel in the late 1940s, earning her the personal thanks of Israeli Labour Minister Golda Meir during a visit to Buenos Aires in 1951.

Although Argentina initially abstained in the 1947 UN vote on the partition of Palestine (in part in order to avoid damaging good relations with Arab states that Perón had been cultivating), it would become the first Latin American country to open diplomatic relations (and an embassy) with the State of Israel and the first to conclude a trade agreement with it. Perón would have a warm relationship with the Israeli ambassador, Yaacov Tsur, and would name a Jewish ambassador to Israel, Pablo Manguel, over the protests of the Catholic Church and even the Vatican; on at least one occasion he would say that 'an Argentine Jew who does not help Israel is not a good Argentine'.[6] Unquestionably at least part of this rhetoric was designed to burnish Perón's credentials as a champion of the underdog (and, incidentally, as a democratic-leaning rather than Nazi leader). However, this effort at defining Argentina as an immigrant society that could have an overarching national identity (solidarity, social justice, the common good) sought not to exclude, instead accepting that those of Spanish, Italian, Arab, Jewish or other descent could all come together as Argentines.

This approach was at best only partially successful – much of the Jewish community preferred to elude Perón's embrace, whether due to political convictions, suspicions of his purported pro-fascist leanings, or the anti-Semitic bent of some of his more right-wing supporters such as the *Alianza Libertadora Nacional* (National Liberation Alliance, ALN), an ultra-nationalist Catholic right-wing strongarm force founded in the late 1930s and led for decades by Guillermo Patricio Kelly. The ALN attached itself to Perón early on and often performed, or was suspected of performing, informally some of the dirty and violent work the government preferred to avoid direct involvement with. Some members of the Jewish community may also have been unwilling to be perceived as too close to a government that might eventually be overthrown, as was indeed the case. Yet his efforts to modernize Argentina through incorporating a range of long-marginalized groups into the mainstream, while self-serving, also represented some of the most progressive elements of his legacy. (Twenty years later, many of the children of those Jewish sceptics, like the children of many anti-Peronist Catholics, would join the JP and fight for his return.)

Two years into his presidency, Perón was already a prolific speechmaker and also a writer, publishing numerous opinion pieces under the pseudonym of Descartes. (In part, this reflected his conviction that 'I must take upon myself the job of being the one who informs public opinion'.[7]) However, the rise in efforts to codify and give substance to the Peronist party and Peronist doctrine would give him greater scope to return to the roles of both pedagogue and historian – both of which he greatly enjoyed – and to seek to turn his wide (if not invariably profound) reading into a theory that could in turn serve as a basis for a new national identity. Given his dedication to the principle that 'if I define, I exclude', this definition would prove necessarily both broad and vague, and perhaps for that reason verbose and lofty in the extreme. This burst of philosophical and pedagogical activity may also have hinted at a degree of boredom with the repetitive affairs of state, which arguably held less excitement than the process of reaching power in the first place.

Third Position

The Peronist position on international relations, to be known as the Third Position, was announced during Eva's visit to Spain, although in practice it had made its first appearance on 5 June 1946, when Argentina resumed diplomatic ties with the Soviet Union. While it would later be taken to be akin to the subsequent Non-Aligned Movement in the Third World, Perón sought to invest it with more significance than merely taking a middle course in foreign affairs. He would say that 'our Third Position is not a central position. It is an ideological position which is in the centre, on the right or on the left, according to specific circumstances.'[8] While vague in the extreme, in practice it was in line with Perón's preferred approach of making his audience infer that he was saying what they wanted to hear (and indeed, of avoiding exclusion by avoiding definition). Equally, also like many of Perón's strategies, it was not without common sense and practicality; it allowed the government alternatively to criticize or ally with foreign governments of whatever stripe based purely on the convenience of the moment, while at the same time providing a veneer of moral high ground and suggesting that the 'position' was superior to that adopted by others (e.g. noting that 'we are always on the side of the humiliated and scorned peoples'[9]). In far more practical and less exalted terms, Perón would note that 'we believe that nations do not have permanent friends. Two friends with conflicting interests quickly become enemies and two enemies with parallel interest quickly become friends. We think we should mix and link our own interests with those of countries we want as friends.'[10] Domestically it gave Perón scope to inveigh against both US imperialism and the Soviet communist threat while taking no hostile measures against either; Perón would frequently remind Washington that his government represented a bulwark against communism in the region and, Braden apart, had cordial relations with US ambassadors during his tenure. Certainly, despite anti-imperialist rhetoric, he did not move against US companies and would increasingly come to seek investment from that quarter.

Despite a relatively positive reception at home, the Third Position would play less well abroad, prompting governments on all sides to believe that it was directed against them and revived questions abroad over both supposed communist and fascist leanings in the Perón government. (Perón himself would suggest to US diplomats that it was nothing more than 'a bit of political demagogy for domestic consumption',[11] in a bid to reassure them that Argentina would not remain neutral in the event of conflict with the Soviet Union.) Those suspicions were accurately rejected by the British ambassador, who dismissed the theory that Perón 'was acting for the Soviets in Latin America'. 'Nor am I disposed to believe that Perón is acting as a cat's paw of Franco. On the contrary, the attitude of the regime towards Spain … is tinged with the condescension of a rich and benevolent colonial nephew for a struggling and impoverished uncle from the Motherland.'[12] This was again highlighted by Perón's condescending claim that 'we must replace misery with abundance, without falling into the unpardonable mistake of turning aid into charity …. We must take to the Old World, in particular, which nourished the culture of the new hemisphere, everything we have learned.'[13] Equally, it would not succeed in convincing other Latin American countries to follow Argentina as a leader of 'an alliance of weak Catholic nations'.[14] Yet while it may have had 'no basis more substantial than a belief that the political and social system created by General Perón is superior to either [capitalism or communism]', that was enough to recommend it to many Argentines who felt that the country was finally taking its rightful place as an important world player, one it had long felt was its destiny.[15]

Peronist doctrine

In 1948 Perón would ask rhetorically 'what is Peronism?' before responding that it 'is humanism in action; Peronism is a new political concept, in the social sphere, it makes all men a bit more equal … and ensures a future where in this land there is no one who does not have what he needs to live.'[16] Also that year the even more high-sounding Peronist doctrine (*doctrina peronista*) would be set out and codified in a how-to guide for Peronists entitled the Peronist Manual (*Manual del peronista*). Again, this is a repetitive and somewhat turgid work incorporating platitudes, authoritarianism, idealism and sound common sense. Divided into three sections – a synthesis of Peronist doctrine, directives from General Perón and the regulations of the Peronist party – the Manual is didactic and prescriptive in the extreme. It fluctuates between demands for absolute loyalty to the party and its leader – 'the man of our movement must be Peronist, and only Peronist, in body, soul and intelligence' and 'to be Peronist … it is necessary and vital to feel it deeply' – and far more widely patriotic sentiments – 'it is vital to understand that above all bias and all personal ambition is the collective interest of the nation's people'.[17] It proposes 'a new Argentina, profoundly Christian and profoundly humanist' to be built on united 'armed forces, economic forces and creative forces' in order to 'keep ourselves economically free and politically sovereign'.[18] 'We divide the country into two categories: the men that work, and those that live off the men that work. In this situation we have placed ourselves openly on the side of the men who work'.[19]

In somewhat more practical terms, the Manual goes on to explain that 'until now the economy was at the service of capital; from now on capital will be at the service of the economy'. On various occasions Perón repeats one of his favourite ambitions – 'fewer rich and fewer poor' – as well as the position that the masses can only be governed through force or through justice. The latter point is not only ethical but practical: 'a government has a single intention: to exercise government over the Argentine masses, because the government today that does not control the masses is a government that does not control anything'.[20] Here again Perón's frequently expressed fear of the 'inorganic mass' and the need for a controlled and organized society. Moreover, while he asserts that 'agitation by the masses is an effect of social injustice',[21] he warns against agitation and strike action in the new context in which the government is looking out for the worker and in which the new Argentina requires love and unity rather than division.

Also in more practical terms, this synthesis sets out a plan of action for government, which includes the recognition of the right to housing, pensions and health coverage as a basic, universal human right which must be given priority in any government spending plan. It also sets out Perón's vision for industrialization, in which machinery rather than human beings will do the most backbreaking labour and the need for greater tertiary education for workers and for university education to be open to all classes to end the breach between workers and the educated; 'rather than teaching many things, we should be teaching useful things'.[22] In sum, the vision is one of creating greater wealth through greater production and industrialization and better exploitation of resources, and of distributing that wealth more equitably. What it does not hint at in any concrete way is how this is to be achieved (beyond a commitment to greater public spending on housing, welfare, health and education) or how difficult the process is likely to be. It is difficult to argue with many of the concepts, but in practical terms the amount of public spending needed to hold up one half of the bargain looks difficult to sustain until the productivity side of the bargain kicks in – something that in a best-case scenario could be expected to take years to achieve.

The second and third sections of the manual are similar in tone, although they throw up a few interesting insights into Perón's thinking – and indeed its sometimes contradictory nature. Deliberately or not, the statement that 'Peronist doctrine is exclusively Argentine' is probably accurate and provides some insight into why it has prompted much misunderstanding abroad. Claims that 'our doctrine is a moral, humanist and patriotic doctrine' and constant references to spiritual unity did considerably less to bolster Catholic support than might have been supposed, not least given that it was not assumed to be the government's or a political party's role to instil spiritual unity.[23]

Perhaps the most contradictory observations refer to the fact that 'politics cannot be the work of one period, one man or one system. Politics imposes organs that ensure continuity ...' and 'it is necessary to replace personalist leadership [*caudillismo*] with the permanent, organic state of the political masses'. Although Perón goes into considerable detail as to the qualities of a leader [*conductor*], this is scarcely a role that appears to be transferrable, given his frequent insistence that they must be born anointed by the 'holy oil of Samuel'. He is at pains to distinguish between the two roles: 'the *caudillo* improvises, while the *conductor* plans and executes; ... the *conductor* creates new things; while the *caudillo* produces circumstantial things, the *conductor* produces permanent things'.[24] All of this is an attempt to highlight the belief that 'personalism is a very common political phenomenon, especially among our people' which 'must be replaced by the organisation',[25] yet all of Perón's actions and pontificating run in the opposite direction. Moreover, the directives note that 'the most perfect thing is that which evolves permanently, adapting to new circumstances' – precisely the virtue that Perón and his nascent movement had had prior to 1946, and which was increasingly being lost amid the verbiage of bureaucratization and institutionalization and Perón's mounting obsession with top-down order.[26]

Perón's rather lengthy perorations throw up various hostages to fortune in the light of his own long and sinuous career and his evident personal ambition. The rules governing the party are not dissimilar to those for most political parties, although they stipulate that members are obliged 'to vote for the party's candidates in all national, provincial and local elections'[27] and establish the system of *unidades básicas* as the base of the party's structure in highly bureaucratic and prescriptive terms. Perhaps more interestingly, they set out various directives from Perón himself that could and would later be used against him, including the statement that 'everyone must be the architect of the common destiny, but no one should be the instrument of anyone's ambition'.[28] In later years his emphasis on morals and discipline would also come back to haunt him ('men who lack moral value are a threat to the security and efficiency of the party'), as his perceived deterioration in that regard would be seen arguably as a more serious defect than in someone who had always taken such values more lightly. Moreover, the statement that 'whoever in our movement fights against another Peronist group to defend personal interests is a traitor to our cause' would be remembered later during Perón's long exile, when many of his efforts were directed at avoiding the return of any Peronist government or leadership that did not include him.[29]

In broader terms, the enforced inclusiveness of the vision set out might be (and was) anathema to the opposition, as well as to sectors such as the Church, which saw the state impinging on its own role in moral, education and family spheres. However, while scarcely a practical formula for government – such unity is impossible to achieve outside Utopia barring a level of repression that the Perón government did not and could not impose – in many respects the tract is touchingly optimistic and idealistic, as well as highly flattering to its readers who can be supposed to be part of the lofty Peronist mission. If it is viewed more with scepticism than alarm, it is notable more for its naivety than for its sinister qualities. And however far Perón is interpreted as being sincere (and his belief that he had found an effective, if simplistic, means to tackle the nation's ills suggests that he was more sincere than some critics have supposed), many of his followers were sincere and fervent converts to the system – for those who had long been marginal, being included, and in such a high-minded enterprise, was a heady and emotional experience that they would not forget. To read it or to sit through the lengthy explications that characterized party conferences and speeches by Perón and Evita – 'notable largely for the number of words spoken and the endurance displayed by orators and audience'[30] – required stamina and the willing suspension of disbelief, but for many it was more than worth it.

The Organized Community

Speaking at the First National Philosophy Congress in Mendoza in 1949, Perón would go even further into the details of his vision for Argentina as an organized community (*la comunidad organizada*). The marathon-length reflection included a rash of classical and modern references ranging from Plato and Aristotle through St Thomas Aquinas, Hobbes, Hegel, Kant and contemporary international philosophical conferences. It was apparently designed at least in part to underscore the erudition of the speaker, in which it succeeded at least to a degree, although it was light years away from his earlier 'popular' and down-to-earth approach. While its length and somewhat pompous tone of the text must have represented a trial for at least some listeners, in the Organized Community Perón sought to identify Argentina as the logical heir to the train of classical and Christian philosophy from ancient Rome through Aquinas and Roman Catholic thought. Pompous it may be, but again it represented a flattering take on the destiny of a people who 'do not content themselves with being one nation among others: they hunger for an overarching destiny, they demand of themselves a proud future.'[31] In this respect, as in many others, Perón did not differ from many of his compatriots; he too wanted an overarching destiny and a proud future for Argentina, and indeed wanted to lead it.

The Organized Community, which in the version published in 1975 runs to 116 pages (and which it can only be hoped included rest breaks when Perón first delivered it), sets out from the starting point of the 'nobility' of 'the pedagogical mission' (which he clearly believed to be his) and its responsibility to 'illuminate' and to trace 'man's direct relations with his beginnings, with his end, with his peers and with his realities.'[32] This, then, is a responsibility of a leader and of a government. Comparing the contemporary circumstances with a new Middle Ages, he predicts that an even greater Renaissance may be coming, 'because ours, with the same faith in destiny, also has men who are freer and thus have greater awareness.'[33] 'The man who must be dignified and put on the path to wellbeing must first be recognised in his essence.'[34] If this is vague and somewhat posturing, it does at least suggest that the government should have an obligation to assess, recognize and ennoble its citizens, a far cry from the approach of past governments to their lower-income citizens.

Perón then goes on to posit that the social upheavals of the eighteenth and nineteenth centuries brought down barriers and established new identities, but that 'these results were obtained only in the face of a common enemy and in short-term fashion .... Love among men would have produced better results in less time.'[35] Love, ethics and moral values are key to the community that Perón claims to be creating. In contemporary times, class struggle is inappropriate (a position Perón had adhered to since his GOU days): 'the notion that social collaboration and dignifying humanity are not just desirable, but inexorable, is gaining ground.'[36] The purpose of such an 'organized community' is to avoid the 'insectification' of man as a means of benefiting the community: 'what characterises healthy and vigorous communities is the level of their individualities and the path they seek to engender in the collective. This sense of community is arrived at from below, not from above.'[37] (This disregards, evidently, the fact that the community is precisely being defined from above, not below.) 'We trust that the day is not far off ... when the full realisation of the "I", the fulfilment of its most substantive ends, is found in the common good.'[38]

Following these somewhat long-winded musings, Perón returns to the substance of his vision of an organized community, citing Plato's belief that the common good lies in order, harmony, proportion and justice and Aristotle's thesis that man is designed for social co-existence and that 'the supreme good is thus not realised in the individual human life, but in the organism of the State; ethics culminates in politics'[39] (a statement that might strike many people around the world as ironic at best). From here, he argues that the Greek state reached its ultimate expression in the Roman Empire, the expression whose legacy he is seeking to claim. This, he argues, has had to struggle against growing materialism, which has led to Marxism, and the fact that both materialism and Marxism have led to 'the annulling of man, his progressive disappearance in the face of the external apparatus of progress, the Faustian state or the mechanised community.'[40] The dangers inherent in being unable to find agreement between the two extremes are clear, he says, having led to two world wars. The antidote to this is that 'our community, to which we should aspire, is that where liberty and responsibility are cause and effect .... A community where the individual really has something to offer to the general welfare .... This community seeks both spiritual and material ends, ... seeks to improve and be more just, better and happier.'[41]

This concept represented at least in part Perón's belief that the military structure in which all levels worked for a common purpose was a sort of ideal, and that his government's efforts to strike a balance between capitalism and communism were an advance on, and superior to, the ideologies on offer elsewhere. However, while it might be seen as risible or Quixotic, it could also be seen as sinister in many quarters – not least the Church, given the apparent breadth and depth of state involvement in personal matters of moral education and values. It would also take on a more ominous tone in the light of the increasing 'Peronization' of the country, not least in the statement 'society must be a harmony in which there is no dissonance.'[42] Alarm would grow as legal means to consecrate Peronism and its doctrine gathered pace, notably in the reform of the Constitution.

The 1949 Constitution

Arguably the most divisive and ultimately destructive innovation over this period was the decision to reform the 1853 Constitution. As early as 1947 the Peronist legislator and newspaper editor Eduardo Colom had presented a reform proposal in the Lower House, a move Perón himself had blocked. However, following the March 1948 mid-term elections, which saw the Peronists gain every Senate seat and over two-thirds of the Lower House, the timing appeared propitious for a project that had undoubtedly been in Perón's mind as well as Colom's. In May 1948 Colom again presented a proposal to convene a constitutional reform convention, this time with Perón's backing, and the bill passed in August, with elections to the convention called for 5 December. Opposition parties were divided as to whether or not to participate, but eventually the Radicals, Communists and Progressive Democrats did so, while the Socialists called on their supporters to cast blank votes. Predictably, the Peronist candidates gained a two-thirds majority at the convention; the most-voted candidate was Buenos Aires Governor Domingo Mercante, who would also be chosen to preside over the convention.

In his May Day speech in 1949 Perón set out reasons why he believed reform of the 1853 Constitution was urgent and necessary, saying that 'in the last 30 years social issues acquired capital importance and completely transformed the world'. According to him, the Constitution could only be considered still viable if its dictates were largely ignored, the same sort of political fraud that the 1943 coup d'état had been designed to end, or if politics 'was maintained within the predominant concepts of the last century in political, economic and social terms'.[43] The new, 'Peronist', Constitution must set out and uphold the social, economic and political dogmas that formed part of Peronist doctrine and its new style of government. 'We have taken the reins not only of political government but also of economic and social government. We orient the three activities in order to have an integral government.'[44]

Logic would suggest that all of the attempts to codify Peronism as an ideology, a way of life or an overarching national identity were intended as a means of ensuring that it would be able to outlive its founder, and indeed that new generations would be trained up to take increasing responsibility and political leadership. Yet, despite the frequent exhortations to eschew personal ambition, it became increasingly clear that its founder had no such intention of relinquishing control or political power. If anyone were still in any doubt, those doubts would be dispelled by the constitutional reform – a reform which could reasonably be justified on the basis of the need to modernize an ageing and derivative document (based largely on the US Constitution rather than local exigencies and realities). It could also be justified from the Peronist point of view as a means of ensuring that its concepts of social justice would be maintained.

Yet the reform increasingly focused on a single question: Article 77, which prohibited immediate re-election of the president. Despite Perón's initial protestations that the article should remain as it was, and subsequent claims that he would not stand for re-election anyway, the constitutional convention would focus almost exclusively on the reworded Article 77, which provided that 'the president and vice-president of the Nation will remain in their posts for six years and may be re-elected' – a formulation that did not even include any limit on the number of times they could seek re-election. The proposed change raised the spectre of his indefinite election – and the possibility, seen as even more horrifying by many, that Evita could be shoehorned into the vice-presidency and eventually the presidency. While it may be unrealistic to believe that all of these dots had been joined up quite so neatly in a well-planned and long-germinated conspiracy, by this time it was evident that things might be moving in that direction. Even among many Peronists, the move would prompt disquiet, given that it appeared to remove the possibility of a succession to which other figures could aspire.

Perón's own approach to Article 77 was typically roundabout, initially indicating that it should not be modified, then expressing agreement that voters should be free to choose a president without the re-election limitation being imposed, and then suggesting that he personally would not stand for re-election if he believed that the country's best interests would be better served by another leader. (Privately, he would tell Mercante that he would stand aside in his favour when his term expired and then perhaps seek a new term after Mercante's. Whether this was aimed at gauging Mercante's reaction to determine his loyalty, or an attempt to keep him on side, or even a fleeting intention, is uncertain.) It was clear to those who knew him best, including Mercante, that he would publicly oppose the re-election clause while allowing himself to be 'persuaded' by others. Even this strategy ran into various risks that Perón may not have envisaged, such as the hope of many of Evita's personal supporters (including Lower House leader Héctor Cámpora, who had replaced Ricardo Guardo) that she might succeed him if re-election were not permitted, now that women were enfranchised and she herself was making great strides in organizing the PPF, which could as easily provide a support base for the First Lady as for the president. Supporters of Mercante within the party were also opposed to re-election, seeing it as a means of sidelining the governor who had long been Perón's heir apparent.

The constitutional convention opened on 27 January, headed by Mercante with the Radical bloc led by Moises Lebensohn, one of the party's more youthful and articulate figures. As was the case in his own provincial government, Mercante forged a cooperative relationship with Lebensohn and ensured that opposition voices were heard unimpeded during the sessions; indeed, many of the additions to the new Constitution were approved of by the Radicals, who shared Perón's notions of economic independence and nationalism. Many of the amendments relating to the rights of the elderly and families, the right to universal access to education and the rights of workers (which, somewhat curiously, did not include the right to strike) were relatively uncontroversial. However, the modification of the original clause stating that 'property is inviolable' to read 'private property has a social function', and the constitutional requirement that all public services be state-owned and private companies could be expropriated in the national interest, were far more controversial; natural resources were also required to be the property of the state. The new Article 40 eliminated the requirement that Congress authorize expropriations and also required that all public services still privately owned must be sold to the state. While in line with government policy up until that time, the reform prompted a storm of protests from foreign embassies and caused Perón to order that it be dropped, although he wavered on the issue several times. Mercante managed to ensure that the article was voted before Juan Duarte could deliver instructions to reject it, and it became part of the new Constitution.

Nevertheless, Article 77 remained the chief bone of contention. Sometime around the end of January, Perón told Mercante and other delegates that he thought it should not be changed, whereupon Mercante took the initiative to publish a proposed draft Constitution for debate that did not alter the ban on immediate re-election. The move was met with surprise and dismay on the part of many Peronists, and with some scepticism by the opposition, which proved to be well founded. Following this announcement, Evita ordered that all copies of the draft already printed be destroyed and called a meeting of several delegates, including Mercante, at which she told him 'Mercante, convince the General to accept re-election. We need to have him as our president now and forever.'[45] Under duress, Mercante did as instructed, including in the new draft text the provision that 'the president and vice-president are elected for a term of six years and can be re-elected'. The text was hotly debated by the opposition, and after a day of angry argument Lebensohn led the Radical delegation out of the chamber, tearing up the draft as they went. Thereafter, the text was voted and the new Constitution finally approved without opposition participation on 10 March 1949.

In addition to changes at the national level of government, the new 'Peronist' Constitution also required that provincial elections should be brought into line with the national timetable, implying that governors' terms of office – hitherto four years – would be extended to six. In the case of Buenos Aires province, Mercante would retain the prohibition on immediate re-election in the provincial constitution, and refused to allow his mandate to be extended for a further two years by the provincial legislature, insisting on calling new elections for those final two years after his original term ended on 16 May 1950. Mercante would easily win that re-election, with strong support from Perón and Evita, the latter campaigning actively for the man she called 'the heart of Perón'. Yet his effective sidelining as Peronism's 'second man' by the re-election clause, and his evident unwillingness to follow the same course in the province, made it clear that his time as a close friend and ally of the presidential couple was drawing to an end.

Nor were the new Constitution and the form of its adoption the only development prompting disquiet. The adoption of the so-called *Ley de Desacato* (Contempt Law, or 'law of aggravated defamation') made any insult to the head of state an imprisonable offence. What constituted such an insult was of course open to broad interpretation, and could include disagreement rather than slander. Admittedly the opposition in Congress had often not conducted itself in a particularly democratic or professional fashion, and could indeed often have been accused of behaving in an insulting manner towards the president and his wife. Yet the new law implied that any such deviation from the official line could render opposition legislators subject to prison; indeed, Radical leader Ricardo

Balbín would be given a ten-month sentence for contending that Perón did not enjoy any immunity merely by virtue of being the leader of the majority party. Even following the *Ley de Desacato*, the Perón government was still some distance from being the dictatorship its opponents claimed: it was not characterized by political assassinations or disappearances, the death penalty was not imposed and parapolice forces did not attack opponents or their property. Yet arbitrary arrest and detention, vengeful acts of humiliation (such as the appointment of the blind writer and librarian Jorge Luis Borges, in truth an intransigent opponent whose writings were often vitriolic and defamatory, as a poultry inspector) and increasing doubts as to what was permitted would make the atmosphere more and more tense and fretful, and make the trip across the river to exile in Uruguay increasingly attractive to those who fell outside the great Peronist fraternity.

The 1949 Constitution would become a point of inflexion in Perón's government, which at the time was still popular with a majority of Argentines. Its provisions on private property were deeply disturbing to many, including the elites who were on the whole most closely linked to the Catholic Church (which itself saw such measures as leaning dangerously towards communism). But it was the introduction of what in effect was the possibility of unlimited re-election that represented not the peak of Perón's dominance but the seeds of his demise. Despite the vitriolic nature of much of the opposition to his government, many political figures and others had been willing to endure his six-year term in the belief that it had a legally determined end that would prompt a change of president – whether Mercante, more palatable to many, or a representative of another party. The elimination of that limit marked the end of the general acceptance of playing by any political rules: if Perón were to remain immovable through legal means, then illegal means could be brought to bear. The notion that Perón was now in theory eternal, that the popular Mercante had been excised from the succession and, even worse, that Evita could become vice-president (and commander-in-chief in the event of Perón's demise) was all anathema to the armed forces, and Perón's support in that vital body began to slip. With only the trade unions left as a reliable base of institutional support, his grip on power would weaken even as it seemingly strengthened; the re-election misstep would set him up for a fall.

Moreover, while much of the overwrought discourse on humanism, justice and spirituality was employed at least in part in service of an attempt at defining a more inclusive national identity – and a flattering one at that – that went beyond earlier narrow definitions which incorporated only a landed and cosmopolitan elite, that definition would also prove divisive rather than unifying. Perón's attempt at defining a portrait of Argentina was too much in Perón's own public image, and in practice defined 'Argentine' as 'Peronist' – which by definition implied that 'anti-Peronist' equated to 'anti-Argentine'. As Perón himself had recognized, when he sought to define, he excluded.

Chapter 11

AT THE PINNACLE

Sus ojos se cerraron y el mundo sigue andando ....
Y ahora que la evoco hundido en mi quebranto,
Las lágrimas trenzadas se niegan a brotar, y no tengo el consuelo
    de poder llorar ....
Por qué esta mueca siniestra de la suerte?
Quise abrigarla y más pudo la Muerte ...
Como me duele y se ahonda mi herida ....
Hoy está solo mi corazón.

Her eyes closed, and the world goes on ....
And now when I imagine her, engulfed in my sorrow,
The tears refuse to come and I don't have the solace of weeping.
Why this sinister smirk of fate?
I tried to protect her but death was stronger ...
How it hurts me and deepens my wound ....
Today my heart is alone.
Sus ojos se cerraron (tango), Carlos Gardel and Alfredo Le Pera[1]

By 1949 Perón was arguably at the peak of his power – a position that might be considered favourable but also dangerous, given that from the top there is nowhere to go but down. His government could unquestionably boast many real and tangible achievements which are worthy of recognition whatever the opinion of his political bent. In the first two years of his presidency, gross domestic product expanded by 16 per cent and urban salaries rose by 44 per cent. Despite the somewhat muddled industrial policies set out in the First Five-Year Plan and the limited achievements in heavy industry, imports of consumer goods fell sharply over the period even as consumption increased, symptomatic of healthy development in both light industry and purchasing power. Between 1945 and 1948, purchases of shoes rose by 133 per cent, of refrigerators by 218 per cent and of radios – the key source of entertainment, information and political propaganda – by 600 per cent, highlighting the level of previously pent-up demand.[2]

Figure 8 Perón and the poodles in 1950 (Photo by Michael Ochs Archives/Getty Images).

Yet, somewhat paradoxically, it could be argued that most of Perón's greatest achievements were already behind him; indeed, many of them had been attained before he became president, during the 1943–1946 de facto government in which he was a leading light. As noted earlier, the favourable economic environment of the early years had deteriorated – due in large part to international developments, but also to the fact that rises in production were not keeping up with increased consumption. Real wages had begun to decline, with inflation quadrupling the cost of living between 1943 and 1951; although the rise in wages for unskilled workers exceeded this level, wages in other sectors failed to keep pace. (Average real income rose steadily from 1943 to 1949 but began to decline after 1952 before rising again by 1955.) Nevertheless, labour's participation in total income rose by eight percentage points between 1945 and 1954, reaching a maximum of 50.8

per cent in 1954.³ In practice many lower- and middle-income sectors continued to enjoy a standard of living and consumer choices much greater than pre-1943, but they had now become accustomed to ever-rising wages and consumption and would become increasingly restive when the government's largesse and support for juicy wage packages began to diminish. Later in his term, the British ambassador would say that Perón was 'always on the look-out for slights and always ready to take offence. Somewhat gloomy by nature, he lacks the gift of being able to laugh at himself.'⁴ An earlier assessment by an earlier British representative, in early 1944, had described Perón as having 'a sense of humour'.⁵ Whether the difference was in the eye of the beholder or due to a change in Perón's humour, it seems highly likely that he enjoyed life more in 1944 as his career took off and he was able to resolve the low-hanging-fruit problems that abounded, than he did five years later as a head of state in an increasingly vexed context.

Times were becoming more difficult for many Argentines, and also for Perón himself. Having been in the enviable position of being able to redistribute plentiful resources at a time of great national prosperity, Perón was now faced with adverse economic currents outside his own control, an increasingly fractious labour force that, while largely loyal, was demanding continued improvements in living conditions at a time when circumstances did not readily permit, and obdurate opposition on the part of both political parties and landed interests. He had also by this time spent more than five years in power (both de facto and de jure), the exercise of which was beginning to take its toll. Although he continued to maintain a strict work schedule and to display remarkable levels of energy and focus, by 1949 a Perón in his mid-fifties increasingly appeared to be frustrated, impatient and perhaps weary of the demands that power made – not least given that those demands were far less gratifying in times of austerity than they had been in times of plenty, when he was so frequently the recipient of popular gratitude for the generosity that he and the country could still afford. Unquestionably he enjoyed being beneficent and doling out favours more than he enjoyed being dour and imposing austerity. This may in part explain an increasingly authoritarian bent; if several years earlier opposition allegations of repression had been largely overstated, the reality was now increasingly coming to resemble the myth. The British Embassy would note 'increasing sensitiveness to criticism and the adoption of stringent means to suppress it'.⁶ One prominent casualty of the downturn would be economic 'czar' Miguel Miranda, who departed in January 1949, although this implied little immediate shift in economic policy. Equally, greater repression appeared increasingly pointless in a context in which no serious opposition remained – arguably another factor that Perón, who enjoyed challenging and circumventing his adversaries, found unappealing.

As noted above, some of the difficulties facing the economy were down to government error and to the failure to plan prudently for more adverse international currents. Yet many were down less to Perón's sometimes haphazard government than to the fact that Argentina, for all the rhetoric of economic independence, remained a somewhat marginal country deeply affected by global events. The US decision not to allow Marshall aid to be used to buy Argentine foodstuffs, if unsurprising, cut Argentine farmers out of their most reliable market, and unwillingness to seek international lending or tone down nationalist rhetoric that played well at home also limited economic options. In practice, Perón was one of the first but certainly not the last of a long list of 'populist' leaders elected on promises of ensuring a better deal for their country and their people who would later be undermined by the very fact that they were unable to bend the international system to their purposes and thus far more limited than they or their constituents had believed in terms of their options for change.

In a bid to address the shortages plaguing an increasingly consumer-driven society, in April 1949 Perón made his first speech as president specifically on agriculture, saying that the first part of the Five-Year Plan had focused on industry and that the second part would now focus on supporting agriculture. In particular, he promised to facilitate imports of agricultural machinery in order to increase productivity at a time when labour costs had risen; the government estimated that the country needed over 27,000 tractors, 250,000 grain sowers and 35,000 harvesters more than it had. However, his proposal that exports should account for only 10 per cent of output, with 90 per cent to be consumed domestically, was not met with enthusiasm by farmers, despite the promise that the government would not intervene in the domestic market. Moreover, the prices being offered by the government for grain remained below production costs, which the sector was unwilling to accept in return for promises that higher productivity would lower those costs.

At the same time, while Perón remained a charismatic and ubiquitous figure, and maintained his rigorous work ethic that ensured he was in action and in the public eye, curiously he was losing the starring role in the ever-more-Peronist Argentina. In these years he would begin to be overshadowed, not by opposition leaders or figures such as Mercante, but by the figure of someone with no elected office or political experience – his wife. Evita would prove even more energetic and tireless than her disciplined husband, and with her non-institutional role she would come to dominate many aspects of the Peronist government's activities and image. Even a less-than-sympathetic British envoy would note that she had 'a certain genuine interest in the welfare of her more unfortunate compatriots', an understatement and a quality that would prompt a frenzy of social welfare activities unlike anything ever seen until that time.[7]

Already a key interlocutor for the trade union movement, which was by this time more linked to the First Lady than to the government, Evita had also made great strides in the organization of the PPF, launched in July 1949. Evita organized a 'national census of women Peronists' as the basis of the party, for which she appointed young women whom she sent to all twenty-three provinces and territories to work for months organizing the foundations of the party. Those young women would themselves become the first in a generation of politically oriented women, and some of them would be elected to office in the 1951 elections, the first in which women could vote or stand as candidates. By the beginning of 1950, the women's party had opened some 3,600 *unidades básicas* across the country, which not only affiliated members but offered medical, legal and beauty services, as well as classes in skills such as sewing, typing and literacy.

While all these activities contributed greatly to exalting the government and the figure of Perón himself, there is no question that they raised Evita's personal profile even more. Her own rhetoric remained strongly (not to say embarrassingly) florid in her praise of Perón – whom she compared to a giant condor while comparing herself to an insignificant sparrow – and her injunctions to the women's party focused on the obligation of absolute loyalty to the General, yet it was she who was the PPF's president and unquestioned leader and the figure to whom many women felt their key allegiance. 'What we wanted was to collaborate with her, not the Peronist Party.'[8]

Moreover, Evita's punishing schedule increasingly curtailed their intimate personal relationship. Perón continued to enjoy 'down time' at home or San Vicente. Evita, by contrast, increasingly resented any such leisure time as the theft of hours that could be dedicated to her feverish activities in favour of social justice. When obliged to spend the weekend at San Vicente, she would hide the telephone from Perón and use every opportunity when he was out of earshot to communicate with subordinates, give orders and remain informed about events elsewhere. Perón himself would complain that he felt he had lost his wife, while she herself would insist that it was only through her intense social and political activities that she felt that she truly *was* his wife.

While Evita had begun operating the María Eva Duarte de Perón Social Aid Crusade in late 1947, not long after her return from Europe, she stepped up her activities the following year when the Crusade formally became the María Eva Duarte de Perón Social Aid Foundation. By then the Crusade was already reportedly receiving 12,000 letters per day and had distributed some 5 million toys at Christmas 1947; the creation of the Foundation greatly increased its financial resources and its operations, which included subsidies to the elderly with no pensions and the construction of temporary housing for working women. The first residence for the elderly was opened on 17 October 1948 and the so-called Ciudad Evita, with 5,000 low-cost homes for working-class families as well as schools and hospitals (and built in the shape of her profile), was also inaugurated that year. The Foundation, launched with a donation from Evita and of Perón's salary cheque as president, also received funds from the national lottery, the casino at the beach resort of Mar del Plata and other funds from the state, including revenues arising from tax debts; it also received donations in cash and kind from companies and trade unions, some of them voluntary and some of them not. It would come to have around 14,000 employees, including 6,000 construction workers, and when it was wound up in 1955 its assets reached some 120 million dollars.

On one level, the Foundation was designed to work more rapidly than the state bureaucracy; given that in practice it was answerable to no one but its leader, it could mobilize projects and assistance without waiting for red tape to be completed. Over its few years of life it constructed five important public hospitals, lavishly appointed residences for working women, a nursing school and 1,000 schools across Argentina, which were then handed over to the government to run. It also organized children's sports championships in which an estimated 500,000 participated (all of whom received medical attention and treatment if required) and ran holiday camps for working-class families. Millions of families received a bottle of cider and fruitcake for Christmas, decorated with photos of the president and his wife. It also constructed thousands of homes for working-class families, built to a level of comfort and elegance decried by her opponents (which produced the urban myth that the beneficiaries of the new houses tore up the parquet floors to use the wood to barbecue their meat). Evita would counter such objections by insisting that she wanted the poor to aspire to better things and 'to get used to living like the rich',[9] and doubtless she was sincere. Perón also wanted the poorer classes to become more aspirational and felt that he had given them the means to do so, through higher wages, and greater access to education and mortgage credit; in part for this reason, he would become increasingly irritated at times by the strikes and protests that appeared to be asking for more rather than making use of what they had been given. Yet neither appeared to accept that the mere fact that so many needed the first couple to 'give' made them more, not less dependent.

While the Eva Perón Foundation and its founder would often, and rightly, be accused of political patronage, personalism and wastage, in point of fact the Foundation was remarkably efficient at undertaking many useful projects; later allegations that its funds made their way into private accounts appear to be unfounded and indeed the investigators appointed after Perón's overthrow to look into the Foundation found no evidence of fraud. Moreover, Evita's increasing presence as a combination of Madonna with good fairy would be disparaged by many, while also attracting well-founded criticism that her brand of 'social justice' in many ways differed little from the charity she despised. Nevertheless, it is worth bearing in mind that Evita created an example of new roles for women – not a feminist in any modern sense, she understood that women needed to be able to earn their own living if they were not to be dependent on a sometimes unreliable man or fall into penury if they lacked one. She created a public role for women not seen before, pressing for the expansion and professionalization of the nursing profession and opening the way for women to participate in politics – nominally in order to vote for Perón, but also to stand for elective office and undertake public responsibilities. Her energies and organizational capacity were remarkable, and despite her lack of formal education and apparently unpromising origins, she was the first and arguably still most prominent example of a woman exercising executive power in Argentina; she may still be the most politically powerful woman Latin America has seen. 'Her personality has permanently changed, not only the position of women here, but the whole social structure of Argentina.'[10]

If Evita's role as president of the women's party and of the Foundation, as well as the sponsor of the CGT, were not enough, she had also acquired by this time a number of media outlets, grouped in the ALEA group (managed by Major Carlos Aloé, who would succeed Mercante as governor of Buenos Aires). These included the newspaper *Democracia*, as well as a number of national and provincial expropriated from their former owners and the magazines owned by the Editorial Haynes, including important women's magazines such as *El Hogar*. She was thus well able to control her own publicity and that of others – as well as curtailing it, as when she ordered that Bramuglia should be excised from photos published in the media. (She would later do the same to Mercante, when she became convinced that he had ambitions to succeed Perón – a notion that her husband may have planted in her mind to that end.) She also kept up a staggering pace of public appearances, not only state galas in which she and her husband appeared glamorous in full evening dress, but more frequently political speeches up and down the country, sometimes exceeding seventy per month.

Evita's method of attending to requests for assistance was famous. She would arrive at her office (still at the Ministry of Labour) to find long queues of supplicants, who had been given appointments but no guarantee of punctuality. Visitors such as diplomats, journalists or politicians were often required to empty their wallets in order to ensure that there was enough cash to meet immediate demands. Requests might include anything from a set of dentures to a job, a house, a bicycle or, most famously, a sewing machine, a source of some financial independence for poor women. All those attended would receive enough money to get home; on some occasions Evita would send visitors home in her own car and have to await its return. Her days went on far into the night, and she would sometimes arrive home at the presidential residence in the early morning, just in time to cross paths with Perón as he left for work.

Not only was Evita's profile at risk of eclipsing her husband's at home, but she unquestionably enjoyed more prestige abroad, not least due to the shipments of aid and provision of medical personnel provided by the Foundation to countries including Israel, Ecuador and even the United States. Although often criticized abroad for the clientelistic nature of her activities, Evita had also won grudging praise even from the US magazine *Time* during her 'Rainbow Tour'. In 1949 she had hosted the Inter-American Commission of Women in Buenos Aires, and while her interventions were predictably politically biased and extravagantly flattering to her husband, she would gain the support of many of the international delegates, not least when she called 'for others to join the [...] Third World struggle, which must include, fundamentally, the active and lucid participation of the woman'.[11] Perón, by contrast, continued to face often excessively negative coverage abroad – notably in the United States, where the Braden view still prevailed – and despite somewhat half-hearted efforts to promote Peronism across the region and his pontificating about the virtues of the Third Position, he stayed at home and did surprisingly little on the international stage. (One of his more widely publicized ventures proved to be a farce. Ronald Richter, one of the German scientists Perón had wooed to come to Argentina, had claimed to be able to generate energy through controlled nuclear fusion, prompting Perón to set him up with a laboratory near San Carlos de Bariloche. In 1951 Perón announced to the international press that Argentina had produced atomic energy, based on Richter's claims which were subsequently proven false, to Perón's substantial embarrassment – although the adventure led to the establishment of the Argentine Nuclear Energy Commission.)

Given her obsession with work and her unsociable hours, Evita had by now moved into a separate bedroom, ostensibly to avoid disturbing Perón, who now rarely saw her. This can only have been a difficult contrast with the early days of their relationship, when they were virtually inseparable and could enjoy each other's company both in politics and in relaxation. Any sexual relationship seems likely to have been truncated, and Perón in this way also began losing his last key friend, companion and sounding board. Given that she would sometimes go for a meal at the working women's home established by the Foundation in Avenida de Mayo after finishing work, usually with a group of trade unionists, assistants or others whose company she enjoyed, it would appear that she made little effort to get home to the presidential residence earlier.

However, the need for separate bedrooms was not due solely to her long hours. Evita's health had been fragile for some time, and in 1948 she had been diagnosed with anaemia. By 1949 she reportedly suffered from haemorrhages and intense pains that occasionally caused her to faint but she adamantly refused to see a doctor or receive medical treatment, and it appears that keeping her distance from Perón was a means of trying to keep him in the dark and prevent him from ordering her to undergo treatment. Evita's mother had had uterine cancer and had been operated on successfully, and Perón's first wife Aurelia had died of the disease; it is thus reasonable to imagine that both of them were aware of the symptoms. (Perón would later say that the symptoms had begun in 1949 and that he had warned her repeatedly that she would die if she did not rest, to which she would reply 'if I rest, who will help these people?'[12]) She was eating little – a glass of juice or a sandwich in her office – and would sometimes have the staff at the residence serve her dessert to make Perón believe that she was finishing off a full meal.

In January 1950 Evita fainted at a public event, redoubling concerns over her health which had hitherto been described as flu, anaemia or exhaustion. Education Minister Oscar Ivanissevich, also the first couple's personal physician, convinced Perón to insist on her hospitalization a few days later; thereafter, Ivanissevich announced that she had had surgery for 'acute appendicitis'. However, he believed the problem to be a different one and reportedly urged a hysterectomy, which earned him a blow from Evita's handbag and encouraged his resignation from the cabinet. It is not certain when Perón became aware of the gravity of Evita's illness, although Ivanissevich is believed to have conveyed his suspicions to him in early 1950.

Others say he was told in September 1951, when doctors who had carried out a full examination were forced to break the news to him. Following exploratory surgery, the biopsy had confirmed that that news was not good: Evita had uterine cancer which by this time was far advanced and offered little prospect of a cure. The gynaecologist Jorge Albertelli was tasked with informing Perón of the news, setting out the seriousness of the illness and proposing an operation followed by radiotherapy. Albertelli would later recall 'the General's face showed his state of mind. He did not interrupt my statement at any time. His sadness was evident; I thought I could detect a furtive tear.' When Albertelli had finished presenting the diagnosis, Perón said finally 'what I have just heard, although I suspected it, has affected me deeply. I want you to know that Eva represents something very important to me as a wife, companion, friend, counsellor.'[13]

Many key events would occur between Evita's faint in January 1950 and her final diagnosis some twenty months later, which would if anything only underscore her importance to Perón and to Peronism. However, despite her hold over the trade unions, she was unable to halt rising strikes and protests, including by railway workers in January 1951, who were unmoved by her frantic personal calls for them to return to work (the union was subsequently 'militarized' in order to break the strike, which was declared illegal). Both Perón and Evita would become increasingly angered by this 'disloyalty' and 'egoism' on the part of the workers, which also highlighted the fact that Evita, in her unofficial capacity, was limited in her ability to resolve such disputes.

Some of those events would also raise renewed tensions with the Catholic Church, now the only potential source of real pushback against a dominant regime. Evita had long been the subject of a degree of religious hagiography, as well as the source of much religious imagery which described Perón in somewhat heretical terms, such as 'the face of God in the darkness'. On 17 October 1950 the 'Twenty Truths of *Justicialismo*' (the party now being officially called the *Partido Justicialista* (PJ), the latter term a corruption of 'social justice') were launched, describing 'a new philosophy of life, simple, practical, popular, profoundly Christian and profoundly human', while priorities were established as 'first the fatherland, then the movement and finally men'. (Another such 'truth', that 'for a Peronist there is nothing better than another Peronist', would prove ironically and tragically inaccurate in coming years.) Also at the 1950 Loyalty Day celebrations, Perón for almost the first time praised his wife for her outstanding contributions, saying 'I know she loves you as I do and maybe more than she loves me. My gratitude cannot omit to name this woman that you and I call by the same name: Evita.'[14] CGT leader José Espejo then decorated her with an honour designed especially for her – unusual moves that appeared to suggest a realization that her remarkable career might be drawing to an end.

With the political, economic and personal panoramas looking increasingly uncertain, the decision was taken to bring forward elections from February 1952 to November 1951. While there was no question at all as to who would be the government's presidential nominee, the vice-presidential post remained a question mark. Incumbent Hortensio Quijano was elderly and ill, and Domingo Mercante, long considered the clear favourite, was 'in the dog house' and on the brink of political exile. However, a number of factions – the PPF, the CGT and Evita loyalists in Congress such as Lower House leader Héctor Cámpora – had little difficulty in coalescing around the name of an alternative. When the presidential campaign was in effect launched in February 1951, the PPF overwhelmingly endorsed Perón but also expressed 'the vehement desire of all the workers that Señora Eva Perón be consecrated vice-president of the nation'.[15] While it is not clear that Evita would have gained any personal power from such a nebulous position as vice-president, it is clear that for whatever reason she wanted the post; it is unthinkable that either the CGT or the PPF would have put forward her name with such insistence without her blessing.

It is also unclear whether Perón ever seriously contemplated the possibility of Eva's candidacy, although the use of her name (like the use of Mercante's in the past) helped to keep other candidates at bay. Although in the past he had stressed that a married couple could not form a presidential ticket, he did not say so publicly at this time. Whatever he thought of the plan, it seems likely that he was already aware that her health would not allow it. More to the point, he must have been entirely certain that the military would not allow it; if he was not, they lost no time in telling him so in no uncertain terms, warning that large elements of the Army would move against the government. This left him in a quandary as to how to keep both the armed forces and the CGT on side, although of the two the military represented the more important factor: Perón himself was a career army officer and was well aware of the need for military support, and neither the CGT nor the PPF would realistically have voted for an opposition candidate regardless of Perón's running-mate. It can only be speculated whether he was subjected to pressure at home, but in practice his options were limited.

By early August, the CGT had called on Perón to accept the nomination and continued to press for Evita to be included on the ticket; the PPF would also proclaim the Perón-Eva Perón slate in advance of the huge *Cabildo Abierto* (open meeting) scheduled for 22 August to bless Perón's re-election drive. The *Cabildo Abierto* had been months in the planning, with transport, accommodation and food laid on for the *descamisados* coming from the interior, and international media put the eventual crowd at some 250,000 on the day. The stage had been set up in front of the Public Works Ministry, at the intersection of two wide avenues, 9 de Julio and Belgrano, dominated by a huge sign proclaiming 'Perón-Eva Perón, the ticket of the fatherland'. However, all the forward planning had failed to contemplate the complications that ensued. Eva initially did not appear to join Perón on the platform, and when Perón attempted to speak he was drowned out by shouting from the crowd after CGT leader José Espejo called for her presence, saying that the event could not 'continue without the presence of Comrade Evita'. Evita appeared shortly thereafter with Espejo, and for once seemed at a loss for words; in tears, she asked Perón what she should say, and instead of telling her to accept the nomination, he told her to 'say yes without saying yes'.[16] In an emotional dialogue with her supporters, not unlike that protagonized by Perón on 17 October 1945, Evita sought to evade the question of her candidacy and to laud the greatness of her husband, only to be constantly interrupted by shouts of 'Evita with Perón'. One of the greatest oddities of this dialogue, however, was the virtual sidelining of the president, who had been forced into a subordinate and almost unnoticed role. When he attempted a speech, he was interrupted by calls for Evita to speak instead; thereafter, when she refused to confirm her acceptance, there were shouts calling for a general strike. After a long and tearful exchange, and following Perón's terse admonition to end the event, she was heard to say 'I will do what the people want', taken to be acceptance and reported as such.

Several days later, on 31 August Evita would broadcast her 'irrevocable decision to renounce the honour that the workers and the people of my country wanted to confer upon me'.[17] Thereafter the decline in her health would be increasingly pronounced and she would be able to undertake fewer and fewer public duties, although her presence would become overwhelming in the months running up to the election. (As an afterthought, Quijano was persuaded to take the vice-presidential slot, although he died before the inauguration in June 1952.) Efforts to exalt her became more and more exaggerated and competitive and her influence and image expanded even as she herself faded away.

During 1950 Evita had been approached by a Spanish journalist, Manuel Penella de Silva, about collaborating on an autobiography, and in early 1951 a first draft of what would become *La razón de mi vida* (The Reason for My Life) was presented to her. Evita was reportedly greatly moved by the work, but Perón was less enthused and the project was temporarily shelved. Thereafter, Technical Affairs Minister Raúl Mendé and Information Sub-Secretary Raúl Apold did some substantial rewriting, during the course of which the book became increasingly a panegyric celebrating the greatness of Perón rather than an autobiography in any meaningful sense. Nevertheless, Evita appeared to be satisfied with the result, not least given that her own views on pro-Perón propaganda largely coincided with those of Mendé and Apold. (Privately she was wont to say that 'Perón is like the sun – he gives light but if you get too close you get burned.'[18]) The book would rapidly become required reading in schools, another source of propaganda that irritated the opposition and yet another example of Peronism's counter-productive habit of over-egging the pudding – demanding universal rather than simply majority support and quasi-deification rather than realistic recognition of achievements. Like the ubiquitous images of the first couple, and the use of primary school readers containing useful texts such as 'Evita loves me', *La razón de mi vida* and its inclusion in the curriculum generated more negatives than positives for a government whose finest hours were behind it.

Despite Evita's 'renunciation' of the vice-presidency, which was predictably lauded as a heroic gesture, tempers within the armed forces were not entirely soothed, and on 28 September General Benjamín Menéndez led a brief and rapidly repressed uprising. Most of the forces remained loyal, as did the CGT, and the rebellion represented little threat in itself, but did point to a sign of worse things to come. Evita, who was bedridden and receiving blood transfusions, later made a radio broadcast to thank the *descamisados* for again coming to Perón's defence, and promising to try to return to the struggle. In tangible terms, on 29 September she called together various union leaders and Army chief Humberto Sosa Molina and ordered the purchase of 1,500 machine guns and 5,000 automatic pistols, to be paid for by the Foundation and handed out to workers in case of another rebellion. (The weapons were never handed out and Perón would subsequently have them confiscated and handed over to the border guards.)

Evita was even unable to attend the launch of her autobiography in mid-October, as her condition worsened, although it would appear that she herself had not yet been told what her diagnosis was. According to her confessor Hernán Benítez, she would find out accidentally only near the end of her life and would be furious that nobody had had the courage to tell her the truth. Yet she surely knew her prognosis, even if she remained in denial. Her appearance at the 17 October 1951 Loyalty Day celebrations (marking Argentina's first television broadcast) left little doubt that she and all around her knew, even if they still maintained the fiction that a recovery was possible. Awarded the Great Peronist Medal (the first and last time it was bestowed) by Perón on the balcony, she was unable to speak and could only stand in a prolonged embrace with her husband, who made 'public my gratitude and my profound thanks to this incomparable woman'.[19] When she was finally able to speak, she made a dramatic and passionate speech reiterating her 'love for this people and for Perón' and warning her people to remain alert in the face of Perón's enemies, asking them to chant 'my life for Perón' and begging them to take care of him if her health prevented her from doing so. It was a deeply emotional event, with tears, love and despair on both sides, and an evident awareness that there would be few more such events to come.

Evita had surgery on 5 November, only six days before the 11 November elections, for which she recorded a radio message describing a vote against Perón as a betrayal. Although she believed that the surgery (purportedly for an ulcer) was to be conducted by Argentine surgeons, led by the distinguished doctor Ricardo Finochietto, a US cancer specialist, George Pack, was secretly brought in for the operation and kept out of the room until Evita had been anaesthetized. She was allowed to vote from her hospital bed, surrounded by electoral officials, media and well-wishers, and had the satisfaction of learning that the women's vote significantly boosted Perón's final majority: the Perón-Quijano ticket received 66 per cent of the vote, double the support attained by the Radical ticket of Ricardo

Figure 9 Perón and Evita on the balcony of the Casa Rosada, on 17 October 1951 (Wikimedia Commons)

Balbín and Arturo Frondizi (who in practice had been unable to campaign in any meaningful way, with media largely closed to them). Perón got 4.6 million votes, more than half of them women voting for the first time, while a number of women entered Congress and provincial legislatures on the Peronist ticket.

Evita returned to the presidential residence on 14 November and would rarely again leave the bedroom in which she received delegations and remained much of the day in bed with her poodle lying beside her. Only a few weeks after the operation a new biopsy indicated that the cancer had metastasized and was incurable, giving Eva only a few months to live. She would occasionally go for a drive with Perón and would pass much time surrounded by colleagues and family, making a few broadcasts or distributing gifts on Epiphany. But by January she was again suffering severe abdominal pains; radiation treatment, then in its early days, provoked severe burns and even more pain without arresting the progress of the cancer. She also received twenty doses of intravenous chemotherapy, also still an experimental treatment, which weakened her but not the cancer. She seldom appeared in public, except to attend Quijano's funeral on 3 April.

Evita's final public speech was on May Day 1952, and it was also her most violent, probably reflecting the fact that she knew it would be her last. Warning against the risk of an uprising against Perón, she said that 'I will come out with the women of the people, I will come out with the *descamisados* of the fatherland, dead or alive, and leave no brick standing that it not Peronist'.[20] Although sustained to an astonishing degree by her own determination and emotional energy, she thereafter collapsed and Perón had to carry her in from the balcony, more dead than alive.

On her thirty-third birthday, six days later, Evita would be awarded the title of 'Spiritual Leader of the Nation', an offence to the Catholic Church and others. Although barely able to get out of bed and reduced to skin and bones, she would make another superhuman effort on Inauguration Day, 4 June, insisting on accompanying Perón in the open car with the help of several injections of painkillers. While Perón was often criticized for his 'exploitation' of her illness, it is unlikely that he or anyone could have dissuaded her from assuming what she regarded as her rightful place, especially since she now knew she would have no further opportunities. The inauguration would be her final public appearance and the last time she would leave the presidential residence.

As her end clearly drew nearer, the competition to offer exaggerated tributes and titles increased. It would later be reported by detractors that Perón avoided the sickroom as much as possible, but he began working from home in the afternoons in order to be close at hand. Her erstwhile designer, Paco Jamandreu, would later write that he was called to the residence late one night by a tearful Perón, who asked him to prepare some sketches of new clothes in order to lift the dying Evita's spirits by making her think that they would be able to go on a long trip together. When Jamandreu brought the sketches the following day, she was enthused and Perón thanked Jamandreu profusely, asking him to make at least some of the dresses to distract her; she died four days later.[21] Having already lived through a similar experience with Potota, the situation can only have been deeply distressing for Perón, and gestures such as the request to Jamandreu suggest that he was far from indifferent. (Much later it would also be claimed, not without some evidence, that he had agreed to a lobotomy shortly before her death in a bid to alleviate her pain.[22])

When she was conscious, Evita purportedly began working on a second book, *Mi mensaje* (My Message), although this version is still disputed, and the fact that it contained a 'will' exalting and leaving all her worldly possessions to her husband has been questioned. While this element might have been promoted by Perón in his own interests, other elements of the text, which come across as revolutionary and anti-military, were by no means in his interests and might well have been suppressed if they were authentic at all, although they would provide grist for other mills in coming years.

On 18 July Evita entered a coma for what was expected to be the last time; the mourners gathered around her bed were amazed when she awoke a few hours later and got out of bed. At Perón's request, on 20 July Father Benítez held an open-air mass to prepare the public for her death, attended by thousands who remained in the rain to pray for her recovery. Hundreds also spent days kneeling outside the residence to pray; elsewhere, anti-government graffiti such as *viva el cáncer* and *viva Perón viudo* [widower] spread around the city. By this time Benítez would say that she was calm and prepared for death; farewells to other friends also suggested this.

On 26 July Benítez administered last rites and Evita again fell into a coma surrounded by her husband, friends and family. It was reported at 3.00 pm that her condition had deteriorated, and a subsequent report at 8.00 pm indicated that it was 'very grave'. Some time later, Apold's Under-Secretariat of Information announced 'that at 20.25 Sra Eva Perón, the Spiritual Leader of the Nation, passed away'. She was only thirty-three. Thousands continued to pray and to weep in the heavy rain outside, while public places spontaneously closed their doors.

Plans were already in place to embalm her body; a well-known embalmer and functionary at the Spanish Embassy, Dr Pedro Ara, had been on alert for some days and arrived at the residence soon after her death. He and an assistant worked all night to leave the body in a fit state for what would prove a lengthy wake; her hairdresser and manicurist thereafter came in to prepare the body aesthetically. Thereafter, she was taken to the Ministry of Labour for public viewing, where an estimated 65,000 people per day filed past the casket; florists sold out within hours and nurses from the Foundation handed out food and attended to mourners who fainted while waiting their turn. Although Perón had promised that she would lie in state until everyone had had the opportunity to pay their respects, by 9 August Ara was becoming nervous that the body could begin to decompose if work were not completed, and the public viewing was brought to an end. On that day the casket was taken to Congress for a further ceremony, accompanied by a parade of 600,000 torches organized by the CGT. The next day Evita was taken to the CGT headquarters, where her body would remain for the next three years and Ara continued his efforts. Some 2 million people were said to have lined the route from Congress to the CGT; although the opposition could rightly grumble that some of the mourning was obligatory, there is no question that much of the grief on display was spontaneous and genuine. Perón himself was astonished at the depth of feeling displayed at Argentina's largest-ever funeral. Thereafter, it was over, and he would return to the presidential residence alone, in the company of his poodles, to carry on the complex business of government in isolation.

Evita's meteoric rise and very public and dramatic death served to distract public opinion from deteriorating economic realities and provided a peerless source of political propaganda for a regime no longer in its first flush of success. Yet her real emotional hold and the impact of her death went far beyond that. The public figure most committed to the socially marginal in Argentina's history, Evita struck a genuine emotional chord among millions who felt for the first time that they mattered, and to someone important. Her ability to do so may have owed something to her acting career and her understanding of public speaking and image, but it owed more to her own experience and real comprehension of what ordinary people's lives were like. If Perón was often more opportunistic, Evita was deeply sincere and deeply motivated, as well as fanatical and divisive. Both her virtues and her defects were considerable, and while her symbolic value in death as a martyr could not be denied, the loss of her presence was a severe blow to Perón himself and to his government. While she herself had often referred to Mercante as 'the heart of Perón', in reality Evita was the heart of Perón and the Peronist movement, and her loss was irreplaceable.

In 1945 Perón had remarked to Mercante that he had what his enemies lacked, 'a loyal friend and a woman who loves me and whom I adore'. Now he had neither.

Chapter 12

DECLINE AND FALL

Adiós, Pampa mía; me voy ... me voy a tierras extrañas ...
Si no volvemos a vernos, tierra querida, quiero que sepas que al irme dejo la vida.

Farewell my Pampa; I am going ... I am going to strange lands ...
If we do not meet again, beloved land, I want you to know that in going I leave
my life.
Adiós, Pampa mía (tango), Francisco Canaro, Mariano Mores and Ivo Pelay[1]

Evita's death represented a turning point in Perón's government and indeed in Argentine history. Despite scornful assertions by the opposition that the display of public grief was artificial and government-sponsored (a claim to which the government lent itself by insisting that public employees use black armbands and attend the funeral events), there is no question that her death prompted genuine outpourings of grief and fears over the future. Although the staging of the massive public events required considerable choreography, the estimated 2 million who lined the streets for her funeral cortege or the many thousands who filed past her coffin visibly did not all do so under duress; most of the displays of emotion were clearly real, although one can only wonder how the soldiers required to accompany the body and render honours to a woman they had loathed may have felt inwardly. Smaller ceremonies took place across the country, leading the opposition to joke about a 'wake with branch offices' as altars and floral tributes multiplied in towns and villages.

Nor was the importance of the death ignored abroad, with widespread press coverage both critical and admiring noting the significance of the event. Queen Elizabeth II would send a telegram to Perón extending her 'deepest sympathy and that of my people for the tragic loss which you and the Argentine people have suffered in the premature death of your brilliant and devoted partner',[2] while from London AFP noted that she had faced her illness 'with such courage and energy' and the fact that the British press had published numerous articles which 'reflected the deep admiration caused by her devotion to the cause of the "descamisados", her loyalty to President Perón and the great power of attraction she exercised over the Argentine masses'. A New York newspaper headed its obituary 'A woman who will never be forgotten: Eva Perón. One of the most important women in the world has fallen into the arms of death.' In early August *Paris Match* began its article by saying 'the disappearance of this beautiful woman is a true political catastrophe.'[3]

Perón would be accused by many of inflating and profiting from the 'necrological bacchanale' that followed Evita's death, and it is true that the Secretariat of Information in particular lost no opportunity to try to build both Evita's image and Perón's own. Yet on both the personal and political level Perón was left deeply damaged by her death; the documentary film *Y la Argentina detuvo su corazón* (And Argentina's heart stopped) produced by the Secretariat, which remains a valuable record of the funeral, shows a Perón who may be in command of himself and his emotions but is scarred by the events. During both the funeral and at home, walking with his poodles in the grounds of the residence, he looks stiff, vacant and almost shell-shocked. A military man who was trained to contain his emotions and carry on with his duties, he did so, yet it appears virtually inevitable at this remove that the emotions he repressed would find a way to escape, as indeed they did. With grief counsellors now normally advising people not to make important decisions after a significant bereavement, with hindsight it would seem that Perón could scarcely have been in a position to take decisions of national importance, yet he continued to soldier on dutifully, and alone, when all best interests might have been better served by another course. As early as October 1951 the State Department had noted that 'the precarious state of his wife's health has seriously affected Perón,'[4] and having lived under this stress both before and after her death took a heavy toll.

For Perón, Evita's departure left not only a gaping hole in his personal life, but also a vacuum in managing the levers of political power. As noted earlier, Evita had acquired as much if not more power over the CGT, the Foundation and the PPF than her husband, and given his reluctance to allow any potential challenger, he was unwilling to see those important factors of power in the hands of another. He would attempt to take over her duties at the Foundation three days per week, attending personally to multifarious petitions from an endless queue of supplicants. The British Embassy would note that 'it is doubtful whether General Perón can possibly add to his own work the feverish activities formerly carried out by his wife .... It is at the same time obvious that he is loath to entrust the power and patronage which went with these activities to anyone other than himself.'[5] Inevitably, the Foundation's activities would begin to be wound down at least at the personal level; Perón himself admitted that he could not stand the degree of personal contact involved and did not understand how Evita had done so. But, as he intuited, his inability and unwillingness to sustain the personal role would create some distance between the government and its supporters that had not previously existed. 'There is even some speculation whether General Perón could long survive the disappearance of his wife, who has been so much the driving, revolutionary force behind his regime.'[6]

Moreover, as noted earlier, Evita's death robbed Perón of a voice that could not be replaced. On the one hand, the exaggeratedly superlative way in which she always spoke of him in public was offensive, repellent or risible to some but accepted by many of their supporters, if for no other reason than a belief that it was respectable for a wife to have such an adoring view of her husband. Only an adoring spouse might have had licence to speak in such a way; Perón clearly could not laud himself in the same effusive terms, nor could mere political allies or even Apold's propaganda machine. At the same time, Evita had always been the more violent and revolutionary in her rhetoric, leaving Perón to adopt a more conciliatory tone as befitted a head of state. Indeed, her incendiary speeches were often followed by a more emollient Perón's addresses, cooling down the inflamed crowd and getting some credit for his greater moderation at the same time. Evita's absence would see Perón adopt inflammatory language on an increasingly frequent basis, with disastrous results; in the first lady it could be brushed aside as sincere but uncontrolled passion, but in the president it took on the more sinister tone of official incitement.

Following Evita's death it was widely observed that Perón maintained his rigorous schedule but often seemed distracted or lost in thought, drumming his fingers on the table during meetings and taking little active part. (Speaking after Perón's 1955 overthrow, his former Vice-President Alberto Tesaire would say that 'after 1952 Perón didn't work any more and spent his time on secondary things …. He came to think that Perón was mentally unbalanced.'[7]) Nor was the political and economic situation a source of comfort, as the economy continued in the doldrums. The Second Five-Year Plan maintained austerity measures, as well as wage and price controls; it also increased emphasis on the role of the private sector and corporate investment, a shift away from earlier statism and labour promotion. In practice, real wages had been falling since 1949 but remained well above pre-Perón levels, suggesting that the tightening envisaged in the Second Five-Year Plan was unwelcome but not intolerable. However, consumers faced not only reduced purchasing power, but increasingly, shortages of key staples such as beef which were widely blamed on speculators.

In April 1953 Perón gave an angry speech promising to root out and punish speculators and all those using their government functions for purposes of self-enrichment. However, one of the key suspects was none other than his private secretary and brother-in-law, Juan Duarte. Duarte had long been accused of involvement in corrupt practices, and his devoted sister's death had robbed him of any protection he might have enjoyed. Duarte was also known for his addiction to nightlife, show business and the pursuit of actresses, several of whom were known to be involved with him, and he was said to be suffering from the final stages of venereal disease. (Paco Jamandreu would describe him as having been known as 'Lux soap', 'because nine out of ten film stars use him' in the phrase of Lux's advertising.[8]) Not an intelligent or resourceful man, he may well have seen the writing on the wall following Perón's diatribe, and he resigned as his secretary on 6 April.

Three days later, his body was found kneeling by his bed, with a gun still in his hand and a bullet lodged in his head, together with an apologetic note to Perón saying 'I came with Evita and I go with her, shouting Viva Perón'. Predictably, his death was widely questioned and there were strong suspicions that someone else had done him the favour of performing the suicide for him; his mother would insist that Perón had killed both of her children, although the evidence for this was also limited. The military dictatorship that overthrew Perón would conclude that Duarte had been murdered, although given its avowed intention of discrediting Perón with as much fact and fiction as it could muster, this is hardly conclusive either. (During the military government one of its interrogators, known by the pseudonym Captain Gandhi, kept Duarte's head in a box in his office, and took it out to frighten two of his former girlfriends, the actresses Fanny Navarro and Elina Colomer, placing it on his desk when they were questioned about his business dealings; Navarro never recovered from the shock.) One version suggested that Raúl Apold participated in the killing, whether or not on Perón's orders, despite the fact that nothing in Apold's life suggested participation in physical violence as opposed to political propaganda and character assassination.

It would seem most out of character for Perón to have ordered his brother-in-law's killing; his record indicates that he was happy to divest himself of people who were no longer useful and sometimes hound them into exile (as in the case of Mercante, who left for Uruguay with Isabel Ernst when his term as governor ended), but not to have them killed. Whether Duarte in fact shot himself or whether someone else within or close to the government believed that his removal would be convenient may never be known (documents relating to his death in the hands of the Duarte family's descendants have not been made public), but his death represented yet another worrying event and the departure of another long-time ally.

Late the following month, Perón's mother Juana would die in the southern city of Comodoro Rivadavia; their relationship had been distant for many years but he attended her funeral in June 1953, when she was interred in the Perón family crypt at Chacarita cemetery in Buenos Aires, and the event perhaps served as another reminder that fewer and fewer of his old relationships remained. The last member of his immediate family, his brother Mario Avelino, would die in January 1955 of heart failure, leaving behind a wife and nine children. Again, they had not been close since childhood but Perón had persuaded his brother to come to Buenos Aires to take charge as director of the zoo, where Mario would sometimes lend the president animals to grace the gardens around the presidential residence.

Days after Duarte's death, on 15 April 1953, two bombs exploded near the Plaza de Mayo, where Perón was making a speech setting out his anti-inflation programme, prompting him to launch into the sort of diatribe in which Evita had specialized, inviting his listeners to respond to violence with violence. Although he finished by urging the crowd to disperse peacefully, right-wing groups attacked and burned the Socialist Party headquarters and the newspaper *La Vanguardia*, the Jockey Club and Radical and National Democratic Party offices. Thereafter, members of those opposition parties were detained and released only several months later, another sign that the repression they had long denounced was becoming more pronounced.

In 1953 the British ambassador would observe that Perón 'seems to have no close friends of either sex. His daily routine is enough to tax anyone's strength. He arrives at his office from Monday to Friday at 6.20 and remains there until after 12 noon, rests after luncheon and works in his house, if he has no speeches or public functions, until 9 or 10 pm when he retires.'[9] Although the economy was recovering somewhat by this time, both Perón's personal and political life appeared rather thankless. Efforts to boost the economy further through seeking a loan from the US Export-Import Bank and attempting to attract investment by Standard Oil served largely to create ammunition for the opposition; this was the president who had said he preferred to cut off his arm rather than to accept foreign loans, and who had included resource nationalism as part of his overarching message of economic independence. Greater pragmatism offered few political rewards.

Although Perón could scarcely be said to have had idle hands, his sterile personal life and apparent loneliness would provide something of a playground for the devil. He continued to enjoy sports and in particular riding motorcycles and driving fast cars, fencing and attending boxing matches. He would enjoy publicly entertaining the US boxers Jack Dempsey and Archie Moore when they visited Argentina; Moore would give Perón the gloves he had been wearing when he first won the world light heavyweight championship and they would appear so close that the opposition began to make derogatory suggestions about the nature of the relationship. (Supporters would respond with the slogan 'fairy or thief, we love Perón'). However, the vacuum in Perón's life and his love of sports would produce another, more destabilizing creation: the *Unión de Estudiantes Secundarios* (Union of Secondary Students, UES).

Figure 10 Perón greets racing champion Juan Manuel Fangio in 1955 (Photo by Keystone/Getty Images).

The brainchild of Education Minister Armando Méndez San Martín, the UES aimed to 'Peronize' young people, a proposal that could only arouse criticism among opposition-oriented families and the Church, which saw the formation of young people as its own role. Enthusiastic about the suggestion, Perón offered the president's summer residence in Olivos for the group's activities, in which he soon began to take part. Olivos would become host to dozens of teenaged girls who would participate in athletic activities and, when Perón was there, socialize with the ageing president, who still enjoyed teaching and interacting with young people and delighted in the fact that they began to use his childhood nickname, 'Pocho'. A sportily dressed Perón was often to be seen riding scooters (which would become known as *pochonetas*) followed by a flock of young girls, a vision considered undignified at best and suggestive of much more sinister things at worst. Before long the rumour would spread that the UES was nothing more than a ruse to provide teenaged girls for the president and his friends (whoever his friends were supposed to be). The figure Perón cut, which he may have perceived as jaunty and fun-loving, was undignified and undisciplined; the latter, striking in a man whose life had been so characterized by rigorous discipline and austere habits, was particularly damaging to his reputation within the military.

Many former participants in the UES have insisted that there was no impropriety and that the organization served only to provide an outlet for young people who might have had limited opportunities to practise sports elsewhere. Nevertheless, while this is almost certainly broadly true, it did not apply to Nélida (Nelly) Rivas, a fourteen-year-old student who participated in the UES and who would become Perón's mistress until he went into exile in September 1955. Nelly, the daughter of working-class parents, would begin to dine with the president, holding long conversations with him and eventually attending sporting and cultural events with him until she gradually moved into the presidential residence with her parents' blessing (where he would attempt to interest her in reading Plutarch). Nelly would later say that Perón needed someone by his side; 'when he arrived the general told me all his problems and I was a kind of haven for him. I tried to give him my opinions.'[10] Others saw Nelly herself as ambitious and scheming, and seeking to cause schisms within the presidential household.

Inevitably, Nelly's presence prompted scandal, although perhaps not entirely for the most obvious of reasons. While the thought of the relationship between a man of sixty and a girl of fourteen would now immediately be defined as illegal and immoral, in the 1950s it probably prompted more outrage because it was public knowledge than because it was occurring. The concept was hardly novel; for young girls working in domestic service it was probably the norm, and more widely the notion that both parties might benefit from the differences in experience and vitality was common. Yet respectable men who had sex with the teenaged servant or prostitute did not do so publicly, and the fact that a head of state would have the temerity to do so was shocking. In many respects the most striking things raised by the relationship are Perón's astonishing lack of judgement and his isolation. However much he may have enjoyed flouting social norms at various times in his life (in part to compensate for the many times he felt the need

Figure 11 Perón (right) riding a scooter with the members of the UES in 1955 (Photo by Keystone-France/Gamma-Keystone via Getty Images).

to excel at maintaining them), it must have been obvious that such a relationship brought the president and his office into disrepute and raised serious questions over his mental stability.

The thought that a sixty-year-old president was seeking support and advice from a fourteen-year-old girl is no less startling. What both these facts point to is that Perón no longer had friends, advisers or ministers competent and trusted enough to offer either support or the obvious advice that his behaviour was deeply damaging. The departure of the most competent and the presence only of those who wished to pander or to ensure personal gain were increasingly a threat to both the government and Perón himself. It would appear that Perón himself had little respect for those advisers and ministers; photos show cabinet ministers accompanying Nelly Rivas to public events and Perón's military escorts required to act as her bodyguards, something that can scarcely have been regarded as appropriate to their functions. Perón himself, in seeking to defend himself from charges of malfeasance, would later say that 'the moments I spent among the students and the children of workers who came to the sports fields of the UES were the most beautiful of my life. Only there, in the few free hours I had after finishing work, could I overcome the melancholy and unease that grew out of my solitude.'[11] While the memoir is hardly unvarnished truth in many of its claims, it is difficult not to believe that this is true.

The UES – both its existence and that of Nelly Rivas – would become yet another thorn in the side of the government's relations with the Catholic Church. Shortly after Evita's death, 'her' trade unions would begin to present petitions seeking her canonization, a move that was premature at best and which inflamed the touchy sensitivities of the Catholic hierarchy, which had been at least temporarily soothed by the upsurge in popular religious observance during her illness and death. The titles bestowed on her, such as the Martyr of Labour, the Guiding Angel of the People and the Standard-Bearer of the Suffering, also added to the earlier insult of her designation as the Spiritual Leader of the Nation, as did claims that 'she died to save us. Like Christ.'[12] The Vatican gave short shrift to the canonization petitions, not unreasonably given the short time elapsed since her death and the fact that a miracle is supposed to be documented and attributed to the candidate for canonization. (It is not clear whether Evita's influence, had she lived, would have averted or increased the conflict, although after her death her confessor, Hernán Benítez, appeared to lose much influence. It is most unlikely, however, that she would have favoured an open clash with an institution she cautiously respected – and she certainly would not have tolerated the UES/Nelly Rivas scandal.)

Much has been written to suggest that Perón's conflict with the Church was the principal cause of his downfall, and indeed that the Catholic Church was the primary mover behind his overthrow. This is exaggerated: despite its formal position in Argentina, the Catholic Church was not a very powerful institution and it had historically been at pains to avoid confrontations even with governments (such as those of Yrigoyen) regarded as deliberately anti-clerical. Yet, whether the hierarchy wished it or not, the Catholic Church was one of the few institutions remaining that could still harbour elements of opposition (not least as it had its greatest strength in the social classes that were most likely to be anti-Peronist), given the complete disarray of the opposition parties and the closure or censorship of most of the opposition media. Possibly for that reason, a president who had seemingly defeated every other potential challenger began to look to the Church as a key antagonist. Despite the rhetoric surrounding the Organized Community, Peronism had by its nature an oppositional discourse, and in order to flourish it required an opposition – something it now lacked. Equally, the signs of boredom and distraction noted in Perón during this period may have led him to seek a new battle and a new enemy, while the signs of poor judgement may also give some explanation as to this particular choice of battleground. It was a poor choice, and if he thought that the crisis with the Church would distract from the less buoyant economy or the climbdown on foreign debt and investment, he was much mistaken.

As noted earlier, the Peronist insistence on seeking to corner the market in encyclical-based social justice concepts and the persistent attempts to define Peronism and the Organized Community, first as an expression of religion and then as a form of state religion, were inevitably going to cause more long-term difficulties than harmony. In particular, the fact that both the Catholic Church and the Peronist movement regarded themselves as having a sort of universal jurisdiction, and a mandate to try to mould national life and individual choices through education and/or indoctrination, made it inevitable that heads would be butted at some stage. Yet the Church remained diplomatically silent for some considerable time, welcoming Perón's public displays of religiosity (such as the consecration of the country to the Virgin in December 1953). Those displays can only have increased the surprise with which Perón's early salvos were received; certainly whatever the position of the hierarchy, it was Perón who fired the first shots. Although he was careful to avoid attacking the institution per se, and invariably limited his verbal rebukes to 'certain priests', from 1954 these salvos would become more and more persistent.

It is unclear whether the breakdown in Church-State relations represented a diversionary tactic on Perón's part or a genuine belief that he was invulnerable (although in the latter case it is difficult to see why a gratuitous dispute with the Catholic Church would be productive). Following the April 1954 elections, in which they received 65 per cent of the vote, the Peronists further increased their congressional majority and a long-standing ally, Admiral Alberto Teisaire, was overwhelmingly elected vice-president to replace (albeit belatedly) the deceased Hortensio Quijano, with double the vote for the Radical candidate, Crisólogo Larralde. The economy had also stabilized, though in a climate of greater austerity; if the years of bonanza had passed, at least there were signs of growth and the working classes continued to enjoy higher standards of living than previously, even if the frequent pay rises were now a thing of the past and depended on increased productivity. (Whereas beef had been rationed in late 1953, described in Perón's New Year's message as a need for a change in the national diet, this extreme had now passed.) The British Embassy would express surprise at the conflict, but remarked that Perón was 'an extremely astute politician and must be presumed to have carefully weighed what would be the results of his actions'.[13] In the past that would have seemed a reasonable assumption, but now it perhaps looked less so.

While the conflict with the Church may have appeared to Perón to be a useful distraction, it also coincided with various rumours regarding his health and his judgement. Many of those rumours can be taken as either maliciously intended or wishful thinking, but there were some signs that the president was perhaps less hale and hearty than in the past. On one occasion, when riding a scooter he swerved to avoid hitting a pedestrian and fell, hitting his head, prompting rumours in mid-1954 that he had developed a tumour as a result. He had also developed a tic in one eye and, unknown to the public, had also lost his famously brilliant teeth after being treated by a quack dentist a few years earlier, forcing him to use a set of dentures. (He would confess to Ricardo Gayol, his host in Paraguay following his overthrow that 'everyone praises my charm and my teeth, but they are all false'.[14])

As in the case of Evita, it is reported that a US medical specialist came to examine him at the request of the Argentine military attaché in Washington, and diagnosed smoking-related arterial problems, something that would return in later years although he did reduce his cigarette consumption somewhat. However, the diplomats who saw him regularly believed him to be in 'fine fettle' and put most of the rumours down to intentional efforts to undermine him. 'He is obviously not the man he was three years ago, but it is difficult to believe that there can be anything very seriously wrong with a man who daily arrives at his office soon after six and completes so full a programme.'[15]

Perón would later attribute the conflict with the Church primarily to the foundation of a Christian Democratic Party (PDC) in mid-1954, despite the fact that the hierarchy was not behind the move and was at pains to stress that 'the Church has nothing to do with this …. It is not convenient to tie the Church to the vehicle of a party, no to link a party to the vehicle of the Church.'[16] Nor is it apparent that the foundation of yet another opposition party would have done much damage to a government already facing an atomized opposition. Yet the PDC appeared to be encroaching on Peronism's turf of Christian political doctrine (in which Peronism was already encroaching on the Church's turf), which might have stood it in good electoral stead with some voters who approved of the policies but increasingly disapproved of the government.

Another source of civic and political activism was the lay *Acción Católica* (AC). The AC was apparently encouraged by both the Vatican and the Argentine hierarchy to take a more political role which it was by no means reluctant to do. It was composed largely of white-collar sectors affected by economic downturn and political exclusion, as well as nationalist tendencies critical of Perón's efforts to improve relations with the United States and the concessions made to US oil companies: 'so now we know that the "third position" is kneeling! Right now Perón is in the correct third position: on his knees before the United States.'[17]

In late 1954 Perón began a series of attacks against 'certain priests' meddling in politics, citing supposed complaints of 'clerical infiltration' from organizations such as the CGT. (These attacks also touched on Spanish *caudillo* Francisco Franco, who was suspected of stirring trouble in Argentina through Spanish priests working there.) Several priests were briefly arrested, and the bishops of Córdoba and Santa Fe were accused of political opposition. Perón would claim that 'I have never had a conflict with Christ. What I am exactly trying to do is defend the doctrine of Christ that … priests like these have tried to destroy'[18] ('This was the same Perón who had earlier said that 'when a leader thinks he has become a messenger from God, he starts to lose his way'.[19]) CGT Secretary-General Eduardo Vuletich would tell a rally that 'if any man preached Perón's doctrine before Perón, that man was God' (as though God were Peronist rather than Perón being Christian), while the legislator and PPF president, Delia Parodi, would refer to 'this shining living Gospel that is Perón's doctrine'.[20] While most of these verbal excesses were doubtless encouraged by members of the government such as Apold, Perón himself did nothing to stop them.

The verbal assaults on 'certain priests' were accompanied by a series of new laws curtailing the Church's temporal power, including greater government oversight of religious activities, the granting of equal legal rights to illegitimate children, the prohibition of public religious demonstrations, the legalization of divorce and prostitution, abolition of religious education in state schools and the calling of a referendum on the separation of Church and State. While many of these laws might be regarded as justifiable in themselves, they were anathema to the Church, and represented a new attack on its traditional spheres of influence. The hierarchy responded with a series of agitated communications denying clerical support for any party and repudiating the divorce law. Lay Catholics such as the AC, on the other hand, responded to these measures and to increasing press censorship through the time-honoured use of pamphlets as a form of propaganda and opposition.

Religious processions also became a vehicle for political dissent, and thus attracted far greater participation than in more normal times. The first religious procession to compete with the government to 'win the street' took place on the Feast of the Immaculate Conception in December 1954. Although official statistics are unreliable, photographs indicate that attendance far exceeded that at a rival government-sponsored rally in honour of the boxer Pascualito Pérez. However, the Church-State conflict would climax in the wake of the Corpus Christi procession on 11 June 1955 (in which Pérez was again the focus of the government's competing demonstration). The Corpus Christi procession filled the Cathedral and much of the Plaza de Mayo, Perón's symbolic stomping ground.

Following the mass, the march proceeded to Congress, where some sort of assault on the national flag purportedly took place. According to the official press, Catholics burned the flag flying at Congress, while various opposition pamphlets accused Interior Minister Angel Borlenghi of burning it. Other observers claimed that the Argentine flag was torn in a scuffle but no flag was burned. However, it was noted that 'whoever is responsible for the flag incident had planned it in advance since both the Papal and Argentine flags involved … were carried to the Plaza Congreso. … No Argentine flags were originally flying.'[21] This would later be confirmed by Vice-President Alberto Teisaire, who said that the burned flag had been burned elsewhere, probably at Perón's instigation.[22] Clashes were reported between the AC and the nationalist ALN.

Two days later, the auxiliary bishop and the deacon canon of Buenos Aires were relieved of their posts by decree and expelled from the country, departing for Rome shortly thereafter. In return, the Vatican issued a decree excommunicating all those responsible for violations of the rights of the Church. The excommunication did not name Perón explicitly, although the intention was implicit. It was suppressed in Argentina, although it was reproduced as a pamphlet; it was widely believed to have sparked off an unsuccessful military revolt on 16 June. It is perhaps more realistic to say that the armed forces were already increasingly alarmed by many of the same developments that had alarmed the Church.

The rebelling officers bombed the Plaza de Mayo, leaving an official death toll of some 355 and 600 wounded and making it the bloodiest such coup attempt until that time. One of the first bombs dropped fell on a trolleybus, killing all sixty-five on board. Another aerial attack near the presidential palace in Palermo killed several other people. As Perón would later say, 'bombs and bursts of machine gun fire rained down on the heart of Buenos Aires, astonished and unarmed. …. I was the rebels' only objective. They wanted to finish me off and to eliminate one man they did not hesitate to kill five hundred.'[23] Perón was taken to the basement of the War Ministry and was unhurt, drinking *mate* and chatting with the surprised staff. However, many of the civilian casualties were trade unionists who responded to a call by the CGT to go to the plaza to defend the president, some of them arming themselves on the way with weapons taken from gun stores; others went bare-handed or carrying sticks. As on 17 October, many commandeered public transport to take them from the suburbs to the plaza. A horrified Perón countermanded the instruction, ordering that all civilians should avoid the area, but this was too late to avoid the high number of deaths.

On the night of 16 June twelve churches were burned in Buenos Aires, a number of priests were arrested and one died after a beating. It was never entirely clear who was responsible for burning the churches, although they had government acquiescence at the very least, given that the arsonists were able to go about their business freely despite the state of siege imposed after the bombings. Borlenghi was again blamed by some; others believed that Perón had orchestrated the events in order to undermine Borlenghi, who resigned shortly thereafter. (Others believed Education Minister Armando Méndez San Martín, the 'genius' behind the UES, to be behind the anti-clerical campaign.) According to at least some opinions, Perón authorized the burning of churches as a means of retribution that made the point while avoiding political killings, which he did not condone.[24]

Following these dramatic events, the Church-State conflict suddenly disappeared from the official discourse, possibly under pressure from the army. Perón sought to ease tensions with both the Church and the opposition, promising in mid-July that his 'revolution' was now at an end and that peace and normality must now prevail. In response, Radical Arturo Frondizi broadcast a speech saying that 'there can be no pacification until urgent measures are adopted to re-establish the full effectiveness of the constitution … ' as well as 'an immediate and ample amnesty for all those who are suffering persecution, imprisonment or exile.'[25]

This phase of sweet reason was short-lived. On 31 August it was announced that Perón intended to resign. At the mass rally called to the Plaza de Mayo to persuade him to change his mind, he made an improvised and vitriolic speech calling for violence against violence: 'when one of ours falls, five of theirs will fall'. This was most likely too much for the remainder of Perón's support in the armed forces, alarmed by his seeming lack of control and the risks of violence (and humiliation) on both sides. The army reportedly demanded, and gained, a number of resignations in the cabinet and the CGT. However, none of these steps would keep Perón in power.

Intelligence reports in early September indicated that another rebellion was under way, led from Córdoba by retired General Eduardo Lonardi (the officer expelled from Chile as a result of Perón's machinations nearly twenty years earlier). On 16 September artillery troops attacked loyal forces in Córdoba, which surrendered rapidly, while similar Army and Navy uprisings occurred around the country. Despite government insistence that the rebellion had been quelled, it was widely reported that a final assault was expected by 19 September, led by Admiral Isaac Rojas; in the interim, there was general astonishment that neither Perón nor any other member of the government was visible or made any broadcast statement. Following days of heavy rain and deep suspense, on the 19th Perón's resignation was suddenly announced, apparently in order to avert a planned naval attack on the oil refinery in La Plata. Although Perón would later say that the resignation was intended as a bargaining counter rather than a real departure (any actual resignation would have been directed to Congress rather than the Army, he claimed[26]), the following day the chiefs of staff agreed that the government should resign and Lonardi should assume the presidency.

Despite stunned popular surprise over the resignation, it is notable that no one made any serious attempt on this occasion to dissuade Perón from going. Whether he had in fact expected them to do so is uncertain; indeed it is not entirely clear that he wished to continue in a role that had become increasingly thankless. Offering no resistance, Perón would pack a bag and seek asylum in Paraguay.

Typically, Perón would later blame obscure forces for his overthrow, including the machinations of freemasons whom he blamed for stirring the conflict with the Church (including 'a well-known English prince' belonging to the Royal and Sovereign Lodge of London – presumably Prince Philip) and imperialist forces seeking to control Argentina's oil, a plot he likened to the overthrow of Iran's Mohammad Mossadegh two years earlier. On these forces he pinned the blame for spreading the belief that he wished to destroy the Church as opposed to being 'in conflict with priests who were politicians like him'. However, while there were doubtless many foreign interests that did not lament his departure, these attempts to divert blame for his own errors are hardly credible.[27]

The ease with which Perón was finally overthrown surprised everyone. The British Embassy, which blamed Perón's fall primarily on his 'ill-judged quarrel with the Church', noted that 'never since the evolution of the modern State has such a system been brought down by purely internal stresses ...' and that the collapse 'was so quick, so complete, and so utterly ignominious'.[28] Yet it reflects not only expanding dissatisfaction with economic development and mounting authoritarianism, but also the sometimes supine nature of his supporters' relationship with their leader. As noted earlier, the most dynamic phase of Peronist development was now a decade behind, and the workers had become increasingly accustomed to doing what they were told; when the order to come out in his defence did not come, they stayed at home. (The exception was the right-wing ALN, led by Guillermo Patricio Kelly, which put up resistance until their headquarters was stormed by the army, killing many – a move which may also have represented a warning to the CGT.) At the same time, as the Embassy noted, 'possibly, if Perón himself had shown more spirit his followers would have reacted differently'. 'It was an ignominious end to the rule of the man who, for better or worse, brought about greater changes in Argentina than had any in the last hundred years.'[29]

Moreover, the mounting insistence on indoctrination and on dominating every aspect of public life (and increasingly the private sphere) had had the counter-productive result of alienating many sectors, undermining some of the government's genuine early achievements. Although many still remembered these, and still loved Perón, the willingness to risk death for an increasingly erratic president had dwindled, and many hoped that his departure would now lead to the end of the exhausting melodrama that had been national life for so long.

If anything, it is difficult not to attribute Perón's lack of 'spirit' to what appeared to be an increasingly negative mental and emotional state. The loss of a second wife to cancer, the arduous workload and the increasingly difficult task of governing may have been behind many of the behaviours that concerned his followers and alienated the military. Although Perón had in the past been prepared to defy convention, as in his early relationship with Evita, he had never been given to the lack of discipline and erratic behaviour that characterized the last period of his presidency, and which caused many, with some reason, to question his sanity. Perhaps even the weight of responsibility attached to being virtually deified was exhausting as well as absurd and offensive. In all likelihood he was on some level quite happy to go, despite his evident resentment at the fact that immediate resistance to his overthrow was relatively muted. Moreover, as he would always insist, he was horrified 'to think that, through my fault, Argentines could suffer the consequences of a heartless civil war'. '[O]nce before, finding myself in a similar situation, I took the same decision and resigned power. It happened in 1945, when I was war minister.'[30]

As in other dark moments of his life, Perón appears to have reacted with resignation and some courage, returning to the presidential residence where 'I wandered through the house I had lived in for ten long years and where Evita's memory was more alive than I …. Every portrait, every object brought memories of a moment of my life, an instant of those years when my wife and I dedicated all our energies to the country.' He packed a small bag with some clothes and 'a miniature of the Virgin of Lujan … and a portrait of my wife. They are the guides of my existence.'[31] He departed from power with, in the end, little resistance and almost no material sustenance; the amount of money he was able to marshal was minimal and the subsequent military government (the 'Liberating Revolution') would halt his military pension and embargo his relatively modest properties. Evita's jewels remained in the residence. Despite allegations that he had amassed a vast and corrupt fortune, no traces of his supposed wealth were ever discovered (the new government despatched emissaries to Switzerland to attempt to uncover the numbered bank accounts Evita was alleged to have opened), and throughout his exile he lived a modest existence bolstered by contributions from his loyal friend, the businessman Jorge Antonio. (According to his sometime secretary Rodolfo Martínez, Perón managed to take about 70,000 dollars with him on leaving Argentina and subsequently received cheques for 500 dollars per month, probably from Antonio. Even in 1955 this hardly constituted great wealth.[32])

From the presidential residence, in the early hours of the 20th Perón made his way to the gunboat *Paraguay*, where he was forced to wait for several days to be given a safe conduct to leave the country; en route to the port his car broke down and he was forced to ask an astonished bus driver to help tow it through the pouring rain. Finally, on 25 September he was given permission to depart and was transferred to a hydroplane which struggled to take off for some time in the bad weather, lifting off and falling back once before finally heading for Asunción. 'I said, see you later, Argentina, not goodbye.'[33]

Before his departure he sent a letter and cash to Nelly Rivas, asking her to bring his poodles and meet him in Paraguay, telling her that 'you are all I have and the only beloved thing I have left', although he also noted that 'what I miss most is my little girl and my little dogs …. I love those bandits very much.' In terms very reminiscent of the letter he wrote to Evita from Martín García a decade earlier, he promised that 'the two of us alone will make a peaceful life somewhere. I am very tired and need some quiet time.'[34] (Nelly and her parents would be detained trying to cross the border into Paraguay; she was sent to a reformatory, the cash was confiscated and the poodles would wait in Buenos Aires for some months before being reunited with Perón in Caracas.)

For both Perón's supporters and opponents, his sudden departure was a shock and prompted trepidation that chaos and civil conflict would follow. He himself attributed his decision to the desire to avoid destruction of the kind he had witnessed in Spain after the Civil War. Referring to the threat to attack oil installations, in his resignation statement he would note that 'in the face of threatened bombardments of the invaluable wealth of the nation and its innocent people, I think nobody can fail to put aside other interests and passions.' 'If my spirit as a fighter impels me to the fight, my patriotism and my love for the people induce me toward every personal sacrifice.'[35] However, his rapid departure would leave his supporters at the mercy of a military government and other sectors keen for vengeance after nine years of Peronist government. Moreover, the truncating of his term would carry the seeds of his eventual return.

That vengeance would only expand after the initial days of the Liberating Revolution. Although Lonardi had promised 'neither victors nor vanquished', he himself was terminally ill with cancer and would be replaced as president two months later by General Pedro Aramburu, whose far harder line would see mounting repression. Many Peronist politicians and unionists would be jailed, and efforts to make Perón a non-person expanded. Laws were passed prohibiting the display of photos of Perón or Evita even in private homes (punishable by up to three years in prison), banning the use of party symbols or the Peronist march, and even banning the use of the names of the former president and his wife. (The media would for a considerable time refer to Perón as 'the fugitive tyrant', the title accepted by the regime.) Many of the public works constructed by the Peronist government were destroyed or truncated; installations of the Eva Perón Foundation were also destroyed and its initials painstakingly removed from sheets and towels at its residences and hospitals. The presidential residence, the Unzué Palace, was torn down, to be replaced decades later by the long-delayed National Library. The collections clothes, jewels, cars, *pochonetas* and other extravagant possessions of Perón and Evita were put on public display in a bid to shock and horrify their supporters. However, given that they had used these things publicly throughout their careers, the display shocked and horrified no one. In arguably the most symbolic move, Evita's body was taken from the CGT headquarters where it had remained, and hidden in various places (all of them rapidly discovered by loyalists, terrifying army officers who routinely discovered flowers and candles next to its anonymous locations) before finally being smuggled out of the country and buried in a Milan grave identified as that of an Italian widow.

Although Perón initially went to neighbouring Paraguay, where he held honorary citizenship and an honorary commission in the Army, by November he had decided to move on. This was partly due to assassination fears and partly due to pressure from the Stroessner government, itself under pressure from Buenos Aires to remove him from the scene and stop him from making political statements. (A lengthy interview with United Press on 5 October, in which he made numerous sharp criticisms of the de facto government and hinted that he might return to the political fray in Argentina one day, was the chief cause of this pressure.) While he told United Press that he planned to remain in Paraguay and that he would not travel to Europe 'because it is not necessary and because I don't have enough money to be a tourist at the moment, despite the wealth my detractors claim I have',[36] shortly thereafter he made plans to relocate to Nicaragua.

On his way there, however, he made a brief stop in Panama, where he expressed to President Ricardo Arias a desire to remain. As a result he would stay in Panama for nine months, living a quiet and somewhat penurious existence, and adjusting to life in a small flat with only his driver Isaac Gilaberte and one or two local supporters for company, amid continuing fears of an attempt on his life. Even so, he appeared somewhat more his old self, attending boxing matches and cabarets and looking more relaxed and rational than he had done in the months leading up to his fall. He would later recall that he dedicated time to *footing* as an effective form of exercise, and became a 'tourist attraction' for the *gringos* staying in the hotel for whom he signed autographs.

He also spent his time finishing a somewhat turgid and self-justifying memoir he had begun on the gunboat, *La fuerza es el derecho de las bestias* (Force is the Law of Beasts, a phrase taken from Cicero), which nevertheless contained trenchant and accurate criticisms of the military regime – some of which might have been applied to his own government. (Apparently aware of the irony of his charge that generals are unlikely to make good political leaders, he hedged this by observing that 'a military man can only govern if he is able to throw his inner general out of the window, renounce violence and submit himself to the law'.[37]) While the book is repetitive and much of it a restatement of Perón's doctrinal dictates elsewhere, and it glosses over major political and economic errors in a lofty manner, it contains a largely accurate and impressive list of some of his government's achievements in terms of workers' rights, infrastructure and education with which the 'Liberating Revolution' would never compete. Lacking money to pay a secretary, Perón would tell a journalist that he had callouses on his hands from typing.

Yet even now Perón was not entirely without more entertaining company. While in Panama he met a 27-year-old woman from Chicago, Eleanor Freeman, who worked for a restaurant chain and was on holiday in Panama. Perón would refer to her affectionately as *la gringuita* and they were frequently seen dining at a local restaurant; she would help him with his English and he would seek to improve her Spanish. The only photo of such a dinner shows a stylish, attractive and smiling young woman. Perón would later speak of her attractiveness but described the relationship on his part as 'a warm friendship' although he suggested that she had something more substantial in mind and that this pleased him. He would praise her discretion and charm but described the relationship as 'excessively platonic'.[38] Those around Perón would coincide in describing her as attractive, educated and charming; had the relationship prospered, one can only assume

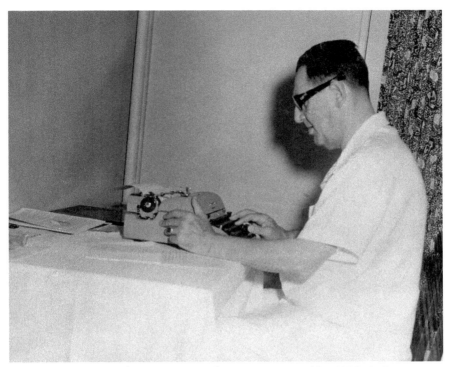

Figure 12 Perón typing his memoirs in exile in Panama, 1956 (OFF/AFP via Getty Images)

that much subsequent history would have been different. Perón's later secretary, Rodolfo Martínez, who met her in Panama would describe Eleanor as 'if not the only, at least one of the very few people I met close to Perón in whom I saw no exaggerated ambitions, ignoble interests or shameful ends.'[39] But Eleanor, although she extended her holidays somewhat, succumbed to pressure from her parents to return home. They in turn were reportedly under pressure from US authorities to present an allegation of kidnap against Perón, whose relationship with Nelly Rivas perhaps lent itself to such accusations (although Eleanor herself, while much younger than Perón, was certainly not an adolescent). In order to avoid any further difficulties, Eleanor would depart for Chicago, leaving Perón alone in Panama. But not for very long.

Chapter 13

ISABEL

Un Otoño te trajo..! Tu nombre era María,
y nunca supe nada de tu rumbo infeliz ...

Si eras como el paisaje de la Melancolía,
que llovía ... llovía, sobre la calle gris ...

An autumn brought you! Your name was María
And I never knew anything of your unhappy route.
You were like a landscape of melancholy that rained ... rained on the grey street.
María (tango), Cátulo Castillo and Aníbal Troilo[1]

Most improbably, María Estela Martínez, usually known as Isabel or Isabelita, would be the first woman president of a republic, despite having few apparent political talents beyond discretion. Discretion has perhaps been her signal characteristic (together with an apparent blankness that has sometimes been interpreted as stupidity and sometimes as astuteness). Her discretion allowed her to carve out a place at Perón's side for the last years of his life and to become both a companion and a successor of sorts. Once she departed the political scene, following a disastrous and brief presidency and several years as prisoner of the military government that succeeded her, she would retire to Madrid and make virtually no public comment about anything for the remainder of her life. She has published no memoir, given almost no interviews and has left few undeniable biographical facts available. Even during her short presidency the normal brief biography usually made available to the press by the Casa Rosada never appeared. She has often been sneered at, despised and blamed for the catastrophe of the 1970s from which Argentina has yet to recover fully, although perhaps more as a scapegoat than as an actual evil mastermind. It is perhaps convenient to place the blame squarely on the head of one person who commands little respect – as it has been convenient to blame Perón for Argentina's many woes, in many of which his role was marginal at best – thus liberating millions of others of culpability. A figure lacking in warmth or spontaneity as well as charisma or political gifts, she is an easy target; whereas Evita generated passionate love and passionate hate, Isabel generated condescension. For a woman who reached the presidency of her country, she remains remarkably unknown and indecipherable. She came seemingly from nowhere and, after the trauma of the 1970s, returned there.

Yet this implausible first woman president has been at least in some respects mischaracterized, by the Peronist faithful who initially saw her as his messenger, those who saw her as usurping Evita's rightful position, and by the anti-Peronists who derided her for her supposed background as a cabaret dancer, comparing her with Evita as yet another disreputable woman who seduced a weak and easily led Perón. (Indeed, Isabel has suffered by both comparisons with Evita, whether as a similar sort of 'fallen woman' or as the upstart who did not deserve to be mentioned in the same breath, who was often received by chants of 'there is only one Evita'.) In many respects, however, she had more in common with Aurelia Tizón – Potota – whose middle-class background and discretion should have made her an obvious choice as the wife of an army officer.

María Estela Martínez Cartas was born in the provincial capital of La Rioja on 4 February 1931, the sixth and last child of Carmelo Martínez and María Josefa Cartas. La Rioja is a remote and highly traditional Hispanic and Catholic province; even the provincial capital was small, hidebound and dull, with few pastimes beyond keeping an eye on – and gossiping about – the neighbours. The Martínez Cartas family was respectable and middle class: Carmelo was an official and eventually the manager of the local branch of the Mortgage Bank, and his children were raised to take their place in respectable middle-class society.

When María Estela was three years old the family moved to Buenos Aires, to a house in the Belgrano district, where she would begin primary school. The few memories of her are as a quiet child who had few friends and played by herself at home. Her father died when she was seven, a blow to her security and also to the family's fortunes; while still middle-class in habits and thought, the family's economic situation became difficult and her older siblings (two sisters and three brothers) were forced to go out to work. Yet this does not initially seem to have affected María Estela's education, and in addition to primary school she also continued to receive piano and French lessons – skills clearly aimed at ensuring that she would be a good candidate for a respectable young man when the time came and would have a secure future as a wife and mother. She is said to have practised piano by the open window looking onto the street, and when other children came to listen to have offered to teach them to play. Yet this would never become a job or a revenue stream, at a time when the family could ill afford her lessons. She finished primary school and may have begun secondary school but does not appear to have advanced very far. As in the case of Evita, the fact of having only a primary school education did not make her altogether unusual among women of her generation, for whom the basics of education were generally considered sufficient and the skills of housekeeping, managing money and looking after children were more crucial; the number of women who had greater professional or academic ambitions was relatively limited.

When she was seventeen years old, María Estela would leave the family home for reasons that are not entirely clear. It has been suggested that her older siblings resented the fact that she was not working to contribute to the family budget and that she resented their pressure. There seems to have been little in her deportment up until that time to suggest that she would take a more unconventional route.

Yet after the split with her family (a rift which never healed), she approached a spiritist group, the San Pantaleón school, run by a married couple, José Cresto and Isabel Zoila Gómez. They virtually adopted the young woman, who began to take an active role in the practice of learning to communicate with the dead. She also seemingly discovered another vocation, that of dance, and began to study dance and eventually to participate in small touring troupes (authorized by José Cresto *in loco parentis*). In 1951, at the somewhat advanced age of twenty, she would enrol in the National Dance School, although she remained there for only one year. According to María Sáenz Quesada, she received only middling marks for her performance and the teachers thought she was too old to begin studying dance.[2]

It is difficult to deduce how María Estela made the journey from drab respectability to spiritism and dreams of a dance career, but it can only have been a more interesting life, and one in which, perhaps like Evita, she hoped to stand out in her art and 'be someone'. Nevertheless, throughout her life she maintained her both middle-class education and discretion and Catholic faith, which somehow managed to co-exist peacefully with her spiritist beliefs.

At the age of twenty-two María Estela took the stage name Isabel Martínez, a tribute to Isabel Zoila, and began working with a small company that offered folkloric and Spanish dance performances. At this age she was small, slim, straight-backed, with light brown hair and hazel eyes and a pleasant smile and demeanour. She was also, as described a few years later by one of Perón's clique, as a 'young woman without youth',[3] a strangely stiff and wooden figure who even as a young woman often had an expressionless, masklike face sometimes interpreted as stupidity. Subsequent claims by detractors that she was in fact a stripper are difficult to reconcile with Isabel's persona; neither physically nor in personality did she seem in any way seductive, sexy, suggestive or even warm or open. She had a wary quality and a closed expression that suggested a very shy young woman passed over at a dance rather than the 'scarlet woman' imagined by the anti-Peronist rumour mill.

After beginning a regional tour in Montevideo with a Spanish dance company, Isabel left the group for reasons that are unclear but joined another, based in Chile, with which she took part in a tour including Peru, Ecuador and Colombia. In Medellín the group closed down and she joined a folklore group run by a dancer called Joe Herald. The group performed at a low-end cabaret in Caracas before arriving in Panama in late 1955, shortly after Perón, where they performed at the Happy Land cabaret. The various photos extant show the dancers wearing folklore costumes at times and skimpier and more suggestive costumes at others, suggesting that as a low-end troupe working in low-end facilities, they performed whatever sort of dance was required.

From here the story of Isabel and her relationship with Perón becomes even stranger. There are various versions of how they met: either Perón went to see the show and then invited the troupe to a Christmas Eve barbecue on the beach, or she was introduced to him by the former Argentine ambassador, or she herself approached him. According to some versions, after their first meeting she turned up at the door with her suitcase and rang the bell. Perón and his small entourage ignored her in the hope that she would go away but she remained there; at dinnertime Perón relented and invited her in. She reportedly told him that she had left Joe Herald's troupe because he had tried to force her to entertain men and encourage them to buy drinks (the sideline of *copera* or *alternadora* could be a relatively good second income for poorly paid dancers, who would receive up to 50 per cent of the price of the drinks the clients bought) and that she now had nowhere to go. She offered herself to Perón as a secretary, although she had no typing skills and Perón could not afford to pay an assistant. In any case, Isabel and her suitcase stayed. She and Perón would move to the former ambassador's flat where they lived together, but in separate bedrooms, Isabel in the maid's room. Isaac Gilaberte the chauffeur and another Argentine exile, Ramón Landajo, made up the rest of the menage, which would move subsequently to a chalet in Colón.

In his own frequently unreliable memoirs, Perón would later say that he had met Isabel following the folklore performance and that he had noticed the 'little, fragile-looking girl' and in particular her 'sharp chin, which signifies firmness, and her gentle and sweet but curious eyes'. According to him, she reminded him that they had met once before, at a general store near San Vicente, where she had been with her mother as a little girl. 'She is an obliging and silent little person who knows how to smile inwardly, is self-assured and only appears fragile, ... she is not a frightened little mouse nor a sly cat, she is a beautiful woman. The ballet continued its tour but Isabelita stayed with me forever.' He noted yet again that he had always needed a woman's companionship, and that he had no particular preferences as to type, except that he liked 'useful women'.[4] This she would certainly become, albeit within limitations. In a slightly different vein, and in line with the story that she had left the troupe and had nowhere else to go, he would observe pages later that she was depressed and had stayed behind in a *pensión*, and that he had gone himself to persuade her to come and join his household as she had offered to do after their first meeting.

At least in the initial stages, Isabel remained decorous and unobtrusive, providing refreshments for visitors and retiring to allow the political conversations to flow freely (unlike Evita, who intervened from the first). In part this may have reflected her insecurity as to her place in the household, not least given the suspicions she aroused in them. According to many sources, she was suspected of being an agent sent by either the Argentine authorities or the CIA to monitor Perón's activities. Landajo would later say that Perón had told him that he had been warned of her coming by informers in Buenos Aires and ordered Landajo and Gilaberte to keep a close but discreet watch on her.[5] According to Landajo, Joe Herald was an Argentine hired by the intelligence services to find a woman whom he could introduce into Perón's household, and that Perón was immediately suspicious both of the presence of this middle-class woman in a third-rate dance troupe and her various 'cover stories' (including, supposedly, a claim that she had left the family home to avoid being married off to an army officer) but allowed her into his household under surveillance.[6]

Landajo would later say that Isabel would tiptoe downstairs at night when they were all in bed, apparently to look through Perón's correspondence and documents, and would later meet other agents when out doing the shopping. Perón continued to send Gilaberte to report on her movements, and also apparently used her contacts to send misleading information to the Argentine authorities. Subsequently, she would reportedly admit to Perón that she had been sent by the Argentine services and had acted under duress, owing to threats against her family. Another observer, Rodolfo Martínez, would describe her as entirely motivated by 'cold, calculated and exaggerated ambition'[7] and also remarked on her cold, mechanical gestures and tendency to 'declaim' like a third-rate actress – qualities that would be noted far more widely when, as president, her shellacked hair, robotic gestures and monotonous, high-pitched and accusing tone would be on display to the entire nation. Martínez also noted that, as he had done in the past, Perón allowed her to become involved in political discussions far beyond her understanding and to take an increasingly dominant role in his household despite continuing suspicions.

Yet Perón let her remain – initially, perhaps, because he thought it better to keep her close by where she could be watched – and the relationship would become more established and more affectionate. Perón enjoyed the company of women and did not enjoy living without one; in this case the woman in question was young, attractive, discreet and reasonably well educated in the traditional sense. Moreover, the cohabitation and routine of life seemed to have made Isabel increasingly part of the Perón 'camp', an ally rather than an adversary. They would take walks and dine together and play cards in the evening while listening to music – activities perhaps better suited to a person of his age than hers. Arguably they shared an interest in spiritism and a predilection for discipline and moderation; as a dancer Isabel was also careful about her diet and inclined to physical rigour and training.

They also shared the perpetual nervousness of not knowing whether or when an attack might come; it was well known that elements of the Argentine government were anxious to remove Perón from the scene permanently. In early 1956 they were informed that Argentine agents were in the area planning to assassinate Perón; Isabel, armed with a revolver, joined the men in keeping watch and preparing to fight off any attack. As it became clearer that Isabel's loyalties, whatever they were, were shifting to Perón, he became less distrustful and more fond. Early that year he would write to Rodolfo Martínez that 'she plays the piano, sings, dances, cooks, looks after the house and makes our life more agreeable' – in other words, the kind of pleasant domesticity he had enjoyed with Potota during a less stressful time in his life and must surely have valued now.[8] They would sometimes be seen dining out together, when observers described her as 'a very quiet blonde, who looked more like a lady than a cabaret dancer'.[9] From her perspective, for a young woman who had lost her father as a child and who had looked to José Cresto as a surrogate, Perón might have represented a kind of *uber* father figure – a man who had been the strongman and then president of Argentina since Isabel was in school, and also one who had been married to Evita, whom Isabel always professed to admire above all others. In many ways he must have seemed a 'good catch' and indeed a far more prestigious one than she could ever have hoped for.

However oddly the relationship had begun, and however ill-assorted they might have seemed, given the age gap of some thirty-eight years and Isabel's seeming lack of intellectual or political prowess, she had clearly become important enough to Perón as a stabilizing factor in his life to ensure that he would not leave her. In mid-1956, when the Organization of American States held its General Assembly in Panama, de facto Argentine President Pedro Aramburu put pressure on the Panamanian authorities to ensure that Perón was not in the country during his visit. Under duress, Perón made a week-long visit to Nicaragua during the General Assembly, during which time Isabel remained in Colón at his insistence, seemingly fearing that she would be abandoned. However, he returned within the week with the news that they would be moving from Panama to Caracas, on the invitation of Venezuelan President Marcos Pérez Jiménez. Perón and Isabel travelled to Caracas together (seated separately on the plane for the sake of discretion, although she managed to be photographed by journalists, making the relationship public). Once in Caracas they would move into Rodolfo Martínez's flat together. Shortly thereafter Perón became seriously ill with pneumonia, possibly due to the constant reported threats on his life; again, Isabel would stay with him constantly in hospital and would become increasingly indispensable to his life and comfort. So much so, in fact, that she was able to ward off another potential threat – the arrival of Eleanor Freeman, who travelled to Caracas with the apparent intention of rekindling the relationship with Perón.

The fact that Isabel's anger was sufficient to convince Perón to break off the relationship makes clear that she was now a fixture in his life. Perón would describe Isabel's jealousy as 'incalculable', and said that 'she made so many scenes … that I had to distance Eleanor permanently from my life'.[10] Some of his intimates remained suspicious and cool towards her; Perón's former ambassador to Washington, Hipólito Paz, who met her in Caracas in May 1956, would say that 'her welcome to me is amiable. However, during the course of lunch I could not help noticing the coldness that she tries to hide with an attempt at a smile that breaks down at the corner of her mouth.'[11] Perón also seemingly used her in the same way he had sometimes used Evita, distancing those he distrusted by claiming that Isabel did not wish to have them around. But she perhaps represented a degree of comfort, companionship and care during a difficult, uncertain and impecunious time of his life, just as he represented a degree of comfort, companionship and protection for a young woman who had little of those things. Her very odd road from the provincial middle class through seances, folklore and apparent espionage had seen her established as a leading player in a new real-life drama who, whatever her lack of skills for the role, would not leave the stage for another twenty years.

Chapter 14

UNSETTLED EXILE

Si arrastré por este mundo el dolor de haber sido, y el dolor de ya no ser ....
*Ahora, cuesta abajo en mi rodada, las ilusiones pasadas yo no las puedo
arrancar.*
Sueño con el pasado que añoro, el tiempo viejo que lloro y que nunca volverá.

*I carried through the world the pain of having been, and the pain of no longer
being ....*
Now, going downhill, I can't root out the illusions of the past.
*I dream of the past that I yearn for, the old times I weep for that will never
return.*
Cuesta abajo (tango), Carlos Gardel and Alfredo Le Pera[1]

If some aspects of Perón's life were becoming slightly more settled during his stay in Panama (despite the continuing threat of assassination), the same could not be said for the country he had left behind. As noted earlier, Lonardi was strongly anti-Perón, but not entirely anti-Peronist per se, and he was sympathetic to many of the economic and social policies adopted during the 1943–1946 military government in particular. However, his attempt at 'neither victors nor vanquished' was far too conciliatory for the liking of the Navy and for many in the Army, and on 13 November he was forced out of office and replaced by General Pedro Eugenio Aramburu.

Aramburu, as noted, took a far harder line against the Peronists than Lonardi, ordering the intervention of the CGT, replacing its leaders with naval officers and putting many political and union leaders in prison. His government openly sided with the landed oligarchy that had been marginalized if not supplanted during the Perón government, and with an attempt to return to the old agro-export model which, by seeking to reduce the emphasis on industry, also sought to reduce the influence of the industrial working classes. Economic policies such as a sharp devaluation and a string of privatizations also aimed to redistribute wealth away from the working classes and back to the landed elites.

On 9 June 1956 two generals, Juan José del Valle and Raúl Tanco, attempted to mount a coup against Aramburu and call new elections. The two were not especially committed Peronists, and Valle's call for elections made no mention of whether Perón would be allowed to participate. Yet the repression of the attempted rising would be the most violent experienced in Argentina to date. Military intelligence was aware of the conspiracy and it was quickly snuffed out and most of the participants detained. Martial law was declared and, under its terms, the officers involved were summarily shot, with anyone involved in any further act of rebellion subject to the same fate; a total of twenty-seven people would be executed. Valle handed himself over in a bid to stop the bloodshed, and was executed on a site that is now a public park in Palermo. Tanco and others took refuge in the Haitian embassy, from which they were removed by troops in a violation of international law; Aramburu was forced to apologize and allow them to return to the embassy, from where Tanco would make his way to Caracas.

Perón showed little sympathy for the attempted uprising, which he referred to contemptuously as a *chirinada* (one of his preferred terms of derision, implying a cock-up and referring to Sergeant Chirino, who had been in charge of the clumsy capture and killing of the outlaw Juan Moreira in Lobos in 1874). Yet he was aware that it offered him potential opportunities. Although overt opposition to the government was limited in the wake of the executions, they represented another source of resentment against a government that had repressed his supporters, barred Peronist trade unionists from holding union posts and imprisoned a number of important figures. Indeed, 'the Liberating Revolution [would] suffer the boomerang effect of its own excesses',[2] increasing nostalgia for Perón and his government among the broad sectors that had benefited from its policies and had not mourned the loss of democratic freedoms they had seldom enjoyed before.

Perón himself, together with Isabel, would arrive in Caracas in August 1956; Gilaberte and the poodles would travel by car and arrive some days later. As was often the case, he was rapidly surrounded by Argentine exiles (including Tanco) and hangers-on, notably Rodolfo Martínez (known as Martincho) who would host the couple and then designate himself as Perón's spokesman. He was soon rivalled by an army captain and Perón's former aide-de-camp, Pablo Vicente, who would become Perón's assistant and begin to plot Martincho's downfall; when it came, he would write a vindictive book, *Grandezas y miserias de Perón* (Perón's Greatness and Wretchedness) containing substantial if disputed information about the early months of Perón's exile. While Martínez's book is vengeful and contains many racist, anti-Semitic and sexist observations, at least some of the detail he includes as to the power games and intrigues within Perón's household is doubtless fairly accurate and highlights Perón's continuing preference for allowing his associates to cannibalize each other as a means of dominating them. However, arguably as he aged his ability to manage these running battles declined and the fallout would gradually become more extensive and damaging.

The fracas within his inner circle, the number of dubious hangers-on in the outer circle and the generally fraught circumstances of life in somewhat penurious exile did little to improve Perón's frame of mind and interviewers often described him as bitter, vengeful or simply out of touch with reality. Yet in general terms he again seems to have adapted well to the routine of a modest existence in a two-bedroom house in Caracas. His routine as usual included an austere diet, an afternoon nap, walks to the supermarket or to a bar or café, writing and receiving visitors. Often he was accompanied by a new member of the household: Manuel Sorolla, an Argentine sergeant who claimed to have been imprisoned after the Liberating Revolution, escaped and to have made his way to Caracas to see Perón. Sorolla would be in charge of maintaining Perón's Opel car and also accompanying him on his walks, often carrying his gun.

Perón and his household continued to carry guns in fear of a possible assassination attempt. This came to pass on 25 May 1957, at the hands of Sorolla himself. Sorolla was in fact working with the head of Argentine army intelligence, Colonel Héctor Cabanillas; the two had been responsible for transporting Eva Perón's body out of the country under a false name and burying it in Milan. Cabanillas arranged for Sorolla to receive the bomb, which was to be set to explode when Perón next rode in his car on 25 May, an Argentine national holiday. Sorolla planted the car bomb and then departed on the pretext that his mother in Buenos Aires was dying. When Gilaberte took the car out to buy supplies for a holiday barbecue, the car bomb destroyed the car and neighbouring windows but miraculously caused no serious injuries.

Unsurprisingly, Perón felt under threat and believed (rightly) that the Argentine government was putting pressure on the Venezuelans to revoke his asylum. The Venezuelan president, General Marcos Pérez Jiménez, was a long-standing military dictator kept in office through repression, corruption and the vast revenues supplied by Venezuela's oil sector. Perón was critical of his lack of social programmes and the two men had chilly relations at best, although Pérez Jiménez was unwilling to bow to Argentine pressure. The risk that he would be turfed out was limited, but his feeling of insecurity persisted.

However, and despite the fact that the Venezuelan secret police monitored his political activities, it was during his stay in Caracas that Perón would again begin to engage seriously in (meddling in) the Argentine political process. Notwithstanding his evident anger at having been allowed to depart unceremoniously with so little public resistance, it would appear that the return to the game of political chess lifted his mood somewhat. Having always preferred playing the political game to administering the bureaucracy in office, Perón's reaction seems to have been in line with the Sherlock Holmesian 'the game's afoot' enthusiasm. Although events in Argentina were in no way propitious for any thought of return, the hardline approach of the Aramburu government was generating nostalgia and resistance, while the removal of the union leaders in place at the time of Perón's fall would see their gradual replacement with a new generation of far more combative and more autonomous figures. In 1957 the CGT would split between Peronist and anti-Peronist unions, with the former, grouped in the so-called 62 Organizations, taking an increasingly dominant position in organized labour.

Sensing a shift towards resistance, Perón would appoint the imprisoned former legislator John William Cooke as his representative in Argentina (although, typically, he would constantly undermine him by communicating through different channels, often with contradictory messages). On 2 November 1956 Perón sent Cooke a letter directed also to 'the whole Peronist movement' authorizing Cooke 'to represent me in all acts or political action. In that respect his decision will be my decision and his word mine.' Perón even went so far as to name Cooke as his successor in the event of his death. However, only a few months later, on 5 April 1957 he authorized his last foreign minister, Ildefonso Cavagna Martínez, 'to act in my name and representation in all the political and personal affairs necessary to carry forward the ends of the movement'.[3] It would not be the only such additional 'anointment'.

Cooke, a highly intelligent and radical thinker and the son of the former foreign minister and diplomat Juan Isaac Cooke, was in prison in the southern city of Río Gallegos in early 1957 together with other important figures such as Jorge Antonio, Héctor Cámpora, former CGT leader José Espejo and ALN leader Guillermo Patricio Kelly, when Antonio concocted a plan to escape. On 17 March the party managed to drug the other prisoners and reduce the guard on duty, finally crossing into Chile and asking for asylum. All were arrested but with the exception of Kelly were deemed to be political prisoners and released. (Kelly would subsequently escape from a Santiago prison in women's clothes provided by Perón's one-time Uruguayan collaborator Blanca Luz Brum.)

Cooke began coordinating the Peronist resistance from Santiago, but rapidly ran up against the difficulties implied by Perón's deviousness and his own qualities: aged only thirty-seven, Cooke was a middle-class intellectual and left-wing ideologue whose authority with the trade union movement was minimal. His conviction that Peronism was a left-wing movement did not sit well with either the trade union movement or the realities on the ground, and his belief that the traditional leftist parties had become an elitist and 'anti-popular' movement, if not entirely inaccurate, did nothing to help him approach other groups that in theory might have been allies in recovering a working-class and anti-imperialist discourse. Despite his considerable and ever-expanding corpulence, metaphorically he also carried little weight with many of Perón's long-term associates; speaking in 2004 Antonio would say that 'Cooke had a great relationship with the resistance. I had a great relationship with Perón.' Probably accurately, Antonio also noted that Perón 'used [Cooke]. He distrusted him very much. Cooke's ideology disturbed Perón. Perón was not a communist or anything like it. And Cooke's tendency was very leftist. Perón used people according to the circumstances and according to his strategy.'[4]

The voluminous correspondence between the two and Perón's own actions would tend to support Antonio's comments. Cooke doubtless proved useful in organizing the clandestine groups that operated outside the party to maintain national resistance through strikes, acts of sabotage and other distracting but not game-changing activities. However, these activities could only be useful to Perón up to a point, beyond which they risked becoming counter-productive. Moreover, Cooke's constant criticism of the 'reactionary' and 'bureaucratic' leadership within the party implied that he was at loggerheads with many of those on whom Perón depended to maintain a party and trade union structure in place. Perón would alternately encourage and dismiss Cooke's more radical plans, usually in vague enough terms that he could maintain deniability if things went wrong. Only in later years would he become more concrete in his rejection of Cooke's views, insisting that 'it is necessary to maintain unity at whatever cost …. A position that dissociates and creates anarchy cannot obtain anything.'[5] For his part, Cooke would insist on believing that Perón had become an ideological prisoner of imperialist forces, not an entirely credible proposition. At the same time, Perón maintained substantial flows of correspondence with many others of widely differing political views, giving them all to understand that he was in agreement with them and would back them as factors of power.

Perón's own machinations reflected changes in the domestic political environment in Argentina, which contained both the opportunity for him to extend his influence and the risk that he could lose influence to others. The Aramburu government continued to promise elections in the near future, although it was clear that the Peronist party would be proscribed. This opened the prospect of an advance by a 'neo-Peronist' formation based on the concept of 'Peronism without Perón' – an obviously unappealing concept for the man himself. Those beginning to explore this possibility included former Peronist heavyweights such as Juan Atilio Bramuglia and Domingo Mercante, the latter still in exile in Uruguay. A newer potential threat would also come from the ascendant metalworkers' leader, Augusto Vandor, a pragmatic and talented figure whose weight within his own union and the 62 Organizations was far greater than that of Cooke.

At the same time, in early 1957 the UCR fragmented into two separate parties, the Intransigent Radical Civic Union (UCRI), led by Arturo Frondizi, and the People's Radical Civic Union (UCRP), led by Ricardo Balbín. The latter was more closely associated with the Aramburu government and therefore deeply unattractive to both Perón and his supporters, but the UCRI under Frondizi began to make overtures to the unions in particular, despite Frondizi's earlier vocal opposition to Perón and to his plans to attract foreign investment into the oil sector in particular. This would open up the prospect of reaching some kind of an understanding with an electorally viable option that did not represent Peronism without Perón. (In a patently insincere comment, in 1958 Perón would write to another of his interlocutors whom he played off against Cooke, Oscar Albrieu, that 'I am and have been the first Peronist without Perón. Nobody can have a greater interest than I in the appearance of a young Peronist who can replace me.' The only drawback, according to him, was that no individual nor organization was yet capable of doing so and that it was thus his duty to continue. 'If I had accepted Peronism without Perón I would have found a comfortable way to free myself from my commitments to the people and the Peronists, but I would have liquidated Peronism.'[6])

A key opportunity to test his strength came Perón's way in July 1957, when the government called elections to a constituent assembly to reform the 1949 Constitution. Perón ordered his supporters to cast blank votes, and over 2.1 million did so, outnumbering the votes cast for the UCRP by around 2,000 nationwide; the UCRI received some 1.8 million. The result, a disturbing reminder for the government of how little the Liberating Revolution had succeeded in undermining Perón's authority, set Balbín and Frondizi up as the obvious contenders for the presidential elections called for 23 February 1958. It also set up Perón as kingmaker and potential spoiler; a new blank vote would seriously undermine the legitimacy of the winner (who would certainly be Balbín in that scenario), while the backing of his supporters would likely see their beneficiary reach the presidency. In this context, Perón was unwilling to back Bramuglia's candidacy outside the party but was willing to pursue negotiations to see which of the alternatives could prove the most beneficial.

With any deal with Balbín out of the question, Frondizi was in little doubt as to the need to strike a deal with some of Perón's more sympathetic interlocutors. His economic adviser Rogelio Frigerio would become the key backer of a deal and the key negotiator; on the Peronist side, Ramón Prieto would take the prime role, meeting not only Frigerio but also Cooke in Santiago and Perón in Caracas. Cooke himself was opposed to any plan to shift Peronist votes in favour of Frondizi, preferring 'insurrection', a plan in which Perón and many of his older followers had no faith. Cooke remained adamant that votes for Frondizi represented supporters lost to any 'national revolution' and defined Frondizi's movement and any national front with the Peronists as 'artificial creations in doctrinal and revolutionary terms'.[7] Perón, of course, was not a devotee of either doctrine or revolution, and adopted a somewhat ambiguous line with Cooke, apparently in a bid to force Cooke to take charge of any pact and to take the blame if it failed.

Perón, who as ever continued to play both sides for as long as possible, constantly giving his contacts to understand that he agreed with their positions whatever they were, finally called Frigerio to Caracas at the beginning of 1958. By this time he perhaps realized that another order to cast blank votes – as Cooke demanded – might not be as widely adhered to in a presidential election, thus undermining his authority, with many of his supporters already seeing Frondizi as potentially opening the door to a gradual return to electoral access and economic policies more favourable to labour.

Here, however, Perón's electioneering activities in Argentina ran up against another unexpected development, and the drama surrounding his talks with Frigerio came primarily from outside. A coup attempt against Pérez Jiménez was launched in January, prompting hundreds of arrests in reprisal. On 20 and 21 January a series of violent strikes added pressure on the regime, prompting the military to give Pérez Jiménez an ultimatum, and on 22 January he left the country for exile in the Dominican Republic. His departure was almost not enough to avert a civil war; the backlash was swift as mobs began pursuing officials and others linked to the fallen ruler.

Among those targeted was Perón himself, after unsubstantiated newspaper reports claimed that he and Patricio Kelly had been involved in Pérez Jiménez's repression of the opposition. With mobs on the streets seeking revenge, this represented a greater threat to his life than the somewhat ineffectual attempts previously orchestrated from Buenos Aires. He went into hiding until the Dominican ambassador offered help, allowing Perón, Isabel and an entourage including Gilaberte, Cooke and Kelly to take refuge in the embassy. As they waited tensely inside, the following day a large crowd assembled outside the embassy, but the ambassador managed to persuade them to depart. Later that day Perón was informed by the new government that he would be allowed to travel to the

Dominican Republic alone, an imposition that raised fears over his safety and indeed that of the contingent still in the embassy. Finally, on 27 January and accompanied by the ambassador, Perón flew to Ciudad Trujillo.

Several days later he was joined by Isabel, Cooke and Perón's secretary Américo Barrios; the Argentine radio and television presenter Roberto Galán remained in Caracas with the poodles and promised to bring them as soon as it was safe to do so. Here again, Perón moved from an expensive beach hotel to a more modest one and then finally to a house owned by the son of Dominican dictator Rafael Trujillo, who helped him to cover the rent. For the first time since leaving Buenos Aires, Perón was in a country where he was welcomed by the government and felt himself both free to pursue his ends without interference and free from fears over his physical security. Trujillo assigned him security and himself approved visa applications from Argentina, blocking questionable visitors and allowing supporters free access. Trujillo and Perón would also dine together and Perón would become friendly, for reasons that are not entirely clear, with the dictator's playboy sons. Indeed, the warmth of his welcome and his amicable relations with Trujillo are somewhat surprising, given the deeply repressive and grotesquely extravagant nature of the regime and its total lack of social programmes. (Trujillo would inform Perón that Peronist-type policies were impossible in the Dominican Republic because the population was largely black and required paternalism rather than social welfare, an outrageous explanation that Perón accepted although it did not stop him lecturing his host on social welfare policy.)

The self-indulgent and predatory Trujillo was a by far crueller and more despotic ruler than even Perón's adversaries had claimed him to be, and it is notable that even after Trujillo and his son Ramfis were dead Perón continued to speak well of them. It suggests that he remained grateful for a warm welcome, security and some financial assistance and thus refused to look beyond at the more sordid and repressive elements of the Trujillo regime. This is in line with Perón's lifelong habit of seeing what he wanted to see and of refusing to be convinced of what he did not: having been impressed by some doubtlessly impressive achievements in Mussolini's Italy, he would later refuse to condemn its excesses, and equally he would seemingly find it impossible to accept that interesting and accomplished professionals with prior Nazi links might have been mixed up in anything unsavoury. It was one of his more negative characteristics, and it was one that often prevented him from learning lessons that his intelligence would otherwise have grasped and profited from.

In the light of his greater security (both physical and financial), Perón appeared more relaxed in the Dominican Republic, despite being uncomfortable in the Caribbean heat. He had greater freedom of movement, a small house in which the poodles could be accommodated, free access to his supporters and the time to return to leisure activities. Notably, he was able to exercise his passion for both sports and pedagogy, teaching Isabel to fence and to ride a motorcycle, both of which they did together. For a man in his mid-60s whose health had been the subject of much rumour and conjecture, he appeared to be in fine physical fettle (far better, in fact, than he had appeared in the final year or so of his presidency).

This more relaxed and sporting existence did not, however, imply that his change of lifestyle and residence represented more than a temporary interruption of his political activities. Not long after his arrival in the Dominican Republic, Prieto arrived with a copy of the so-called Perón-Frondizi Pact, the fruit of his Caracas talks with Frigerio, supposedly accepted by Frondizi. The contents would remain disputed: Frigerio would claim that Frondizi had agreed to no specific commitments, while Frondizi would later make the implausible claim that he had been unaware of Frigerio's dealings. Under the terms of the supposed agreement, Perón would instruct his supporters to withdraw any candidacies and vote for candidates best placed to reverse the policies of the Aramburu regime. Frondizi, for his part, apparently agreed to return to Perón's economic policies, end legal actions against the former president and his supporters, return the body of Evita to her husband and return the assets of the Eva Perón Foundation to it. Moreover, the pact called for a new constitutional reform and new general elections. All of these demands would clearly be unacceptable to the military and create a Frondizi presidency that was deeply fragile from the outset. Yet in electoral terms the pact was effective: Frondizi received 4 million votes in the presidential elections, to 2.4 million for Balbín, and the UCRI won every provincial governorship, the entire Senate and a greater-than-two-thirds majority in the Lower House.

Frondizi would be sworn in on 1 May 1958, representing a return to electoral democracy but one born with the seeds of its own destruction already sprouting within. For the military, the obvious success of the Peronist vote in the elections was an unacceptable threat, and rumours of a coup began to circulate before Frondizi had even taken office. On the other side, the new president was in no position to make good on many of the promises he had made to Perón (of which he would attempt to deny knowledge). A highly intelligent, cerebral and professional politician, Frondizi must have known how weak a hand he had been dealt, unless hubris prompted him to believe that his intelligence would somehow allow him to find solutions that did not exist. Lacking solid support from either the military or the working classes, Frondizi began his presidency with only narrow room for manoeuvre that tightened like a noose almost immediately. The looming economic crisis forced him to pursue foreign investment in the oil sector, precisely the policy for which he himself had attacked Perón only a few years earlier, and his decision to appeal to the IMF had not only the same anti-nationalist image as the entry of foreign oil companies, but it implied austerity measures that would place greater strain on the working classes.

Whether or not they were orchestrated by Perón and by Cooke, strikes and protests mounted through the rest of 1958 and into 1959; Frondizi declared a state of siege in November 1958 and was forced by the military to dismiss his economy minister, Frigerio. The perception at least that Perón was driving labour unrest undermined any inclination Frondizi might have had to seek accord, had he even had the ability to implement much in the way of policy. In July 1959 Perón made public the text of the so-called pact which Frondizi continued to deny, prompting demands for his resignation. (Given that Frigerio had finally admitted to the deal, it is clear that Frondizi was aware of what his deputy had committed to, even if technically he might have signed no piece of paper in a bid to maintain deniability.)

Labour unrest was a factor bolstering the leadership claims of the metalworker Augusto Vandor, whose star rose in 1959 in much the same period as Cooke's faded. Following the Cuban Revolution Cooke would relocate to Havana (after having attempted to press for a similar revolution in Argentina), where he died in 1968. Vandor met Perón in Ciudad Trujillo, and the relationship rapidly became one of wary respect. Both probably sensed early on that it could easily become one of rivalry.

Following the success of the Cuban Revolution, Cooke was not the only Peronist who saw in the ageing leader a potential figurehead for the wider revolution they hoped would soon sweep Latin America. The attempt to make Peronism a more region-wide phenomenon had little historical basis: despite Perón's much-vaunted Third Position and supposed desire to extend his movement's influence more widely, as president he had travelled very little beyond a 1953 visit to Chile, and his relationship to Latin America had been, in line with Argentina's historical position more generally, somewhat distant. The only relatively serious effort at spreading the gospel of Peronist-type trade unions across the region, a supposedly pan-American union confederation known by the acronym ATLAS, existed more on paper than in practice. The fact that he was now living in a country run by an outstandingly repressive dictator potentially a target for revolution also undermined this position. Nevertheless, the image would take hold in some sectors, helped later by Perón's subsequent writings in exile, *La hora de los pueblos* (The Hour of the Peoples) and *América Latina: ahora o nunca* (Latin America: Now or Never), which emphasized a far more radical line than he pursued in power.

The Cuban Revolution also had more far-reaching implications for Perón than the ideological direction and new homeland it gave to Cooke. The deposed Cuban dictator Fulgencio Batista also arrived in Ciudad Trujillo, increasing the number of controversial exiles in residence and prompting Cuban pressures on the Dominican Republic. More widely, the political climate in Latin America became more rarefied, and there were signs that change could also come to Ciudad Trujillo. With no obvious host countries now available in Latin America, Perón sought asylum in Spain; the move had the blessing of the Argentine government, happy to see him removed further away. All signs are that General Francisco Franco was not pleased to receive the visa request, but he could not readily refuse, given the substantial food and monetary aid Spain had received from Argentina in the 1940s and the popularity of Evita's 1947 visit. In late 1959 Perón was authorized to travel to Spain, a trip largely paid for by his still-generous host, Trujillo. Trujillo met the cost of a chartered Varig flight which was to take Perón, Isabel, assistant Américo Barrios, a few hangers-on and the two surviving poodles across the Atlantic.

After an engine failure delayed the first attempt, the flight finally took the contingent to the Azores, where they were informed that Franco had ordered that they land in Seville, not Madrid. It was a sign of the chilliness of the reception Perón would enjoy at the hands of the *generalísimo*, but at least it meant a greater degree of personal security, far from the troubles in Latin America and any potential further assassin. The chill continued, as Perón was sent by the government to a hotel in the southern city of Torremolinos and there was no sign of a personal welcome or any intention on Franco's part to recognize his guest. However, not long afterwards he was offered the use of a house in a Madrid suburb, and the government made no move to prevent him relocating to the capital. He would stay there for thirteen of the remaining fourteen years of his life.

Chapter 15

MADRID

Lejano Buenos Aires, qué lindo que has de estar ....
Ya van para diez años que me viste zarpar ....
No sabés las ganas que tengo de verte!
Acá estoy parado, sin plata y sin fe ....
Quién sabe, una noche me encane la Muerte
Y chau Buenos Aires, no te vuelvo a ver!

Distant Buenos Aires, how beautiful you must look ....
It's been nearly ten years since you saw me go ....
You don't know how much I long to see you!
Here I am, marooned, without money or faith ....
Who knows, one night death may take me prisoner
And goodbye Buenos Aires, I won't see you again!
Anclao en París (tango), Enrique Cadícamo and Guillermo Barbieri[1]

While in Madrid, Perón would be joined by his long-time friend, adviser, confidant and financial backer Jorge Antonio, a somewhat questionable figure who was nonetheless arguably one of Perón's few true and loyal friends. He would purchase a plot of land in the Puerta de Hierro neighbourhood and give it to Perón who built his Madrid home, called 17 de octubre, there.

Born in Buenos Aires to Syrian immigrants in 1917, Antonio became a wealthy businessman in the 1940s and 1950s, due in part to his relationship to Juan Duarte and increasing friendship with Perón. In the late 1940s he became the Argentine representative of both General Motors and Mercedes Benz, and his friendship with the presidential couple grew on the back of his proposals to expand vehicle production in the country, as well as imports of vehicles that Evita distributed to members of the taxi drivers' union. In an interview with Felipe Pigna in 2004, Antonio himself recognized that he had employed former Nazis including Adolf Eichmann at Mercedes Benz after they arrived in Argentina with passports allegedly obtained by the Vatican, although he denied that Perón had Nazi connections. He would become even closer to Perón after Evita's death, saying that the president consulted him more frequently than ever and appeared to be in a 'slump'. 'Eva's death was a terrible blow to the general. He felt more alone.' (Antonio would also make the interesting observation that 'she was in love with Perón, and Perón in his way was in love with her'.[2])

While Antonio was seen in many respects as the face of cronyism in the Perón government, a man who had used his connections to attain a significant fortune, on the other hand, he demonstrated his continuing loyalty and friendship throughout the rest of Perón's life, helping to support his somewhat modest life in exile, in part by giving him shares in some of his own companies which were later sold, and giving him advice and friendship that he did not easily find in other quarters. (From the mid-1960s the trade unions would also send Perón monthly cheques to finance his exile.)

Under some pressure from the Franco government and the prevailing conservative Catholicism in Spain, Perón married Isabel in November 1961, albeit not without some protest (he later claimed to have been obliged to do so). Witnesses noted that Isabel, by contrast, had considerably more to gain from the marriage and was anxious to formalize her position (and perhaps her inheritance). A former maid would later say that immediately following the wedding Isabel called the staff together and ordered them to refer to her as '*señora*' thereafter.[3] If Perón was not overly enthusiastic about the marriage, he seems to have been genuinely fond of Isabel and to have enjoyed a comfortable and companionable relationship – one that fell within his pattern of preferring relationships that did not make heavy emotional demands on him, Evita being the one notable exception. (Perhaps the deep loss he experienced on her death discouraged him from forming any other such close bond.)

Although Perón was in theory excommunicated following the events of 1955 and thus not able to receive the sacraments, including marriage, a Catholic ceremony was engineered under the pretext of freeing Isabel, still a practising Catholic, from the sin of unwed cohabitation. It did, however, represent an initial step in gradually improving relations with the Catholic Church – something that would be necessary if Perón's plan of eventually returning to Argentina, and the presidency, were to be feasible. In particular, as many of his letters from the period make clear, he was convinced that renewed ties to the Argentine clergy would be key to any return of Peronism to power. In 1963 he made a formal petition for pardon to Pope John XXIII, who acceded to the request (although the fact that the excommunication had been lifted was not made public in Argentina until 1971).

In 1962 Perón received a visit from John William Cooke, now installed in Havana, with an invitation from Fidel Castro to relocate to Cuba, a move that would have implied more than a wink and a nod towards the more insurgent sectors of the Peronist movement. Cooke saw this as an opportunity for Perón to free himself from the 'ideological prison' of Puerta de Hierro and his inner circle and to join in the increasingly revolutionary fervour gripping much of the Third World with which he felt Peronism to be associated.

Perón himself had taken a fairly positive tone with regard to the Cuban Revolution, noting its (perhaps somewhat spurious) similarities with his own 'revolution', and this tone would become stronger as the 1960s continued. For their part, Castro and Che Guevara, an Argentine from an anti-Peronist family (who would subsequently also visit Perón in Madrid), had become increasingly convinced that Peronism did represent a kind of indigenous Latin American socialism with which the Cuban Revolution could side. From this perspective, having Perón in Havana might have been a sort of trophy. Yet while residing in Spain could give Perón the image of a reactionary, his distant relationship with the Franco regime made it more feasible for him to continue playing off both ends against the other. A move to Havana would have placed him irremediably in the revolutionary camp where he was not altogether comfortable and would have shaken much of his Argentine support base. Moreover, he was comfortable in Madrid and seemed to have little inclination to leave it, at least unless and until he had an opportunity to return to Buenos Aires. Nevertheless, on Guevara's death in 1967 Perón would describe him as 'one of ours, perhaps the best' and noted that Peronism, 'as a national, popular and revolutionary movement, pays homage to the idealist, the revolutionary, Comandante Ernesto Che Guevara, Argentine guerrilla dead in action taking up arms to seek the triumph of national revolutions in Latin America'.[4]

Cooke and Guevara were, of course, far from Perón's only Argentine visitors during this period; the house in Puerta de Hierro would become the destination for a wide range of political and other figures from across the spectrum. Perón would receive them all with his noted hospitality, an attentive host who made his guests feel welcome and made them all believe that he agreed with them. This had of course been the key to his early political success, but it again raises the question of his apparent indifference to many around him and his willingness to utilize them and dispose of them if they were no longer useful. This attitude contrasts with the genial host and with the man who once fell and injured himself trying to rescue a hen from a marauding dog or who interrupted an important visitor to go and find some milk for a stray kitten. As he himself had observed, he had a gift for presenting himself as people wanted him to be and society was willing to see itself reflected in him. As Richard Gillespie noted, 'all ... created a Perón in their own image and proved more willing to listen to rhetoric than study political history'.[5] However, the affection and empathy he often showed to animals (which perhaps did not represent competition) were oddly lacking in his courteous but distant relations with most people.

Perón also maintained a voluminous correspondence with dozens of people, both in Argentina and in exile, as well as continuing to write books that would also traverse a wide range of political views, from the left to a defence of at least some aspects of fascism. Indeed, during the 1960s and, despite also courting elements of the left, Perón would begin to express more clearly than ever his admiration for aspects of the fascist state he had seen in the 1930s (although his host government in Madrid was never singled out for such words of admiration). In part this was more feasible now that some years had elapsed since the end of the Second World War, and indeed, in the midst of the Cold War in the 1960s it was easier to argue, as Perón did, that fascism had been a response to the dichotomy between capitalism and communism (and, indeed, the alliance of convenience between capitalism and communism to combat it). Perón would continue to defend the idea of the state-driven economy organized for the benefit of society as a whole (something that could be sold to both left and right), and the idea that across the world peoples were seeking 'liberation from one of the two imperialisms at the international level and the liberation of their people at the national level'.[6] In this reading fascism could fit comfortably into the rhetoric of both anti-communism and anti-US imperialism.

Much of this line of thinking would in fact be included in Perón's 1968 book *La hora de los pueblos*, generally cited as evidence of his more 'leftist' credentials, in which he observed that 'in 1938 the world, absorbed and confused, watched the bitter confrontation of capitalism and communism, while fascism and national socialism maintained an ideological third position'. Thirty years later, at the time of writing, 'the third position is now much stronger and the imperialisms have left us the experience of 1938 when ideologies were transcended'. Thus, again, the third position was reclaimed as above and beyond ideologies, and as the direction in which the world would go. This vindication of fascism (which never included its worst excesses but rather its outward achievements) was arguably more readily swallowed by a younger generation who did not remember fascism, and arguably also finessed by the fact that during the 1960s many left-wing intellectuals had no qualms about vindicating the worst abuses of the Soviet Union under Stalin.

Perón's continued affinity for the broad-brush, 'if I define, I exclude' approach to political allies was of course directed in large part towards continuing to stir political trouble in Argentina, where little additional stirring was required. President Arturo Frondizi remained under pressure on a range of political and economic fronts, weakened by his evident dependence on the Peronist vote in 1958 and by economic policies that stirred union and public protest. Economic policies aimed at stabilizing the weak economy promised long-term gains but no short-term improvements, and an IMF-backed devaluation and a series of wage cuts brought further union resistance. Frondizi's hopes of gaining some trade union backing were also damaged by his decision to sign contracts with foreign oil companies despite having made his reputation a few years earlier by attacking Perón's decision to do the same.

Politically, Frondizi was also weakened by what was seen by the military (and the United States) as leftist leanings that prompted him to receive Che Guevara during his only visit to Argentina, and to abstain in the Organization of American States vote to expel Cuba in 1961. The decision to break diplomatic ties with Havana early the following year did not reduce military and US pressures, while trade union resistance was also mounting again as another bout of hyperinflation and recession hit workers' purchasing power despite a series of price freezes and wage rises.

In March 1962 Frondizi took the perilous decision to allow Peronist candidates to participate in gubernatorial and legislative elections, although the party itself remained proscribed and they were obliged to join 'neo-Peronist' forces – most notably the Popular Union. The party presented textile workers' leader Andrés Framini as its candidate for governor of Buenos Aires province, with the backing of metalworkers' leader Augusto Vandor. As an added challenge, the party announced that Perón himself would be Framini's candidate for vice-governor; this was predictably rejected by the authorities, but Framini nevertheless won the governorship, while Peronist candidates won around one-third of the national vote, forty-one Lower House seats and nine provincial governorships.

If Frondizi had hoped to demonstrate that Peronist influence was waning, the result was a disaster for him. Although he announced the federal intervention of five of the provinces won by the Peronists, the move was too little, too late to save him and he was, predictably, removed by the military on 29 March 1962. Also predictably, Perón, who had already undermined Frondizi by making public the existence of the 1958 electoral pact, was unsympathetic, noting later that 'Frondizi did not fulfil any of his commitments to the people, because he never planned to fulfil them …. There was no choice but to organise a defeat for him, just as we had organised his victory.'[7]

Although internecine struggles between the hard-line anti-Peronist and more moderate military factions prevented the establishment of a military government, and Senate President José María Guido assumed the provisional presidency, his weakness vis-à-vis the military was evident from the beginning. In a new round of presidential elections in mid-1963, the Popular Union was not allowed to present a presidential candidate, although it formed part of a coalition, the National Popular Front, that backed Perón's chosen candidate, the conservative Vicente Solano Lima (who in the end was barred from standing). Frondizi's UCRI presented former Buenos Aires Governor Oscar Alende as its candidate, while the elderly Córdoba doctor Arturo Illia stood for Balbín's UCRP. Illia would eventually win the election, with the unconvincing figure of 25 per cent of the vote, to 16.4 per cent for Alende and nearly 19 per cent of blank votes. Again, a presidency born of weakness and buffeted by lack of political support and economic challenges was taking office. Like Frondizi, Illia would find it impossible to balance the competing demands of the CGT, industry, agriculture and the military.

During this period Perón continued to hold court in Madrid, with his new wife appearing decorously as a hostess but taking no apparent interest or active role in politics. Isabel would become quite a social figure, forming friendships with influential figures such as Franco's sister, Pilar. She would also accompany Perón on his frequent walks and in looking after the poodles. The couple were joined during this time by Isabel's spiritist mentor and foster father, José Cresto, whose wife Isabel had died. He would live with them in Puerta de Hierro for some time, not only accompanying Isabel but joining Perón on his morning constitutional and sometimes at lunches; regarded as a strange and somewhat incoherent being, he would nonetheless become another long-term member of the household.

True to form, Perón also continued to turn his pedagogical skills on his new wife, taking pride in her prowess at fencing. Whether due to hubris or necessity, he would also undertake to tutor Isabel in the skills of politics, despite the fact that her talents appear to have lent themselves more readily to fencing. It is not entirely clear whether at this stage he was seriously considering her political deployment or whether the lessons represented another pastime, such as building a house of cards. Perón ensured that she was acquainted with the trade unionists and other figures who visited the house, although they later could not remember any notable contribution on her part to the discussions. Most likely he remained suspicious of other individuals (most notably Vandor) and their potential to pursue 'Peronism without Perón', and wanted to ensure that he had another card to play. He may also have been influenced by issues of health: in early 1964 he had a prostate operation and, despite an apparently full recovery, rumours regarding his health began to circulate, fuelling the race for a potential succession battle. (At a New Year's Eve party in 1963 he had told guests, with whatever degree of seriousness, that he intended it to be 'the last New Year I celebrate outside my country'.[8]) Later in 1964 it was decided that he would attempt to return to Argentina to take control of the movement himself, a plan orchestrated with the connivance of several leading associates including Jorge Antonio, Vandor, Framini and the former legislator Delia Parodi, who had been president of both the PPF and the Eva Perón Foundation after Evita's death. The stage was set by a series of union actions including strikes and factory occupations designed to put further pressure on the Illia government.

On 2 December Perón left Puerta de Hierro concealed in the boot of his own car, driven by Antonio, thus eluding the police guard, who had been informed that he was in bed with flu. Perón boarded a flight from Madrid to Buenos Aires using a Paraguayan passport under the name of Juan P. Sosa, accompanied by Delia Parodi posing as his wife and by Antonio, Vandor, Framini and others. Despite the use of false documents, it was, predictably, known that Perón was on board and that the Argentine military had no intention of allowing his return. When the Iberia flight landed in Rio de Janeiro it was surrounded by Brazilian forces who, at the request of the Argentine government, removed the party from the plane and returned them to Madrid. The failed attempt strengthened Vandor's conviction that Perón would be unable to return and that another leader would have to emerge – in other words, himself. At this point Perón decided to make use of his wife and latest pupil, announcing that she would travel to Paraguay (where Jorge Antonio had relocated following the so-called *Operación Retorno*) in May 1965, following the mid-term elections in Argentina. The results of those elections only served to roil political tensions in Argentina further: when Illia permitted Peronist candidates to stand, they received some 3.4 million votes nationwide to 2.6 for Illia's Radicals, incensing the armed forces and making a new coup d'état almost certain. Moreover, it inflamed tensions within the Peronist movement, with the trade unions, the traditional political wing and the left-wing elements jockeying for position at a moment when it appeared that a political earthquake was on the horizon.

Isabel arrived in Asunción in May 1965 with a message from her husband for long-standing Paraguayan dictator Alfredo Stroessner, Perón's first host at the start of his exile – and, it was widely assumed, more messages for others in Argentina. She held numerous meetings with a range of Peronist and less-Peronist figures who brought gifts for her and letters for her husband, although in a rare press interview with the Argentine magazine *Primera Plana* she stressed that she did not get involved in politics, was a devout Catholic and not a spiritist, and had only come to Asunción to rest. The reporter noted her Madrid accent, luxurious wardrobe and tendency to seek Jorge Antonio's approval for the comments she made, as well as her claim that their one-time neighbour in Madrid, the actress Ava Gardner, 'swore that she had never eaten as well anywhere as in her home'.[9] So far, so unremarkable.

A few months later, however, Isabel would return to the Southern Cone, this time to Buenos Aires, where she arrived in October 1965 and installed herself in the de luxe Alvear Palace Hotel in the Recoleta district. Her function on this occasion was to monitor the activities of Vandor, whose activism and independence were a cause of concern to Perón; they were likewise of concern to the Illia government, which tolerated her low-profile visit (made under the name of María Estela Martínez). However, she managed to retain her low profile for only a short time, and the Alvear Palace soon became the target of anti-Peronist protests.

In a context of mounting tensions between the government and the unions, and of increasing rumours of an impending coup d'état (fuelled further by the fairly open contact between Vandor and some military leaders), Isabel would make a tour of several provinces. She was supported by Vandor (both of them perhaps operating on the principle that keeping one's enemies close was the best policy), who provided funds, transport and security for a tour in which her primary function was to seek to undermine his political autonomy. This could have been said to be her true political education: she met with political and union leaders wherever she went, as well as Peronist supporters who received her gladly as her husband's emissary. Although not a natural public speaker, she began to make occasional short speeches and seemed to gain in confidence – even when Vandor, increasingly aware that her purpose was to undercut him, halted financing for her travels and left her stranded in Rosario. Perón subsequently named Isabel as his delegate in Argentina, in charge of the movement's political leadership there, and threw her support behind Vandor's main rival, textile workers' leader José Alonso, who at the start of 1966 launched a rival union movement, known as the 62 Organizations Together with Perón. Both the unions and the neo-Peronist members of Congress increasingly divided between Vandor's leadership and the putative leadership of Isabel.

The face-off between Vandor and Perón via Isabel came to a head in the gubernatorial elections in Jujuy and Mendoza provinces in the early part of 1966, where both factions presented candidates. Although Vandor's candidate won in Jujuy, Isabel succeeded in dividing the waters in Mendoza sufficiently to ensure that a third-party candidate won – not an absolute triumph, but a result that saw Vandor's candidate place fourth while Isabel's ally came second. How much of this success can be attributed to Isabel per se is questionable, but her physical presence and her identity as his wife (and arguably as Evita's putative successor) helped Perón to recover much of the authority over the movement in Argentina that had begun to slip. In a letter to Cooke, Perón would observe that Isabel's efforts in Argentina would play a key role in the party's fortunes there, and that he had spent ten years preparing her for that role.

Whether or not she was the proximate cause, Isabel's stay in Argentina also coincided with the 28 June 1966 coup d'état, a long-foretold event that saw the elderly and honourable President Illia turfed out of the presidential residence in his pyjamas and General Juan Carlos Onganía installed in the presidency. Onganía was the leader of the so-called *azul* faction within the army which had hitherto favoured a constitutional approach, unlike the rival '*colorado*' faction which had long been spoiling for a return to military rule. Although there were many factors underlying the coup, both political and economic, there is no question that Isabel's activities had placed Onganía in something of a bind, given his earlier support for Illia and mounting military anger over Illia's apparent tolerance of Isabel and Vandor's shenanigans. Moreover, Onganía had favoured overtures to Vandor and other union leaders, and Vandor's loss of influence vis-à-vis Isabel had also undermined the strength of Onganía's position in this respect.

The coup would devolve into a lengthy military government, known as the 'Argentine Revolution', which would prove more interventionist and more repressive than any military government to date; in this respect it would provide grist to Perón's mill as it became increasingly divisive and its economic policies inflicted considerable pain on the working classes in particular. Although Perón would initially make some positive noises about Onganía, and many sectors of public opinion also hoped for some improvement in social and economic conditions, such thoughts were short-lived. A respected professional as a military man, Onganía was also highly authoritarian, rigidly conservative and imposed a strict and increasingly repressive regime which in particular targeted the urban intelligentsia and progressive sectors such as students, generating an alarming rise in both dissent and the use of torture and violence to suppress it. A month after he took power, police would invade the University of Buenos Aires to break up occupations by students and teachers protesting against the military government's suspension of university autonomy, resulting the over 400 detentions, the dismissal of hundreds of lecturers and a migration of others to provincial universities less affected by the repression. While 'The Night of the Long Batons' was a far less bloody affair than the repression that would follow the 1976 coup a decade later, it represented a sharp break between the government and the educated classes that undermined Onganía's popularity and arguably contributed to Perón's increasing attractiveness for disaffected and educated youth.

Isabel returned to Madrid, her husband and José Cresto in July 1966 after nine months away. She did not come alone. With her was one of the more outlandish personalities ever attached to Peronism, and one whose implausible influence would have catastrophic consequences.

José López Rega, a former police corporal who had once been part of Perón and Evita's security detail, a would-be opera singer and a passionate student of astrology, esoterism and the occult, was born in Buenos Aires in 1916. Having pursued his musical ambitions with limited success, he had a similarly mediocre career in the police, never rising above the rank of corporal and retiring in 1962 when he began to operate a small printing press; the newspaper *Clarín* would describe him as possessed of 'unwavering idiocy'.[10] The author of a number of self-published and incomprehensible works such as *Esoteric Astrology* and *Alpha and Omega: A Message for Humanity* (the latter of which purportedly stemmed from a literary collaboration with the Archangel Gabriel, who dictated some of the content in dreams), López Rega shared this passion with Isabel. How they met remains an open question. Some have claimed that they had met earlier, during Isabel's days with Joe Herald's troupe (and indeed, that both had been agents of either the CIA, Argentine intelligence or both), while others say they met through the so-called Anael Lodge to which he belonged, where he was known as 'Brother Daniel'. (He would become more widely known as *el brujo*, the warlock.) Most likely he was introduced to her by Major Bernardo Alberte, Perón's former aide, who put Isabel up at his home briefly during her stay and who may have known López Rega from the mid-1950s. López Rega reportedly offered his printer's shop to print leaflets for the Jujuy and Mendoza gubernatorial contests and was seemingly recruited by Alberte as part of Isabel's security detail. In any case, their shared interest in spiritism and his weird charisma (heightened by his very pale white skin and glassy light blue eyes) appear to have enchanted Isabel, who returned to Madrid with him and brought him into the Perón household as her husband's valet.

Although at least in the early period he lived apart in a rented room and occupied himself with relatively menial tasks, López Rega would gradually insinuate himself into the house and into Perón's confidence, becoming increasingly influential in later years as Perón's health and mental faculties began to deteriorate. While Perón at first seemed to regard him with a mixture of amusement and benign disdain (referring to him with the diminutive nickname 'Lopecito'), in time he would appear to fall increasingly under his control. As has been noted, Perón's lifelong predilection for surrounding himself with mediocrities while distancing those talented enough to challenge him would in this case have dire results; whether or not he believed that he continued to maintain enough authority to keep such mediocrities under control, in practice he was no longer the man he had been. Although the relationship had its ups and downs – Perón once dismissed López Rega after learning that he was using his image to market a patent medicine in Brazil, with the claim that Perón had retained his youthful appearance thanks to its use – Isabel would intercede on 'Daniel's' behalf, ensuring that he remained within the entourage. (An early casualty of his influence was José Cresto, who found himself dispatched back to Buenos Aires as his place in the household and Isabel's affections was usurped.) Indeed, it was said that she threatened to leave if he was not allowed to move in with them.

Despite ironically continuing to insist on the need for unity, Perón continued to play off different factions of his movement against each other as he held court in Madrid, meeting with both elements of the far right among the military and trade unions and also with the leaders of the so-called Peronist left, nascent guerrillas (referred to by Perón as 'special formations') whose origins in fact came largely from right-wing sources such as the Falangist Tacuara armed movement active in the early 1960s, and frequently from middle- and upper-middle-class Catholic backgrounds; some had been members of the AC. This was particularly the case of the leadership of the largest such group, the Montoneros, some of whom had studied at the Institute of the Immaculate Conception, a Jesuit secondary school in Santa Fe, under the then Jesuit priest Jorge Bergoglio. (An influential figure who swam in the opposite direction was Norma Kennedy, the daughter of a Radical family who became a communist activist trained in Cuba before becoming a virulent anti-communist and a member of the Peronist right.)

Figure 13 Perón and Isabel in Madrid, late 1972 (Photo by Central Press/Getty Images)

These younger activists had grown up, often in anti-Peronist families, with little awareness of what Peronism in power had actually been like and the image they had was thus blurry. The Liberating Revolution had, ironically, been a key contributor to this state of affairs: while the Aramburu government had believed that banning all reference to Perón and Peronism and attempting to erase the movement from history would lead to its disappearance, instead it promoted both an idealized notion and an ignorant one. In particular, they appeared unaware of the fact that Perón had always been avowedly a reformer rather than a revolutionary, and indeed that their attractiveness to him lay not in ideological affinity but in the fact that they could be played off against, and limit the influence of, the proponents of 'Peronism without Perón' such as Vandor. For his part, Perón's years in exile had skewed his own views of Argentine realities and of the 'special forces' he would find himself dealing with. Montonero leader Mario Firmenich would later say that 'Perón had trouble understanding that the relationship with us was different from the rest of the movement. And we had trouble understanding that the flesh and blood Perón was different from the historical image.'[11]

The Montoneros would take some of their ideological concepts from the writings of Cooke, who had posited that the Peronist movement contained the seeds of a revolutionary movement by virtue of its working-class base. Although this vision was facilitated by the fact that Peronism had lost much middle-class and business support by the mid-1950s and was thus in practice more class-based than in its origins, it sat uncomfortably with the fact that its trade union base was largely seen as more right-wing and reactionary, while the traditional left was historically in opposition and the so-called leftist Peronist factions came from middle-class and intellectual backgrounds that had little in common with the 'workers'.

However, if he continued to receive a broad range of political contacts, his social life more generally became increasingly circumscribed by the efforts of Isabel and López Rega, who restricted the access of those they preferred to marginalize. Jorge Antonio was an early casualty; although Perón would continue to consult him privately he no longer came to the house and relations became increasingly distant. According to one account, from early on López Rega had threatened to destroy Antonio if he did not cooperate with him; Antonio's clear contempt for him doubtless only strengthened that determination.[12] Early on López Rega had reportedly suggested a pact with Antonio in which they would seek to control Perón between them; when Antonio angrily rejected this *el brujo* purportedly told him that he would 'regret it because Isabel will be the one in control and I control Isabel'.[13] In 1970 he seems to have convinced Isabel that Antonio was involved in a plot against Perón; whether this is so or whether she simply also wished to reduce competing sources of influence, she banned him from the inner circle and he himself, justifiably offended, refused to return to the house and spoke to Perón only elsewhere and alone.

In parallel, López Rega's influence would rise, from a somewhat marginal and jokey figure on the outer edges of Perón's circle to a central position. During a 1970 visit, the journalist Tomás Eloy Martínez would note that López Rega would interrupt Perón's reminiscences and adjust them, often claiming to have accompanied him at events early in his life – such as Perón's boyhood attendance at the funeral of former President Bartolomé Mitre, a decade before López Rega's birth. Perón would not contradict his insertions, even when his valet began to use the pronoun 'I' when in theory speaking of Perón.[14] Into the late 1960s and early 1970s a series of health problems, combined with his advancing age and increasing isolation, raised doubts among various interlocutors as to Perón's state of mental health and his dependence on his valet/secretary.

In the case of Eloy Martínez, the confusing interviews annotated by López Rega would become the basis of his hugely successful and surreal work *The Perón Novel*, primarily because he believed the story too incredible to publish as a non-fiction biography. López Rega would tell him on one occasion that 'I am the lightning rod that halts all the evils sent against this house. I am less and less López Rega and more and more the health of the general.'[15] Increasingly, he would believe himself to be able to maintain Perón's health better than the doctors and to intervene to keep him miraculously alive. While it is unclear how far Perón shared these views, his own interest in spiritism and his fading energy seem to have made him at least complicit in the fantasy. Certainly López Rega's more esoteric pursuits fascinated Isabel, who, according to their housekeeper, spent much time alone in her bedroom with him. Perón either 'trusted them very much or didn't care'.[16]

Others differed as to how much Perón had deteriorated during this period. In January 1969, the author Felix Luna found Perón to be 'the same erect, sturdy, robust man he has been all his life. He exudes authentic cordiality: he is one of those men who is offering a light when one is halfway through getting out a cigarette.'[17] However, a few years later, shortly before his return to Buenos Aires, Perón was visited in Madrid by the former Israeli ambassador in Argentina, Yaacov Tsur, whose reaction was considerably different. 'I remembered him in his military uniform, erect, self-assured, smiling .... Now he was old, stooped, wearing a dressing gown. He was 78, but he looked old, tired and sick, more than an octogenarian .... The man seemed sick and broken, pathetic.'[18] Arguably it was this latter view that would make it increasingly urgent to plan his return, before death or infirmity intervened forever.

Abetted to a degree by the ageing former president in Madrid, events in Argentina were in some ways propitious for that return, despite the fact that the complications of the deteriorating situation would have taxed a far more vigorous leader. Economic pressures, trade union reaction, government repression and mounting guerrilla violence were the order of the day by the late 1960s. In May 1969, protests over food price increases at the state university in the city of Corrientes prompted police repression that was met by mounting resistance elsewhere. Major demonstrations in the cities of Rosario and Córdoba saw troops sent in, which in the latter city caused a major outbreak of civil unrest, known as the *Cordobazo*. The characteristics of the *Cordobazo* were somewhat unique, the city having a strong history of both student and trade union activism, and the uprising was the work of a range of elements often regarded as having little in common: Peronist trade unions, students usually associated with the UCR and unions with socialist or communist leadership. At least fourteen people died during the protests, marking the largest-ever show of resistance to the military regime, and both Vandor's CGT and the rival CGT of the Argentines (CGTA) led by a more hardline Perón loyalist,

Raimundo Ongaro, declared a general strike. The *Cordobazo* captured the scalp of the unpopular economy minister, Adalbert Krieger Vasena, but did not bring rapid economic policy shifts nor a return to calm.

One month following the *Cordobazo*, Vandor was shot to death at the metalworkers' headquarters in Córdoba, ostensibly at the hands of one of the 'special formations' of Peronist youth encouraged by the leader from Madrid, who regarded Vandor as a traitor to the working classes and to Perón given his own leadership ambitions within the 'Peronism without Perón' scenario. The members of the so-called Descamisado Command were not identified, but a state of siege was declared and the number of violent incidents attributed to both left-wing and right-wing activists would mount.

The appeal to violence was not the only path Perón sought to follow; as noted earlier he had already begun to build bridges to the Catholic Church and in particular to the sectors of it who might see in Peronism a political expression of the Second Vatican Council's 'preferential option for the poor'. That option was increasingly espoused by priests working in shantytowns who saw their role as defending social as well as spiritual issues, and for whom Peronism was seen as a precursor of Liberation Theology. The Argentine Third World Priests Movement attracted only a small minority of Argentine priests, but argued that 'the Peronist movement, revolutionary, with its massive force, … will necessarily lead to the revolution which will make possible an original and Latin American socialism'.[19] This coincided with Perón's own apparent shift to the left in his writings, notably his statement in *La hora de los pueblos* that 'evolution will lead us imperceptibly toward revolution …. The reign of the bourgeoisie in the world has ended. The government of the peoples begins'.[20] Highlighting that supposed shift, he would return to the prediction for Latin America he had first made in 1951 to the effect that 'the year 2000 will find us united or dominated'.

Perón's appeal to the more radicalized clergy (some of whom, like Perón himself, were reluctant to reject violence although many clearly did not take violent actions themselves) was also abetted by the image of Evita, whom the Third World priests adopted as a more classist and revolutionary figure – in contrast to the more saintly image preferred by sectors of the Peronist right. The lack of a clear rejection of violence would later provide the excuse for ferocious repression of the Third World Priests as well as other Peronist groups – for example, the *Juventud Peronista* (Peronist Youth, JP), came to be considered by the military to be synonymous with guerrilla groups such as the Montoneros, despite the fact that there was only limited overlap and that many of the 'glorious JP' were involved only in political rather than violent activism. Some priests would also see Peronism less as a revolutionary path, but simply as the representation of the aspirations of the poor; most priests who worked in slum areas would become deeply aware that the poor were Peronist and many would become Peronist themselves.

This would also inform the positions articulated by the hierarchy when one of those priests influenced by Peronism, the Jesuit Jorge Bergoglio, would become archbishop of Buenos Aires and later Pope Francis. Never noted for his radical tendencies, Bergoglio did not form part of the Third World Priests Movement and had little sympathy with Marxism (being, like Perón, arguably a reformer rather than a revolutionary) but did spend much of his career working with the *curas villeros* (shantytown priests). As well as having taught some of the sons of well-off Catholic families, Bergoglio was also widely believed to be associated with the *Guardia de Hierro* (Iron Guard), a right-wing intellectual Peronist organization, some of whose members were active in the leadership of the Jesuit University del Salvador in Buenos Aires when Bergoglio was the order's leader (Provincial) from 1973. Although as a priest he never confirmed any political affiliation, he has often been described as Peronist, and it was widely believed that he had been named the Jesuits' Provincial in 1973, despite his very young age, precisely because he was expected to have good relations with the Peronist government.

Whether or not due to any real influence, Bergoglio would over the years express many views similar to those espoused by Perón during this period. His first apostolic exhortation after becoming Pope in 2013, *Evangelii Gaudium*, focused in part on 'the inclusion of the poor in society', which

> means working to eliminate the structural causes of poverty and to promote the integral development of the poor. .... It presumes the creation of a new mindset which thinks in terms of community and the priority of the life of all over the appropriation of goods by a few. Solidarity is a spontaneous reaction by those who recognize that the social function of property and the universal destination of goods are realities which come before private property.[21]

Whether deliberately or not (or because Perón had himself co-opted much of his social doctrine from Catholic texts), this description of the 'social function of property' is entirely in line with the Peronist doctrine of the 1940s and prompted wide disquiet with the new Pope's purportedly 'anti-capitalist' stance. During the Pope's 2013 visit to Brazil, the liberation theologian Father Leonardo Boff would remark that Francis was 'clearly defining that the enemy of the peoples is capitalism, and to say that he must have great courage: he has to be Argentine, he has to be a Jesuit and he has to be a Peronist.'[22]

One year after the *Cordobazo*, on 29 May 1970, two men in military uniform appeared at the home of General Pedro Aramburu. They turned out to be Fernando Abal Medina and Emilio Angel Maza, members of the hitherto unknown Montonero guerrilla movement, who held Aramburu at a remote property owned by the family of another Montonero member and subjected him to 'revolutionary justice' over his role in the Liberating Revolution, the June 1956 executions and the disappearance of Evita's body. His 'execution' was announced on 31 May. The move represented a challenge not only to the government but to Perón himself: Perón had had no hand in the formation of the Montoneros and they sought from the start to negotiate with him from the position of strength gained from Aramburu's spectacular kidnapping and death, capitalizing on the strong feelings of resentment among the Peronist resistance (in which they had played no part). One Montonero would later say 'we aimed to occupy the empty space left between

Perón and the people. And we challenged him for the leadership from the first moment.'[23] The question remains to a degree as to who would co-opt whom.

Its apparent helplessness in the face of Aramburu's abduction and killing marked the end of the Onganía government, in part due to initial suspicions that Onganía and his interior minister might have had a hand in it. The government had not given Aramburu any security detail, and Aramburu represented a potential challenge to Onganía, seeking a political role even including negotiations with some Peronist elements. Onganía was replaced on 8 June by General Roberto Levingston, who would then himself be succeeded by a more high-profile general, Alejandro Lanusse, in March 1971. Lanusse, a more ambitious man than Levingston, had hopes of making the leap from de facto leader to elected president in much the same way Perón had done twenty-five years earlier. Violence by the Montoneros and other left-wing groups, including the killing of trade unionist José Alonso in August 1970, as well as right-wing violence such as the killing of sixteen political prisoners in the southern city of Trelew following a prison escape from Rawson in 1972, was undermining Lanusse's potential path to elected power, and as violence spiralled he saw no alternative but to seek negotiations with Perón. To that end, the proscription on political parties was ended and an emissary, Colonel Francisco Cornicelli, was dispatched to Madrid the month after Lanusse assumed office with a view to brokering talks. (Perón would insist on referring to the mediator, scornfully, as Vermicelli.)

One olive branch offered by Lanusse was the return of Evita's body, which was disinterred from a Milan cemetery in September 1971 and transported to Puerta de Hierro where it was received by Perón, Isabel, López Rega, her sisters Blanca and Erminda and the embalmer Pedro Ara. The anti-Peronist Argentine ambassador, Jorge Rojas Silveyra, who was also present, would later note that Perón was in tears and told him 'I was much happier with this woman than everyone thinks'.[24] Damage to the body was repaired, Isabel herself dressed her predecessor in a new tunic and arranged her hair, and the body was ensconced in the attic of their home. (In *La novela de Perón*, Eloy Martínez would write that Isabel would lie on top of the coffin while López Rega attempted to make Evita's spirit enter her body, an invention by the novelist that would nonetheless be taken as fact by many sources, probably because it seemed entirely plausible within the general strangeness of the household.)

However, Lanusse's plans would founder on the fact that Perón, possibly to Lanusse's surprise, wanted to return to the presidency and was disinclined to bless Lanusse's own candidacy. Moreover, his efforts to persuade Perón to call a halt to violence by his supporters fell on deaf ears, with Perón insisting that violence would disappear when the political climate changed and it was no longer required. In a bid to outflank Perón, in October 1971 Lanusse announced that presidential elections would be held in March 1973, with candidates to be chosen in 1972. Isabel and López Rega were dispatched to Buenos Aires at the end of 1971 to prepare for the process of selecting candidates, while Perón yet again began negotiating a pact with former President Arturo Frondizi to present an alliance to be called the Civic

National Liberation Front (FRECILINA) as well as a 'social pact' with the CGT now led by the right-wing metalworkers' leader José Rucci.

Despite the many concurrent negotiations in train, violence continued to mount among the guerrillas, death squads and the security forces, with a spate of kidnappings and murders of prominent figures and a mounting threat to Lanusse from within the armed forces that risked a new internal coup before elections could take place. (The Montoneros in particular had thus far retained a fair degree of public sympathy by virtue of the fact that many of their armed actions such as bank robberies had a Robin Hood quality and that they by and large avoided killings of low-ranking police and military who belonged to the working classes.) Lanusse would later justify his determination to call elections and restore democracy on the grounds that it was necessary '"to deprive the subversives of all their arguments", and the ageing Perón had to be brought back to Argentina if his myth were to be exploded'.[25]

In July 1972 Lanusse announced that all presidential candidates would be required to be resident in the country by 25 August 1972, an attempt to scupper any attempt to present Perón as a candidate which prompted the sharp termination of negotiations. In a further attempt to bait Perón, Lanusse would charge that he would not return ahead of the deadline due to cowardice; Perón kept quiet for several weeks before announcing via his representative, former Lower House leader and Evita loyalist Héctor Cámpora, that he would return to Argentina by the end of the year.

On 7 November it was announced that Perón would return ten days later, in a bid to demonstrate his continuing support. He arrived on 17 November on an Alitalia flight from Rome after spending several days in Italy with Isabel and López Rega, and was met at the airport by a number of political figures although not by his young supporters, who were prevented from holding a rally at the airport. The entourage would be held overnight at an airport hotel before being allowed to leave the following day. Perón and Isabel would move to a rented house in the northern suburb of Vicente López, where he would appear at the window to wave to supporters (on such a regular basis that he was referred to as 'the cuckoo') but largely kept a low profile. Nevertheless, rumours soon began to spread that he was largely under the control of Isabel and López Rega, although he managed to hold meetings with other political leaders including his long-time rival Ricardo Balbín. Several visitors reported that Perón seemed somewhat cowed by his valet, who increasingly interfered and limited his communications. However, among the meetings he held there were with representatives of the Third World Priests Movement and with the well-known shantytown priest Carlos Mugica, who lived and worked in the Retiro slum in Buenos Aires and who was 'absolutely convinced that the liberation of my people will be through the Peronist movement. .... I know from the Gospel, from Christ's attitude, that I must see human history through the poor. And in Argentina the majority of the poor are Peronists'.[26] (A few years earlier, as spiritual advisor of the Catholic students' organization at the Colegio Nacional in Buenos Aires, Mugica had become an influence on several students who would later become leading members of the Montoneros, including Fernando

Abal Medina, Emilio Maza, Norma Arrostito and Mario Firmenich, although Mugica diverged from their position, often saying that he was prepared to die for the poor but not to kill for them.)

Less than a month later, Perón would return to Madrid on 14 December, having designated Cámpora as his chosen proxy candidate. He did not withdraw without indulging in some inflammatory language defending the use of violence against the 'gangster' regime, saying that 'if I were 50 years younger I would be planting bombs or taking justice into my own hands'.[27] Such language was in line with Perón's frequent references to 'generational change' and exhortations to the younger generation to assume leadership responsibilities, which was politically useful but far from an accurate reflection of his immediate desires. It also prompted the government to ban him from returning to the country before the 11 March 1973 elections. However, to a considerable degree he had already done what he had set out to do, and had ensured the nomination of a candidate who was biddable, loyal and presented no competition (whether to himself or to the rising power of Isabel and López Rega has been disputed). The campaign's most famous slogan, 'Cámpora to the presidency, Perón to power', could not have made the position clearer.

There must be some question as to the extent to which by this time Perón himself actually relished a return to Argentina and to what could only be an arduous presidency. There is no doubt that he had spent his years in exile driven by the desire for self-justification and the remarkable triumph that such a return would signify. Having been driven ignominiously and relatively easily from power that had once seemed unassailable, a victorious return would represent the pinnacle of all he had hoped to achieve in the intervening seventeen years. Yet Perón by late 1972 was not the same man who had left Argentina in 1955, any more than Argentina was unchanged. At seventy-nine, he had suffered a series of ailments, some of them serious, including his prostate surgery and cardiovascular problems that may also have had an impact on his cognitive capacity. These medical contretemps had also facilitated the expansion of López Rega's role as nurse.

Perón enjoyed holding court in Madrid and he enjoyed playing the political games that had so complicated the panorama in Argentina and the options for alternative political leadership; as in the 1940s, it may have been the case that he preferred the political games to the actual exercise of power. It is also slightly unclear to what extent he grasped the violent and complicated reality of the country. Although he was known to be extremely well informed about the situation in factual terms, with a telex machine providing him with constant updates, it is uncertain that the realities on the ground and the virtual impossibility of coming to grips with them were entirely clear. While at times he appeared to acknowledge the impossibility, at other times he appeared confident that he could restore order and bring his warring compatriots into line. He was also perhaps influenced by the fact that his constant visitors tried to tell him what he wanted to hear (just as he told them what they wanted to hear). Even with a remarkable range of information to hand, it was sometimes noted by his visitors that he was not entirely lucid in his vision of the present, often preferring to reminisce about the past.

To make the leap from elder statesman and virtual obligatory destination for visiting Argentines to a role of intense day-to-day decision-making may have been something that was more appealing as a dream than a reality. After difficult initial years in exile, Perón was comfortable in Madrid, he enjoyed his house, his walks, his domestic comforts and his social life, and being uprooted again to return to a country from which he had long departed (not without bitterness) was perhaps a more daunting prospect than he let on.

Unquestionably his age and health increased the urgency of any return, but is it the case that Perón himself felt that urgency? Although he was known to fear dying in exile, the fate of leaders such as San Martín and Rosas, the question of the presidency is a somewhat different one. It seems at least as likely that it was a matter of great urgency for his wife and López Rega, whose ambitions depended entirely on his safe return to Buenos Aires, as well as to the myriad political figures who hoped to increase their personal influence but were unable to represent a serious alternative power base – not to mention the millions of supporters who had for many years maintained the illusion of Perón's triumphal return. Almost certainly it had been his long-held ambition to return to power, and his years of machinations to achieve that end had in essence painted him into a corner even as the realities of his age and stamina were making achievement of that ambition almost a worst-case scenario. For him it was perhaps a fantasy that seemed less and less likely to become hard reality. Yet even if this is the case, he bore the greatest responsibility for this predicament, being the chief architect of a situation in which other potential leaders had been undermined, all roads were designed to lead to Perón and the ambitions of both hangers-on and genuine devotees were pinned ineluctably to his return to Argentina. In the end, both for Perón and for Argentina this may have been a harsh object lesson as to the need to 'be careful what you wish for'. Getting what they wished for may have proved a catastrophe for all concerned.

Chapter 16

RETURN

Volver con la frente marchita, las nieves del tiempo platearon mi sien …
Sentir que es un soplo la vida, que veinte años no es nada ….
Tengo miedo del encuentro con el pasado que vuelve a enfrentarse con mi vida
….
To return with my brow withered, the snows of time have silvered my temples …
To feel that life is a puff of wind, that twenty years is nothing ….
I fear the encounter with the past that returns to confront my life ….
Volver (tango), Carlos Gardel and Alfredo Le Pera[1]

As the presidential campaign got underway ahead of the March elections, with Cámpora and conservative Vicente Solano Lima confirmed as the *Frente Justicialista de Liberación* (Justicialist Liberation Front, FREJULI) slate, it became apparent that the submissive Cámpora might prove a more effective campaigner than expected. This was due in no small part to the affection he gained among the JP, who referred to him as '*Tío*' (uncle) because he was 'the brother of *el Viejo* [the old man]'. However, violence by the Peronist left, other guerrilla movements such as the Trotskyist *Ejército Revolutionario del Pueblo* (People's Revolutionary Army, ERP) as well as right-wing death squads and the security forces would deeply mar the campaign and the prospects of the incoming government. At the same time, Cámpora remained clear in his position that it was Perón who was in charge, sending his son Héctor to Madrid in January 1973 to receive the leader's campaign instructions. Those instructions were clear as to the need to 'win the street', which would require the organization and support of the JP and the armed movements, as would a successful electoral result: some 3 million young Argentines would be eligible to vote for the first time. (As Perón had bragged at the time of the 1951 elections, he won that contest with the newly enfranchised women's vote and would win his third election with the children.)

Simultaneously, however, via Isabel and López Rega, Perón was also negotiating the backing of the Italian mafioso Licio Gelli, leader of the Propaganda Due masonic movement and in practice the controller of the Vatican Bank. Gelli had a particular interest in averting any risk of Marxist expansion in Latin America, for which Perón was seen as key, and had influence with elements in Argentina such as the Christian Democrats and some high-ranking military officers who could help to achieve that end. As Cámpora became increasingly identified with the left, he would become an obstacle to this aim and to Perón's hopes of attracting investment into the economy.

Cámpora would premise much of his campaign on stressing his loyalty, as well as on the work of a team of young strategists focused on the youth vote, which included his son Héctor and his nephew Mario, an intelligent career diplomat. In this he proved highly successful, and his rallies were punctuated by thousands of young supporters enthusiastically chanting slogans such as 'how beautiful it will be, Uncle in government and Perón in power' or 'Perón, Evita and Uncle Camporita', as well as the more strident and more ominous chants of '*Montoneros CARAJO!*' (Montoneros damn it!) and 'they'll see, they'll see, when we revenge the dead of Trelew'. However, Perón himself took no direct part in the campaign. Although he had been prohibited from returning before the presidential handover on 25 May, the fact that he spent much of the period travelling in Italy and Romania suggested that he had no desire to become involved, perhaps in the belief that Cámpora might perform poorly. Cámpora's son made another visit to Perón, this time in Rome, in mid-February with a report from his father and a proposal that he return with a view to ensuring a first-round victory. His reply offered some advice but no mention of any more active participation.

The elections finally went ahead as scheduled on 11 March, without Perón's presence. Although initial unofficial reports suggested that Cámpora had received as much as 52 per cent of the vote, the final result was delayed for a considerable period – perhaps because Lanusse's own candidate, Ezequiel Martínez, received only about 3 per cent of the vote, a far worse defeat than expected. Perón continued to receive constant updates by telex; 'only his eyes reflected the satisfaction of the strategist who has won the decisive battle',[2] although the figures would fluctuate substantially over the coming days. On the 12th he would send a message of congratulation 'to electors and the elected, to supporters and adversaries' and a call for 'patriotic efforts for national reconstruction'. That message contained a handwritten note to Cámpora, sent by facsimile, which read, 'Dear Cámpora, with my most affectionate embrace I send my congratulations. Greetings to the boys. Juan Perón.'[3] This suggested that at least he was satisfied of victory. In fact the final result (released only at the end of March) gave Cámpora 49.6 per cent of the vote to 21.3 per cent for Ricardo Balbín, who congratulated Cámpora for his win and announced that he would withdraw from any run-off (50 per cent being the required minimum for a first-round victory). The result prompted mass demonstrations of joy and enthusiasm reminiscent of 17 October. 'When the victory was confirmed, the country that had been hidden away took to the streets.'[4] As thousands of supporters gathered in front of Cámpora's campaign headquarters in Palermo, from the balcony the names of those who had died in the Peronist resistance were read out, starting with General Juan José Valle, producing a thunderous response of 'present!' after each name. The FREJULI also won in twenty-one provinces, losing elections only in the capital and the provinces of Santiago del Estero and Neuquén (the latter long governed by the Sapag family's 'neo-Peronist' provincial party).

However, there were stirrings of disquiet surrounding Cámpora even before he could take office, many of them originating from Madrid. In particular, Isabel and López Rega appear to have feared that Cámpora and his own circle might begin to believe him to be president and to act independently – in other words, presumably, that he might prove unwilling to step down in favour of Perón when the time came. In particular, perhaps, his close ties to many younger members of the movement, including his own relatives and the party's then secretary-general Juan Manuel Abal Medina (brother of one of Aramburu's kidnappers) suggested both a tendency towards more radical factions and a belief in Perón's often-mentioned but not immediately plausible 'generational transfer'. Abal Medina, another Catholic activist who was not linked to the 'special formations' but in fact had good relations with some union leaders such as the metalworkers José Rucci and Lorenzo Miguel, as well as fluid contacts with sectors of the military, would find himself increasingly marginalized by the machinations from Madrid.

The concerns of Isabel and López Rega were made more pressing by new worries over Perón's health: new studies showed that he had already had a serious heart attack, probably during his visit to Buenos Aires the previous November, and that he was suffering from advanced arteriosclerosis. He had also earlier had both prostate and gall bladder surgery, as well as an operation to remove a malignant polyp from his bladder, and appeared to be beginning to suffer from kidney problems. Doctors' reports suggested that his life expectancy was around one to three years, the latter if he lived a quiet and health-conscious existence.[5]

Those stirrings of concern became more evident during a visit by Cámpora, this time in Rome, on 26 March, in which Cámpora made strenuous efforts to convince Perón to attend his inauguration on 25 May and sought his approval of potential cabinet ministers. He was accompanied by the Montoneros Mario Firmenich and Roberto Quieto, who far from taking a secondary role attempted to 'impose' their own cabinet choices on Perón. The president-elect had some important meetings in Rome, including with the president and prime minister, but the most important was an audience with Pope Paul VI, to which his family was invited but Perón and Isabel were not. Although publicly at least Perón made light of this and showed understanding of the protocols in place, the fact that Cámpora's wife María Georgina met the pope appears to have been too much for Isabel, as was the attention she garnered in the press, however respectful she was of Isabel's position when speaking of her in interviews. (Nor was Isabel impressed when, on a brief visit by Cámpora to Madrid, he and Perón were received by General Francisco Franco – for the first time during Perón's long stay in Spain – and she was forced to remain outside making small talk with Franco's wife Carmen Polo.)

Having failed yet again to extract a promise that Perón would accompany him at his inauguration, Cámpora once again sent his nephew Mario, together with his wife Magdalena, to plead his case, this time in Paris, where they were met by López Rega, Perón and Isabel at the Hotel Claridge. Magdalena would later describe them, in horror, as 'an absurd couple': he elderly and 'incredibly tall', with implausibly black hair and an impassive face, and she 'a vulgar little woman' who was 'horribly hysterical'.[6] Both began to realize that he was distancing himself from

Figure 14 Perón, his secretary José López Rega (left) and President-elect Héctor Cámpora in Rome, March 1973 (Photo by Keystone/Getty Images)

Cámpora; according to Mario later, he rejected the invitation to the inauguration by saying 'I won't go, so as not to steal the show from Dr Cámpora', before adding 'I'll go later and then the balcony will be for me.' Mario would subsequently inform his uncle that he believed that Perón aimed to supplant him in the presidency, to which Cámpora merely replied 'here we will do what the General wants. We are here to fulfil his will.'[7]

So much was this the case that Cámpora spent considerable effort in gaining Perón's approval of his cabinet. Contrary to some reports, Perón largely accepted Cámpora's suggestions (although he would later take issue with the young interior minister, Esteban Righi), imposing only a single nomination: his valet cum secretary, López Rega, as minister of social welfare. Although Cámpora had proposed to offer this post to Isabel, Perón preferred that she lead a reconstituted Eva Perón Foundation. For his part, López Rega would bring in retired Lieutenant Colonel Jorge Osinde, a former army intelligence officer, as sub-secretary of sports, a seemingly innocuous post that would in fact be key in arming what would become the ministry's primary activity – the establishment of a clandestine right-wing death squad, the Argentine Anti-Communist Alliance (Triple A). Cámpora himself would suggest Raúl Lastiri, López Rega's son-in-law, as president of the Lower House. (Lastiri, a non-entity a year older than his father-in-law, became known primarily for his extensive collection of neckties, which he boasted numbered some 300.) López Rega, moreover, would represent Perón at Cámpora's inauguration.

That inauguration, attended by the presidents of Chile and Cuba, was marked by the massive presence in the Plaza de Mayo of the 'special formations' and other leftist groups: banners of the JP, Montoneros and FAR were everywhere, and the chants included 'long live the Montoneros who killed Aramburu'. Although the left was largely successful in 'winning the street', there were also many traditional Peronists, trade unionists and rightists alike, who clashed with the left. Cámpora himself made a speech exalting Perón and Evita, as well as 'the marvellous youth that responded to violence with violence',[8] a probably well-meant tribute that would only undermine Cámpora's position with the broader movement and the armed forces. Despite the great enthusiasm surrounding the inauguration, the event was marked by fights between those demanding the 'socialist fatherland' and those calling for the 'Peronist fatherland', while abuse faced by the military increased resentments.

Even more controversially, the new president let himself be pressured by the militant groups into declaring a pardon for political prisoners, rather than awaiting the proposed amnesty law before Congress. Thousands thronged to Devoto prison to free the prisoners, including individuals jailed for terrorist offences, driving a new wedge between Cámpora and the other forces with which he had to contend; attempts to free other prisoners ended with two demonstrators being shot dead. (By contrast, the announcement of his cabinet later that day, and the inclusion of López Rega, did nothing to improve relations with either the left or centre.) It also doubtless did nothing to improve his standing with Perón, whose own willingness to condone leftist violence when it suited his purposes did not make him genuinely sympathetic to such disorder; his distaste for the 'inorganic mass' and uncontrolled violence persisted, although he apparently continued to believe that his own eventual arrival in Argentina would force the troublemakers into line.

Despite the theory that Peronism's return to power would discourage violence, Cámpora's early days in government were marked by further serious events such as kidnappings and killings, some of them involving non-Peronist guerrillas such as the ERP and some of them involving right-wing movements angered by the liberation of political prisoners. While the Montoneros had left the underground and temporarily focused on political rather than guerrilla activities, their frequent presence in Cámpora's office undermined him in the eyes of many, including moderates – and the leader still lurking in Madrid. Shortly after Cámpora's inauguration, on 4 April the Montoneros assassinated Colonel Héctor Alberto Iribarren, head of the Third Army Corps information services, which they announced through a communiqué titled 'with the ballot box to government, with arms to power'. Only a few days later, JP leader Rodolfo Galimberti proposed the creation of 'popular militias', a proposal that aroused Perón's ire and saw Galimberti removed from his post. Although on 8 June Cámpora managed to preside over a 'social pact' between the CGT and the Peronist-dominated business organization the General Economic Confederation (CGE), there was little opportunity to implement an economic plan. Moreover, Cámpora remained engrossed in the question of Perón's future – which in turn was seemingly influenced by the failure of his proxy to restore order.

Finally it was announced that Perón would return home on 20 June, Argentina's Flag Day. Cámpora dropped everything to travel to Madrid on the 15th to accompany him, an evidently subservient attitude for an elected head of state that won him no favour from the General – Perón did not meet him at the airport, took no part in official events and largely ignored his presence in Madrid, even rebuffing him when the tuxedoed president appeared in person in Puerta de Hierro to plead with him to attend a formal reception. This may have been a show of power and of disapproval, but it also appears likely to have represented an attempt to make clear that he was distancing himself from Cámpora and would not long support his continued stay in the presidency. Shortly he would have another reason to criticize his proxy's ability to organize and control events.

The group departed Madrid on a chartered Aerolíneas Argentinas flight; the contingent included Cámpora and his wife, Perón and Isabel, López Rega, Lastiri and Perón's physician Pedro Cossio. The flight was due to land at Ezeiza at 3.00 pm on the 20th, where Perón, Isabel and Cámpora would be transported by helicopter to the platform, adorned by huge photos of Perón, Evita and Isabel, and Perón would be the sole speaker. In many respects the event was more than even Perón could ever have imagined. With up to 3 million people waiting to greet him, his return was being welcomed by a far wider range of society than had ever accepted him during his nine years in the presidency. Not only had some memories faded, while others were strengthened or distorted by the long years of proscription and repression, but the increasingly disastrous situation in Argentina had led many to believe that Perón alone was the man able to restore order and some semblance of a future. However, both Perón and the public had been deceived by distance: he would find that Argentina was not the country he had left eighteen years earlier, and Argentines would find that he was not the man they remembered but an elderly and ailing man who had had an urgent prostate operation only days before travelling. (On the flight itself, there are strong suggestions that he may have had another heart attack, suffering severe pains only hours before landing.)

As described earlier, the joy of the event rapidly turned to horror, not least as Perón's proximity made it imperative for both wings of the movement to display their power and thus seek the upper hand. With the exception of Abal Medina, the welcoming committee charged with organizing the event was a select group composed of the Peronist far right: López Rega, Osinde, metalworkers' leaders José Rucci and Lorenzo Miguel, and Norma Kennedy. Osinde's men having taken charge of the arrangements, and control of the platform, the left sought to circumvent their own marginalization by employing a pincer movement to elude the security. Carrying chains to swing in a bid to force their way through, they were met by gunfire from the platform. Clashes between left and right segments started early, with the first shots fired around 10.30. Shortly before the flight was due to land, the Ezeiza massacre began in earnest: according to the left, the right-wing shock troops launched an unprovoked assault on them, while according to the right the guerrilla movements had planned to assassinate Perón (an unlikely claim given their sustained and often violent campaign to ensure his return). As bullets began to fly and those near the front of the crowd were wounded in the crossfire, a stampede of people attempting to escape prompted further injuries. Both the left and right would blame foreign elements for increasing polarization and violence, with the left pointing to the CIA and imperialism and the right to the infiltration of foreign Marxist ideologies.

The vice-president, Vicente Solano Lima, was waiting at Ezeiza when he was informed of the catastrophe; he radioed the aircraft and told Cámpora that he would have the flight diverted to Morón to prevent any assassination risk, despite Cámpora's protestations that this would ruin an already devastated *fiesta*. Cámpora then faced the unenviable task of informing Perón, who disembarked in Morón in high dudgeon, leaving Cámpora to make a radio speech blaming 'anti-national elements' for the events. Perón and Isabel would then depart by helicopter for Buenos Aires and the presidential residence in Olivos, where he made a brief speech thanking those who had turned out to welcome him and reassuring them that he was safe. He began by saying, 'I return without rancours nor passions, other than the passion that informed my whole life: to serve the fatherland loyally' and that 'we have a revolution to carry out, but for it to be valid it must be constructed peacefully, without costing the life of a single Argentine.' However, he went on to warn 'whoever disturbs the principle of coexistence … will be the common enemy we must fight without respite' and that 'those who try to infiltrate popular or state classes are going the wrong way'.[9] Beatings and torture of those captured carried on into the night.

There is evidence that Perón was convinced that the Montoneros or other guerrilla groups had planned to murder him in Ezeiza in order to launch a socialist revolution; this may in part explain the violent splits that would occur only months later.[10] In any case, the following day, newly ensconced in the house in Vicente López, he made a major speech denouncing terrorism and the infiltration of 'foreign ideologies', which should have made it clear to the 'marvellous youth' that they had lost any influence they might have believed they had – and indeed that Perón had no vision of presiding over revolution. (That impression was underscored by the company of Isabel, López Rega and Lastiri in the frame.) In general terms, the speech was well received by many others, being moderate, centrist and calling for hard work, discipline and unity, a statesmanlike rather than partisan speech. The following day he held a lengthy meeting with Ricardo Balbín in which they agreed in broad terms on a framework for moving forward and a possible consensus between the two large parties. All of this made clear rapidly that any leadership had passed from Cámpora's hands. Two days later Perón visited López Rega at his office at the Social Welfare Ministry, a further signal of his support. (A popular joke would later sum up Perón's supposed strategy: on arriving at a crossroads, his chauffeur asks him what to do, to which he responds 'signal left and turn right'.)

Only six days after his arrival, on 26 June Perón suffered a major heart attack requiring medical treatment, although he remained at home rather than going to hospital. Two days later he was diagnosed with acute pleuropericarditis, apparently linked to bowel problems. Thereafter a permanent medical team was established in the premises with a small intensive care unit set up to deal with any urgencies. The team would be led by Perón's personal physicians Pedro Cossio and Jorge Taiana (the latter also the education minister) and include a group of younger personnel on a rota system.

Perón's health then seemed to stabilize for some time and their ministrations were not required, although it would deteriorate again from November 1973. In the meantime, Perón, who had always fancied his medical knowledge, seemed to enjoy their company and reportedly made various revealing comments to Cossio in particular, expressing his distaste for Righi and complaining of Cámpora's performance, asking rhetorically, 'Is it possible that there is no young Argentine who could be president now? ... I'd like to be a counsellor and supervise what needs to be done ... although sometimes I'd like to go back to Spain for a while.'[11] Cossio believed, accurately or not, that Perón felt he had no choice but to assume the presidency, despite the fact that his health was not up to the job. (On visiting his doctor in Barcelona for the last time before his departure, Perón reportedly said, 'I have no choice but to go back and put things in order. Cámpora opened the prisons and infiltrated communists everywhere.'[12])

Both Cossio and a young doctor who formed part of the team, Carlos Seara, would also claim that Perón was entirely lucid during these final months, although this was disputed by other interlocutors: the CIA would say that he 'has lucid periods, interrupted by periods of depression during which he becomes a dependent old man' and that he was at those times very dependent on Isabel and López Rega.[13] Others would note that he seemed alert in the morning but grew tired and less lucid as the day wore on. Perhaps more revealingly, Seara would also note that 'he was very agreeable, very friendly ... but I could not help but notice, although unconsciously I tried to deny the reality, that he was old, he seemed tired'. This unwillingness to see Perón as he really was in 1973 represented a widely shared and deliberate blind spot, an unwillingness to see the weary reality in place of the vigorous myth. At the same time, despite the cordial exterior, 'Perón was a very distant person, in practice he spoke with very few people and had no physical or emotional closeness with anyone, not even Isabel or López Rega, who was very close at hand (at his own initiative, not because Perón called him).'[14]

After Perón's heart attack, it should have been evident that the handwriting was on the wall for any return to the presidency. However, the handwriting was also on the wall for Cámpora's own presidency. However much Perón may have deliberately undermined Cámpora, the reality was that *el Tío* lacked the authority or the political skills to manage an unmanageable situation – and indeed, as Buenos Aires vice-governor Victorio Calabró observed, 'with General Perón in the country no one else can be president of the Argentines'.[15] Once Perón had recovered sufficiently to appear in public, Cámpora and Solano Lima announced their resignations on 13 July, forty-nine days into their term. Prior to their resignations, Senate president Alejandro Díaz Bialet (under the constitution next in line to the presidency) was persuaded to undertake a visit to Madrid, allowing Raúl Lastiri as president of the Lower House to take over as interim head of state. Cámpora's last act as outgoing president was to call new elections for 23 September.

The precise circumstances of Cámpora's resignation are unclear. He reportedly offered his resignation a week before it was finally announced, possibly pushed by Isabel and López Rega; whether or not Perón was himself directly involved in the defenestration is uncertain. Suggestions that he might have resolved to remove him after being told that Cámpora had delayed signing a decree returning Perón's military rank of lieutenant general appear unlikely in such a deliberate tactician more given to extracting humiliation for the error than to throwing away any real strategy for such a reason.

The fact that Perón seldom publicly accepted responsibility and that his followers were often eager to offer up other scapegoats made it easy for the left in particular to blame Isabel and *El Brujo* for Cámpora's ouster (just as Evita had been blamed for those of Bramuglia and Mercante years earlier). Similarly, the organization of the Triple A was usually laid at the feet of López Rega, often with the excuse that Perón was too ill and confused to know what was happening – scarcely an argument in favour of him assuming the presidency.

In fact, although there is no question that López Rega was the driving force behind the Triple A, it is far more dubious whether Perón was really ignorant of its sinister activities; the daughter of Buenos Aires governor Oscar Bidegain would subsequently admit her suspicion that 'the Triple A had not been born in López Rega's head, but in Perón's'.[16] In all likelihood, Perón had adhered to his lifelong habit of hints and ambiguity rather than clear instruction, leaving his inferiors free to act in unpalatable ways while retaining a degree of plausible deniability, perhaps even to himself. (Perón himself would cruelly refer to the rise of right-wing violence as the appearance of 'anti-bodies' to attack the 'microbes' of left-wing groups infiltrating the body politic.) The Triple A would announce itself for the first time in November 1973, with an attack on the Radical politician Hipólito Solarí Yrigoyen, although it had existed quietly for some time; at the end of January 1974 it issued a blacklist of people it intended to kill. Although the Triple A was not responsible for all of them, the number of right-wing attacks including bombings, shootings, kidnappings and assassinations by security forces or clandestine groups would mount throughout the period: during the year between Perón's return and his death there were around eight such attacks in July 1973, seven in August, eighteen in September, thirty-two in October, thirteen in November, thirty-four in December, twelve in January, twenty-three in February, thirty in March, eight in April, nineteen in May (including the murder of the shantytown priest Father Carlos Mugica) and twelve in June. Worse would be to come.

Following Cámpora's resignation Perón appeared on television to try to generate calm, although his physical appearance should have had the opposite effect. While making no specific statements, he promised to follow the will of the people – which by this time was genuinely clear at least insofar as the wish that Perón should return to the presidency to try to heal the deep rifts in society and in the battered economy. In the latter respect at least he had already showed himself to be astute, seeking to woo European investment in particular while also seeking to build regional bridges and also closer economic ties with Asia as an alternative; the decision to send Isabel and López Rega to China and North Korea during the previous months had represented a clever move. Moreover, despite the belief on the left that the old man would still turn to socialism and the belief on the right that he would hew to the hard line of the unionist right and the security services, for much of the rest of the population, weary of extremism, he looked increasingly statesmanlike and conciliatory. His hopes were pinned on accords with other political parties and between business and labour; whatever the hopes of the left, in an October meeting with business leaders he made it clear that he did not intend to deviate from prudent economic policies. The 'social pact' reached envisaged a gradual increase in labour's share of national income from 35 per cent to 48 per cent, allowing the Montoneros to cling to the hope that there was "'no difference between the Peronist Fatherland and the Socialist Fatherland, since the Peronist Movement led by General Perón serves the workers' interests'".[17]

A British Embassy report, while styling him a 'complete opportunist', observed that he also seemed entirely pragmatic, shifting 'away from nationalism via "continentalism" towards "universalism"' and seeking to mend fences and champion regional unity while also seeking investment from anywhere it could be found. This implied that, although Europe would be the preferred partner, East Asia or the Middle East would be palatable alternatives, with Argentina well placed as a leading supplier of food and raw materials (a significant shift from his earlier hopes of industrialization, perhaps reflecting the reality of how that policy had foundered). 'During his exile Perón has clearly done a lot of reading and absorbed ideas from various sources …. [H]is philosophy is based on his largely borrowed understanding of world history.'[18] This, at least, was nothing new. However, it did imply, as he must have understood, the need for a stable government that could bring a degree of social and economic order necessary to attract investment and trade partners.

If there was then absolutely no secret as to who the Peronist candidate for president would be in September, the most contentious issue was who would be his running-mate. This was a particularly vexed question, given not only the wildly divergent factions within the movement and the animosities among them but also the realization that the vice-president would almost certainly be required ultimately to complete his term. One possibility widely discussed was to form an alliance with the Radicals that would see Balbín as the vice-presidential choice; whether or not this was ever seriously mooted, Perón himself fuelled the rumour when he said, 'I have great respect for Dr. Balbín and would go anywhere with him.'[19] However, even if Perón himself might have seen this as a desirable outcome, it was not one he ever discussed with Balbín and would never have been a feasible one, with the Radicals still determined to present an opposition ticket and the Peronists unwilling to be left off the ticket and out of power should Balbín succeed as president. The difficulty would be to strike a balance between competing demands: the left hoped to see the battered Cámpora as the running-mate, while moderates backed Education Minister Jorge Taiana and the right backed Isabel.

At the party convention on 4 August, from which the 'glorious JP' was excluded, Perón was nominated unopposed but the vice-presidential slot was left blank. Perhaps taking a leaf from the playbook of August 1951, Perón did not appear and made no indication of his preference, but a delegate nominated Isabel and she was also approved by acclamation. Isabel herself then arrived and, echoing Evita twenty-two years earlier, expressed her willingness to serve and promised that Perón would always do what the people wanted, describing herself as 'the General's best pupil'. Unlike Evita, the widely despised Isabel made history and a place on the ticket. However evasive Perón may have been, there can be no doubt that he backed the decision, otherwise it would not have gone ahead. Whether this was due to pressures from within his household that he no longer felt able to withstand, or a genuine belief that as his pupil he had trained Isabel sufficiently for the role, or simply that she was the one candidate that all factions of the movement would have to accept, as his wife, he engineered a situation in which a disastrous decision was taken (and, again, one for which he could claim not to have been directly responsible).

If Perón did believe Isabel to be competent to assume the presidency, this view was not widely shared. Yet the process continued, in part because it had long been widely accepted that Perón took decisions and others followed, and in part due to considerable unwillingness to accept the reality of Perón's age and infirmity persisted. For thirty years he had been the driving force in Argentine political life, even when in exile, and for many it was difficult to believe in the reality that he would soon die. This feeling was even greater than in the past, given that for the first time Perón had achieved wide consensus across Peronist and anti-Peronist sectors alike that he was Argentina's single greatest hope; as 'God is Argentine', in a popular saying, surely he would not let Perón die when he was most needed.

This stubborn refusal to accept realities was arguably greatest among the Peronist left, who remained deeply committed to *El Viejo* despite the fact that the choice of Isabel as running-mate and the consequent strengthening of López Rega must have made it obvious that the balance had shifted irrevocably away from them in the struggle for influence. Nevertheless, after the candidates formally accepted their nominations on 18 August, the JP participated in mass demonstrations on 31 August organized by the CGT and attended by around 1 million people, at which both sides made sure there was no repeat of the Ezeiza massacre. Yet the demonstrations represented a competition to see which side could bring out more supporters; according to those keeping score, the CGT delegations took 165 minutes to march past Perón's platform, while the left took 162 minutes.[20] Prior to the 23 September elections López Rega was also kept in the background and Perón met with leaders of the Montoneros and FAR in a bid to sustain the appearance of balance and to deter factional struggles that would have impacted on his ability to carry on an electoral campaign.

The Perón-Perón ticket would win the 23 September elections with over 60 per cent of the vote, inevitably trouncing the Radical ticket of Ricardo Balbín and Fernando de la Rua. Perón's return to the presidency almost eighteen years to the day after his ignominious departure was an unprecedented triumph for Perón himself, a moment of great joy for his followers and one of hope even among many of his opponents that a moment of national reconciliation and reconstruction might be at hand. That optimism would be marred rapidly by the assassination of the right-wing CGT leader José Rucci two days later, probably by the Montoneros. The crime infuriated Perón, who regarded Rucci as almost a son as well as a key part of his political strategy; he would say that the killers 'cut off my legs'. It perhaps also forced him to face, fearfully, that he now had to find a way to address the violence that continued to wrack the country. A member of the JP was murdered the following day. Either way, the moment of hope and glory would be short-lived. The long years of institutional erosion, economic crisis, inflation, trade union conflicts and guerrilla actions had undermined governability and an increasingly frail man with only months to live had no hope of reverting this, whatever his intentions.

Chapter 17

THE MOST MARVELLOUS MUSIC

Adiós muchachos, ya me voy y me resigno; contra el Destino nadie la talla …
Se terminaron para mí todas las farras, mi cuerpo enfermo no resiste más.
Dos lágrimas sinceras derramo en mi partida por la barra querida que nunca
    me olvidó
Y al darles a mis amigos mi adios postrero, les doy con toda mi alma mi
    bendición.

Goodbye friends, I am going and I am resigned,
No-one can defeat destiny ….
The good times are over for me, my ailing body can resist no more.
On departing I shed a sincere tear for my beloved supporters who never forgot
    me
And in saying my last farewell to my friends I give them my blessing with all my
    heart.
Adiós, muchachos (tango), César Felipe Vedani and Julio César Alberto Sanders[1]

Perón was sworn in as president for the third time on 12 October 1973, making his first appearance on the famous balcony of the Casa Rosada since his ill-advised 'five-for-one' speech more than eighteen years earlier, as well as his first public appearance in his general's uniform. Again, the factions within the movement saw to it that the event passed off peacefully and without clashes, although the Montoneros would mark the event by announcing a fusion with the FAR. The inauguration was relatively low-key for such a long-awaited event. Perón made a relatively bland and brief speech – promising, as ever, to reappear on May Day to ask the workers if they were satisfied with the government – and the prospects for a degree of national consensus seemed, at least fleetingly, better than they had been in some years. The Montoneros would (briefly) lay down arms and opt instead to work with the poor and with the JP, which they would come to dominate as an ideological force. Yet more ominous undercurrents were already growing.

As noted earlier, before his inauguration Perón had increasingly focused on imposing order on the unruly movements whose activities he had encouraged from Madrid but now repudiated as a threat to his government. Following Rucci's death the Peronist Superior Council had ordered all purportedly Peronist groups to combat the 'terrorist and subversive Marxist groups' 'infiltrated' into the Peronist movement.[2] Despite this, and despite the fact that that document was signed by Perón himself, the left appeared unable to believe that Perón had come down on the side of the right and appeared to be frozen in the headlights for some time, opting to accept orders from above rather than defending themselves. However, the number of attacks on the left would escalate rapidly and would be widely attributed to López Rega and the Triple A; although they were not directly or demonstrably linked to the government per se (and the Montoneros clearly preferred to think that they were not), it was evident that the government was making little effort to halt them. (Even despite this willing suspension of disbelief, Montonero leader Mario Firmenich would observe in March 1974 that 'we created our own Perón, someone greater than the person he really is. Now that Perón is here, Perón is Perón and not the man we wish him to be.'[3])

As Perón's health faltered, too, López Rega would become more ubiquitous, accompanying the president permanently in public and continuing to act as his private secretary as well as cabinet minister. He also insisted that Perón continue to walk long distances in order to maintain his physical fitness. Firmenich would later say, 'Perón was an old man …. He had his own ideas, but he had almost no capacity for action … in some ways he was a prisoner of his age.'[4] As he had during his earlier presidencies, Perón continued to sustain a demanding schedule, getting up at 6.00 am every day and reaching his office at 7 am before returning home for lunch and a nap. This may have been well advised, given that he was often said to be more lucid in the morning than in the afternoon, yet for a man of his age it was scarcely a pace that could be maintained for any period of time.

Weeks after assuming the presidency, in early November Perón made a visit to the aircraft carrier *25 de mayo* in bad weather and was subsequently diagnosed with a respiratory infection and prescribed antibiotics and bed rest, notwithstanding which he participated in another outdoor event with the military high command a few days later. During the night of 21 November Perón suffered a serious arrhythmia which required his medical team to be sent for and compressions to be administered. Although he recovered, the event made clear to his doctors that his heart condition was worse than they had believed; Perón himself would say to Dr Cossio 'the scythe wasn't ready this time, but I saw it up close'.[5] The scare prompted the strengthening of a permanent emergency medical team which would be present at the presidential residences, the Casa Rosada and any travel undertaken by the president. Although Perón recovered at least in part from these difficulties, by January the doctors were noting instances of fluid in his lungs and changes to his heart rhythm which did not bode well.

On 19 January 1974 members of the Trotskyist ERP attacked a tank brigade in Azul, Buenos Aires province, killing a colonel and his wife. Although this riposte to the wave of right-wing violence did not come from the Montoneros, Perón accused the leftist Peronist governor of Buenos Aires province, Oscar Bidegain, of tolerating subversion, prompting his resignation and replacement by his right-wing vice-governor, metalworkers' leader Victorio Calabró. (The other left-wing Peronist governor, Córdoba Governor Ricardo Obregón Cano, was forced to resign in March together with his vice-governor when the federal government intervened in the province after the provincial police rebelled against the governor.) Shortly after these events the government presented to Congress a severe anti-subversion law that curtailed even non-violent protest – the move prompted JP members of Congress to resign, which served only to increase the legislative influence of the right.

The killings clearly shook Perón, who also cancelled a planned river trip on the presidential yacht in mid-January after a launch carrying a police officer was blown up in the Tigre Delta, possibly in the belief that an attempt would also be made on his life. At a February press conference, Perón would say that extremism was acceptable within the movement only so long as it was 'useful', suggesting that this was no longer the case now that he was in power and remarking that 'we are not sectarian but we are not fools either'.[6] Over the same period, killings by shadowy right-wing groups were also mounting; twelve left-wing activists were killed and a number of their headquarters bombed. Perón refused to condemn the killings, and the apparent real rupture with the Montoneros came when they refused to attend a meeting he had called to establish a General Youth Confederation which included the participation of far-right groups.

Despite these many concerns, Perón nonetheless decided to make a spontaneous appearance at the Formula 1 Grand Prix run in Buenos Aires on 13 January, in which the Argentine driver Carlos Reutemann was competing. Perón arrived by helicopter, accompanied by Isabel, López Rega and members of his medical team, who would later note the adulation with which he was greeted – the ovation and chants of Perón! Perón! entirely eclipsed the race. (Perón himself still loved to drive and, despite security and health concerns, would sometimes take his Fiat out for a spin around Olivos where he would greet the neighbours and enjoy a brief respite before returning to routine.)

In political and economic terms, this third mandate would see little progress on any front, apart from a university reform carried out under the auspices of Education Minister Jorge Taiana, which granted the universities substantial autonomy. Perón had also retained many other members of Cámpora's cabinet (obviously including López Rega), among them Economy Minister José Ber Gelbard, a one-time member of the Communist Party and a leader of the Peronist CGE who had earlier served as an informal economic adviser to Perón during his second term. Gelbard, who had arrived in Argentina as a child as a Jewish refugee from Poland, was a successful and self-made businessman and an astute functionary, but he had little scope to address serious challenges such as a European ban on Argentine meat imports and inflation which had hit 61 per cent in 1973 (although it fell to around 23 per cent in 1974, partly as a result of the social pact, before soaring to 183 per cent in 1975 and 444 per cent in 1976). Whatever the promises of economic independence of three decades earlier, Argentina remained a country largely dependent on agricultural exports and imports of finished products, and the times globally were no more propitious than the domestic panorama. Nor was Perón, ailing and increasingly distracted by attempting to end the factional infighting he himself had encouraged, in any position to focus significant emphasis on the economy.

Although Perón had made a brief speech from the balcony of the Casa Rosada on 12 October, the 1 May celebrations were intended to mark his true return; together with 17 October, the International Labour Day holiday was one of the key moments of the Peronist calendar and his appearance would hark back to the golden days of the 1940s and 1950s. Or so it was intended. The fact that Perón had rebuffed overtures from the Montoneros to distance himself from right-wing elements and to ban them from the May Day rally should have represented a warning that conflict was coming. Given the date, it should perhaps have been unsurprising that the main protagonists were the trade unions, but that did not stop the Montoneros from organizing a large presence, representing over half the 100,000 or so gathered in the plaza. As only the Argentine flag and trade union banners were permitted, the left brought aerosol cans and banners with Montonero slogans hidden in drums which were brought out once the rally started. This was the spectacle that greeted Perón when he stepped out onto the balcony, along with chants of 'if Evita were alive she would be a Montonera' and the reading out of the names of fallen Montoneros, each followed by a shout of 'present!'. They jeered as Isabel was crowned Queen of Labour (the honour that Evita had once graciously refused). The disobedient display 'infurated Perón. Perón was the prototype of a rational politician, a strategist, a cold man, a man who took decisions without emotions. And that day ... he was an emotional man and reacted emotionally, reacted with insults that were not part of the political discourse. That set off a tragedy.'[7]

Flanked by Isabel and López Rega, a visibly irate Perón began his speech, which had been intended to be a call to unity and, in particular, a paean to the labour movement. 'Nineteen years ago today, on this same balcony and on a bright day like this, I spoke to the Argentine workers for the last time.' Before he could continue, he was interrupted by loud chants of 'what's happening General? Why is the popular government full of gorillas?' and 'it's going to end, the union bureaucracy'. His voice shaking, Perón continued, 'I was not mistaken either in my appraisal of the days ahead or of the quality of the union organisation, which has held for 20 years, regardless of these idiots who are shouting.' 'Over these 20 years the union organisations have stayed immovable, and today some beardless youths think they have more merit than those who struggled for 20 years.' The response to his praise for the unions came back from the Montoneros: 'Rucci, traitor, say hello to Vandor.' Then the leftist groupings began to withdraw from the plaza; although unions and groups such as Guardia de Hierro attacked them and prevented some from leaving, the departure of the left resulted in a plaza that was more than half empty. As had occurred on 31 August 1955, Perón's wrath ran away with him and he continued to improvise an increasingly violent speech, emphasizing the position of the unions as the backbone of the movement and calling for national reconstruction and liberation, 'not only from colonialism ... but also these infiltrators who operate from within, and who traitorously are more dangerous than those who work from outside'.[8]

On 6 June Perón would make a visit to Paraguay on the invitation of his long-time friend and one-time host General Alfredo Stroessner. The trip would prove physically demanding and damaging. As the doctor who accompanied him later described it, the committee flew to Formosa, where on a cold and wet day Perón spent some thirty minutes reviewing the troops before continuing his trip in helicopter to Puerto Pilcomayo, where again he stood in the inclement weather to review troops before embarking on a minesweeper that would take him on to Paraguay, another hour up river in which he was forced to stand on deck. He was received in Asunción by a huge crowd and by Stroessner, who made a lengthy speech before they were taken to their hotel – a trip that took some six hours door-to-door, much of it outdoors in bad weather. This was followed by various visits and a reception and gala dinner in the evening, before the return journey the next morning.[9]

The impact of that visit on Perón's health would prove damaging, whether or not it was decisive in his final decline. Although the greatest deterioration would not become apparent for several more days, by mid-June he himself clearly felt fatigued and unwell. (During a visit by Balbín, Perón told him bluntly that he was dying.) It had already been announced that he would speak from the balcony of the Casa Rosada on 12 June, but to wide surprise he appeared suddenly on television that morning, railing against fractures in the social pact, union criticism of Gelbard and others, and implicitly suggested that he might resign (following on from earlier private threats to return to Madrid). In traditional fashion, the CGT called a rally for that afternoon to convince him to change his mind.

Again, it was a cold day, and Perón's speech sounded undeniably to the millions who heard it, whether in person or on television, like a final farewell. Sounding hoarse, Perón began by reverting to some of his earlier warnings about violence, saying that 'there are many who want to divert us in one direction or another, but we know our objectives perfectly and will march directly towards them without being influenced by those who pull either from the right or from the left'. Calling for prudence, he went on to say that 'we want no one to fear us, but we want them to understand us', urging his listeners to become 'vigilant observers' and 'neutralise the negative of those sectors that still have not understood us and will have to understand'.

Notwithstanding the warning note sounded in much of the speech, Perón ended on a far more gentle and perhaps melancholy note, thanking those gathered and saying,

> I will carry this marvellous spectacle etched on my retina, in which the working people of the city and province of Buenos Aires bring me the message that I need. *Compañeros*, together with my thanks I want to transmit to all the people of the Republic our desire to continue working to reconstruct and liberate our country. These watchwords, which more than mine are those of the Argentine people, we will defend to our last breath. To finish, I desire that God will bless you with all of the good fortune and happiness you deserve. I thank you profoundly for having come to this historic Plaza de Mayo. I carry in my ears the most marvellous music which, for me, is the word of the Argentine people.[10]

Although Perón would continue working in his office, albeit on a reduced timetable, and would continue to take an active line on combating insurgency (on 17 June, he would say 'we should employ repression a bit stronger and more violent'[11]), by 16 June his health was visibly deteriorating, starting with a chest infection. Nevertheless, his symptoms were not yet considered serious enough for Isabel (and López Rega) to suspend a planned trip to Geneva, Rome and Madrid on 15 June, which implied that his second-in-command was not in the country in the event he was incapacitated, and his next of kin was not present to take personal medical decisions. He suspended official activities, and press statements referred to a mild case of bronchitis; Perón himself passed some of his time watching news reports of Isabel's official visit to Italy (including crowds chanting slogans in favour of Perón and the Third Position).

From the 18th Perón began to suffer more frequent and more serious chest pains. On the 25th his general state, both physical and mental, appeared to decline. The medical team brought in equipment to enable them to monitor his heart rate continuously, and on the 27th he was awakened twice by fierce chest pains which the electrocardiograms indicated were heart attacks. The doctors informed Isabel that it would be wise to cut short her visit to Italy and return, which she did on the 28th. By then his heart rate was increasingly rapid and the doctors began to suspect a pulmonary oedema; Perón himself would gasp out that he was drowning, prompting the team to put him on a drip. The intravenous medicine saw a rapid improvement in the short term, but by the following day he was only semi-conscious and showing signs of renal failure. The medical team maintained a permanent presence in his bedroom, while Isabel and López Rega appeared intermittently. On the 29th Perón signed the handover of presidential power to Isabel.

On Monday 1 July Perón suffered a heart attack at 10.20. Although he was still only semi-conscious, the nurse who was with him would insist she heard him say 'it's over'. The doctors sprang into action, laying the president on the floor and beginning compressions, mouth-to-mouth resuscitation and inserting a breathing tube as well as administering adrenaline and electric shocks with a portable defibrillator. A team of eight doctors took turns keeping up compressions. At one point López Rega entered and, somewhat bizarrely, offered to ennoble one of the doctors if they could keep the president alive (although two of the doctors present have denied widely repeated claims that López Rega attempted to keep Perón's soul from leaving his body by grabbing his ankles and muttering incantations).[12] More than three hours after Perón's heart attack and resuscitation efforts began, time of death was called at 13.15. (The date of his death, precisely mid-year, would prompt ironic jokes about his refusal to commit to one side or another, even in death.)

Despite the relatively realistic communiqués issued about Perón's state of health over the preceding days, his death was a deep shock to a country still clinging to the hope that he might be able to bring unity to an Argentina sinking deeper and deeper into crisis. Moreover, few people could remember a time when Perón had not been the central presence in the political life of the country (even when proscription and exile made that presence an absence for eighteen years). To say that many experienced it in the way they would have reacted to the death of a parent and the gap that would leave in their lives is not an exaggeration. It was suddenly time for Argentines – Peronist and anti-Peronist alike – to face the reality of a future without Perón as a central figure of either hope or hatred. Perhaps more to the point in practical terms, Argentines now faced a deep crisis with a president of minimal experience and political skills, who could scarcely be expected to fare well where her husband had failed.

For all his own claims that he had trained her up for political duties, Perón himself clearly had doubts about Isabel's fitness for office. In June during his final illness he reportedly attempted to refloat plans to seek a constitutional means to pass the presidency to Balbín; as difficult as this would have been legally in any case, the failure to pursue it has been attributed to the machinations of López Rega, who prevented Perón from undertaking consultations that would have seen his acolyte and path to power sidelined.[13]

It was left to Isabel, as president and widow, to make the announcement, flanked by her cabinet. Perón had given specific instructions that his body was not to be embalmed like that of Evita, which implied that the funeral would be by necessity of shorter duration. His body was taken to the cathedral for a mass and then, on 2 July, to Congress where many thousands were waiting to pay their final respects. (The body, dressed in his general's uniform, would eventually require an injection of some three litres of formaldehyde in order to preserve it sufficiently to allow the crowds time to file past, which as it would later prove made it quite resistant to decomposition.[14]) The public mood was perhaps best captured by Balbín, who dispensed with his prepared speech and made a few warm comments ending with 'this old adversary says farewell to a friend'. On Thursday 4 July the casket was closed and taken to the chapel at the presidential residence at Olivos.

Although Perón had not been embalmed for permanent display, as in the case of Evita questions arose as to what to do with his mortal remains. In particular, one of López Rega's pet projects was the construction of an 'Altar of the Fatherland', whose construction was approved by Congress in the days before Perón's death, harking back to the original proposal to erect a monument to Evita and the *descamisado* where Evita's body would have reposed. López Rega's grandiose plan envisaged a giant monument opposite the place where the presidential residence in Palermo had once stood, where the mortal remains of the full pantheon of Argentine national heroes would eventually reside: Liberator General José de San Martín, Juan Manuel de Rosas, Hipólito Yrigoyen, Evita and even General Pedro Aramburu, together with Perón and, presumably, López Rega himself at a later date. (A less congenial group could scarcely be imagined.) Subsequent events would again scupper the plans for the monument, but Perón's remains, like Evita's, would nevertheless have a long and chequered afterlife.

*****

A biography might in theory be expected to end with the life of its subject, but Perón's life after death would prove to be almost as durable and unpredictable as that of Evita. Although much of the near-term aftermath is well known, it cannot be disregarded either as part of Perón's life or his legacy.

Perón himself may have said on 12 June that the Argentine people would be his only successor, but in practice that immediate successor would be Isabel, both as president and as leader of a movement accustomed to take its orders from the leader. Her orientation and her dependence on López Rega were already well known, and it should not have come as a surprise that within hours of Perón's death she signed a decree permitting draconian short-term security measures, apparently on the advice of *El Brujo*. The following day she called together the cabinet and the armed forces chiefs to launch a sharp attack on those rumoured to be conspiring against López Rega, a move that would soon lead to the departure of several other ministers. If Isabel had been expected to stand aside rapidly or to listen to the advice of experienced hands such as Balbín, as Perón himself had urged her, it soon became clear that this was not her intention.

Violence rapidly mounted again, both from the left and the right, with the Triple A claiming responsibility for a number of killings including the former vice-governor of Córdoba, Atilio López, and the brother of former President Arturo Frondizi, as well as issuing a death list including Taiana and various other public figures from both the Peronist left and the opposition. The Montoneros published an inflammatory account of the kidnapping and killing of Aramburu; they returned underground after the publication, *La causa peronista*, was closed down by the authorities. In September 1974 the Montoneros would carry off the spectacular kidnapping of the millionaire brothers Jorge and Juan Born, who were released on payment of a reported 60-million-dollar ransom, and followed this up, just ahead of the 17 October Loyalty Day celebrations, with an even more outrageous move, stealing the body of Aramburu from the Recoleta cemetery and demanding the return of Evita's body to Argentina in exchange for its return.

Accompanied by López Rega, Evita's body arrived in Buenos Aires on 17 November, the second anniversary of Perón's first return. As promised, Aramburu's body was returned and Evita was put on display in the chapel in Olivos, together with Perón's coffin, marking the only brief time they would be reunited in whatever remained of their eternal life.

In February 1975, Isabel signed a decree ordering the armed forces to 'annihilate subversion' in the province of Tucumán, where the ERP had begun a Cuban-style guerrilla action the previous year. 'Operation Independence' would mobilize some 5,000 members of the security forces to combat a guerrilla force estimated at between 120 and 600. It would also make Tucumán the testing ground for the methods that would be used following the coup d'état, notably the enforced disappearance of those believed to be part of what Isabel described as the 'anti-national subversion' (the word *apátrida* is difficult to translate in a way that conveys exactly the same meaning in English, implying stateless or unpatriotic but also lacking roots in or fealty to a country or system).

Isabel's evident incapacity was constantly underscored by her obvious submission to López Rega, who would stand behind her while she spoke mouthing her words, claiming to be a medium transmitting Perón's instructions. He also persuaded her to dismiss Gelbard as economy minister and to adopt austerity measures which prompted the first-ever mass protest by the CGT against a Peronist government, followed by a two-day general strike that put paid to austerity. In the end, both the CGT and the armed forces became convinced that López Rega's departure was necessary. Trade unionists who rallied on 27 June 1975 against austerity shouted insults and jeers against him, which helped to puncture the aura of absolute power and fear that he had projected, and opposition to him from various quarters became increasingly fierce. Following an ultimatum from the military, Isabel removed him from the ministry on 20 July, naming him 'special ambassador'. He left for Brazil and then Spain before disappearing for nearly a decade. (After being spotted in Geneva in 1982 he left for the United States, where he was arrested and extradited to Argentina in 1986; he died of diabetes in prison in 1989 while awaiting trial on homicide and corruption charges.)

Although the removal of the hated and feared López Rega gave Isabel a brief breathing space, Peronists, Radicals and others urged her to stand down and call early elections, mindful that the economic and political chaos mounting would make it virtually impossible to sustain the government until elections were due in 1977. For whatever reason, she stubbornly refused, continuing to disregard rumours of an impending coup until she was taken away in a helicopter in the early hours of 24 March 1976 and placed under arrest. She would be held, first in military installations and then at Perón's weekend home in San Vicente, until 1981, when she was finally released without trial and allowed to return to Spain. This would prove to be a much kinder fate than that reserved for many Argentines.

The 'National Reorganization Process' under the new military government proposed to 'eradicate subversion and promote economic development'.[15] To achieve this, Congress, civil courts and the Supreme Court were closed, provincial authorities replaced with military appointees and an unprecedented bloodbath began. Although the counterinsurgency methods employed had been initiated in Tucumán under Isabel, they now extended across the country and affected not only those with links to the guerrillas but also the JP, trade unions, students and many others with no affiliations at all. Although members of all parties were affected, the Peronists were by far the most targeted group. The National Commission on the Disappearance of Persons (CONADEP) established after the return to democracy in 1983 would document 8,961 disappearances (distinct from outright killings), although other estimates put the total as high as 30,000. The dictatorship did opt on this occasion for Christian burial as a means of disposing of the bodies of Perón and Evita, still in Olivos: Perón's body would go to the family crypt in the Chacarita cemetery, while Evita would be handed over to her family to be interred in a steel-reinforced vault beneath the Duarte crypt in Recoleta to prevent further attempts to steal it. (One can only imagine that Evita would have preferred to remain alongside her husband rather than in a different cemetery and in Buenos Aires' most aristocratic final resting place at that.)

The military government's economic results proved little more stellar than its human rights record; public foreign debt rose by 500 per cent during the dictatorship, poverty rose and the share of wages in the economy fell. The military's ill-starred decision to invade the Falklands/Malvinas Islands in April 1982, which led to a disastrous military campaign and a rapid and ignominious surrender, would prove the final nail in the dictatorship's coffin, with elections finally held in October 1983.

The first presidential elections to be held following Perón's death raised serious questions over Peronism's viability and longevity without its leader. These would become more pointed after the uninspiring Peronist candidate Italo Luder lost to Radical Raúl Alfonsín, although Alfonsín's charisma, dynamism and oratory made him appear as the more 'Peronist' of the two. Alfonsín would become the first Radical to defeat a Peronist presidential candidate, although the victory of the Peronists in congressional and provincial elections four years later would make it clear that they were far from a spent force. Alfonsín's government would face not only three military uprisings which prompted the curtailment of historic human rights trials but also an attack on the La Tablada barracks in January 1989 by a hitherto unknown left-wing group called *Movimiento Todos Por la Patria* (All for the Fatherland Movement, MTP) which prompted a twenty-five-hour siege and dozens of deaths. Although not on the scale of the 1970s, bomb attacks also became commonplace. In the face of a vertiginous political and economic crisis in 1989, Alfonsín would be forced to step down six months early and hand over to his elected successor, the Peronist governor of La Rioja, Carlos Menem.

On 26 June 1987, just before the thirteenth anniversary of Perón's death, two Peronist party leaders, Vicente Saadi and Carlos Grosso, received identical letters signed by a mysterious 'Hermes Iai and the 13'. The letters informed them that they had 'amputate[d] the hands of the remains of ... Lieutenant General Juan Domingo Perón' and that his hands, ring and military sabre were being held until the sum of 8 million dollars was paid for their return. According to the letter, 'in the year 1973 General Perón contracted for services subsequently rendered a debt of eight million ($8,000,000 USA) which subsequently was never paid'. The letter threatened that in the event of non-payment 'or any occurrence unfavourable to our interest those remains will be destroyed or pulverised leaving that illustrious forebear incomplete for all eternity'.[16] Both copies of the letter also contained half of a sheet of paper containing a poem which Isabel had written and deposited in the tomb on a visit to Argentina after the end of the dictatorship.

Subsequent investigations proved that the hands had indeed been removed in the recent past (the death of a cemetery night watchman, apparently following a beating, in April suggested that date, although the letter pointed to early June), but little more was ever proved. The terms of the letter suggested that the writers were aware of private telephone conversations, which seemed to point the finger at the intelligence services, angry at the purge of their ranks being undertaken by the government. It was also widely suggested that the motive was the theft of a signet ring believed to contain the number of a secret Swiss bank account, as well as a political message that power remained in Perón's hands.

Arguably the most solid theory attributed responsibility to the disbanded army intelligence services, whose leader during the dictatorship, General Guillermo Suárez Mason, was a member of the Propaganda Due (P-2) masonic lodge led by Licio Gelli – as were, at one time, Perón and López Rega. The most apparent motive might have been to throw blame on an already tottering Alfonsín government (which, if so, proved unsuccessful), although it has also been suggested that among the more mystical elements of P-2 was the adoption of elements of Egyptology, in which Hermes represented the judge of the dead, Iai the 'rebellion of the soul' and 13 the hour of reincarnation.[17] Under this interpretation, the decision to cut off Perón's hands might have represented a judgement on him, preventing his body from remaining intact as required by ancient Egyptian rites. Perhaps more prosaically, it was also the case that prisoners disappeared and killed during the dictatorship often had their hands cut off to make identification more difficult. Either way, the purported involvement of P-2, the remains of the Triple A and army intelligence would offer an explanation for the impenetrable nature of the case.

In May 1987 Perón's Puerta de Hierro home was broken into; nothing was taken but his clothes and various religious images were stolen, and two small statues of Christ and the Virgin Mary had had their hands removed. Jaime Far Suar, the judge originally assigned to investigate the case, would suffer a series of threats, an attempted car bomb and the attempted kidnap of his wife (whose elderly mother died following a beating). Far Suar and his partner died in an October 1988 car crash widely considered suspicious, accurately or not. Despite many false leads, Perón's hands were never returned and the mystery remains unresolved. Nor would this be the last of the afflictions suffered by Perón's mortal remains.

Although Carlos Menem appeared on the surface to be in the traditional *caudillo* mould, with his flamboyant style and bushy sideburns reminiscent of the nineteenth-century La Rioja *caudillo* Facundo Quiroga, he soon proved to be a very different type of Peronist leader. Despite a 'populist' election campaign promising a 'productive revolution' and based on the slogan 'follow me, I won't defraud you', he rapidly set about dismantling the Peronist-originated state, privatizing companies, imposing a one-for-one currency peg with the dollar and pursuing policies that favoured crony capitalism over labour. Much of the money from privatization would disappear through corruption and borrowing soared, contributing to the economic collapse and default at the end of 2001. Nevertheless, Menem would be re-elected in 1995 under a newly reformed Constitution and would supplant Perón as Argentina's longest-serving president before handing over to the hapless Radical Fernando de la Rúa in 1999. Within two years De la Rúa would be swept away by his inability to halt the economic slide and the burgeoning impact of the debt burden, choosing to depart in the helicopter in December 2001.

Following a series of days-long interim presidencies, the Senate would designate Senator Eduardo Duhalde, briefly Menem's vice-president before becoming governor of Buenos Aires and losing to De la Rúa in 1999, as interim president for the remainder of the term. Duhalde would succeed to a great extent in stabilizing the post-default crisis and laying the ground for new elections in 2003 that would throw up yet another face of Peronist leadership: the little-known Santa Cruz Governor Néstor Kirchner would win the presidency with only 23 per cent of the vote after Menem withdrew from a second-round run-off. Kirchner and his wife Cristina Fernández, a glamorous and combative senator, had come out of the leftist Peronist youth movements in the early 1970s and would prove to have more affinity with Evita and with Cámpora than with Perón, although like Perón Kirchner was a pragmatist who put ends above ideology.

Duhalde, arguably the most traditional of the Peronist leaders who would emerge following Perón's death, largely retired from politics following Kirchner's election but would nonetheless play a key role in one of the last acts in Perón's own saga. Duhalde had earlier acquired the *quinta* in San Vicente with a view to creating a museum there, as well as a final resting place for Perón and Evita. Although Evita's family would refuse permission to reinter her remains there, Perón's body was removed from Chacarita and transported to a newly built mausoleum in San Vicente on 17 October 2006 in a procession that aimed to hark back to greater times, with an estimated 100,000 lining the route. In the end, it appeared more of a ludicrous recreation of Ezeiza; scuffles broke out between different trade union factions and stones and bottles were thrown as they sought to reach the front of the procession and gain access to the speakers' platform. Finally guns were drawn, shots were fired and the provincial police intervened with tear gas and rubber bullets as the Peronist march played over the loudspeakers and veteran Peronist leader Antonio Cafiero ended his speech by shouting 'rest in peace my General', with no apparent intention of irony. Perón would finally be laid to rest there but the distance from Buenos Aires, the increasing historical distance from the man himself and the economic difficulties that would mark subsequent years made the museum difficult to sustain. With relatively few visitors, the house and museum have fallen into disrepair and Perón's mutilated remains lie largely alone and isolated, a far cry from the days of multitudes but perhaps after all an unsurprising end for a man who for much of his life was alone and isolated even among the crowds.

Chapter 18

LEGACY

Imitemos el ejemplo de este varón argentino
Y siguiendo su camino, gritemos de corazón Perón, Perón!

Let us follow the example of this great Argentine
And following in his path, let us shout from the heart Perón, Perón!
La marcha peronista

More than four decades after his death, Perón and Peronism in various guises remain central to Argentina and to Argentine identity, still often defined by its position vis-à-vis Peronism. This does not imply that Perón himself is universally loved even among Peronists: the generation who participated in youth movements in the 1970s have often preferred to identify more with Evita or with Cámpora than with 'the general'. Indeed, the (increasingly middle-aged) youth movement surrounding the Kirchners is known as 'La Cámpora', and Cristina Kirchner has been reported to have refused to sign a petition to erect a statute of Perón saying, 'I wouldn't sign anything for that old son of a bitch.' Yet they have sought to adhere to the personalism and verticalist control that characterized the party's founder, also often with negative consequences, as well as to the types of social welfare policy with which he and Evita will always be associated. The geographical structure of Peronist support also remains largely unchanged; provinces with traditional Peronist bases remain solidly Peronist, and the city of Buenos Aires remains consistently resistant to the charms of the party. (The only statue of Perón in the capital was only erected in 2015 by opposition Mayor Mauricio Macri when he was trying to woo Peronist support for his presidential bid.)

By definition, the world has changed, Argentina has changed, and Peronism has retained its central place by adapting to circumstances while harking back to its glory days, but the policies of the 1940s – often if not always appropriate at the time – are no longer altogether viable nor applicable in a very different economic and political context. Yet some elements of Peronism, which are emotional rather than political, are non-negotiable: it is required to have a social conscience not always demanded of other parties and to implement social welfare policies that often amount to clientelism rather than measures to boost citizen welfare and autonomy. The party has been permanently identified with the concept of social justice, to the extent that this is reflected in its formal name, the Partido Justicialista. Peronism was the first party to recognize deep levels of inequity throughout society and to seek a greater degree of inclusion for the most marginal. In this respect, it was the heir to the UCR, without which it could not have existed in the forms it took, but it went beyond the UCR's middle-class focus to encompass the working classes and the destitute (and, by doing so and by attracting progressive sectors of the UCR such as the FORJA, it drove the UCR to a more conservative position than it originally espoused). This concept of social justice, however ingenuous or even mendacious at times, has allowed Peronism to maintain (at least in its own eyes) a mantle of being on the side of right – something cemented by the violently revanchist anti-Peronism that culminated in the Liberating Revolution and the National Reorganization Process, which by persecuting Peronism both increased its self-belief as the righteous side and embedded it even more deeply in social and political structures. This is not to deny its more cynical and corrupt side or the numerous supporters who became 'Peronists to steal'. Moreover, Peronism was and is uniquely and innately Argentine – a 'melting pot' of peoples, cultures, ethnicities, philosophies and ideologies, like Argentina and Perón himself. It has characteristics in common with political movements elsewhere but also stark differences and contradictions; it does not travel easily outside its native land.

While its clientelism and social welfare policies have been widely criticized, not without reason, for generating dependence and a self-sustaining cycle of underdevelopment, the long series of political, economic and social crises that have marked Argentina since 1955 have repeatedly made this course of action necessary and limited the scope for alternatives; the short-term imperatives that require assistance and aid (whether termed charity or social justice) never give way to a stability that might allow for long-term policies that would change realities on the ground. Arguably the perception of Peronism as the arbiter of social justice was strengthened by Mauricio Macri's 2015–2019 neoliberal presidency, the first genuine conservative government elected without fraud since 1916. Although Macri was somewhat unfairly accused of reducing social welfare (which his government actually expanded in some areas), his policies helped to foment a new social, economic and debt crisis that the successor Peronist government of Alberto Fernandez and Cristina Kirchner was expected to ameliorate with social justice. The Fernandez-Kirchner ticket itself exemplifies some of the continuing contradictions within Peronism: while Fernandez himself is a moderate whose instinct is to conciliate and to deal with interests across the board, Kirchner and her supporters have taken the increasingly radical tone of 'vamos por todo' ('we're going for everything'). Rather as Perón tended to do, this attitude presupposes that electoral victory implies that the victor is entitled to define the nation as they see fit, with little reference to those whose views differ. In the case of Kirchner and La Cámpora, the 'vamos por todo' reflects a belief that they owe it to the revolutionaries of the 1970s, dead or disappeared, to pursue the revolution they were unable to complete and bring it to fruition. While also mixing idealism and cynicism, it is unlikely to make for a more governable country or break with Argentina's history of polarization.

Perón enjoyed an opportunity denied to his successors – a moment of economic prosperity that allowed him to redistribute and to create options for modernization

– and he seized that moment, distributing largesse and opening up possibilities for greater opportunities across society. He did so at least initially in an often improvisational way, finding ways around the lack of institutional channels, but he would find the grind of administering long-term problems and greater austerity less sustainable, and he would not create institutions capable of sustaining policies long-term. This is not altogether surprising – efficient institutions reduce the need for the individual touch cherished by individualist leaders like Perón, who had little desire to reform himself out of a job, whatever he might have claimed to the contrary. They also run counter to the personal touch appreciated by his supporters, as Evita would stress, as opposed to administration by faceless bureaucracies. This personal and improvisational approach was arguably essential in the early days but has not served well as a long-term form of government.

Perón could be said to have 'led from the rear' – as he himself would recognize, he was perceived as channelling and realizing the aspirations of the working classes, rather than creating or defining those aspirations himself. The attachment to Peronism was arguably a response by the working classes to a system that did not meet their needs and which indeed excluded those needs. In this respect Peronism was 'populist' but a forward-looking populism driven primarily by hope of taking charge of a better and more inclusive future, not by resentment over lost empire or industry. While other strands of national thought or identity were backward-looking and wanted a return to the 'breadbasket' past and a society based on an agricultural elite, professional middle class and obedient working classes, Peronism aimed to look forward to that 'proud future' the Argentines demanded. If it played on an undercurrent of resentment, this was about what had not been achieved in the past rather than what had supposedly gone. However, in later life Perón himself would focus on the past and attempt to apply it to the present, a mistake his followers would also make. In 1972 the historian Félix Luna observed that 'it is easy to talk to Perón, establish an immediate human relationship with him. But it is very hard … to penetrate his mental structure, in his closed and unvarying world.'[1] This led him to imagine that things could be managed in the same way in a different world and made him unresponsive to efforts by his younger followers to transmute him into a different person and a different reality.

Arguably the most accurate summary of Perón's appeal was set out by the socialist writer Ernesto Sábato, unquestionably an opponent of Peronism if not one of the 'gorilla' variety.

> There was a justified desire for justice and for recognition, in the face of a cold and egocentric society which had always forgotten [the poor]. …. This is fundamentally what Perón saw and mobilised. The rest is only detail. …. If it is true that Perón awoke in the people their latent hatred, it is also true that the anti-Peronists did everything possible to justify and increase it.[2]

Anti-Peronism has marked the scorched earth of Argentine politics at least as much as Peronism since 1955 in particular. Arguably, had Perón been allowed to finish out what was unquestionably an increasingly turbulent second term or had his supporters not been politically proscribed for the better part of two decades, Peronism might have evolved in a different direction or even seen its importance dwindle over time. But the revenge taken post-1955 and the attempts to annihilate Peronism (and, on occasion, its founder) cemented it in a central and frequently combative position, and one in which its evolution was hindered by proscription, confusion, ignorance and, of course, Perón himself. The fixed image of the Peronist decade as a golden age for many Argentines would exaggerate its achievements as well as exacerbate the post-1973 debacle. Yet Perón and Peronism remain quintessentially Argentine in both their virtues and their defects, their divisiveness and their inclusivity. As Perón himself said, 'in Argentina 30 percent are Radicals, 30 percent are conservatives and the same number are socialists'; when asked by his interviewer where that left the Peronists, he replied, 'ah, no, we're all Peronists!'[3]

NOTES

Preface

1   D. Michaelis, *Eleanor*, 506.
2   R. Potash, *Perón y el G.O.U.,* Document 3.5, 225.

Introduction

1   J. Page, *Perón*, 6.
2   D. Kelly, *The Ruling Few*, 307.
3   Ibid., 310.
4   Quoted in J. Page, *Perón*, 6.
5   J. D. Perón, *La comunidad organizada*, 35.
6   P.D.S. Chesterfield, *Letters to His Son*, 13 of 661.
7   Ibid., 96 of 661; 266 of 661.
8   T. Eloy Martínez, *La novela de Perón*, 45.
9   J. Hedges, *Argentina*, 89.
10 FCO 7/2394, 1973.
11 Ambassador Sir David Kelly to the Foreign Office dated 12 June 1944, in FO 118/730.
12 F. Luna, *El 45*, 513.
13 Quoted in G. Varela, *Perón y Evita Memoría íntima*, 18 of 638.

Chapter 1

1   C.A. Cosantino, *Letras de tango*, 142–3.
2   Quoted in E. Pavón Pereyra, *Yo Perón*, 20.
3   Interview published in July 1974 and quoted in I.M. Cloppet, *Eva Duarte y Juan Perón: la cuna materna*, 96.
4   H. Barreiro, *Juancito Sosa*, 20.
5   Ibid., 256.
6   E. Pavón Pereira, *Yo Perón*, 26.
7   Ibid., 22.
8   Ibid., 40.
9   See H. Barreiro, *Juancito Sosa*; and I.M. Cloppet, *Eva Duarte y Juan Perón*.
10 T. Eloy Martínez, *Las memorias del general*, 21, 73.
11 Quoted ibid., 22.
12 Quoted ibid., 21.
13 T. Eloy Martínez, *Las memorias del general*, 26; E. Pavón Pereyra, *Yo Perón*, 29.
14 T. Eloy Martínez, *Las memorias del general*, 77–8.
15 Quoted ibid., 80.

16 Quoted in J.I. García Hamilton, *Juan Domingo*, 49.
17 Quoted in T. Eloy Martínez, *Las memorias del general*, 83.
18 E. Pavón Pereyra, *Yo Perón*, 43.
19 Ibid., 43.
20 T. Eloy Martínez, *Las memorias del general*, 27; E. Pavón Pereyra, *Yo Perón*, 32.

Chapter 2

1   E. Pavón Pereira, *Yo Perón*, 41.
2   Ibid., 52.
3   Ibid., 56.
4   Ibid., 57.
5   J.I. García Hamilton, *Juan Domingo*, 47.
6   E. Pavón Pereyra, *Yo, Perón*, 61, 60.
7   E. Pavón Pereyra, *Diario secreto de Perón*, 18.
8   Quoted in T. Eloy Martínez, *Las memorias del general*, 90.
9   E. Pavón Pereyra, *Yo Perón*, 60.
10 Quoted in J.I. García Hamilton, *Juan Domingo*, 56.
11 Quoted in A. Bellotta, *Las mujeres de Perón*, 33, 34.
12 Ibid., 37.
13 Quoted in T. Eloy Martínez, *Las memorias del general*, 99.

Chapter 3

1   Quoted in A. Bellotta, *Las mujeres de Perón*, 38.
2   T. Eloy Martínez, *Las memorias del general*.
3   H. Barreiro, *Juancito Sosa*, 186.
4   See J. Hedges, *Evita*, 62; H. Vázquez Rial, *Perón: tal vez la historia*, 106–11.
5   E. Pavón Pereira, *Yo Perón*, 101.
6   Ibid., 96.
7   Ibid., 98.
8   T. Eloy Martínez, *Las memorias del general*, 38.
9   Ibid., 39.
10 E. Pavón Pereira, *Yo Perón*, 101.
11 Quoted in A. Rhodes, *The Vatican in the Age of the Dictators*, 25.
12 Quoted in J.O. Frigerio, 'Perón y la Iglesia', *Todo es Historia*, October 1984, 12.
13 N. Stack, 'Avoiding the Greater Evil', 28.
14 M. Murmis and J.C. Portantiero, *Estudios sobre los orígenes del peronismo*, 33.
15 Quoted ibid., 36.
16 See, e.g., W. Little, 'The Popular Origins of Peronism'.
17 Quoted in T. Eloy Martínez, *Las memorias del general*, 103.
18 Quoted in A. Bellotta, *Las mujeres de Perón*, 47.
19 T. Eloy Martínez, *Las memorias del general*, 101–2; J.I. García Hamilton, *Juan Domingo*, 83.
20 Quoted ibid., 100.
21 Quoted in A. Bellotta, *Las mujeres de Perón*, 50.
22 Quoted ibid., 50.

Chapter 4

1 C.A. Cosantino, *Letras de tango*, 38–9.
2 Quoted in T. Eloy Martínez, *Las memorias del general*, 39.
3 J.I. García Hamilton, *Juan Domingo*, 85–6.
4 Quoted Ibid., 89; 88.
5 Quoted in R. Crassweller, *Perón and the Enigmas of Argentina*, 88.
6 T. Eloy Martínez, *Las memorias del general*, 106, 109.
7 Quoted in E. Pavón Pereira, *Yo Perón*, 124.
8 Quoted in P.R. Cossio and C.A. Seara, *Perón: Testimonios médicos y vivencias (1973–1974)*, 76.
9 E. Pavón Pereyra, *Yo Perón*, 127.
10 Ibid., 129, 133.
11 D. A. Mercante, *Mercante: El corazón de Perón*, 18–22.
12 B.C. Carvalho Lopes Rogério, 'History with Some Evidence: Inequality Levels of Argentina and Australia at the Turn of the 20th Century'. M.A. thesis, Lund University, June 2016.
13 F. Alvaredo, G. Cruces and L. Gasparini, 'A Short Episodic History of Income Distribution in Argentina'. *Latin American Economic Review* 27, Art. 7 (2018).

Chapter 5

1 C.A. Cosantino, *Letras de tango*, 20–1.
2 Quoted in *Revista Criterio*, November 2015; E. Pavón Pereyra, *Yo Perón*, 149.
3 Quoted on Twitter in @gabrielsoglio, 1 June 2018.
4 Quoted in F. Pigna, *Evita*, 35.
5 British Embassy to Foreign Office, in FO 371/33512.
6 R. Potash, *Perón y el GOU*, 11.
7 Quoted in C. Becker, *Domingo A. Mercante*, 997 of 7451.
8 E. Pavón Pereyra, *Yo Perón*, 135.
9 Quoted in A. Rouquie, *El siglo de Perón*, 39.
10 E. Pavón Pereyra, *Yo Perón*, 141.
11 Quoted in R. Potash, *Perón y el GOU*, 15.
12 Document 1.1, ibid., 25–42.
13 Ibid., 39.
14 British Embassy telegram to Foreign Office dated 5 June 1943, in FO 371/33512.
15 Document 1.2, *Perón y el GOU*, 47.
16 Quoted in FO 371/33512, 8 June 1943.
17 Argentine personalities report in FO 371/37744, 1944.
18 Quoted ibid., 7 June 1943.
19 Quoted in F. Luna, *El 45*, 58–9.
20 R. Potash, *Perón y el GOU*, Document 3.2, 202.
21 *Criterio*, 10 June 1943, 128.
22 J.D. Perón, *Del poder al exilio*, 34.
23 J.D. Perón, *Diálogo entre Perón y las Fuerzas Armadas*, 26.
24 FO 371/33516, 28 October and 6 November 1943.
25 FO 371/37744, 1944.
26 Quoted in C. Decker, *Domingo Mercante*, 1488 of 7451.

27 Quoted in F. Luna, *El 45*, 32–3.
28 Quoted in C. Reyes, *Yo hice el 17 de octubre*, 189.
29 Quoted in E. Pavón Pereyra, *Diario secreto de Perón*, 63.
30 C. Reyes, *Yo hice el 17 de octubre*, 27–8.
31 Ibid., 187.

Chapter 6

1   C.A. Cosantino, *Letras de tango*, 117–18.
2   FO 371/37671, 11 March 1944.
3   Ibid., 26 February 1944.
4   Ibid., 11 March 1944.
5   GOU Documents 2.18 and 2.8, quoted in R. Potash, *Perón y el GOU*, 399.
6   Ibid., 309–11.
7   Quoted in E. Pavón Pereyra, *Yo Perón*, 172–3; E. Pavón Pereyra, *Diario secreto de Perón*, 77.
8   FO 118/755, 7 March 1947.
9   Quoted in V. Pichel, *Evita íntima*, 59.
10 Quoted in N. Galasso, *Yo fui el confesor de Eva Perón*, 27.
11 E. Perón, *La razón de mi vida*, 54.
12 J.I. García Hamilton, *Juan Domingo*, 109.
13 P. Jamandreu, *La cabeza contra el suelo*, 75–6.
14 FO 371/68127, 9 November 1948.
15 Quoted in M. Navarro, *Evita*, 79.
16 Quoted in S. Mercado, *El inventor del peronismo*, 791 of 5638.
17 Quoted in E. Pavón Pereyra, *Diario secreto de Perón*, 77.
18 Ibid., 78.
19 FO371/68127, Special Memorandum No 41: Five Years of Perón's Labour Policy, December 1948.
20 Quoted in L. Monzalvo, *Testigo de la primera hora del peronismo*, 79.
21 C. Reyes, *Yo hice el 17 de octubre*, 152–9.
22 Ibid., 158.
23 Ibid., 161–2.
24 J.D. Perón, *Discurso en la Bolsa de Comercio*, 25 August 1944, www.archivoperonista.com
25 FO 371/37672, 1944
26 *Conferencia pronunciada el 10 de junio de 1944 por Coronel Juan D. Perón, en calidad de Ministro de Guerra, en la inauguración de la Cátedra de Defensa Nacional de la Universidad de La Plata.* Downloaded from www.argentinahistorica.com.ar.
27 J. Page, *Perón*, 74.

Chapter 7

1   Quoted in V. Pichel, *Evita íntima*, 57–8.
2   Ibid., 57–8.
3   Ibid., 59.

4   Colonel Gerardo Demetro, quoted in O. Borroni and R. Vacca, *La vida de Eva Perón*, 114–15.
5   British Embassy annual report, FO 371/51838, F. Luna, *El 45*, 151.
6   Ibid.
7   Quoted in J. Page, *Perón*, 94.
8   S. Braden, *Diplomats and Demagogues*, 1.
9   Ibid., 114.
10   Ibid., 153.
11   Ibid., 260.
12   FO 371/51838
13   S. Braden, *Diplomats and Demagogues*, 316.
14   Sir D. Kelly, *The Ruling Few*, 307.
15   Ibid., 311.
16   C. Reyes, *Yo hice el 17 de octubre*, 193.
17   F. Luna, *El 45*, 45.
18   S. Braden, *Diplomats and Demagogues*, 322-3.
19   Quoted in F. Luna, *El 45*, 156.
20   Ibid., 92.
21   Ibid., 90.
22   Ibid., 166.
23   S. Braden, *Diplomats and Demagogues*, 333–4.
24   Quoted in F. Luna, *El 45*, 99.
25   Sir D. Kelly, *The Ruling Few*, 307.
26   Quoted in J. Page, *Perón*, 104; F. Luna, *El 45*, 100–1.
27   *Review of the River Plate*, 21 September 1945.
28   *Buenos Aires Herald*, 20 September 1945.
29   C. Reyes, *Yo hice el 17 de octubre*, 207.
30   Quoted in C. Becker, *Domingo A. Mercante*, 3099 of 7451.
31   Quoted in F. Luna, *El 45*, 353.
32   Quoted ibid., 355-6.
33   Quoted in F. Luna, *El 45*, 356.
34   E. Perón, *La razón de mi vida*, 37-8.
35   C. Reyes, *Yo hice el 17 de octubre*, 252.
36   Quoted in F. Luna, *El 45*, 294.
37   Ibid., 307.
38   Quoted in C. Reyes, *Yo hice el 17 de octubre*, 237–9.
39   Ibid., 93.
40   E. Perón, *Clases y escritos completos*, 144.
41   F. Luna, *El 45*, 513.

Chapter 8

1   C.A. Cosantino, *Letras de tango*, 134–5.
2   Quoted in F. Luna, *El 45*, 362.
3   Ibid., 414.
4   Pamphlets from author's personal collection.
5   Quoted in M. Murmis and J.C. Portantiero, *Estudios sobre los orígenes del peronismo*, 95.

6   Quoted in F. Luna, *El 45*, 454.
7   FO 371/51774, 19 March 1946.
8   *Libro Azul y Blanco*, 7, 12.
9   L. Lagomarsino de Guardo, *Y ahora hablo yo*, 87.

Chapter 9

1   H.A. Benedetti, *Las mejores letras de tango*, 216.
2   D.A. Mercante, *Mercante: El corazón de Perón*, 89–90.
3   Quoted in J.I. García Hamilton, *Juan Domingo*, 181.
4   Quoted in R. Crassweller, *Perón and the Enigmas of Argentina*, 187.
5   Quoted in J.I. García Hamilton, *Juan Domingo*, 169.
6   E. Pavón Pereyra, *Yo Perón*, 207.
7   Ibid., 208.
8   Quoted in A. Bellota, *Las mujeres de Perón*, 200.
9   J.D. Perón, *Doctrina peronista*, 166.
10   Ibid., 148.
11   See D. Guy, *Creating Charismatic Bonds in Argentina*.
12   J.D. Perón, *Doctrina peronista*, 335.
13   Quoted in FO 371/68127, 30 October 1948.
14   Ibid., 22 December 1948.
15   Quoted in R. Crassweller, *Perón and the Enigmas of Argentina*, 184.
16   Adela Rodas, quoted in L. Lardone, *20.25, Quince mujeres hablan de Eva Perón*, 300 of
     2160.
17   Buenos Aires Herald, 28 June 1947; US State Department, Despatch from Vatican
     City, 1 July 1947, Microfilm 341, Reel 2:0312.
18   P. Jamandreu, *La cabeza contra el suelo*, 74.
19   Quoted in O. Borroni and R. Vacca, *La vida de Eva Perón*, 201.
20   Quoted ibid., 132–3.
21   Carta Pastoral Colectiva, 15 November 1945, reproduced in *Criterio*, No. 923, 22
     November 1945, 496–8.
22   *Criterio*, No. 933, 31 January 1946, 97.
23   Quoted in M. Lubertino Beltrán, *Perón y la Iglesia*, 37.
24   FO 371/68127, 17 October 1948; 9 November 1948.

Chapter 10

1   J.D. Perón, *Doctrina peronista*, 61, 26, 53–4.
2   Ibid., 70.
3   Quoted in R. Rein, *Los muchachos peronistas judíos*, 97.
4   Ibid., 102.
5   Quoted ibid., 16.
6   Quoted ibid., 198.
7   J.D. Perón, *Doctrina peronista*, 50.
8   Quoted in J. Hedges, *Argentina: A Modern History*, 132.
9   J.D. Perón, *Doctrina peronista*, 309.

10 Ibid., 311.
11 Quoted in R. Rein, *Los muchachos peronistas judíos*, 170.
12 Note dated 15 December 1948, in FO 371/68127, 1948.
13 J.D. Perón, *Doctrina peronista*, 322.
14 L. Zanatta, *Eva Perón, una biografía política*, 2362 of 9278.
15 FO 371/74288, 1948 political report from the British Embassy.
16 J.D. Peron, *Doctrina peronista*, 69.
17 Ibid., 9, 11, 15.
18 Ibid., 17.
19 Ibid., 20.
20 Ibid., 23, 22.
21 Ibid., 27.
22 Ibid., 28.
23 Ibid., 38, 39.
24 J.D. Perón, *Doctrina peronista*, 146-7.
25 J.D. Perón, *Manual del peronista*, 38, 43.
26 Ibid., 40.
27 Ibid., 52.
28 Ibid., 72.
29 Ibid., 71, 72.
30 FO 371/74409, 3 April 1949.
31 J. Ortega y Gasset, quoted in D. Rock, *Argentina 1516-1982*, xxii.
32 J.D. Perón, *La comunidad organizada*, 16.
33 Ibid., 19.
34 Ibid., 32.
35 Ibid., 39, 41.
36 Ibid., 51, 98.
37 Ibid., 76.
38 Ibid., 80.
39 Ibid., 89.
40 Ibid., 105.
41 Ibid., 109, 116.
42 Ibid., 111.
43 Ibid., 75-6.
44 Ibid., 139.
45 Quoted in C. Becker, *Domingo A. Mercante*, Loc. 5420 of 7451.

Chapter 11

1 C.A. Cosantino, *Letras de tango*, 137-8.
2 A. Rouquie, *El siglo de Perón*, 68.
3 F. Alvaredo et al., 'A Short Episodic History of Income Distribution in Argentina'.
4 FO 371/108791.
5 FO 371/37744.
6 1949 political report to Foreign Office, in FO 371/81148.
7 Report dated 9 November 1948, in FO 371/68127.
8 H. Castañeira, in Castañeira et al., *Legisladoras de Evita*, 34.

9   Quoted in J. Hedges, *Evita*, 168.
10 Letter to the Foreign Office dated 16 March 1951, in FO 371/90467.
11 Quoted in J. Hedges, *Evita*, 177–8.
12 Quoted in F. Chavez, *Eva Perón sin mitos*, 244.
13 Quoted in F. Pigna, *Evita, jirones de su vida*, 279.
14 Quoted in J. Hedges, *Evita*, 188.
15 Quoted ibid., 193.
16 Quoted ibid., 199.
17 Quoted ibid., 202.
18 Quoted in J.I. García Hamilton, *Juan Domingo*, 200.
19 Quoted in J. Hedges, *Evita*, 206.
20 Quoted ibid., 210.
21 P. Jamandreu, *La cabeza contra el suelo*, 103–4. Days before going into exile, Perón would give Jamandreu a new car to express his gratitude.
22 See, e.g., N. Castro, *Los últimos días de Eva*, 280–308. A much earlier anecdote cited in O. Borroni and R. Vacca, *La vida deEva Perón*, 292–3, might also give credence to the claims.

Chapter 12

1   C.A. Cosantino, *Letras de tango*, 18–19.
2   Telegram dated 27 July 1952, in FO 371/97426.
3   Quoted in V. Pichel, *Evita íntima*, 293, 311–13.
4   Quoted in FO 371/90469, 25 October 1951.
5   FO 371/97426.
6   FO 371/90469, 9 November 1951.
7   J.B. Yofre, *Puerta de Hierro*, 57.
8   P. Jamandreu, *La cabeza contra el suelo*, 63.
9   FO 371/108791.
10 Quoted in J.I. García Hamilton, *Juan Domingo*, 213.
11 J.D. Perón, *Del poder al exilio*, 52.
12 *Democracia*, 30 July 1952.
13 FO 420/305, 1954 Annual Review.
14 Quoted in J.I. García Hamilton, *Juan Domingo*, 240.
15 FO 371/108791, 27 July 1954.
16 *Revista Criterio*, No 1241, 11 August 1955, 563–6.
17 Pamphlet No. 64, in F. Lafiandra (ed), *Los panfletos*, 176–81.
18 Quoted in *La Nación*, 11 November 1954.
19 J.D. Perón, *Conducción política*, 38.
20 Quoted in *La Nación*, 26 November 1954.
21 Memorandum from US Embassy, 14 June 1955, US State Department Files on Argentina, Microfilm 337, Reel 24, 991–3.
22 Quoted in *Libro negro de la segunda tiranía*, 210–14.
23 J.D. Perón, *Del poder al exilio*, 15.
24 Interview with Dr Emilio Mignone, 29 August 1990.
25 Quoted in FO 371/114022, 28 June 1955.
26 Interview with United Press, 5 October 1955, quoted in J.D. Perón, *La fuerza es el derecho de las bestias*, 5; J.D. Perón, *Del poder al exilio*, 43–4.

27 J.D. Perón, *Del poder al exilio*, 10, 31.
28 FO 371/119862, Annual Report 1955.
29 FO 371/114022, 22 September 1955.
30 J.D. Perón, *Del poder al exilio*, 25, 24.
31 Ibid., 27, 18.
32 R. Martínez, *Grandezas y miserias de Perón*, 103.
33 J.D. Perón, *Del poder al exilio*, 56.
34 Quoted in J.I. García Hamilton, *Juan Domingo*, 237.
35 Quoted in FO 371/114022, 22 September 1955.
36 Quoted in J.D. Perón, *La fuerza es el derecho de las bestias*, 7.
37 Ibid., 3.
38 Quoted in E. Pavón Pereyra, *Yo Perón*, 323–4.
39 R. Martínez, *Grandezas y miserias de Perón*, 40.

Chapter 13

1 C.A. Cosantino, *Letras de tango*, 94–5.
2 M. Sáenz Quesada, *Isabel Perón*, 37.
3 Quoted ibid., 44.
4 Quoted in E. Pavón Pereyra, *Yo Perón*, 321–2, 327.
5 A. Bellota, *Las mujeres de Perón*, 182–3.
6 M. Sáenz Quesada, *Isabel Perón*, 41–2.
7 R. Martínez, *Grandezas y miserias de Perón*, 49.
8 Quoted ibid., 43.
9 *Revista Somos*, 23 February 1977, quoted ibid., 43.
10 Quoted in E. Pavón Pereyra, *Yo Perón*, 325.
11 Quoted in M. Sáenz Quesada, *Isabel Perón*, 48.

Chapter 14

1 C.A. Cosantino, *Letras de tango*, 49–50.
2 A. Rouquié, *El siglo de Perón*, 105.
3 In E. Pavón Pereyra (comp), *Diario secreto de Perón*, 134–5.
4 Interview with Jorge Antonio, *Revista Noticias*, January 2004.
5 Letter from J.D. Perón to J.W. Cooke dated 25 August 1964, quoted in A. Recalde, *El pensamiento de John William Cooke en las cartas a Perón, 1956–1966*, 203.
6 Letter to Oscar Albrieu dated 28 November 1958, in J.C. Chiaramonte et al. (eds), *El exilio de Perón*, 417–18.
7 Letter from J.W. Cooke to Perón dated 28 August 1957, quoted in A.T. Serafini, 'El pacto Perón-Frondizi en la correspondencia entre Perón y Cooke', 9.

Chapter 15

1 C.A. Cosantino, *Letras de tango*, 23–4.
2 Interview with Jorge Antonio, *Revista Noticias*, January 2004.

3 M. Sáenz Quesada, *Isabel Perón*, 61.
4 Letter dated 24 October 1967, in C. Belini et al., *El exilio de Perón*, 94. This letter may in fact have been written by Cooke, not Perón.
5 R. Gillespie, *Soldiers of Perón*, 71–2.
6 Quoted ibid., 259.
7 Quoted in L.E. Meglioli, *Perón Frondizi, La conversación*, 25.
8 Quoted in J.I. García Hamilton, *Juan Domingo*, 272.
9 Quoted in M. Sáenz Quesada, *Isabel Perón*, 68.
10 *Clarín*, 2 September 2020.
11 Interview with F. Pigna, at www.elhistoriador.com.ar/mario-firmenich.
12 R. Crassweller, *Perón and the Enigmas of Argentina*, 343–4.
13 Quoted in M. Sáenz Quesada, *Isabel Perón*, 96.
14 T. Eloy Martínez, *Las memorias del general*, 11, 28.
15 Ibid., 140.
16 Quoted in M. Sáenz Quesada, *Isabel Perón*, 95.
17 F. Luna, *El 45*, 513.
18 Quoted in R. Rein, *Los muchachos peronistas judíos*, 340.
19 *Revista Así*, 13 July 1971.
20 J.D. Perón, *La hora de los pueblos*, 172, 20.
21 Pope Francis, *Evangelii Gaudium*, 188–9.
22 Quoted in A.C. Tarruella, *Guardia de Hierro*, 326.
23 I. Vélez Carreras, quoted in M. O'Donnell, *Aramburu*, Loc. 4230.
24 *Clarín*, 2 September 2020.
25 R. Gillespie, *Soldiers of Perón*, 114.
26 C. Mugica, *Peronismo y Cristianismo*, 58.
27 Quoted in J.I. García Hamilton, *Juan Domingo*, 300.

Chapter 16

1 C.A. Cosantino, *Letras de tango*, 153–4.
2 Quoted in M. Bonasso, *El presidente que no fue*, 396.
3 Quoted in ibid., 398.
4 Ibid., 400.
5 See, e.g., M. Bonasso, ibid., 405–6; P.R. Cossio and C.A. Seara, *Perón: Testimonios medicos y vivencias (1973–1974)*, 39.
6 Quoted in M. Bonasso, *El presidente que no fue*, 425.
7 Quoted in ibid., 426.
8 Quoted in J.I. García Hamilton, *Juan Domingo*, 305.
9 Quoted in S. Bufano and L. Teixidó, *Peron y la Triple A*, 59.
10 See, e.g., P.R. Cossio and C.A. Seara, *Perón: Testimonios medicos y vivencias (1973–1974)*, 22.
11 Quoted in ibid., 24.
12 Quoted in S. Bufano and L. Teixidó, *Peron y la Triple A*, 64.
13 Quoted in J. Page, *Perón*, 473.
14 Quoted in P.R. Cossio and C.A. Seara, *Perón: Testimonios medicos y vivencias (1973–1974)*, 63; 67.
15 Quoted in J.I. García Hamilton, *Juan Domingo*, 312.

16 Quoted in M. Bonasso, *El presidente que no fue*, 442.
17 M. Firmenich, quoted in R. Gillespie, *Soldiers of Perón*, 128.
18 Report on Perón's foreign policy, in FCO 7/2394, 1973.
19 Quoted in J. Page, *Perón*, 567.
20 R. Gillespie, *Soldiers of Perón*, 135.

Chapter 17

1   C.A. Cosantino, *Letras de tango*, 16–17.
2   Quoted in R. Gillespie, *Soldiers of Perón*, 144.
3   Quoted ibid., 146.
4   Interview with F. Pigna, at www.elhistoriador.com.ar/mario-firmenich
5   Quoted in P.R. Cossio and C.A. Seara, *Perón, testimonios medicos y vivencias*, 27.
6   https://www.youtube.com/watch?v=v_oKKKqiats
7   M. Firmenich, interview with F. Pigna, www.elhistoriador.com.ar/mario-firmenich.
8   Speech reprinted in full in https://www.infobae.com/2014/05/01/1561245-hace-40-anos-juan-peron-echaba-los-montoneros-la-plaza/.
9   C.A. Seara, in P.R. Cossio and C.A. Seara, *Perón, testimonios medicos y vivencias*, 90–6.
10 Full text republished at http://gestar.org.ar/nota/ver/id/1384.
11 Quoted in S. Bufano and L. Teixidó, *Perón y la Triple A*, 17.
12 C.A. Seara, *Perón, testimonios medicos y vivencias*, 115.
13 See, e.g., M. Sáenz Quesada, *Isabel Perón*, 160–1.
14 P.R. Cossio and C.A. Seara, *Perón, testimonios medicos y vivencias*, 122.
15 Quoted in *La Gaceta de Tucumán*, 25 March 1976.
16 Reproduced in D. Cox and D. Nabot, *La segunda muerte*, 28–9.
17 Ibid., 215.

Chapter 18

1   F. Luna, *El 45*, 513.
2   E. Sábato, *El otro rostro del peronismo*, 41–3.
3   Quoted in *La Vanguardia*, 15 June 2019.

BIBLIOGRAPHY

Documents

Conferencia pronunciada el 10 de junio de 1944 por Coronel Juan D. Perón, en calidad de Ministro de Guerra, en la inauguración de la Cátedra de Defensa Nacional de la Universidad de La Plata. Downloaded from www.argentinahistorica.com.ar.
Perón, J.D., *Discurso en la Bolsa de Comercio*, 25 August 1944. Downloaded from www.archivoperonista.com.
Reports on the political situation in Argentina from the British Embassy, Buenos Aires, to the Foreign Office, 1943–1955; 1973. National Archives, Kew.
Unión Democrática: pamphlets issued in the context of 1945–1946 election campaign. Author's personal archive.
US Department of State. Confidential Central Files on Argentina, 1945–1955. Microfilm Collection, London School of Economics, Microfilms 336, 337, 341, 342.
US Department of State. *Consultation among the American Republics with Respect to the Argentine Situation.* Washington, DC, February 1946.

Biographies

Becker, C. *Domingo A. Mercante: A Democrat in the Shadow of Perón and Evita.* Xlibris, Bloomington, Indiana (Kindle edition), 19 September 2005.
Bellotta, A. *Las mujeres de Perón.* Editorial Planeta, Buenos Aires 2005.
Borroni, O. and Vacca, R. *La vida de Eva Perón. Tomo I – testimonios para su historia.* Editorial Galerna, Buenos Aires 1970.
Cowles, F. *Bloody Precedent: The Perón Story.* Frederick Muller, London 1952.
García Hamilton, J.I. *Juan Domingo.* Editorial Sudamericana, Buenos Aires 2009.
Gillespie, R. *J. W. Cooke: El peronismo alternativo.* Cántaro editores, Buenos Aires 1989.
Hedges, J. *Evita: The Life of Eva Perón.* I.B. Tauris, London 2016.
Mercante, D.A. *Mercante: El corazón de Perón.* Ediciones de la Flor, Buenos Aires 1995.
Michaelis, D. *Eleanor.* Simon & Schuster, New York 2020.
Navarro Gerassi, M. *Evita.* Editorial Edhasa, Buenos Aires 2005.
Page, J. *Perón.* Random House, New York 1983.
Pigna, F. *Evita, jirones de su vida.* Editorial Planeta, Buenos Aires 2012.
Piqué, E. *Pope Francis: Life and Revolution.* Kindle edition, January 2015.
Rein, R. *In the Shadow of Perón: Juan Atilio Bramuglia and the Second Line of Argentina's Populist Movement.* Stanford University Press, Stanford, California 2018.
Sáenz Quesada, M. *Isabel Perón.* Editorial Planeta, Buenos Aires 2003.
Vázquez Rial, H. *Perón: tal vez la historia.* Editorial El Ateneo, Buenos Aires 2005.
Zanatta, L. *Eva Perón: Una biografía política.* Kindle edition, 1 January 2012.

Books

Adamovsky, E. *Historia de la clase media argentina*. Editorial Planeta, Buenos Aires 2009.

Barreiro, H. *Juancito Sosa: el indio que cambió la historia*. Avellaneda Tehuelche, Buenos Aires 2000.

Belini, C., Bosoer, F., Devoto, F., Mathias, C., Melon, J., and Plotkin, M. *El exilio de Perón*. Editorial Sudamericana, Buenos Aires 2017.

Benedetti, H.A. *Las mejores letras de tango* (9th ed). Booket, Buenos Aires 2011.

Benítez, H. *La aristocracia frente a la revolución*. Copyright L.E. Benitez de Aldama, Buenos Aires 1953.

Bergoglio, J.M. *Biblia: diálogo vigente*. Editorial Planeta, Buenos Aires 2013.

Bonasso, M. *El presidente que no fue*. Editorial Planeta, Buenos Aires 1997.

Bufano, S. and Teixidó, L. *Perón y la Triple A*. Editorial Sudamericana, Buenos Aires 2015.

Chaves, G.L. *Rebelde Acontecer. Relatos de la resistencia peronista*. Ediciones Colihue, Buenos Aires 2015.

Chesterfield, P.D.S. *Letters to His Son 1766–71 by the Earl of Chesterfield on the Fine Art of Becoming a Man of the World and a Gentleman*. Kindle edition.

Cloppet, I.M. *Eva Duarte y Juan Perón: la cuna materna*. ALFAR Editora, Buenos Aires 2011.

Cloppet, I.M. *Los orígenes de Juan Perón y Eva Duarte*. ALFAR Editora, Buenos Aires 2010.

Cosantino, C.A. (comp). *Letras de tango de ayer, de hoy y de siempre*. Andromeda Ediciones, Buenos Aires 2003.

Cox, D. and Nabot, D. *La segunda muerte*. Editorial Planeta, Buenos Aires 2006.

Crassweller, R. *Perón and the Enigmas of Argentina*. W. W. Norton, New York 1987.

Elena, E. *Dignifying Argentina: Peronism, Citizenship and Mass Consumption*. University of Pittsburgh Press, Pittsburgh, Pennsylvania 2011.

Gambini, H. *El peronismo y la Iglesia*. Centro Editor de América Latina, Buenos Aires 1971.

Gambini, H. *Historia del peronismo*. Editorial Planeta, Buenos Aires 1999.

Gambini, H. *Las traiciones de Perón*. Editorial Sudamericana, Buenos Aires 2019.

Gillespie, R. *Soldiers of Perón: Argentina's Montoneros*. Oxford University Press 1982.

Goñi, U. *The Real Odessa*. Granta Books, London 2003 (revised ed).

Guy, D. *Creating Charismatic Bonds in Argentina*. University of New Mexico Press, Albuquerque, New Mexico 2016.

Hedges, J. *Argentina: A Modern History*. I.B. Tauris, London 2011.

Jauretche, A. *Política nacional y revisionismo histórico*. A. Peña Lillo Editor, Buenos Aires 1982 (6th ed).

Karush, M.B. and Chamosa, O. (eds). *The New Cultural History of Peronism*. Duke University Press, London 2010.

Lafiandra, F. (ed). *Los panfletos: recopilación, comentario y notas*. Editorial Itinerarium, Buenos Aires 1955 (2nd ed).

Lubertino Beltrán, M.J. *Perón y la Iglesia (1943–1955)*. Centro Editor de América Latina, Buenos Aires 1987.

Luna, F. *El 45*. Editorial Sudamericana, Buenos Aires 1986.

Luna, F. *Perón y su tiempo*. Editorial Sudamericana, Buenos Aires 1993 (2nd ed).

Mallimaci, F. *El catolicismo integral en la Argentina (1930–1946)*. Editorial Biblos, Buenos Aires 1988.

Marsal S., P. *Perón y la Iglesia*. Ediciones Rex, Buenos Aires 1955.

Meglioli, L.E. *Perón Frondizi, La conversación*. El Emporio Ediciones, Córdoba 2012.

Mugica, C. *Peronismo y cristianismo*. Editorial Merlin, Buenos Aires 1973.

Murmis, M. and Portantiero, J.C. *Estudio sobre los origenes del peronismo.* Siglo XXI, Buenos Aires 1971.

O'Donnell, M. *Aramburu.* Kindle edition, June 2020.

O'Donnell, M. *Born.* Kindle edition, May 2015.

Pérez Gaudio, J.L. *Catolicismo y Peronismo.* Ediciones Corregidor, Buenos Aires 1985.

Perón, J. *La comunidad organizada.* Editorial Pleamar, Buenos Aires 1975.

Perón, J. *Conducción política.* Editorial Megafón, Buenos Aires 1998.

Perón, J. *Diálogo entre Perón y las Fuerzas Armadas.* Editorial Jorge Mar, Buenos Aires 1973.

Perón, J. *Doctrina peronista.* Partido Peronista Consejo Superior Ejecutivo, Buenos Aires 1952.

Perón, J. *Habla Perón.* Ediciones Realidad Política, Buenos Aires 1984.

Perón, J. *La hora de los pueblos.* Editorial Norte, Buenos Aires 1968.

Perón, J. *Libro Azul y Blanco.* Editorial Freeland, Buenos Aires 1973.

Perón, J. *Manual del Peronista.* Ediciones Los Coihues, Buenos Aires 1988.

Perón, J. *Política y estrategia: No ataco, critico.* Editorial Pleamar, Buenos Aires 1983.

Pigna, F. *Los mitos de la historia argentina 4: La Argentina peronista*, Editorial Planeta, Buenos Aires 2008.

Plotkin, M.B. *Mañana es San Perón: A Cultural History of Perón's Argentina.* Kindle edition, 1 October 2002.

Poder Ejecutivo Nacional. *Libro Negro de la Segunda Tiranía.* Editorial Integración, Buenos Aires 1958.

Potash, R. (ed). *Perón y el GOU.* Editorial Sudamericana, Buenos Aires 1984.

Quintana, R. and Manrupe, R. *Afiches del Peronismo, 1945–1955.* EDUNTREF, Buenos Aires 2016.

Recalde, A. *El pensamiento de John William Cooke en las cartas a Perón, 1956–1966.* Ediciones Nuevos Tiempos, Buenos Aires 2009.

Rein, R. *Los muchachos peronistas judíos.* Editorial Sudamericana, Buenos Aires 2015.

Rhodes, A. *The Vatican in the Age of the Dictators 1922–1945.* Hodder and Stoughton, London 1973.

Rouquié, A. *El siglo de Perón.* Ediciones Edhasa, Buenos Aires 2017.

Sacerdotes para el Tercer Mundo – Capital Federal. *El pueblo. ¿Dónde está?,* Buenos Aires 1975.

Sammartino, E. *La verdad sobre la situación argentina.* Montevideo, Uruguay 1951.

Sampay, A. (ed). *Las Constituciones de la Nación Argentina (1810–1972).* Editorial Universitaria de Buenos Aires, Buenos Aires 1975.

Tarruella, A.C. *Guardia de Hierro: de Perón a Bergoglio.* Punto de Encuentro, Buenos Aires 2016.

Yofre, J.B. *Puerta de Hierro.* Editorial Sudamericana, Buenos Aires 2015.

Zanatta, L. *Perón y el mito de la nación católica.* EDUNTREF, Buenos Aires 2013.

Memoirs

Amadeo, M. *Ayer, hoy, mañana.* Ediciones Gure, Buenos Aires 1956.

Braden, S. *Diplomats and Demagogues.* Arlington House, New York 1971.

Castañeira, H., Alvarez Seminario, M., and Chico de Arce, E. *Legisladoras de Evita.* Ediciones del Instituto Nacional de Investigaciones Históricas Eva Perón, Buenos Aires 2014.

Castro, N. *Los últimos días de Eva: historia de un engaño.* Editorial Sudamericana, Buenos Aires 2014.

Chávez, F. *Eva Perón sin mitos*. Editorial Fraterna, Buenos Aires 1990.

Cossio, P.R. and Seara, C.A. *Perón: Testimonios medicos y vivencias (1973–1974)*. Grupo Editorial Lumen, Buenos Aires 2006.

Duarte de Perón, E. *La razón de mi vida*. Ediciones Peuser, Buenos Aires 1951.

Eloy Martínez, T. *La novela de Perón*. Editorial Planeta Bolsillo, Buenos Aires 1996.

Eloy Martínez, T. *Las memorias del general*. Editorial Planeta, Buenos Aires 1996.

Galasso, N. *Yo fui el confesor de Eva Perón. Conversaciones con el Padre Hernán Benítez*. Homo Sapiens Ediciones, Buenos Aires 1999.

Jamandreu, P. *La cabeza contra el suelo*. Ediciones de la Flor, Buenos Aires 1975.

Lagomarsino de Guardo, L. *Y ahora ... hablo yo*. Editorial Sudamericana, Buenos Aires 1996.

Kelly, Sir D.V. *The Ruling Few*. Hollis and Carter, London 1953 (4th ed).

Lardone, L. *20.25. Quince mujeres hablan de Eva Perón*. Kindle edition, 1 July 2012.

Martínez, R. *Grandezas y miserias de Perón*. Biblioteca Esotérica Herrou Aragón, Mexico 1957.

Mercado, S.P. *El inventor del peronismo. Raúl Apold, el cerebro oculto que cambió la política argentina*. Editorial Planeta, Buenos Aires (Kindle edition) 2013.

Monzalvo, L. *Testigo de la primera hora del peronismo: memorias de un ferroviario*. Editorial Pleamar, Buenos Aires 1974.

Pavón Pereyra, E. *Diario secreto de Perón*. Editorial Sudamericana/ Planeta, Buenos Aires 1986.

Pavón Pereyra, E. *Yo Perón*. Penguin Random House, Buenos Aires 2018.

Perón, E. *Clases y escritos completos 1946–1952, Tomo III*. Editorial Megafón, Buenos Aires 1987.

Perón, J.D. *Del poder al exilio*. Ediciones Sintesis, Buenos Aires 1982.

Perón, J.D. *La fuerza es el derecho de las bestias*. Editorial Volver, Buenos Aires 1987.

Perón, J.D. *Yo, Juan Domingo Perón, Relato Autobiográfico*. (Torcuato Luca di Tena, Luis Calvo, Esteban Peicovich (eds). Editorial Planeta, Barcelona 1976.

Pichel, V. *Evita íntima*. Editorial Planeta, Buenos Aires 1993.

Reyes, C. *La farsa del peronismo*. Sudamericana-Planeta, Buenos 1987.

Reyes, C. *Yo hice el 17 de octubre*. Centro Editor de América Latina, Buenos Aires 1984.

Sabato, E. *El otro rostro del peronismo*. Imprenta López, Buenos Aires 1956 (2nd ed).

Varela, G. *Perón y Evita, memoría íntima*. Kindle edition, 1 January 2014.

Newspapers and Periodicals

Buenos Aires Herald, 1945, 1947, 1954, 1976–1977, 1990–2000

Clarín (Buenos Aires), 1984–2010

Democracia, Buenos Aires, July 1952

La Nación, Buenos Aires, 1943–1952

New York Times, 1945–1946

Noticias Gráficas, 22 November 1949

La Prensa, Buenos Aires, 1945–1946

The Review of the River Plate, 1943–1946

Revista Criterio, 1943–1956

Revista de la Universidad de Buenos Aires, 1950–1953

The Times of London, October 1945

Articles

Alvaredo, F., Cruces, G., and Gasparini, L. 'A Short Episodic History of Income Distribution in Argentina'. *Latin American Economic Review* 27, Art. 7 (2018).

Little, W. 'The Popular Origins of Peronism'. In D. Rock (ed), Argentina in the 20th Century, Duckworth & Co., London 1975.

Pigna, F. Interview with Mario Firmenich, www.elhistoriador.com.ar/mario-firmenich.

Unpublished Theses

Carvalho Lopes Rogério, B.C. 'History with Some Evidence: Inequality Levels of Argentina and Australia at the Turn of the 20th Century'. M.A. thesis, Lund University June 2016.

Hedges, J. 'The Catholic Church and Peronismo in Argentina 1943–1974'. M.A. thesis, University of Liverpool 1990.

Stack, N. 'Avoiding the Greater Evil. The Response of the Argentine Catholic Church to Juan Perón, 1943–1955'. Ph.D. thesis, Rutgers University 1976.

INDEX